'This thoroughly readable book adds greatly to the current debate on the Iranian nuclear programme. It should be read by all those who are interested in this topic.'

– Professor Paul Rogers, Professor of Peace Studies,
University of Bradford

'An outstanding book ... the first scholarly work on Iran's nuclear programme that grasps the programme's historical, cultural and political impetus and clearly explains its elements of continuity over time. It will become a valuable resource for researchers on this subject.'

– Dr. Ali Vaez, Director, Iran Project, Federation of American Scientists

'This book is a watershed in the understanding of the Iranian nuclear programme. No other book quite like it exists. It is a cogent, highly readable and very well-written account of the programme's evolution from its inception to the present day that succeeds in unravelling the technical and political complexities which have often clouded our understanding of the programme. It shows both a deep understanding of modern Iran and of its nuclear programme. The book will be invaluable to policy analysts, politicians, diplomats and journalists in Europe and the USA and is a must read for anyone with an interest in international affairs.'

– Siavush Randjbar-Daemi, Lecturer, SOAS

David Patrikarakos is a writer and journalist who has written for the *New Statesman*, the *Financial Times*, the *London Review of Books*, *Prospect* and the *Guardian*.

NUCLEAR IRAN

THE BIRTH OF AN ATOMIC STATE

David Patrikarakos

I.B. TAURIS

LONDON · NEW YORK

Published in 2012 by I.B.Tauris & Co Ltd
6 Salem Road, London W2 4BU
175 Fifth Avenue, New York NY 10010
www.ibtauris.com

Distributed in the United States and Canada
Exclusively by Palgrave Macmillan
175 Fifth Avenue, New York NY 10010

ISBN: 978 1 78076 125 1

A full CIP record for this book is available from the British Library
A full CIP record is available from the Library of Congress

Library of Congress Catalog Card Number: available

Typeset in Janson by MPS Limited
Printed and bound in Sweden by ScandBook AB

CONTENTS

ACKNOWLEDGEMENTS

As is customary, the list of people I must thank for helping to bring this book to fruition is long yet certainly incomplete. Most immediately, for taking the time to read through the manuscript and point out errors and possible improvements I owe a considerable debt to Norman Dombey and Ali Vaez, whose scientific expertise filled the black hole of my ignorance. Their patience and generosity in answering my questions was unending and appreciated. It goes without saying that all errors are mine alone, most likely from a failure to listen or indeed understand their points correctly.

I also owe a huge debt of thanks to Alan Ramon Ward and Bryn Harris, both for their friendship over many years and for taking time out of their own extensive intellectual pursuits to read through various sections of the book, often at very short notice and at times when I could no longer view the page with any objectivity. Their comments and suggestions have made all the difference. Thanks also to my dear 'moon-face' Tanya Lawrence and to Kayvan Sadeghi, whose input also greatly improved the text.

Hossein Heirini Moghaddam and James Piscatori (who also taught me how to think) advised me on this book when it was in embryonic form. Edmund Herzig helped bring it to its early fruition and, with Homa Katouzian, guided me so expertly through modern Iran at Oxford. Dominic Brookshaw did his level best to teach me Persian, Reza Sheikholeslami gave me excellent advice on the Shah's period while Ali Ansari (and his work) has been an inspiration for me in understanding modern Iran. All these men are true scholars of the Middle East; I have only benefited from their teaching and guidance.

I must also thank all the staff (academic and non-academic) at Oxford's Middle East Centre and especially at Wadham College whose kindness (and forbearance) ensured I spent many happy years there. And of course Tom Woodman, without whom nothing subsequent would have been possible.

Ben Judah has been a continual source of support as we begin this long game together. The same is true of Ioanna Koutzoukou while the support of Alexis Hood was also invaluable, and always appreciated. Chris Mitchell and Dai Richards must also be thanked, as must David Mainwaring who was an excellent source of advice about the publishing world in general.

And of course, my mother, who is everything, and my brother, Phillip, who is with me every day. Rene must also be thanked for this support over many years. And my father, without whom this book would most certainly have never seen the light of day. His unyielding support throughout the writing process was, in the end, crucial.

David Patrikarakos, July 2012

A NOTE ON TRANSLITERATION

The transliteration of the Persian words and names in this book is based on a simplified phonetic system, without diacritical accents though distinguishing between the 'ayn and the hamzeh. The aim has been to make the Persian names and terms accessible to non-specialist readers.

LIST OF ACRONYMS

AEOI	Atomic Energy Agency of Iran
CENTO	Central Treaty Organization
HEU	Highly Enriched Uranium
IAEA	International Atomic Energy Agency
IRNA	Islamic Republic News Agency
LEU	Low-Enriched Uranium
MW/MWe	Megawatt
NPT	The Treaty on the Non-Proliferation of Nuclear Weapons
UCF	Uranium Conversion Facility
UF_6	Uranium Hexafluoride
UN	United Nations
WMD	Weapons of Mass Destruction

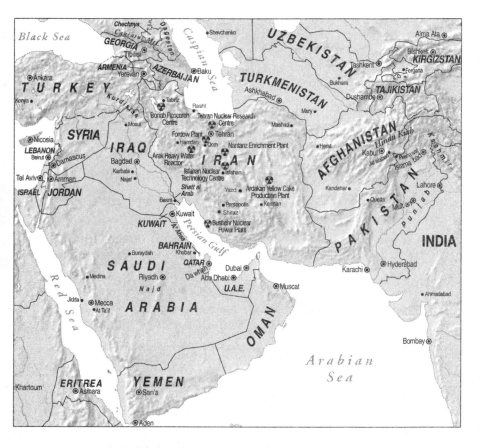

Map of Iran showing enrichment centres and reactors

PREFACE

In war more than in any other subject we must begin by looking at the nature of the whole; for here more than elsewhere the part and the whole must always be thought of together.

Carl Von Clausewitz

The world may be tumbling into another Middle East war. For the last decade, the West's leading powers and Iran have engaged in the most sustained diplomatic clash since the run-up to the 2003 Iraq war, and it is escalating. The Iranian nuclear crisis is everywhere. Thousands of newspaper, magazine and journal articles, dozens of books, almost daily news bulletins, and hundreds of hours of TV and radio (not to mention scores of documentary films) have appeared to judge, analyse and pontificate on Iran's nuclear programme. The crisis now dominates Iranian, European and US foreign policy; Iran specialists have mushroomed in the media and in government; watching its nuclear programme has become a geopolitical cottage industry.

Iran's nuclear ambitions – and the international attempts to stop them – have become the major global crisis of the twenty-first century's second decade. It is a Manichean conflict with the potential to reorder the international geopolitical balance of power. On one side is Iran: a regional giant that lies between two of the world's great energy sources – the Caspian Basin and the Persian Gulf. With the fourth largest reserves of oil and second largest reserves of natural gas in the world, the country will be integral to satisfying the world's forthcoming energy needs. Iran's links to Shi'i groups in Iraq and its ability to influence events in Afghanistan, not to mention its longstanding ties to Hamas and Hezbollah, mean that political stability in the Middle East is also to a large degree dependent on Iran.

Opposing Iran is a coalition of the leading Western states headed by the world's only remaining superpower, the USA; on the diplomatic sidelines is Israel, threatening to escalate the crisis to irretrievable, military levels. Somewhere in the middle, along with the UN Security Council, the EU and the Non-Aligned Movement of Developing Countries, are two of the world's other Great Powers: China and Russia. The nuclear crisis is unquestionably global in its importance, and its effects accordingly severe. Higher oil prices, the increased prospect of war, more division among the UN Security Council powers and a deepening of the already huge rupture between Iran and the West have already occurred. Its resolution – one way or another – will affect the world for at least a generation.

The need to find a solution is both critical and immediate. The international strategy up until now has failed; Iran remains as isolated, and as angry, as ever. The pressure heaped on the country over the past year – greater than anything it has experienced since the Iran–Iraq war – has only been met with repeated Iranian defiance. Israeli threats to strike Iran's nuclear facilities increase by the day – certainly if the rhetoric coming out of Tel Aviv and parts of Washington is to be believed, the prospect may even be imminent. Should Israel (or the USA) launch an attack, the global repercussions would be severe. Iran would more than likely respond by leaving the NPT launching missiles against Israel, attacking US forces in the Gulf, destabilizing Afghanistan and Iraq, and possibly even blockading the Straits of Hormuz through which 20 per cent of the world's oil passes. An increasingly hostile and unstable Middle East, and an Iran even more determined to accelerate any possible drive towards a nuclear bomb, are the very least that could be expected after such an attack.

But for a programme that is now in its seventh decade, there is very little understanding of it: in particular, of what it *means* to Iran, and why. No one has yet tried to tell the full story of Iran's nuclear programme from its birth until the present day. How does Iran make decisions on its programme and why? And how have these changed over the years? What exactly is it that stands at the heart of global concerns? While there have been some excellent treatments of the subject, much of the available literature is often sensationalist, lightweight or too politically charged to be of real use, to either the historian or the policymaker.

This book seeks to redress these problems, and it is written with a bold but clear purpose in mind: to present the most comprehensive account and analysis of the nuclear programme so far written. It is, accordingly, based predominantly on primary sources: official statements, government and parliamentary records, declassified intelligence documents, both in English and in Persian, and of course interviews with key actors, at the national and international levels, throughout the 60-year history of the programme. Secondary literature, mainly newspapers and other media sources, again both in Persian and in English, has also been used.

This book tells the story of Iran's nuclear programme from its beginning in the late 1950s to the present day. It opens with a brief consideration of the birth of nuclear power in the post-war world and Iran's historical experiences over the last two centuries, which drive the modern Iranian state and its nuclear programme to this day. Chapters 4 to 6 then detail the programme's early days – the founding of the Atomic Energy Agency of Iran (AEOI), and the Shah's motivations for a nuclear programme – both spoken and unspoken; the programme's expansion in the late 1970s and the early discussions on Iran's attainment of an atomic bomb. Chapters 7 to 9 cover the arrival of the Islamic Republic in 1979 and the nuclear programme's meandering course through the traumatic war years of the 1980s. Initially discarded for ideological reasons, the programme was restarted shortly afterwards (alongside a covert uranium-enrichment programme) and eventually mutated into a symbol of Iranian defiance in the face of a supposedly hostile world. Chapters 10 to 12 deal with the programme's post-war progress and increasing international controversy, as well as the expansion of its covert activities, which eventually grew into an AEOI drive towards uranium enrichment and plutonium production, the two paths to a nuclear bomb.

The book's later chapters deal with the modern nuclear clash. Chapter 13 begins by recounting the 2002 announcement that publicly revealed the extent of Iran's undeclared nuclear activities and began the nuclear crisis, the resulting negotiations between Iran and the Europeans, Iran's strategic response to them and the Tehran Agreement of 2003. The following chapter deals with the 2004 Paris Agreement and the arrival of Secretary of State Condoleezza Rice and US attempts to engage the Islamic Republic in dialogue. Chapters 15 and 16 then chart the arrival of Mahmoud Ahmadinejad and, later, Barack Obama, detailing both the former's escalation of tensions between Iran and the international community, and the latter's decision to engage Iran at the highest levels. The final chapters analyse Washington's attempts to negotiate with Iran, the increasingly difficult relationship with Israel and Tel Aviv's fear of a nuclear Iran, the seeming failure of diplomacy, and the rise of possible alternatives, including the possibility of military action against the nuclear programme.

To do all this with the necessary degree of rigour has taken six years. I have travelled thousands of miles to three continents to speak to key players in this drama (and it is a drama) in Iran, the USA, Europe, the Arab world and Israel. Access to senior Iranian and non-Iranian decision-makers (the former made considerably more difficult given the near-impossibility of speaking to relevant Iranians after the 2009 Iranian presidential elections) forms a critical part of this book. At all times, the most pertinent, personal testimony has been sought on the most crucial periods of the programme's history. The book would not have been possible without the input of so many of those that have shaped the history of the nuclear programme. Many of the people whose insight was most valuable must remain anonymous as they continue to affect its course today, but there are several who can, and must, be mentioned.

Akbar Etemad, the founder of the AEOI, and the father of Iran's nuclear programme, who so generously devoted countless hours of his time so that I could understand how it all began and what it all meant. Endlessly gracious, he answered all of my questions fully and expertly, and provided this book with that rarest and most valuable of things: a window into the thinking that guided and guides the programme at the very highest levels. Similarly, Reza Khazaneh, former head of the Isfahan Nuclear Technology Centre, was an excellent source of information on the programme's early days under the Islamic Republic and, later, on its drastic and significant change of direction in the 1990s.

Ahmad Salematian, Dariush Homayoun, Mohsen Sazegara, Adeshir Zahedi and Ata'ollah Mohajerani were all of great help in illuminating the internal workings of 1979 Islamic Revolution, and of the modern day Islamic Republic. Former President of Iran Abulhassan Bani-Sadr was an excellent source of information on the early Islamic Republic's thinking on the nuclear programme at the highest level.

Moving into the present day, Alireza Jafarzadeh kindly took me through the events of August 2002, when he publicly revealed the full extent of Iran's nuclear activities to the world and in so doing ignited the nuclear crisis. Ali Asghar Soltanieh, Iran's Ambassador to the International Atomic Energy Agency (IAEA), who has represented Iran at the Agency (and to the world) throughout the nuclear crisis, gave me many hours of his time in Vienna to explain in valuable detail the Iranian position.

Among the many Americans I must thank are the numerous White House and State Department officials, who remain nameless in government and continue to work on the nuclear file today. But special thanks must go to Ambassador Nick Burns, who explained the thinking behind the initial US attempt at détente with Iran under President George W. Bush and behind much of

PREFACE

the P5+1's nuclear diplomacy at the very highest levels. Thanks also to US Ambassador John R. Bolton, a powerful presence in the early stages of international negotiations with Iran. Bruce Reidel, who worked closely with Barack Obama during his 2008 presidential campaign and on the presidential transition team, adeptly explained the reasoning behind President Obama's initial decision as US President to speak directly to the Iranian leadership for the first time in over 30 years, and was also of huge help.

On the European side, Britain's Ambassador to the IAEA, Peter Jenkins, was critical in demystifying the often opaque series of events that comprise the early nuclear negotiations, as was France's Ambassador to Tehran, François Nicoullaud. Officials at the Quai d'Orsay in Paris, and at the British FCO, who continue to work on the Iran file to this day, were also of great help. For the view from Tel Aviv, Kadima MK and former head of Shin Bet, Avi Dichter; the head of Israeli internal security, Amos Gilad; Prime Minister's spokesman, Mark Regev; and former National Security Advisor to the Prime Minister, Giora Eiland, were of great help, as well as the Israeli diplomats who made me understand the gravity with which they view the Iranian threat.

This book is built on a largely linear, chronological structure that traces the history of the nuclear programme over 60 years with several guiding principles in mind. The first is that the problem is political. The crisis is not the cause but the effect of a 'failed relationship' between Iran and the West, and it is this underlying relationship that must be addressed if any resolution is to be found. The second is that the only way to find a solution is to understand, on a political, economic, security and, perhaps most importantly of all, psychological level, what the nuclear programme means to Iran. Which leads into the third principle, which takes the form of a question this book seeks to answer: does the programme have a definite military dimension? Only by assessing as accurately and as completely as possible whether Iran is indeed seeking a bomb, and if so just how close it is to achieving its aim, can the correct policy be found. And this is urgently needed: if the spectre of a possible attack on Iran is deeply troubling, the prospect of a nuclear-armed Iran is worse. It would strengthen the Iranian regime, both domestically and at the expense of its Middle East neighbours, further damage Iran–Israeli relations, embolden Tehran's proxies, Hezbollah and Hamas, and more than likely start a regional arms race. On a wider level, it would inflict an irrevocable blow to the NPT's credibility and likely convince other near-nuclear powers to follow Iran's example. It is a deeply undesirable outcome – one that must be avoided at all costs.

But the nuclear programme also offers an opportunity: it is a window into the enigma of modern Iran, the story of which is, in several important regards, the story of Iran's efforts to engage with modernity, and to negotiate a place within a perennially hostile modern world. The nuclear programme is merely the country's most ambitious attempt to do so, and its history, I argue, is a kind of *tabula rasa* onto which modern Iran's evolution has been and continues to be written; or, more simply, it is the story of Iran's attempt to deal with modernity: ordered, detailed, configured. The degree of political, institutional and financial commitment necessary from any country to pursue a successful nuclear programme is absolute; the state must pour itself into the undertaking, and in so doing it puts on display its own sense of itself – not only its ambitions, its worldview, but also its anxieties and neuroses. Over 30 years after the 1979 Islamic Revolution the question of how to deal with one of the Middle East's largest countries, one of the world's largest energy suppliers and a nation with the ability to drastically alter the global balance of power, still persists. Understand the nuclear programme and you understand modern Iran; understand modern Iran and you have the best chance of resolving the nuclear impasse. This book attempts to do both.

Finally, to fully understand Iran's nuclear programme is to understand that it has a dual history or, perhaps more correctly, two 'histories'. The first is the evolution of the programme itself – the progress of its nuclear facilities and capabilities. The second is what can usefully be described as the 'nuclear debate': the programme's political history that has evolved alongside it – created largely by the diplomatic clash between Iran and the West. The first consists of reactors and centrifuges; the second comprises the constellation of relationships that dominate both international politics and the nuclear world: Sunni versus Shia; Israel versus the Islamic World; Developed versus the Developing World; and the Nuclear-weapon States versus the Non-nuclear-weapon States. And it is informed by organizing principles on each 'side' ('Western perfidy' versus 'Iranian irrationality' to name but one). Politics creates facts on the ground; it prompts decisions on both 'sides'. Iran's desire to acquire nuclear technology meets a corresponding Western desire to block Iran's access to that technology, and both desires are informed by political beliefs and values. In its early chapters, while chronological, this book is accordingly built on a parallel structure – with parallel timelines – that considers the technical progression of Iran's civil nuclear programme in conjunction with the evolution of a (more covert) weapons programme, such as it may exist, and, perhaps more importantly, the debate that has surrounded the nuclear programme since its birth.

Within this, several questions will be answered. How accurate is speculation about Iran's nuclear programme? What was the relationship of first the Shah, and then the Islamic Republic, to nuclear power? How has the programme altered in purpose under different regimes, and how and why have motivations changed over time? The scope and range of possible Iranian desires for nuclear weapons must and will be considered. Iran is, after all, a country with, it believes, very real security threats in a world that it also believes to be fundamentally hostile. And, above all, why does Iran do it? Why does one of the world's great oil producers pursue a programme ostensibly for nuclear energy that has brought it the hostility of large parts of the world, the fear of its neighbours, and possible military attack by Israel or the most powerful nation on earth? Is it just a desperate urge to build a bomb or are other influences at work?

Each day seems to bring news of yet another Iranian scientist assassinated, of more sanctions placed on Iran and of more Israeli threats to strike its nuclear facilities. Obama's failed détente has left hardliners in Washington, Tel Aviv and many European capitals with the belief that diplomacy is now exhausted and only the 'military option' remains viable. Iran, in turn, continues to enrich uranium and becomes ever more belligerent and intransigent. The two sides now seem to be heading, almost ineluctably, towards conflict. The Iranian nuclear crisis is a drama with a panoramic cast of characters and a sweeping 'narrative' now in danger of ending in a disastrous denouement that could seriously alter the global balance of power and, with it, international stability. To be properly addressed, Iran's nuclear programme must be properly understood: only by doing this can we hope to resolve what has become one of the global crises of our age.

To John Gurney

PROLOGUE

Under watchful eyes, a crowd chanted slogans on the street outside my Tehran window. Late morning; early August 2005. I was in the University dormitory on Kargar Avenue, the city's carotid artery that runs from the down-at-heel Rah Ahan Square in the south up into the affluent vistas of the capital's northern reaches, once home to the Western-educated elite that gathered around Sa'dabad, the Shah's old palace. Barring the University entrance, two wary guards studied a crowd of tieless men and veiled women, while assorted university types – my language teacher, some clerical staff, the trio of depressed African students I vaguely knew – passed through the gates. The crowd's roars became louder and more aggressive. It wasn't a demonstration as such, but about 40 people had gathered to 'celebrate' Iran's decision, announced that day, to resume uranium enrichment after two years of suspension. Iranian flags were waved. A few of the more vocal participants held up pictures of Iran's recently elected President, Mahmoud Ahmadinejad, as they shouted about nuclear power and the Great Satan; there was a lot of anger for a celebration. I recognized references to the Iran–Iraq war and the long-overthrown Iranian Prime Minister, Mohammad Mossadegh.

I had come to Iran from Oxford University to study Persian and, only three days into my trip, I hadn't yet spoken to many Iranians. I lived down a corridor in the Tehran University dormitory with two French friends, a Syrian (with whom I had reverently shared a single can of illegally procured Heineken) as well as a German and a Kazakh. Two European engineers lived on the first floor while the rest of the building was populated with Kurds from Iran's Kermanshah province. Iranian students were housed separately, and encouraged not to mix. But everywhere I went I encountered the nuclear programme – only two days earlier a taxi driver had lectured me on the subject at considerable (and tedious) length. A nuclear programme, he had informed me, was the country's 'right' (peaceful nuclear power was the key to economic growth), as was the 'nuclear fuel cycle', a term he kept repeating, but I suspected he didn't fully understand.

He told me that Iran didn't want nuclear weapons; that it was an advanced country and, as the nuclear programme showed the world, one of the 'great nations'. The problem, he added disapprovingly, was the West, mainly my country Britain and of course the USA, which wanted to 'kill' the programme. The 1953 coup that had overthrown Mohammad Mossadegh, *Amrika*'s 'enslavement' of the Shah, and now the endless Western accusations against the nuclear programme were all part of (to paraphrase) a broader scheme of Western oppression that had created a world he decried in a single geopolitical aphorism: 'England: the grandfather; America: the son; Israel: the grandson'. If simplistic, his analysis had the virtue of certainty.

Iranians love talking to Westerners, even if their government does not. Over the coming weeks I was lectured on the nuclear programme by two more taxi drivers, my language teacher (she thought it was all a lot of nonsense), a waiter, the man that owned the local internet café and, most incredibly of all, a gaggle of pre-teen children that accosted me on a side street just off *Naqsh-e Jahan* square in Isfahan. Nuclear power, it seemed, was a national aspiration, and it was about more than just reactors and centrifuges. It was clearly bound up with perceptions of Iranian history and it clearly mobilized the people through an ability to generate intense emotion by tapping into universal registers of meanings for Iranians. The crowd I saw in the street that day was jubilant but angry, and its anger had more to do with Iran's relationship with the West than with uranium enrichment. It was as if the regime had somehow managed to create a causal link between Iran's perceived historical injustices and the rather more prosaic question of its adherence to international law.

Meanwhile, the country seemed to be retreating back into the womb of the early Islamic Republic. On the streets, the Islamist militia, the *Basij*, were already an increasing presence; as if Ahmadinejad's recent election had unchained them from bonds against which, if their fastidiousness indicated, they had so clearly chafed under his predecessor Mohammad Khatami. Female friends were roughly accosted in the street for imperfect veils and 'unsuitable' trousers. One day I ducked into a basement restaurant in the Amirabad district of North Tehran to eat my favoured *chelo kabab* (a lamb and rice dish). 'You have to understand who we are', said the owner grandly, as a flunky served me another cup of saccharin tea. There was a clatter of cutlery and the cup joined several others on the table. 'We are the children of Cyrus the Great, the man who gave the world its first human rights act. This is true', he added with satisfaction. 'The West does not understand this, which is bad. But perhaps it will soon. *Inshallah.*'

The Iranians are great storytellers; they revere the epic tales of their national poets Ferdowsi and Hafez. The people I met variously complained, boasted and expounded conspiracy theories of often bewilderingly imaginative content, but in one form or another, they all told me stories of Iran's problematic relationship with the modern world, which centred on the even more problematic question of Iranian identity. It is fitting that Manichaeism was born in Iran: Iranians are caught between Cyrus the Great and Allah; between democracy and dictatorship; between East and West; and between the future and the past. On my last morning in Iran I went present shopping in Tehran's Grand Bazaar and met a *bazaari* who told me that Iran was 'pure', untainted by Western civilization, as he tried to sell me fake Diesel jeans. Back in the dormitory that evening, a student asked me to teach him to speak English with an American accent.

Over the last century Iran has experienced two revolutions, two world wars (and a resulting occupation), a coup d'état, the end of a centuries-old tradition of monarchy, the arrival of an Islamic Republic, a devastating war with Iraq, a rupture with the world's last remaining superpower, seemingly endless sanctions and international isolation. The country has emerged into the twenty-first century unsure of itself and of its place in the world and the Iranian consciousness is accordingly sundered: a strong sense of Iran's importance combines with the insecurity of a 'fallen' nation. Iranian political rhetoric is filled with pronouncements about national greatness mixed with status anxiety and xenophobia. The nuclear programme clearly straddled both these impulses for the Iranians I met: an example of their country's collective accomplishment and, in the international opposition it faced, of yet more 'victimization' by the West.

I returned to Oxford (via a nervous flight with Azerbaijan Airlines) where the nuclear crisis filled the newspapers and my inbox with stories of a rogue Iran set on a path towards nuclear Armageddon. Two narratives were clearly at work, and if the answers were to be found in Iran's history that is where I would start. I wanted to tell this story, and the way to do it, I now understood, was to tell it *ab initio* – from the beginning.

PART I

A SURGE INTO MODERNITY: THE NUCLEAR PROGRAMME 1957–2001

CHAPTER 1

IN THE BEGINNING WAS THE ATOM BOMB: NUCLEAR POWER AND THE POST-WAR WORLD

In August 1945 the USA dropped two atomic bombs on the Japanese cities of Nagasaki and Hiroshima. 'Fat Man' (a 6.4 kg plutonium bomb) and 'Little Boy' (a 60 kg uranium bomb) obliterated almost 100,000 people in minutes and began the nuclear age. Japanese radio described the view hours after Nagasaki was hit: 'Practically all living things, human and animal', it reported, 'were literally seared to death'.[1] Images of the 'Great Mushroom Cloud' beamed across the world were a perhaps inevitable end to the long funeral march of World War II, and united the victorious allies in agreement that the bloodshed of the previous six years must never be repeated – at least not among themselves. The world would need greater regulation and the UN was created to at least give form to this idea. The very first UN Resolution in 1946 highlighted the 'problem' of atomic energy and called for the 'elimination' of atomic weapons and all other major weapons of mass destruction.[2] Just over a year later, at the third session in 1948, the General Assembly again called for the atomic bomb to be outlawed.[3] Nuclear power had arrived, and it had changed everything.

THE ATOMS FOR PEACE PROGRAMME

But the UN also faced nuclear power's inherent paradox: a clean, renewable energy source that could destroy on an unprecedented scale but could also lift countries into modernity. It was simply unrealistic to try to deny this new energy to a clamouring world, particularly when its appeal was almost universal, stretching from South Asia to the Middle East to Northern Europe; it had to be harnessed, not simply abandoned.[4] While the UN pronounced, a recalibrated world order looked to Washington for a more substantive reaction, which it supplied. At the eighth UN General Assembly in New York on 8 December 1953, US President Dwight D. Eisenhower stepped up to the podium and gave his 'Atoms for Peace' speech, which created the international non-proliferation regime that exists to this day. The speech outlined the extent of global anxiety over atomic energy, the response that sought to assuage it and the reasoning behind this.

Eisenhower grasped that nuclear power's destructive potency had irretrievably changed the world, not least in its military and political spheres; and that it was an international problem. Critically, even then, he (or his advisors) understood the global threat of proliferation:[5]

> ... the dread secret and the fearful engines of atomic might are not ours alone ... If at one time the United States possessed what might have been called a monopoly of atomic power, that monopoly ceased to exist several years ago ... the knowledge now possessed by several nations will eventually be shared by others, possibly all others.

Behind the rhetoric was policy: a commitment to establish a supranational institution devoted solely to the regulation of nuclear power, realized four years later in 1957 with the establishment of the IAEA and with it the internationalization of nuclear governance:

The governments principally involved, to the extent permitted by elementary prudence, should begin now and continue to make joint contributions from their stockpiles of normal uranium and fissionable materials to an international atomic energy agency.

Each state that was able would donate nuclear materials and expertise to the Agency, which would in turn be distributed to those in need. Eisenhower had (with characteristic floridity) set out a simple bargain. The IAEA would provide assistance to any country that wanted a nuclear programme in exchange for a commitment that it would be for civil and not military use: 'Atoms for Peace'. The speech garnered a standing ovation and almost universal acclaim. The European delegations considered it the most significant America had yet delivered at the UN,[6] while Winston Churchill declared it 'a great pronouncement' that would 'resound' through 'the anxious and bewildered world'.[7] Reaction from across the Middle East was almost universally positive, too.[8] But the Belgian delegation sounded a note of prescient disquiet, arguing the proposal was insufficient because it excluded any disarmament commitments and left the USA and the USSR with their nuclear stockpiles.[9] As a critique of the nascent non-proliferation regime's structural flaws it was astute; as a premonition of what would become the major grievance of the non-nuclear-weapon states – the nuclear states' lack of disarmament – it was prophetic.

Washington's determination to encourage peaceful atomic energy was as privately resolute as it was publicly robust. Its nuclear energy establishment was eager to show the world 'the benign possibilities of the atom' and proposals to help other nations set up their own isotope production and training centres, designed after the US nuclear centre at Oak Ridge, quickly occurred.[10] The *zeitgeist* was peaceful nuclear power, and the language of international relations decried proliferation. If you wanted international acceptance, you didn't want nuclear weapons – at least not publicly. And Mohammad Reza Pahlavi, the Shah of Iran, wanted that acceptance more than anything else.

CHAPTER 2

TWO CENTURIES OF LOSS: IRAN AT THE ADVENT OF NUCLEAR POWER

At 4:30 in the afternoon on 17 September 1941, a day after his father, Reza Shah, had left Tehran in an unmarked car, a faltering Mohammad Reza Pahlavi took the imperial oath of office and became Shah of Iran. The Soviet and British legations were pointedly absent from the Parliamentary gallery set aside for the diplomatic corps, though their soldiers had been a presence in Iran for some weeks. 'I swear to the sacred words of Allah', said the young Shah with a strained forcefulness, 'that I will focus all of my efforts towards safeguarding the borders of the nation, and the rights of the people'.[1] As night fell, British soldiers in the Tehran streets bellowed and squawked in triumph; some of the bolder (and drunker) ones donned Iranian army uniforms they had found in an abandoned barrack; others mimicked Reza Shah, painting his bushy moustache onto their faces with regulation army boot polish, and strutting up and down the road like peacocks.

Mohammad Reza Shah had taken 'power' at the height of World War II in circumstances that reflected the precariousness of both his position and Iran's. And he nearly hadn't taken power at all. Only 24 hours earlier, the impending Anglo-Soviet occupation of Tehran had finally convinced Reza Shah to abdicate and flee to South Africa, having persuaded his callow 21-year-old son (whom he never thought up to much anyway) to stay and take his place as they stood outside the palace gates. Meanwhile, Sir Reader Bullard, the British Ambassador to Iran, had already met with Iranian emissaries and described the Crown Prince as 'obnoxious to His Majesty's government', as well as assuring them that the Soviets were also 'unfavourably inclined' towards him.[2] Efforts had been made to see if the Qajar dynasty, specifically Prince Hamid, son of the last Qajar Crown Prince, Mohammad Hassan Mirza, could be re-installed. Now a British citizen (an officer in the Royal Navy calling himself Lieutenant Drummond, no less) and completely unable to speak a word of Persian, he was considered too much of a stretch even for British Middle East policy. So Mohammad Reza Shah it was. Reluctantly.

War had come to Iran in June 1941 after Nazi Germany had launched *Operation Barbarossa* and invaded the USSR, breaking the 1939 Molotov–Ribbentrop Non-Aggression Pact between the two countries. Iran now became a vital strategic 'corridor' to supply the Soviets, who would have to engage German forces on what would become known as the War's Eastern Front. Britain and the USSR had watched Iran and Germany become uncomfortably close since the late 1930s; they now mistrusted Reza Shah's official position of neutrality and on 25 August 1941 launched *Operation Countenance*, invading Iran in order to secure the country's oilfields and supply lines. The invasion was traumatic. The ultimate symbol of imperial machination for Iranians – the Union Jack – flew from Royal Navy ships that attacked from the Persian Gulf and from tanks rolling across the border from Iraq; simultaneously, Soviet forces descended from Transcaucasia to occupy Iran's northern provinces.

The Allies eventually advanced on Tehran, shelling the city and causing mass terror (though few casualties). Even worse was the total implosion of the Iranian military – the pride of imperial Iran. The young Mohammad Reza Pahlavi watched soldiers desert in their hundreds, scuttling (sometimes barefoot) out of army bases, while officers made bonfires in their homes to burn their uniforms as the Allies approached; and those were the ones that didn't flee the city disguised as women. Bombed out ruins and streets emptied by panic all left their mark on the young prince who vowed that Iran would never be so defenceless again. His army, should he ever have one, would be different.

More psychologically devastating was the knowledge that he owed his very position to the Great Powers: they had pressured his father into abdicating and then only begrudgingly 'allowed' him to claim the throne. The new Shah internalized two truths at his political birth: the need for his regime to be militarily strong and the ability of the Great Powers, particularly Britain and Russia, to manipulate his country at the highest levels; in fact, to do whatever they wanted in Iran. And just in case he had not, the British sent him a message (via the Egyptians) to 'read, mark, learn and inwardly digest what had happened to his father'.[3] He did.

Foreigners had decided Iran's future – again. No country is more cursed by its own self than Iran. Its geostrategic location and natural wealth have made it a target for more powerful nations for over 200 years, and while the country never experienced direct colonialism like, say, India, it has repeatedly been subject to deleterious foreign meddling. As with many previously powerful Middle Eastern states, Iran enjoyed relative military and economic parity with its contemporaries until a sharp decline in the nineteenth century, which coincided with the rapid industrialization of the West and a new Great Power focus on the Middle East. With the advent of the British Empire, Persia (as it was then) became a gateway to London's 'jewel in the crown', India, and so of vital importance to Britain, which began to compete with Russia for influence in the country and for supremacy in Central Asia as a whole – the so-called 'Great Game'. Iran had become an arena for superpower battles, which only intensified with what came next.

In the late 1890s, reports began to circulate of great oil potential in Persia, leading a British industrialist, William Knox D'Arcy, to sign a concession with Iran's Shah, Mozaffar al-Din, in 1901 for exclusive rights to prospect for oil in the country. Believing the concession would provide an advantage in the struggle against Moscow, British officials gave full political support to D'Arcy, while their Russian counterparts tried to block the deal and, indeed, succeeded in slowing negotiations until D'Arcy's representative in Tehran offered the Shah an extra £5,000 to sign the agreement. The relatively paltry sum was enough. On 28 May 1901, Shah Mozzafar al-Din signed an 18-point concession granting D'Arcy exclusive rights to prospect, explore, exploit, transport and sell natural gas, petroleum, asphalt and mineral waxes over an area of 1,242,000 km^2 – three quarters of the country – for a 60-year period. In return, the Shah received £20,000 cash, another £20,000 worth of shares, and 16 per cent of annual net profits from the operating companies of the concession. D'Arcy subsequently ran into difficulties but eventually discovered large commercial quantities of oil in 1908 just in time for the Anglo-Persian Oil Company (which later became British Petroleum) to take over the concession in 1909. Anglo-Persian became one of the most powerful oil companies in the world and an asset to British Imperial interests for the next 50 years. For Iranians, it was a shameful 'capitulation' to foreigners.

And it was merely the latest. In several key regards, Knox D'Arcy encapsulates the tragedy of modern Iran in the Iranian mind. Caught between the Great Powers of the day, which meddle in Iran for their own political or financial reasons, an Iranian leader is forced to sacrifice the country's wealth and (perhaps more importantly) 'integrity' to the interests of foreigners through a disadvantageous deal that has the threat of the bayonet behind it: often unspoken, sometimes overt, but always there. Even before the oil concession, Iran had lost substantial territories to Russia following its defeat in the 1826–8 Russian–Persian war. Under the resulting 1828 Treaty of Turkmenchay, Iran was forced to cede most of present-day central Armenia and parts of Azerbaijan. This was in addition to all lands annexed by Russia (including modern day Daghestan and Eastern Georgia) in the Gulistan Treaty 15 years earlier. The Russians had promised Iran's ruler, Fath Ali

Shah, that if he did not sign the treaty, they would conquer Tehran in five days.

And all the while, Iran was trying to grope towards some form of political modernity. From 1905 to 1907 the Iranian people finally awoke into mass political consciousness with a 'constitutional revolution' that led to the establishment of Iran's first parliament, just as the British and Russians were busy dividing the country into 'spheres of influence' between themselves. Almost 20 years later in 1925, Moscow and London 'encouraged' further political change in the country by helping end the Qajar dynasty that had ruled Iran for a century through tacit support of a military coup that replaced Ahmad Shah Qajar with a young Reza Khan (later Reza Shah), who of course fell victim to the same forces less than 20 years after that. The cycle may have seemed endless, but it always ended with Iran as the loser. Even without the trauma of a sustained occupation, this interference amounted to a colonization of Iranian politics that Mohammad Reza Shah experienced so viscerally in 1941 and that would find its inevitable apotheosis in the 1953 Anglo-American Coup that overthrew Mossadegh.

The internalization of these events (and of many others like them) would drive national policy for over 100 years. A perennial concern of successive Iranian governments has been, since the start of the nineteenth century, to achieve some form of 'independence' and to preserve Iran's territory: to protect its shape on the map ('a sitting cat'). Tehran's diplomacy has veered from Prime Minister Mirza Taghi Khan Amir Kabir's attempts in the mid-nineteenth century to try to balance stronger powers by offering concessions to all, to Mossadegh, who tried to deal with the superpowers by offering nothing to either, with predictable results. But the underlying narrative that fuels this spectrum of approaches has remained the same: that Iran is a weak country that must do what it can to protect itself against stronger and more aggressive ones to achieve some kind of 'independence' within a Western-dominated world that is historically hostile. Twinned with this is a second, attendant imperative: the need to restore the national 'self-respect' that has been taken away as a result of Iran's encounter with the modern world.[4] Iranian political rhetoric reflects both the ambivalence of Iran's relationship with its own history and the importance of that history. It is the struggle between pride in a glorious past and shame at more recent subjugations (in which the latter predominates) that would lead Mohammad Reza Shah, in 1971, to spend millions on an extravaganza marking (with questionable historicity) 2,500 years of continuous Iranian monarchy, and almost 40 years later, Iran's Ambassador to the IAEA to tell me, over tea, that Iran is a 5,000-year-old country, the West must not speak to it 'in the language of animals'. Emotive it may be, but the influence of history is undeniable. And it explains much of the way both Pahlavi Iran and the Islamic Republic made and make decisions, especially nuclear ones.

So it was unsurprising that when Mohammad Reza Shah took power in 1941 after a century-long history of foreign meddling insecurity was his default emotion; and his early reign was conducted in the shadow of the occupying British and Soviets (a 1942 *Life* Magazine article described him as a king 'on probation').[5] Perhaps paradoxically, it was also its most democratic era: a time of relative pluralism with no single figure in total control. While he did make efforts to consolidate himself, the Shah was something of a playboy; less concerned with the exercise of power than with playing tennis, going to parties and driving around Tehran very quickly. When he gradually began to engage in politics, he found himself involved in struggles against the Majlis (parliament), successive Prime Ministers (notably Ahmad Qavam) and the landed and religious classes.

The 1953 coup changed everything. Mohammad Mossadegh had been a problem for the Shah since he became Prime Minister on 28 April 1951. He had by then been a force in Iranian politics since the 1905–7 Constitutional Revolution when he had joined the Majlis aged 24. A nationalist, Mossadegh had taken a keen interest in the question of Iran's oil from the beginning of his career and almost 40 years earlier had actually decamped to Switzerland for a year in protest at the 1919 Anglo-Persian Agreement that had guaranteed Britain access and drilling rights to Iran's oilfields. The Shah was naturally desperate to keep the Western powers happy, which of course meant satisfying their oil thirst, and when Mossadegh became Prime Minister with a vocal agenda to nationalize Iran's oil reserves – at this time largely controlled by the British – conflict was inevitable.

Mossadegh repeatedly offered large amounts of compensation in return for his proposed nationalization, but he would not compromise on the fundamental point of Iranian control of its own oil. While better for national self-respect, the move was politically naïve; Iran was simply too weak to pursue such an assertive policy with any success. Once the more hardline Eisenhower replaced Truman in the White House in January 1953, Britain was able to play on US anti-Communist fears, Mossadegh became yet another Iranian victim of Great Power machinations and on 19 August was overthrown in the British-inspired and CIA-implemented coup *Operation Ajax*. The event (which, in effect, imposed a regime change on the country) has lodged in Iran's political rhetoric, historical canon and collective memory ever since – reducing centuries of foreign meddling to a single image that defined the birth of the modern Iranian political consciousness.[6]

The coup did, however, strengthen the Shah, who no longer had the charismatic Mossadegh to oppose him. But Iran remained weaker than ever, now with a ruler who owed his throne, twice over in the space of 12 years, to foreign powers, and he remained cautious. Always tending towards paranoia (he saw communists everywhere and the Soviet Union as a constant threat) he became obsessed with security. In the coup's aftermath he had a new problem: his new, and robust, Prime Minister, General Fazllolah Zahedi, whom the CIA had chosen to lead the coup, and who then insisted on retaining all of the Prime Minister's constitutional powers while demanding that the Shah rule as a figurehead. But in 1955 the Shah managed to dismiss Zahedi and became, in effect, Iran's sole ruler for the first time. The dismissal did not mean an instant consolidation of power – this was to be a gradual process, and one for which he needed, like all dictators, his army, and even more importantly, the USA.

So it is perhaps unsurprising that the Shah explicitly rejected much of what had gone before. In *Mission for My Country* (published in 1961), and which he supposedly wrote himself, he outlined his royal vision for Iran. Mossadegh's ideas were dismissed as mere negativity in favour of his own foreign policy, one of 'greater virility', that he called 'positive nationalism'.[7] This did not mean non-alignment (or as he described it 'sitting on the fence', which had been responsible for foreign 'infiltration and subversion') but engagement with the international order. His Iran stood for the 'ideals and principles' of the UN, and the proactive seeking out of alliances.[8]

The wish to break with the past is common with new leaders. What is important is how opinion had differed between the Shah and Mossadegh over the causes of Iran's 150-year regression. For Mossadegh, Britain's imperial greed and Iran's failure to nationalize its oil industry were to blame. For the Shah, it was two things, both of which would become crucial to his nuclear programme: Iran's lack of security and its technological backwardness. These two matters were subsumed into the overarching goals of his reign: to modernize Iran and restore Persian glory. What most characterized the country during this period was, therefore, that fundamental social feature of modernization – the gradual transfer of the bulk of the population from agrarian to urban employment.[9] But Iran remained economically underdeveloped and struggled with a history of foreign domination; nuclear power would come to a classic modernizing state, one ruled by a man who was dependent on the USA, desperate to 'modernize', and who had an unyielding urge to assuage a deeply felt loss of national self-respect.

CHAPTER 3

THE PEACOCK WANTS TO STRUT: NUCLEAR POWER UNDER THE SHAH

.

The 1950s were a time of change. As a Lacoste-attired Shah posed for photos on the tennis court and Parisian fashion began to appear in Tehran bazaars, the city's high society began to dream of a Persian *Belle Epoque*. Meanwhile, though perhaps of less concern to Iranian socialites, Britain's influence in the Middle East had all but died as Washington's had grown to supplant it (as amply demonstrated by the 1956 Suez Crisis when the Americans virtually frog-marched Britain and France from their imperial excursion to Egypt). The Shah's increased political control of the country was reflected in a national policy increasingly dictated by his desires, most immediately to prevent the emergence of another Mossadegh who might threaten his authority. Even before Zahedi's dismissal he ensured that elections to the 18th Majlis in early 1954 were firmly controlled (with candidates chosen for maximum pliability) to allow the Oil Consortium Bill (the *quid pro quo* for the 1953 coup that guaranteed Britain and the USA a healthy share of Iranian oil profits) to pass.

Post Zahedi, the Shah was finally able to begin the journey to autocratic modernization, which, like his father before him, he prized almost above all else. A more educated population, a more urbanized country and technological advancement were, he believed, the keys to Iran's future, which he also believed lay in close ties to the West. Washington now began to supply more military equipment to Iran as well as increasing its number of advisors in Iranian civilian and military programmes. US aid to a country that it perceived to be strongly anti-communist also increased, as did Iran's resulting dependence on Washington, which would become a source of widespread popular disgust and a serious political vulnerability for the Shah.

The government's 1955 Second Development Plan saw increasingly large sums spent on economic and social projects (often inefficiently). The Shah considered himself an enlightened leader that would lead Iran, finally, into the twentieth century, opposed only by blinkered reactionaries – the 'Black and the Red' (clerics and communists). Even at this early stage, the Shah believed modernization and Westernization were synonymous and Western goods and technology began to flow into the country, which only increased popular perception that the Shah was a Western 'lapdog' (a sin compounded because his 'master' was the Israel-supporting Washington). The display of progress was what counted and the very latest in progress was nuclear power.

By 1957, four years after the coup, Iran was judged stable enough to be trusted with nuclear technology. That year saw a nuclear training centre under the auspices of Central Treaty Organization (CENTO) move from Baghdad to Tehran, the opening of the American 'Atoms for Peace' exhibit in the city and the announcement of a bilateral agreement between Iran and the USA for co-operation on 'the peaceful uses of nuclear technology'.[1] The agreement required Iran to commit to not pursuing nuclear weapons, but allowed it to pursue 'peaceful' nuclear research and provided for technical assistance and the lease of several kilograms of US-enriched uranium. The agreement also laid the groundwork for the delivery of a 5 MW light-water research reactor.[2] Nuclear power was born in Iran; the USA was its midwife.

It was a long infancy, though. Iran's rather limited scientific establishment simply couldn't build on what it had received; the country now had some basic nuclear equipment but no real scientific base capable of operating it and the 5 MW light-water reactor – the Tehran Research Reactor – sat idle in Tehran University for almost the next decade. It was 1965 when Akbar Etemad, a young nuclear physicist, returned home to Iran from studies in Geneva and Paris with plenty of qualifications but no job. With time on his hands he occupied himself, as the unemployed generally do, by watching TV and reading the papers. According to the press, the Shah was angry about the lack of progress on the reactor. Construction had been stopped because the University was simply unable to continue without the necessary expertise, which didn't surprise Etemad, who was used to the European way of doing things and was surprised that the government had no single body dedicated solely to nuclear technology. Rather, all nuclear issues fell under the ambit of Iran's Plan Organization, which was responsible for all the country's development projects.

His dreams of a technologically advanced Iran powering to modernity on nuclear-generated electricity had seemingly been thwarted before they had begun. He publicly urged the organization's head, Safi Asfia, to get things moving, which was simply impossible without anyone able to operate the reactor, something Etemad knew he could do. So one morning, in one of those twists of serendipity that litter history, he put his diplomas in a bag, went to the Plan Organization's office in Tehran and asked to see Asfia. The receptionist was reluctant to let him in but he said that if she told her boss that there was a young Iranian outside who knew about the atom he would see him, which he did. Asfia was a professor of engineering at Tehran University and had enough technical knowledge to understand he was talking to someone whose expertise was far greater. 'God has sent you through the window to us', he told Etemad with obvious and desperate relief.[3]

Etemad left his diplomas at the office; such was the desperation for qualified personnel they would be shown to the Shah himself and Etemad was told that he would receive a call shortly. Two days later he did. He was told to start work at Tehran University immediately and that all funds needed to complete the reactor would be released. When Etemad arrived, his initial reaction was shock: the lack of infrastructure, the lack of qualified personnel and the generally shambolic state of things made the size of the job depressingly clear. The staff consisted mainly of a few nuclear physics professors from the University, but they were academics without the necessary practical know-how to build, run or maintain reactors. Some of the construction work on the reactor had been done, but it was not even installed and anyway appeared to have problems.

The first thing Etemad did was to catch a flight to Illinois to visit American Machine and Foundry (which had supplied the reactor and was helping to build it) where he was able to diagnose and resolve the outstanding technical issues. Then came the hard part: training people to operate it. The University had a few people who could do this at a basic level but Etemad needed to train more to deal with radioisotope production and other more sophisticated procedures. In the end it took two years (1965–7) to finish everything. When he was done he just handed the reactor over to the University for research and educational purposes. It went critical (live and ready for use) in November 1967, using 93 per cent-enriched (ironically weapons grade) uranium supplied by the USA. In 1968, the Atomic Research Centre, affiliated to Tehran University, with a working 5 MW pool type research reactor was officially (and finally) opened, but it was all low-level stuff.

Teaching nuclear physics at Tehran University was his next stop, but Etemad was now too valuable to remain just a professor for long. In late 1969, just one year after the Atomic Research Centre had opened, Prime Minister Amir Abbas Hoveida duly summoned him to his elegant prime ministerial office to discuss how to improve scientific research in Iran. In a fairly brief meeting, Etemad offered to put together a package of recommendations but insisted he do so with the help of relevant experts. What had most struck him during his work on the reactor was the lack of scientific professionalism that existed, almost at a cultural level, within government – there was just no recognition that national scientific projects should be run and staffed by experts not bureaucrats, and he recommended the establishment of an independent, national organization dedicated purely to scientific research. The proposal was approved and became Iran's Institute for Planning and Research in Science and Education with Etemad at its head.

Etemad had introduced the idea of technological specialism into government; technology and research could no longer be subsumed into general government bureaucracy (which had yielded such consistently disappointing results). These early experiences had been technologically remedial but politically instructive for Etemad: the Shah, it seemed, was desperate to overhaul Iran's scientific establishment and, more pertinently, he clearly wanted nuclear power personally. He alone had made the decision to launch a nuclear programme with almost no government consultation; nuclear power had come to Iran not from political consensus or debate, but from one man's will.

Etemad was more right than he knew. Successful nuclear programmes in modernizing countries traditionally depend upon the support of authoritarian leaders that privilege nuclear power on the political agenda. Non-democratic countries are less susceptible to the types of opposition – political groups, public opinion, a reluctant civil service, to name a few – as democracies, and if their leaders want something badly enough it usually happens. The two modernizing countries with the most advanced nuclear programmes throughout the 1960s and 1970s were India and Argentina (though the latter certainly had difficulties with its programme), both of which began their nuclear programmes in the 1950s like Iran, and which were shepherded through their formative years by strong leaders. For 20 years Homi Bhabha presided over the Indian Atomic Energy Agency's swell from humble origins to a world-class institution, employing over 1,800 scientists and engineers and 3,000 technicians; an achievement impossible without the unwavering prime ministerial support of Jawaharlal Nehru. Equally, Juan Perón's desire to go nuclear allowed Admiral Oscar Quihillalt unfettered control of Argentina's nuclear project, and the ability to override tiresome political checks and balances as he saw fit.[4]

As the 1960s slid into the 1970s Etemad returned to higher education and watched the Shah's grip on almost all areas of Iranian life become complete. Pressure from the Kennedy Administration in the early 1960s for its ally to (at least pay lip service to) reform had resulted in various liberalizing measures that the Shah used – along with his earlier creation of a 'two-party' system (with an official 'opposition' to boot) – to assuage both Washington's concerns and his self-image as a modern, just ruler. It is difficult to overestimate the extent of change that took place in Iran from 1953 to the end of the 1970s. Oil set the Shah free: in 1953 oil revenue was $34 million a year; at the end of 1973 it was around $5 billion.[5] Despite huge wastage and corruption, almost $30 billion was spent on economic and social projects in the Second (1955–62), Third (1962–8), Fourth (1968–73) and Fifth (1973–8) Development Plans. GNP rose from $3 billion to over $53 billion and the per capita income jumped from less than $160 to over $1,600, even though the population grew from 18 million to nearly 35 million.[6] From 1953 to 1977 the education system grew by 1,000 per cent and the country experienced unprecedented industrialization as factories mushroomed across Iran.

All of this combined with an increasingly sophisticated army and the ability of government security forces, notably the hated secret police, SAVAK, to repress domestic opposition had emboldened the Shah to the point of hubris. Almost a decade earlier, in 1965, he had celebrated the 25th year of his reign by bestowing upon himself the title Aryan Sun (*Aryamehr*); post 1973 oil wealth merely completed his metamorphosis to the Iranian Louis XIV. In 1974 his Prime Minister, Hoveida, summed up late Pahlavi Iran's rather 'streamlined' policy process: 'In Western countries', he oleaginously declared, 'you talk too much about things, take them from committee to committee. Here we go to the Shah and then act'.[7] What this meant for the nuclear programme was that pet projects – of which nuclear power was one – became policy. Oil prices and nuclear energy were two issues on which the Shah could always be reached, and on which he would make decisions personally.

THE FOUNDING OF THE ATOMIC ENERGY ORGANIZATION OF IRAN (AEOI)

Three things then affected the birth of the nuclear programme and its character and purpose during its formative years. The most important of these were Washington's support and the Shah's desperation for nuclear energy. He had personally driven the project from the beginning, bullying and chivvying his subordinates, demanding more and more progress all the time. The third was Etemad's expertise and in early 1974 he received another call. It was from the influential media personality, Reza Ghotbi, head of Iran's national RadioTelevision and cousin to Queen Farah, who told Etemad he had been out to dinner with the Shah and Hoveida the previous evening and the Shah, who had taken note of Etemad's previous work, had again mentioned that he wanted to set up an independent body devoted to nuclear energy. He had, in fact, given the order two years ago, but, inevitably, it had got lost in Iran's bureaucratic maze and nothing had happened. The Shah was now sick of waiting and told Ghotbi to call Etemad and ask him to do it. After thinking it through for a couple of days, Etemad accepted, more out of duty than anything else. He spent the next month preparing yet another report that outlined the various possible approaches and their respective political implications.

The Shah's goal was characteristically vague: officially he wanted nuclear energy for electricity – beyond that nothing was specified. He was desperate, Etemad thought, for the *idea* of nuclear energy; at times it seemed that it was not even nuclear energy in itself, just anything (and everything) that would modernize Iran as quickly as possible.[8] So Etemad set out a condition:

that the organization would be independent from government, for which it needed sufficient resources; and the Iranian treasury had resources. In October 1973 the Organization of the Petroleum Exporting Countries (OPEC) members had proclaimed a global oil embargo in response to Washington's decision to re-supply the Israeli military during the Yom Kippur War, causing a global spike in the price of oil. Independently, the OPEC members decided to use their leverage over the world price setting mechanism for oil to stabilize their income by officially raising world oil prices, which by 1977 had quadrupled; Iran's oil revenues hit $20 billion. The Shah's desperation to progress on the nuclear front was now more than matched by the means to do so. Etemad was confident his demand wouldn't be a problem, and it was not. After he submitted his report a meeting was convened at the Royal Palace in North Tehran in March. The three of them met in the Shah's large office: Etemad, Hoveida and a casually attired Shah himself. The Shah read the report a few times, asked Etemad a question or two, and then handed it to Hoveida; 'this is how things will work', he told him. The meeting had lasted under two hours.[9]

Things now moved quickly. The proposal needed parliamentary approval but given the nature of the Shah's autocracy this was just a formality. Then suitable premises had to be found, equipped and, finally, staffed. Etemad was fortunate here. The government had trumpeted the founding of the AEOI so loudly that when the news broke internationally many suitably qualified Iranians abroad (mainly in the USA or Europe) made contact and by the end of first year the AEOI had a nucleus of around 100 people. Etemad had also stipulated that the Tehran Research Reactor and its staff be transferred to the AEOI, which further augmented numbers. The organization also had an almost limitless budget (much to the chagrin of other industry sectors) and Etemad had total freedom to pay his employees what he liked – the Majlis naturally approved everything without question.

Etemad had ensured that the Head of the AEOI retained all decision-making powers involving budget, which he then bolstered with a set of internal agency regulations for hiring staff, for which the agency head also had sole responsibility. Nor did the AEOI have to submit reports to the government on the amount of money spent. Instead, a single report on all expenditure went to the treasury at the end of the year – the only financial report ever produced.[10] Unsurprisingly, this caused considerable jealousy. Almost all the top ministers – especially in the oil sector (traditionally Iran's most prized industry) – were against the programme, or at the very least criticized its scale.[11] Following the 1973 oil price boom Iran's oil revenues increased from less than $1 billion to over $20 billion by the end of the decade. The government initiated numerous industrial projects only to find that, very often, promised funds had been diverted to the nuclear programme, which consumed a huge portion of Iran's foreign exchange earnings.

A pattern of sorts emerged: Hoveida and the Finance Minister would go to Etemad and tell him there was not enough money for a particular project, a message Etemad would then take to the Shah, who would get angry and tell the Prime Minister and Finance Minister that their job was to find the money; his personal support made the programme virtually impregnable in cabinet disputes.[12] This was the second and almost equally important benefit of royal support necessary for a successful nuclear programme in a modernizing country. If a leader will not consistently intervene on behalf of a nascent nuclear programme – sustain his or her interest – bureaucratic competitors will invariably take advantage. (In the late 1970s, for example, Suharto's loss of interest allowed the Indonesian nuclear programme to be smothered by the Indonesian Finance Ministry and rival coal interests.)

By statute, two organs were responsible for the AEOI. The first, the High Council of Atomic Energy Policy (consisting of the Prime Minister and some ministers with relevant expertise) was supposed to supervise policy. The Council met two or three times and no more. The second, the Committee of Nuclear Energy, which consisted of three ministers and Etemad himself, was responsible for governmental supervision of the organization as a whole. It met once and never again. The government just didn't interfere. From the beginning the Shah wanted to streamline the channels of communication, and had publicly declared the matter of such national importance that the AEOI would operate under his direct supervision. Any government oversight that occurred took place in regular meetings between the Shah and Etemad himself.

Etemad was also made Deputy Prime Minister of Iran, which many believed was yet another example of the Shah's desire to ally the nuclear industry directly with the centre of political power. The truth is that political manoeuvring was responsible. Hoveida had suggested it at the original, March 1974, meeting – his only real contribution – as he had uneasily witnessed Etemad insist on total independence to a receptive Shah and realized that the AEOI would be totally free of government oversight. If Etemad were made Deputy Prime Minister there would be at least one link between the AEOI and the government, and he would have some kind of channel into the programme.

Hoveida's concern was hardly surprising and Etemad knew what was bothering the Prime Minister. Over the years Etemad had witnessed a change in the charismatic Hoveida. In the early days of their collaboration in the late 1960s Hoveida had genuinely tried to use his office for the national good, especially by supporting the Shah's aims in developing Iran. But little by little he had lost that enthusiasm and grown cynical, and by the early 1970s his main objective seemed to be to stay in power. He was educated, well travelled, well read and sarcastic – a pragmatist – and Etemad liked him; but he knew that Hoveida's goal was to avoid problems wherever possible and if that were impossible, to conceal them. He was a political animal and he guarded his position jealously. Etemad suspected that this was the impulse behind the suggestion to make him Deputy Prime Minister. The Shah had initially considered this unnecessary, but in the end he relented. It made no difference to him what Etemad was called; he would report directly to his king, everything else was irrelevant.

THE OFFICIAL POSITION: ECONOMICS OF THE DEVELOPING WORLD

Shortly after the AEOI was officially opened, the Shah and Etemad met alone for the first time at Sa'dabad Palace. In his early days at the Tehran Research Reactor, Etemad had been told, somewhat vaguely, that the Shah had ordered the programme for 'electricity'. Over the course of a pleasant afternoon in late 1974 the Shah outlined, for the first time, the reasons why he so desperately wanted nuclear power. Most immediately, he said, Iran's biggest obstacle to development was economic (he always fancied himself an economist). Nuclear energy, particularly as a source of cheap power, could significantly improve a country's economic position and raise its standard of living. This was a standard argument of the time: developing countries that embark upon nuclear power programmes invariably argue that they are motivated by reasons of economic growth and energy security.[13] Despite being a member of the Non-Aligned Movement and enjoying good personal relations with developing world leaders like Marshall Tito, the Shah was desperate to ally Iran with the West and always resented identification of Iran as a developing world country. But as he made clear to Etemad, nuclear power was the perfect conduit for industrial and economic progress.

Nor was this a necessarily unrealistic aspiration. Undertaking a project that required a general minimum outlay of $1 billion was simply too great a financial undertaking for most developing countries, many of which struggled with huge foreign debt.[14] Moreover, the general industry rule of thumb that one nuclear reactor should comprise no more than 10 per cent of an electrical grid's capacity meant that the smallest offered nuclear reactor at the time – that of 600 MW – needed to be placed in a 6,000 MW grid, generally too large for those of most developing countries.[15]

As a country with (at this time) a population of 32 million people and a total area of 628,000 sq miles (about the size of Western Europe), Iran was one of the few modernizing states for which such a project was theoretically feasible.[16] Rapid economic growth obsessed Mohammad Reza Pahlavi (he envisaged Iran becoming an industrial power equal to France by the end of the twentieth century) and the ambition only intensified as his wealth and military strength increased.[17] That afternoon in late 1974 in his office, he outlined three unashamedly economic reasons for nuclear power that became the official government 'line' for its need: the benefits of resource diversification, energy competition and technological advancement.

The first of these amounted to an obsession (one of several) for the Shah. One of nuclear power's greatest benefits is the escape it offers from overdependence upon valuable resources like petroleum because the energy needed to power the country can be derived from an alternative energy source. To non-petroleum-producing countries it may free them from vulnerability to international oil price fluctuations (and political dependence on oil producers); for an oil producing country such as Iran where petroleum also represents the primary source of national income, nuclear energy can be life saving. During the 1970s Iran was the third largest producer of oil in the world. As the major base of Iran's wealth, the Shah explained, oil was a valuable but finite commodity. He had strong views on this economic dilemma, and was at pains to repeat his belief to anyone who would listen that petroleum and natural gas were so valuable that it was 'scandalous' to burn them as fuel.[18]

Iran's primary public justification of its nuclear programme from its beginnings under the Shah to Khamenei's Islamic Republic today has always been presented as an economic argument. The domestic use of fossil fuels, especially oil, for domestic energy consumption seriously affects Iran's foreign exchange earnings – every barrel burned is a barrel not sold. Even at this stage, studies indicated that if Iran continued to export its oil at the same rate it would become a net-importer of crude oil and associated by-products within 50 years.[19] As early as 1960, the Shah envisaged nuclear energy as its direct replacement:

> The oil we call the noble product will be depleted one day. It is a shame to burn the noble product for the production of energy to run factories and lighthouses. About 70,000 products can be derived from oil. We plan to get as soon as possible, 23,000 MWe from nuclear power stations. Added to the electricity generated by our dams, this will give us one of the highest per capita supplies in the world.[20]

Supported by Etemad's counsel, he maintained this belief throughout his reign, and as late as 1977 he told US President Jimmy Carter that the programme's ultimate aim was to replace petroleum as the source of industrial energy.[21] With water resources insufficient to support hydroelectric power, and other potential energy sources such as fusion and solar technologies too far off to be feasible, for 1970s Iran, nuclear energy remained the only realistic long-term energy alternative for the preservation of oil reserves.

The Shah also worried about the increasing threat to oil from alternative energy sources. Here, he worked very much within the *zeitgeist*. During the 1970s nuclear power was almost universally considered an energy panacea. In 1974–5 alone Washington ordered 25,000 MW, while Germany and France and Japan also heavily explored civil nuclear power; it was *the* new source of energy. The Shah repeatedly outlined, to the point of boredom, the dangers of over reliance on a single energy source for income and of the threat to oil from nuclear power in particular: 'as a sort of crowning indignity to oil', he argued, 'Germany, Britain and other countries are planning nuclear-powered oil tankers. In the distant future oil may face competition from solar energy'.[22] The supply market had also become more competitive, which could affect both price and potential customer base, with new oilfields discovered in Libya and new French-built refineries in the Sahara.[23] Nuclear power would lessen reliance upon oil revenues and, therefore, upon consistently high petroleum prices for both continued prosperity and short-term economic gains.

26

The final reason especially excited the scientifically minded Etemad. For any country that contemplates a nuclear programme, an important, related benefit lies in the attendant increase in human capital it can bring: nuclear programmes need nuclear scientists and technicians, who need teachers and professors, who need equipment and facilities and universities and so on. Also, once workers are trained in a complex field like nuclear technology they can move on to other development projects, where their skill set can be used to train fellow citizens, which increases national productivity as a whole.[24] This, so the thinking goes, creates a nationwide chain of scientific and industrial improvement. At this time the greatest obstacle to Iran's becoming a world power was its lack of technically trained manpower (though it was successful in 'importing' foreign instructors).[25] Etemad was determined to rectify this and technological advancement became another prominent public trope – especially important for the wider Pahlavi national project. By seeking to increase technological capability, the Shah sought to give his country the 'instruments of power'.[26]

A final economic consideration arose. The programme only began in seriousness with Etemad's founding of the AEOI, which had been largely possible due to the Shah's increased sense of political security and financial clout from the oil windfall. A genuine economic dilemma thereby presented itself: what to do with the colossal oil revenues pouring into the Iranian coffers? What options are available to a developing country, albeit a superficially (and transiently) wealthy one? Iran could not simply invest the money domestically without suffering severe digestion problems likely to cause sharp inflation and other economically undesirable consequences (which actually happened in the mid-1970s). Other investment strategies such as currency speculation were hampered by insufficient expertise resulting from no genuine investment culture among the nation's wealthy elite, more used to haggling in the bazaar and/or owning land. Investing in foreign countries or depositing reserves in foreign bank accounts were tried but foreign assets purchased abroad are always vulnerable, susceptible as they are to 'confiscation' by host governments, something that did in fact occur with the Shah's downfall – money that Iran is still owed to this day.

What had landed, like a slab of marble, at the Shah's feet was an opportunity to push ahead of his Middle East rivals. Nuclear energy required a financial investment only few countries could afford to make, let alone developing ones. In their early meetings Etemad made this point repeatedly to the Shah – 'the country', he said, 'should cash in on its competitive advantage'; particularly as contemporary forecasts showed that the cost of conventionally fired power plants would continue to rise.[27] Nuclear power is so capital intensive, he explained, that a country has to spend a lot very quickly to get returns in ten years. During this time Iran had the means to do this, so it represented sound economic policy. The best way to preserve the value of petrodollars might be to spend them. Certainly, nuclear power was a markedly more sensible way of spending money than ostentatious birthday 'celebrations' or Reza Shah's malfunctioning railways.

BEYOND THE OFFICIAL CASE: ROYAL GLORY

Like all dead kings, even the successful ones, the Shah is condemned to dramatic irony. In this case the leitmotif is hubris. Ever since Nader Shah returned to Tehran with a stolen Mughal throne in 1738, the Peacock Throne has symbolized the Royal House of Persia. For Mohammad Reza Shah, royal glory was both domestic and foreign policy, and he was determined to make the metaphor a reality; the great tail feathers would unfurl in all their Pahlavi splendour and the world, or at any rate the region, would marvel at the display. As early as the mid-1960s those close to the Shah had noticed that a nuclear programme meant more to him than just economics. It certainly brought justifiable economic benefits, but transcended these for one simple reason: it brought the nation prestige. Prestige is a nebulous yet very real idea in international politics and is perhaps best defined as power based upon reputation rather than reputation based upon power. This is instructive because it illustrates the reliance of prestige on a fundamentally intangible quality: 'reputation', which exists only in the perceptions of others.[28]

The Shah was not a complex man. The desire to impress drove him, and with his ostentatious palaces, ceremonies, ultra-sophisticated weapons and solid gold bathtubs, displays of power and wealth were his natural idiom. As his power grew he came to view himself as not just a national but an international leader with a global mission. In November 1956, the Suez Crisis had offered the Shah his first opportunity to play the role of statesman when he chaired a Muslim heads-of-state meeting between Iran, Iraq, Turkey and Pakistan in Tehran. It gave him a taste for international diplomacy that would only increase and combine with his internal reforms to create (in his eyes) a narrative of Iran as the new Persian Empire – with himself at its head, naturally – for which a nuclear programme was the perfect complement. Its economic benefits were clear to him, and any economic improvements to a country logically raise its prestige. But, beyond these, the combination of a modernizing country that wanted greater national self-respect ruled by a man desperate for global admiration fused to make the desire for nuclear power almost irresistible.

This was for several reasons. Most immediately, nuclear power is a political phenomenon that divides the modern and modernizing worlds. *Prima facie*, modernizing countries believe it offers them an escape from backwardness into technological advancement. In 1974, Indira Gandhi defended India's (supposedly) peaceful nuclear test in the face of international outrage on the grounds that it was vital 'for development': 'Only through acquisition of "higher technology"', she argued, 'could a nation overcome poverty and economic backwardness.'[29] In this line of thought, nuclear power is considered a conduit to modernity that (as well as bringing practical benefits) helps to plug a 'prestige deficit' suffered by developing countries, particularly in the Islamic Middle East, shamed by their backwardness compared to the West. Gandhi's defence adumbrated both classic developing world economic justifications for nuclear power and the inherent 'Third Worldism' that characterizes the 'nuclear clash' between the nuclear-weapon states and many of their developing world non-nuclear counterparts. Here, a modernizing state cited its need to progress in the face of the developed world's (perceived) opposition; economic imperatives fused with a desire for greater independence and defiance. In a climate where such countries value anything they perceive to be an equalizer of their positions against the major powers, ideas of prestige, glory, or anything that can bring much-needed *external* acknowledgement, have a special piquancy. They are compensatory – and it is the reason why national nuclear programmes are so often considered a symbol of sovereignty.

Second, the international system of nuclear governance – as embodied in the NPT – is seen by the developing states as asymmetric: a Western 'tool' that has entrenched a system where civilian nuclear energy can (theoretically) be freely distributed around the world while military technology is restricted to a self-selecting elite.[30] This self-selecting elite, moreover, decides which countries are 'trustworthy' enough to receive their largesse in the form of even civil nuclear assistance (via the IAEA or unilaterally). As the developing world sees it, the NPT divides the world into nations that can be trusted and those that cannot and in so doing further embeds the binary division between the nuclear and non-nuclear countries, reinforces their respective prejudices and bolsters the confrontation between the two sides.[31] The nuclear states, so the thinking goes, object to the advancement of their less-developed contemporaries and use the NPT to mire them in backwardness. The proliferation of nuclear power in the modernizing world becomes a largely political enterprise conducted in the shade of confrontation between the developed and less-developed countries, the modern versus the modernizing world. In the Indian nuclear test's aftermath, State Department officials noted that developing countries, many of them India's rivals, nonetheless 'quietly welcomed the Indian demonstration that one of their number could accomplish a technical achievement formerly reserved for the major powers'.[32]

Modernizing world desires for nuclear independence are, therefore, necessarily both aspirational and confrontational. Nuclear power is perceived to offer the chance of redress in a constitutionally unjust world where colonialism persists as 'technological apartheid'; a potential balm for anxieties of comparison with a West that begrudges its developing world counterparts the requisite technology to compete. It is perceived to offer, in effect, what Iran craves, and has craved since the beginning of the Qajar Empire. In 1974, the Indian nuclear explosion showed the world that, despite its industrial and economic modesty, on nuclear terms at least it could compete.[33] For many modernizing nations, nuclear power offers the *sole* means of being taken seriously – of *external* recognition – as an international 'player'. In the case of Pakistan, for example, which lacked even India's economic and political power and autonomy, near autonomy in at least one important area would be even more important as a symbol of national pride.

Assuaging a Western 'complex' underpinned the Shah's reign. What differentiated him from many of his contemporaries (and the later Islamic Republic) was how he tried to do this. Nuclear power was not a battleground between the 'West and the rest', but a means of transmutation by which Iran could become 'Western'. Like his father before him, the Shah believed that Iran's problems could be attributed to its lack of 'modernization' (a nebulous term onto which both men were free to impose their own reductive definitions) relative to the West. What made his desire so idiosyncratic was his belief that modernization *was* Westernization – he even titled a chapter in *Mission for My Country* 'Westernization: Our Welcome Ordeal'. As a worldview the book is illuminating (if lacking in literary merit) as the Shah both displayed classic status anxiety in regard to the Western 'other' and signposted the Pahlavi mandate. 'Western nations', he declared, '[had] forged rapidly ahead'; Iran had to progress and it was not enough to merely 'catch up'.[34]

His urge to modernize was a psychological idiosyncrasy, but there were also pragmatic reasons for a programme of serious reform. Iran was changing at a rate incomparable (and almost incomprehensible) to any of its Western contemporaries. In 1940, 75 per cent of the population were peasants; huge industrialization and oil wealth changed the fabric of society (as well as convincing the Shah that all was well), not least by making it more urbanized and politically aware. The growth of mass media in particular had huge political significance. By the early 1960s, there were estimated to be around 1 million radio sets in Iran (a tenfold increase from 1940) and around 67,000 television sets with the ability to reach an audience of over half a million.[35] The need for a clear and defined political message was imperative and the Shah was a ruler with a clear and defined self-image to promulgate. International pressure (primarily from the USA) combined with increasing domestic unrest had convinced the Shah that Iran needed a 'revolution from above' to abort what would otherwise be the inevitable 'revolution from below'. It was myth making for the TV age.

As early as 1960, he told the outgoing Majlis that Iran could no longer live in the 'Middle Ages'. Modernity was the goal and the West, the home of 'science and reason', not to mention Versace and Dunhill, was the model. The Shah's preferred method of modernization was the grand, showy project – perfect for myth-making narratives designed to bolster the image of his 'revolutionary' Iran – which found its earliest expression with his 1963 'White Revolution' (a term coined by the conservative newspaper *Etela'at*). The White Revolution was essentially a series of land reforms designed to distribute land ownership to the peasants – a perfect project for the Shah, who saw modernity as the antithesis of 'feudalism'.

Guided by the Shah's conception of modernity as embodied in the industrialized West, it was also superficial. In a 1961 speech the Shah had set out his vision for the 'new' Iranian man to the 20th Majlis: 'your income should be such that you and your family are full. That you have smart clothes. That you have a nice house', he said.[36] Leaving aside the banality of the first sentence, the aspiration was clear: the values were not even merely bourgeoisie but encompassed the most meretricious aspects of Western consumerism. The Shah identified himself with 'progress' (repeating this word throughout many speeches on the subject), which was the opposite of backwardness and of 'reactionaries' like Mossadegh, but it was a conception of progress quantified by what could be possessed and, importantly, seen.

The White Revolution eventually morphed into the 'Great Civilization' – an exercise in myth making on a national scale in which government propaganda portrayed the Shah's reign as the harbinger of a 'Great Civilization', which would transform Iran into a leading industrial power; Iranians as Aryan people would be comparable to Europeans, and would re-found the Persian Empire. As the Shah's power increased and Iran's supposed 'constitutional monarchy' became ever more subordinated to the reality of his 'imperial system' (*nezm-e shahanshahi*) with him as its 'commander' (*farmandar*), hubris fuelled by high GNP and oil wealth reached vertiginous levels. The image of modernity espoused in the 'White Revolution' and the 'Great Civilization' – its superficiality, its emphasis on the showy and spectacular, not to mention the idea of Pahlavi Modernism as, critically, Westernization – would find its fullest expression with the nuclear programme. Iran would restore its former glory through its 'modern' character as embodied in the Shah's domestic reforms, the country's increasing global reach and, critically, its technology. As with his domestic reforms, the possible political benefits were not lost on the Shah either. If the Iranian people could bask in the reflected glory of his rapidly modernizing Iran, then they would surely rejoice in the global prestige a sophisticated nuclear programme would bring. The Shah saw himself as a revolutionary monarch, and nothing was more revolutionary than nuclear power.

Technology was the ultimate vessel of modernity. The language the Shah used whenever he discussed technology was always that of pride and, vitally, modernization – but a peculiar view of modernization. In *Mission for My Country*, the country's Abadan oil refinery, for example, was noteworthy not for any specific industrial reason but because it was 'the biggest refinery in the world'; more important still, Abadan itself was a 'cosmopolitan city' with 'visible ties with all parts of the world'; for the Shah, the quality of Iranian technology showed the nation clearly allied to the developed world. Describing a dam, he dwelt not on its purpose but the fact that it was 'one of the highest dams in the world ... two-thirds the height of the Eiffel Tower in Paris'.[37] Equally, he declared the Namazee Hospital in Shiraz an example of Iranian accomplishment because an 'American expert' in hospital administration had declared it 'unquestionably' the best run in the Middle East.[38] Throughout the book, technological achievements were constantly evaluated in relation to the West. For the Shah, Iranian technology was not merely of economic or industrial benefit, it was a display: a medal for the royal breast, but one that could only be pinned there by a Western hand.

Nuclear power was of course the apotheosis of modern technology, the catalyst for economic growth and the future. Nuclear programmes often serve an important symbolic function that reflects a country's identity. They have a 'normative' value similar to flags, airlines and Olympic teams: something some modern states believe they must have to be modern states.[39] Once again, a modernizing Islamic state's need for independence and greater self-respect fused with the Shah's personal thirst for modernity, while some of the more 'compensatory' benefits of nuclear power fused with the Pahlavi view of technology to make the desire for a nuclear programme all consuming. Westernization was the goal, technology the means and nuclear technology – the height of Western achievement – its zenith. All around him the Shah saw 'momentous developments ... taking place in respect to mankind's energy resources', particularly in the nuclear field, among those countries that 'mattered'. Britain, the book tells us, had 'assumed world leadership in nuclear power production' while, with 'fearlessness of the dangers' (or of cliché), 'America's long-range nuclear submarines roam[ed] the seven seas'. Iran would once again be great, just like them.

Nowhere was this more evident than with Iran's own nuclear programme. The Tehran Nuclear Research Centre was 'equipped by the United Kingdom' and 'staffed by British, Turkish, Pakistani and Iranian scientists' and drew 'students from the CENTO region'. Naturally, the academic work compared 'in quality with that of similar courses given in Britain and the United States'.[40] The programme's high academic standard made it yet another monument to Iranian achievement (again the standard was quantified in relation to the West) and its international character affirmed the idea of an Iran wedded to the international community. In 1961 the Shah had told the American Ambassador that Iran had to remain 'tied' to the West; if those ties were ever broken, he would cease being Shah. His nuclear programme was yet another example of the 'Iranian renaissance' he believed he had created that made his country so valuable to the USA.[41] The Pahlavi national project was about creating a narrative of Iran; the nuclear programme was its inevitable apotheosis. It brought real potential economic benefits, but the Shah's own ambitions combined with the particular appeal nuclear power had for many developing countries meant it transcended those benefits and became both a symbol of modernity (read Westernization) and a means of its effectuation.

THE PROGRAMME DEVELOPS

What this meant practically was made clear by the extent of the commercial ties that soon bound Iran to the West. The opportunity to build an indigenous scientific base was largely sacrificed to collaboration with foreign contractors; and while this is often a necessity for modernizing states due to their limited domestic capabilities, it represented a definite choice on the Shah's part. From the first day he walked into the AEOI offices in Amirabad in North Tehran, Etemad knew he faced the problem of Iran's lack of indigenous capability. In the late 1960s, the country had around 150 people at various levels of training in nuclear physics, and while this had improved, Etemad knew he would need around 15,000 trained employees for all the projected plants to become operational.[42] Technology was also a problem; if Iran did not possess it indigenously it would have to get it elsewhere, which is what it ultimately did. As the project progressed, the increases in oil revenue meant the regime was able to substitute wealth for human capital.

Everything, down to the construction of roads and houses for what would be Iran's first nuclear reactor at Bushehr, was farmed out to foreign contractors. While Etemad would oversee a definite improvement, and the buildup of the AEOI's scientific base was impressive, it was far less so than other modernizing countries of the time, such as Argentina and India, which focused on slowly building up a domestic base for their programmes. The Shah, conversely, while wanting a wide array of nuclear technologies (which caused international alarm), was always careful to maintain nuclear links with Western countries. Like his grand dreams of investing in Western companies like Mercedes and Krupp (not to mention his penchant and order for a Concorde) the Shah attempted to bind Iran to the West through commercial ties. Focus was placed on the USA and the major European countries; and he hoped that eventually even Sweden would get involved.[43]

He worked very much within a reciprocal relationship here. If he was happy that progress was finally being made, nuclear suppliers were delighted. Western governments clamoured for a piece of Iran's nuclear pie. The Shah's bold plans – he wanted up to 20 nuclear reactors – meant that billions were there to be made; the French Foreign Ministry even created the post of Nuclear Attaché at their embassy in Tehran.[44] Foreign companies swamped Etemad with requests for meetings, and embassy officials, including Sir Anthony Parsons, the British Ambassador to Iran, wooed AEOI officials over dinner.[45] Staff also received endless invitations to visit foreign nuclear installations and discuss possible co-operation with the USSR, China, Brazil, Japan and many others; not to mention being given repeated tours of US nuclear installations. The financial opportunities were vast. Etemad had drawn up plans for a programme divided into three distinct parts revolving around the ostensible goal of a nuclear-powered national electrical grid. For this it needed nuclear power plants to produce the nuclear-powered electricity, fuel to power these plants, and scientific and technical support for the plants and for the wider programme as a whole.

Top priority was understandably the construction of the power plants to generate electricity. The AEOI directors first debated what type of nuclear reactors to use: heavy-water or light-water reactors. In the end, Etemad selected the light-water variety as they were considered to be the most reliable (they were also, coincidentally, the type least conducive to making weapons). The second, critical, decision was who would build them. West Germany and France were chosen after some discussion and it was a fairly easy decision to make. Both had excellent nuclear industries and were fairly neutral political choices. A preliminary site for the country's first power plant was then chosen, 17 km southeast of the city of Bushehr on the south-western coast of Iran along the Persian Gulf. It would supply energy to the inland city of Shiraz.

A coastal location was considered desirable because much of the equipment, some of which weighed several hundred tonnes, would have to be shipped to Iran, while water from the sea would be needed to cool the plant. The problem was the area's history of earthquakes, but after an investigation the AEOI decided to go ahead. The data was passed across to the West German firm Kraftwerk Union AG, a joint venture of Siemens AG and AEG Telefunken, which had been selected to build the plant. Kraftwerk was instructed to make the plant as earthquake-resistant as possible. In late 1975, having read through all of Kraftwerk's impressive reports, Etemad called Ahmad Sotudehnia (who had been appointed as AEOI manager on the project) into his office and authorized him to sign a contract with Kraftwerk worth US$4–6 billion to build a pressurized water reactor power plant with two 1,196 MW reactors at Bushehr. Construction began the same year, subcontracted to ThyssenKrupp AG. The reactors were based on the Convoy design and identical to the second reactor unit of the German Biblis Nuclear Power Plant.[46]

The 'turnkey' nature of the project (by which Kraftwerk would do everything and at the end simply hand everything over to the Iranians to 'turn the key' to get started) was controversial; and

it caused arguments at AEOI meetings, where Etemad had pro-
moted an atmosphere of open discussion. The directors (there
were about ten under Etemad himself) met several times a week
and few subjects were off-limits. In the weeks before the Bushehr
deal there were many arguments in the smoke-filled conference
room between two clear sides, with some arguing that the
'turnkey' method was a necessity given Iran's limited nuclear
capabilities, while others supported Etemad's thesis that Iranian
industry should benefit from the programme and get involved in
construction.[47] Despite favouring the latter view, Etemad calculated that Bushehr was only one of many envisaged projects and
there would be ample opportunity for Iranian involvement in
power plant construction: the immediate goal was to get Bushehr
finished quickly and get the programme running.[48]

The first reactor was scheduled to be finished by 1980 and the
second one by 1981. The German government was so eager to enter the Iranian market that it guaranteed Kraftwerk's investment
against any loss. The German market was saturated and the USA
had cornered most of the rest of Europe, so the developing world
was the target and Iran's oil wealth made it the ideal client. With
an eager Siemens and a supportive Shah, progress was steady over
the next few years. Etemad visited the site once or twice a year,
as did the Shah, and both were impressed with the quality of the
German work. By the time the revolution came in 1979 the first
reactor (Bushehr I) was 85 per cent complete (on schedule for
its 1981 completion date) and the second (Bushehr II) partially
complete.

The Shah's plans for up to 20 nuclear reactors meant that multiple projects had to be commissioned simultaneously (and
quickly). It was a hectic though enjoyable time for the AEOI. In
preliminary investigations, AEOI engineers had also identified a
second possible site for a power plant, at Darkhovin, 40 km north
of the city of Ahvaz, less subject to earthquakes and also close to
a water source, the Karoon River. This was where France would
come in. In June 1974 Etemad and the Shah took the royal plane
to Paris; while they were in the air the Shah spoke of his pleasure

at the recent developments and his excitement at the prospect of French involvement (he was a Francophile). When they arrived, the two men split up as the Shah busied himself with a few political meetings and a lot of shopping on the Champs-Élysées, while Etemad visited the Paris headquarters of French nuclear company Framatome to discuss nuclear co-operation. At the end of two days of meetings he came to a preliminary agreement for the supply of two 900 MW reactors (the first to be operational in 1982 and the second in 1983), some uranium and a nuclear research centre to Iran.

Contract negotiations would unfortunately not prove as simple as with Kraftwerk; and Etemad's arrival and the founding of the AEOI, notably the element of professionalism it brought, now paid dividends. The system of decision-making that now existed (in place of the amateurishness that plagued its very early years) was simple but effective, and allowed Iran to deal (as effectively as any developing country could) with its Western partners. The Shah's desire for a large nuclear programme had only increased with each new development, and he wanted to know everything that happened. But he also knew his limitations and left the day-to-day running of things to Etemad, who kept him informed at regular meetings. The Framatome deal would go a long way to bringing nuclear-powered electricity to Iran, but after Paris the problems started. The French wanted the contract finalized quickly and were constantly trying to bypass Etemad (who felt things weren't ready) and speak to the Shah directly, hoping he would just give in and sign.

Etemad had to go back and forth to France over the next few months – a frustrating process (though he loved Paris). One morning in late 1976 he met with Framatome's chief nuclear negotiator at his Paris hotel. Over a light breakfast of croissants and coffee the two men chatted amiably until he told Etemad, slightly too casually, that Michel Poniatowski, the French Minister of Finance, was leaving for Tehran the following day to deliver a message to the Shah from President Valéry Giscard d'Estaing. Etemad knew the message would be about the contract, which made him furious. He demanded to see Poniatowski immediately, and half an hour later was standing in the stunned man's office, chastising him for trying to go behind his back while he was in Tehran; if he tried to bypass him again, he said, all nuclear cooperation with France would be cancelled.[49] Poniatowski understandably protested that it wasn't his decision, so Etemad told him to call Giscard, which he did; the meeting was cancelled. It was a bold move by Etemad but he knew just how desperately the French wanted Iranian oil money, and calculated that they wouldn't risk jeopardizing relations with the AEOI.

In any case, the Shah had invited Giscard to come to Tehran a few weeks later in early November, which Etemad regarded as the crucial meeting; the problems would either be sorted out there or not at all. On the morning of 15 November, Giscard arrived at Sa'dabad with a phalanx of ministers in tow, and, after the usual courtesies, went off with the Shah for bilateral discussions. Etemad arrived at the palace just in time for the official five-course lunch (at which it seemed everything was on the menu except caviar, as the Shah was allergic); soon afterwards, he, Hoveida and some ministers retired to one of the palace drawing rooms for coffee with the French President. As the coffee was being poured, Hoveida (while smiling politely at their guests) whispered (in French) to Etemad that at the morning meeting Giscard had told the Shah that the Darkhovin contract had to be signed during the visit, which meant the next couple of days.

'Which one of my hats', replied Etemad, 'are you addressing?' In response to Hoveida's puzzled look, Etemad explained that he had a 'power plant' hat, which he wore when he was totally focused on building power plants as quickly as possible. If the contract was acceptable then great, but he had not been privy to any discussions so he doubted it was. This was a serious problem because, of course, he also had his Iranian nuclear policy hat on (not to mention his fuel supply hat), which demanded he get the best possible deal for Iran on the wider picture.[50]

Sensing a lull in the conversation as the Oil Minister finally finished a very tedious story about the benefits of oil for the rubber industry, Etemad took his chance and addressed Giscard directly. He praised France's success as a nuclear power, especially (he added, somewhat pointedly) since it had developed its programme indigenously. The Americans, he reminded Giscard, hadn't done anything to help their ally; they hadn't even sold them the advanced computers necessary for nuclear research. But France had overcome all these difficulties alone, and was now one of the world's leading providers of nuclear technology. If he, Etemad, as head of the AEOI, failed to defend Iran's interests in the same way, what sort of a patriot would he be? Giscard was in an awkward position, but, with characteristic finesse, merely replied that he certainly had no intention of imposing anything on Iran that wasn't appropriate.

Etemad now enjoyed almost total access to the Shah by virtue of a simple system: he would make a call to the Palace office that arranged all the Shah's meetings and get an appointment. But if it was urgent he just informed the office he was coming over there and then. This was one of those times. He phoned up and asked the startled secretary where he could find the Shah – walking in the Palace gardens, he was told. After a short sprint over to the gardens he found the Shah by some large bushes and told him that whatever he had promised Giscard was his problem and that the contract – technically and financially and legally – was not ready to be signed. The Shah conceded, which allowed Etemad to prepare the contract and it was subsequently signed a month later, but it was a close-run thing. Framatome subsequently surveyed the area and began site preparation when the Revolutionary government cancelled the contract shortly after the Islamic Revolution.

There were also many discussions with other major western powers. Etemad met several times with Walter Marshall, future chair of the UK Atomic Energy Commission (and the man who would 'keep the lights on' in Britain during the 1984–5 Miners' Strike), but nothing much emerged, mainly because much of the UK's technology was outdated. The Shah's strong links with the USA made it the other obvious partner; and Washington also wanted in on the Iranian nuclear bonanza. But there were political difficulties (and Etemad was less keen than his boss on US co-operation). In June 1974, the USA and Iran reached a provisional agreement for it to supply two nuclear power reactors and enriched uranium fuel, and in October the State Department began preparations to negotiate an agreement that would permit the sale of nuclear reactors as well as enriched fuel 'at levels desired by the Shah'. But US proliferation concerns were a problem, and while co-operation increased (in January 1975, for example, the two countries signed a broad trade agreement that called for the purchase of eight reactors valued at $6.4 billion[51]) throughout the 1970s, the relationship became increasingly fraught.[52]

'THE NUCLEAR FUEL CYCLE'

All these plants would of course need nuclear fuel to power them, which was a more problematic area. The nuclear fuel cycle is the progression of nuclear fuel through a series of different stages. It consists of steps in the 'front end' (the preparation of the fuel), steps in the 'service period' in which the fuel is used during reactor operation, and steps in the 'back end', which are necessary to safely manage, contain, and either reprocess or dispose of spent nuclear fuel. Once a country is able to run the complete nuclear fuel cycle from start to finish it is, in theory, nuclear-independent because it does not need foreign expertise or assistance. From a non-proliferation point of view, however, it also enables the country in question to theoretically develop a nuclear bomb.

The fuel cycle begins with the mineral, uranium: the basic raw material of both civilian and military nuclear programmes. The first stage of the nuclear fuel cycle is to mine the uranium from the earth. Uranium ore occurs naturally, but when dug out of the ground it is almost entirely composed of the relatively long-lived U-238 isotope. Only a very small fraction is made up of the unstable U-235, which is the isotope needed for spontaneous fission – the process where the atomic nucleus splits, releasing enough energy in the process to coerce its neighbours into splitting, resulting in a so-called 'chain reaction'.[53] If the reaction proceeds at a sedate level, the fission produces energy in a controllable manner suitable for a nuclear power plant: the energy released is used in the plant to heat water to the point of steam, which then spins turbines connected to generators to make electricity. If the reaction proceeds at an uncontrolled level, however, a nuclear explosion can result – this is what powers an atomic bomb.[54] For either outcome, the ultimate goal, therefore, is to increase the percentage of U-235 in uranium ore to levels suitable to induce and maintain a chain reaction.

Once mined from the earth, uranium ore is taken to a mill to be ground into a fine powder, which is then purified in a chemical process and reconstituted in a solid form known as yellowcake (due to its yellow colouring). The yellowcake (which is Uranium Oxide) is then taken to a Uranium Conversion Facility (UCF) to be converted into Uranium Hexafluoride (UF_6) – the second stage known as 'conversion'. After it is converted, the UF_6 is then enriched (the third stage) to increase the amount of U-235 isotope. To achieve this, it is dissolved in nitric acid and chemically processed before being heated to become UF_6 gas. It is then enriched, usually through a gas centrifuge, where UF_6 gas is spun in a cylindrical chamber at high speeds. The enriched U-235 is then fed into another centrifuge and the process repeated many times through a chain of centrifuges known as a cascade. To enrich uranium to levels suitable for 'civil' use – in power electricity-generating nuclear reactors, for example – it must be enriched to contain 2–3 per cent U-235. For a bomb, it must be enriched to weapons-grade levels, for which the uranium must contain 80 per cent or more U-235 (which requires thousands of centrifuges connected in cascades). With the suitable degree of weaponization, this uranium can be used to power a nuclear bomb.

After the uranium is enriched, it then needs to be 'fabricated' for use as nuclear fuel – the fourth stage, by which the enriched UF_6 is fabricated into Uranium Dioxide powder that is then processed into pellet form, which then undergoes a grinding process to achieve a uniform pellet size before being stacked (according to each nuclear reactor's core design specifications) into tubes of corrosion-resistant metal alloy. The tubes are sealed to contain the fuel pellets, which are called fuel rods. The finished fuel rods are grouped in special fuel assemblies that are then used to build up the nuclear fuel core of a power reactor.

The fuel then enters the 'service period' – where it is used to operate the reactor. After this, reprocessing occurs – the chemical operation that separates useful fuel for recycling from nuclear waste. (If spent fuel is not reprocessed, the fuel cycle is referred to as an 'open fuel cycle'; if the spent fuel is reprocessed, it is referred to as a 'closed fuel cycle'.) Used fuel rods have their metallic outer casing stripped away before being dissolved in hot nitric acid. This produces uranium (96 per cent), which is reused in reactors, highly radioactive waste (3 per cent) and plutonium (1 per cent). The plutonium produced (only relatively small amounts – about 4 kg – are needed) can be used to fuel the second type of bomb available – the plutonium bomb.

For light-water reactors (which the AEOI had chosen and which comprise the vast majority of operating nuclear power plants), the production of fuel involves these four stages: (a) mining and milling, (b) uranium conversion, (c) enrichment and (d) fuel fabrication. (For heavy-water reactors, which run on natural uranium, the enrichment stage is not needed.)[55] The AEOI immediately got to work on the first stage: the extraction of the raw material for nuclear fuel – uranium ore – from the ground. Little was known about Iran's uranium deposits, though various features of geological formation were promising and the AEOI undertook some initial exploration. Time was of the essence, however, so Etemad decided they would source uranium from abroad. Iran signed contracts with South African companies Nufcor and Rossing (also purchasing a 20 per cent share in Rossing at a time when the company was building a huge mining complex in Namibia) to supply 13,000 tonnes of uranium between 1978 and 1990. All these purchases, including a 20 per cent share of a German uranium exploration company, were made through an Iranian company called USICAN, which worked exclusively for the AEOI.[56]

It was the fourth stage of the nuclear fuel cycle – turning the uranium ore into fuel for the power plants – that was to cause problems. For light-water reactors, nuclear fuel is created through uranium enrichment, which (unlike electricity-producing reactors in themselves) is also a classic means of producing the material for nuclear weapons. The possibility of Iran doing this indigenously greatly concerned the USA.[57] Washington knew that Iran needed fuel to power its reactors (especially the ones it hoped to sell the AEOI) and encouraged the Shah to pursue any means of uranium enrichment that did not take place on Iranian soil. In 1974 it notified the Shah of its support for an Iranian proposal to buy up to 25 per cent interest in a US commercial uranium-enrichment plant. A year later Etemad negotiated arguably the most adventurous initiative of the programme – the 1975 Eurodif project with France. Here, Iran agreed to help finance the Eurodif project, in return for 10 per cent of its output of enriched uranium (to produce the necessary LEU fuel to power the Bushehr reactor) from its reprocessing plant in Tricastin.[58] The AEOI also began a small programme of research with high-powered lasers to enrich uranium, but by and large, on this key indicator of technological independence, Iran, despite occasional pronouncements to the contrary, relied on expertise abroad.[59]

Finally, Iran needed to create scientific and technical support for the reactors, which was where Reza Khazaneh came in. Khazaneh had always wanted to be a scientist. When news broke of the AEOI's establishment in 1974, he was one of the many people that contacted Etemad, and, with a degree in electrical engineering from the University of Stuttgart and PhD work from the University of California, Berkeley, he was just what was needed. The two men met soon after, and Etemad made Khazaneh head of the Iranian end of a collaborative project between the AEOI and the Commissariat à l'énergie atomique et aux énergies alternatives (CEA) of France for a new Nuclear Research Centre. Nothing so clearly illustrates how the early nuclear programme worked, what its limitations were and how the AEOI tried to circumvent them as the founding of the Isfahan Nuclear Technology

Centre, which came into being through a combination of Iranian determination and Western expertise.

Within a month of joining the AEOI Khazaneh travelled with Etemad to Paris to discuss the details with CEA. There they met with the head of CEA's foreign relations, who had already prepared an outline, both for the centre and, more generally, for the development of nuclear technology in Iran, based on the firm's experience in France. His proposed programme included laboratories for metallurgy, corrosion, heat transfer and fluid flow, uranium chemistry, hot laboratories and large workshops. Everything. As ever, a turnkey project based on a Western model was the plan. Khazaneh and Etemad then toured four French nuclear research centres and examined the laboratories and the methods of research there.[60]

Back in Tehran Khazaneh and Etemad decided on two possible locations for the centre – Isfahan and Shiraz. The French experts then returned with earthquake, geology and meteorology specialists and together with Khazaneh they explored the areas, selecting four sites around Isfahan and three around Shiraz. Khazaneh reported back to Etemad in Tehran, who immediately flew to Switzerland to get approval from the Shah who was at Survetta Villa, his palatial chalet just outside St. Moritz, overlooking the Engadine Alps. The site selected for the nuclear centre, a large unused tract of land between two mountains about 20 km southeast of Isfahan and 2 km from the Zayandeh Roud River, was chosen because it was one of Iran's most earthquake-free regions. Moreover, the wind direction was eastward, away from Isfahan itself, so in case of accident any radioactivity would blow away from the city towards the desert.

Khazaneh also signed an agreement with the Belgian nuclear company Belgonucleaire for the construction of a 30 MW research reactor, which would be designed and built with Iranian participation to improve indigenous expertise, and the AEOI sent ten experts to Brussels to participate in the programme. Khazaneh also signed an agreement with CEA for the training of personnel, and 100 engineers and technicians were sent to four nuclear research centres in France for two years, followed by a one-year degree course in nuclear engineering. Khazaneh also made similar arrangements with Oak Ridge National Laboratories in the USA.[61]

By this time Khazaneh had decided that the centre should be renamed the Isfahan Nuclear Technology Centre to distinguish it from the nuclear centre in Tehran. At the end of 1978 about 450 people worked there; detailed programmes of works and drawings had been prepared for the laboratories, workshops and services (with provisional labs, offices, dorms and facilities built for the interim period). Water and electricity was supplied and 200 hectares of forest had been cleared. A meteorological tower was erected and provisional laboratories established in two buildings in Tehran where some initial research work had been carried out. Around 120 experts had completed their training abroad and joined about 80 scientific and technical personnel in Tehran.

By the end of 1978 Iran had acquired the basis of a civil nuclear programme, which centred on the two reactors at Bushehr. The power plant was expected to come online in a few years to provide electricity and thus lessen Iran's dependence on oil for domestic power, which would free up more of the 'black gold' to sell internationally and bring foreign currency into the country. In the AEOI it had an agency solely devoted to nuclear power with a royal mandate to do almost whatever it pleased that had grown to almost 5,000 staff with premises spread across the city. Moreover, even turnkey projects like Bushehr involved the training of hundreds of technical staff to manage and operate the power plant and, with the aid of an educational division inside the AEOI, Iran had developed a nuclear base from almost nothing. More and more Iranians were being sent abroad for training, with over 1,000 being sent to Europe, America and Asia for research or education (the AEOI even reached an agreement with MIT to create a Master's degree specifically to cover its needs). In the space of a few years Iran had made more nuclear progress than in the previous 20.

CHAPTER 4

ARMS AND THE SHAH: NUCLEAR WEAPONS UNDER THE SHAH

In 1941, just days after Britain and the Soviet Union had invaded Iran, Sir Reader Bullard, Britain's Ambassador to Tehran, spent a dull but portentous September morning listening to a bumptious young man lecture him on the art of war. London's emissary listened patiently and politely to the young Mohammad Reza Pahlavi, who, he noted, became particularly animated when discussing military hardware. His Majesty, he later reported, appears to think himself a great military strategist; he even offered strong opinions about the conduct of the war, and the military decisions of generals.[1] Bullard was merely the first to suffer what would become a customary trial for visiting dignitaries, and over a decade later in the late 1950s US Secretary of State, John Foster Dulles, wrote to Eisenhower about what he called 'the Shah's military obsession', noting with equal sarcasm the Shah's tendency to 'consider himself a military genius'. US officials were arguably more damning: 'the Shah's interest in military forces is in part emotional rather than logical. [This] psychological bias', they concluded, 'renders him immune to logical persuasion in this field'.[2]

The Shah adored weapons – the more expensive and complex and ostentatious the better. From the early days of his reign, US officials (continuing their psychological analysis) believed that to ask him to 'de-emphasize the military element in the Iranian government would be to attack his most sensitive personal quirk'.[3] They also believed weaponry was probably his 'primary purpose' for formally aligning Iran with the West and as his reign progressed he was given ample opportunity to indulge his tastes.[4] At the post-1973 Yom Kippur War OPEC meeting, he strongly pushed for a redoubling (the prices had already doubled following the OPEC Arab oil boycott on Western suppliers to Israel) of the oil price, arguing that prices had been kept artificially low while other commodities had risen, enabling him to spend billions on arms, mostly from the USA. Such was the strength of feeling on this subject that many US Ambassadors spent tortuous afternoons at Sa'dabad being berated about the quantity and quality of US military aid.[5]

The increased revenues allowed him to implement his 'myth' of Iran domestically, but they also allowed him to implement the second and necessary corollary to the narrative he believed he was creating of dragging his country (kicking and screaming, it sometimes seemed to him) into modernity. If, as he genuinely believed, Iran would soon become one of the world's superpowers, it needed to show this on the international as well as the domestic stage. In the late 1960s it seemed that Britain's imminent withdrawal from the Middle East would give him his chance. In 1967, Richard Nixon, whom the Shah regarded as a good friend, visited Tehran and the two men spent several hours discussing the changing Middle East. After the meeting, Nixon told his Ambassador, Armin Meyer, that the Shah had come up with rather a good idea about Iran becoming the new regional policeman in Britain's absence (following its 1971 withdrawal from the Middle East), which would ease the burden on the already overstretched US military.[6] When Nixon became President two years later, Iran duly became, along with Saudi Arabia, one of the limbs (the military one to Saudi's financial one) of his 'Two Pillar'

Middle East strategy. Trapped in the Vietnam War, Washington needed Iran.

By the late 1970s Iran was launching ambitious aid projects, providing troops to neighbouring countries like Oman, and sending forces into countries as far afield as Somalia (to quell a Marxist rebellion in Dhofar). In short, it was behaving like a regional superpower. Its navy patrolled a 1,175-mile southern coastline, including its islands in the Gulf, southwards around Oman and Yemen, as well as extending its protection to tankers bound for Europe as far south as the tenth parallel. Iranian TV seemed to show almost daily pictures of the Shah in full military regalia inspecting impeccably attired Iranian troops, behind the controls of a helicopter, looking through the sights of an automatic weapon or laughing with a supplicant foreign head of State visiting Tehran (usually to try to borrow money).

He had made his views clear in a 1972 visit to an Iranian navy base: 'Events in the world have taught us that the sea contiguous to the Gulf of Oman, and I mean the Indian Ocean, recognizes no frontier', he said to the gathered sailors. His navy would be able to assume its 'new responsibilities' only by increasing its ability to strike against 'any enemy and win in a wide radius'.[7] With a nuclear programme that was finally beginning to take shape, the awesome capability of nuclear weapons and, perhaps more importantly, their symbolic possibilities for the Pahlavi project, were in many respects an obvious, indeed logical, choice. By the mid-1970s it seemed to many in the region that the Shah might conceivably wish to go nuclear and, more worryingly, that he now had the financial and technological ability to do so.

NUCLEAR WEAPONS: THE OFFICIAL STANCE

Tehran made its case for nuclear power publicly and baldly, but it was only half the story. A government with even only a civil programme must have a policy on nuclear weapons. The demonstrable military threat they pose is too great for it to be otherwise, and all nuclear programmes of NPT non-weapon-state parties are subject to (semi-)regular IAEA inspections – even Sweden's. Any civil nuclear programme raises military possibilities because the 'dual-use' nature of nuclear technology (by which civil nuclear equipment, with slight variations in emphasis and degree, can be used to produce nuclear weapons) means that civil and weapons programmes can never be entirely divorced. A country with a nuclear programme will inescapably consider the nuclear weapons option – even if only to rule it out.

Unsurprisingly, Iran publicly rejected nuclear weapons. Rhetorically, its case was twofold: a denial of any nuclear weapons ambitions combined with a self-conscious emphasis on the programme's peaceful nature. Prime Minister Hoveida himself unambiguously articulated the first limb: 'The atomic bomb does not interest us,' he told the *New York Times* in 1976. 'We want to master nuclear technology.'[8] Beyond this, in *Mission for My Country*, the Shah claimed that the programme, like his CENTO-sponsored road systems, transmitting stations and railway links, proved that Iran was building 'for a future of prosperity and peace, not of war and devastation'. He then went further and claimed that his overall benign posture was actually 'expressed' by the CENTO Institute of Nuclear Science, which was devoted 'entirely' to peaceful applications of nuclear energy.[9] The nuclear programme was, it seemed, an exercise in philanthropy, and the study of radioisotopes at the Tehran Nuclear Research Centre (that, naturally, were to be used for the 'treatment of tumours') an expression of his hope that such 'peaceful possibilities of nuclear energy' might be used for the benefit of the region as a whole.[10]

In this respect at least, the Shah matched words with political action. The single most important thing for the non-nuclear states is the treaty that commits them to staying that way. The NPT, like the IAEA, was a perhaps logical result of 'Atoms for Peace'. The proliferation concerns Eisenhower set out in his 1953 speech had only intensified along with the Cold War – a conflict that ultimately rested on the fragile relationship of nuclear deterrence between Washington and Moscow. It was a political given that more nuclear-weapon states would endanger global security, multiplying the risks of actual nuclear war through mis-calculation, accidents, unauthorized use of weapons, or from an escalation in tensions. Frank Aiken, Irish Minister for External Affairs, first raised the idea of something like the NPT in 1958, and, in 1961, the UN General Assembly adopted what became known as the 'Irish Resolution', which called for measures to limit the spread of nuclear weapons to additional countries and for all states to refrain from transfer or acquisition of such weapons. After much debate (and only after the USA and USSR were able to settle on identical draft texts of the treaty following a meeting between Soviet statesman Alexei Kosygin and President Lyndon Baines Johnson at Glassboro, New Jersey, in summer 1967) the Eighteen Nation Committee on Disarmament and the UN General Assembly agreed on the final draft in June 1968. The NPT opened for signature on 1 July 1968 and came into force on 5 March 1970.[11]

The treaty (which rests on three pillars: (1) 'Proliferation', (2) 'Disarmament' and (3) 'The Right to Peacefully use Nuclear Technology') enshrines the bargain contained in 'Atoms for Peace'. The non-nuclear-weapon states agree never to acquire nuclear weapons in exchange for the nuclear states' agreement to share the benefits of peaceful nuclear technology and to pursue nuclear disarmament aimed at the ultimate elimination of their nuclear ar-senals. The bargain is carried in the key Article IV, which outlines 'the inalienable right of all the Parties ... to develop research, production and use of nuclear energy for peaceful purposes with-out discrimination'. Some also argue that Article VI in which the nuclear-weapon states undertake to pursue 'negotiations in good faith on effective measures relating ... to nuclear disarmament', and towards a 'treaty on general and complete disarmament under strict and effective international control' carries a second limb of the bargain: a promise from the nuclear states to disarm in exchange for the non-nuclear states' promise to never acquire nuclear weapons.[12]

Which is where it becomes controversial. One view, supported by the treaty's negotiating history (and, for example, the view of the British Foreign Office) is that Article VI is not part of the NPT's fundamental bargain: it was introduced to appease the non-nuclear-weapon states and did not appear in the early drafts of the treaty, in particular the agreed US/USSR draft which formed the basis of the negotiations in the Eighteen Nation Committee on Disarmament, and which merely contained some vague words about disarmament in the preamble. The non-nuclear-weapon states insisted that the commitment to disarmament be strengthened, which prompted the nuclear-weapon states to include Article VI in the treaty text. Even so, Washington made it clear that it was not constrained in any way by Article VI. A 1996 judgment of the International Court of Justice on the legality of nuclear weapons stated broadly that Article VI must be respected and that NPT parties work towards nuclear disarmament and nuclear arms control.[13] But it remains a long-term objective rather than a constraint to many of the nuclear states. Their non-nuclear colleagues, by contrast, believe Article VI contains a firm commitment to disarm.

What is not in doubt is that, for NPT signatories, the treaty turns public avowals of peaceful nuclear intentions into a legal obligation with the possibility of Security Council censure for violation. Iran's signature of the NPT is arguably the single most important event in the political history of its nuclear programme; its repercussions are still felt today. Had Iran not signed, like India or Israel, the present-day crisis may not have occurred or, at any rate, would have taken a markedly different form. But it did sign, so while expediency meant a necessary public rejection of nuclear weapons, the Shah's rhetoric was given a legislative concomitant; in fact the two reinforced each other. Even before the introduction of the NPT, Tehran had signed and ratified the 1963 Limited Test Ban Treaty and it signed the NPT on the day it opened for signature on 1 July 1968 – before even the nuclear powers of France and China had officially committed (they did not sign until 1992).

What was more, a minimum of fuss surrounded this. On 20 June 1968 Iran's Foreign Minister Adeshir Zahedi had simply been instructed via a personal phone call from the Shah to sign the treaty as soon as it became possible. No discussion or debate took place and two weeks later, sat behind a desk in London's Foreign Office between three efficient but formal British civil servants on a mild summer morning, he signed the tightly bound, five-page document. The whole process took less than 20 minutes. Later that day he returned to the Iranian Embassy on Princess Gate in Kensington and called the Shah, who was delighted at the news. He was especially pleased that they had signed the very day it opened for signature. He told Zahedi it showed the West that Iran was 'honourable'.[14] As soon as Zahedi signed the document the British diplomats in the room had congratulated him. By signing so promptly Iran had set an example to the rest of the non-nuclear-weapon states they hoped would be followed; it was, they too said, the honourable thing to have done.

But honourable in whose eyes? By signing the NPT the Shah legally precluded the possibility of an Iranian bomb. Any nuclear weapons desires would now have to be covert and therefore that much harder. In many ways it was a surprising thing to have done. The Shah wanted to re-create the empire of Iran; he loved weapons and nothing was more sophisticated, or powerful, than a nuclear bomb. What was more, all his Great Power role models had one; and only a few years previously, nuclear testing had been considered such a sign of status that France had carried out 210 nuclear tests between 1960 and 1966. What the Shah had understood, consciously or not, is that the NPT had brought with it a set of values concerning the non-acquisition of nuclear weapons. It shifted the international 'norm' of what granted a state prestige and legitimacy from the earlier notion of joining 'the nuclear club' to an emerging concept of joining 'the club of the nations adhering to the NPT'.[15] In so doing, it created a further bifurcation in the nuclear sphere by which countries could be divided into 'good' (those that signed) and 'bad' (those that didn't). And it became yet another banner to which the Shah could assign Iran; another chance for him to show what 'side' his Iran was on, and, as a result, the *kind* of state it was. As ever, the Shah's nuclear programme, more than a mere technical concern, was a vessel of Pahlavi identity.

Meanwhile, some other modernizing states refused to sign. Indira Gandhi resisted US pressure, claimed that the treaty was 'discriminatory' and that India would not sign until nuclear-weapon states China and France did (the NPT's values took some time to entrench themselves globally).[16] In the eyes of the more belligerent of the developing world countries it was a clear confrontation once more: the Haves and Have Nots lined up against each other once again. The former urged compliance; the latter cried discrimination. Pakistan also refused to sign and, given both it and India's subsequent nuclearization, 'discrimination' was obviously only half the story; their programmes had clear, technological (military, in fact) goals, and the West, and 'honour', could be damned. Undeterred, Iran ratified the treaty on 2 February 1970, and in 1973 signed the comprehensive safeguards agreement it required, which made its programme subject to international control and inspections to detect and thereby deter any diversion of nuclear material for non-peaceful means.[17] Throughout the Shah's reign Tehran complied fully with all its non-proliferation obligations, promptly and without complaint over the limits placed on national sovereignty or the built-in imbalance of the treaties.

Etemad disliked the NPT, which he believed threatened Iran's national sovereignty. He came too late to affect the decision to sign the treaty, which had been taken before the AEOI's existence and, therefore, without the benefit of expert advice. Ironically, his position – that it was based on an unfair bargain – was the same as that of many of the non-nuclear countries from whom the Shah was so desperate to distance himself. It was, he believed, a colossal mistake for Iran to have joined because the NPT benefited two sets of countries: the nuclear states, which wanted to retain their nuclear monopoly, and the very vulnerable countries with no realistic chance of ever getting a bomb. Iran, he argued, was not the USA or UK, and certainly not Burkina Faso or Nicaragua or Fiji. Admittedly, the Western European countries had signed but this meant little, he argued, because 'everybody' knew they had no intention of going for nuclear weapons. The so-called 'threshold' states, countries that actually had a meaningful chance of proliferating – Pakistan, India, Israel and Brazil – all stayed out. Only Iran had signed and, what was worse, it had done so without hesitation. Frankly, thought Etemad, it was a dishonourable thing to have done.

Etemad's view was both important and instructive. Important because it marked the beginnings of a belief in the fundamental unfairness of the NPT that would consistently inform Iran's nuclear posture – no matter which regime was in power. Instructive because it must be noted that, despite his belief, Sweden, Switzerland and South Korea were just a few of the 'threshold' countries that not only had the capability to build a bomb but were actually doing so until they decided to forgo the option and sign the NPT. Certainly, the overwhelming majority of non-nuclear states were in favour of the NPT (it is the most signed-up to treaty in the world apart from the UN charter itself), aware that their own security depended on the prevention of nuclear proliferation.

Nonetheless, his feelings were sincere, and one afternoon he took the matter up with the Shah. He was told, perhaps unsurprisingly, that little thought had gone into signing the treaty (the concern had been to keep Washington happy). Etemad remained deeply sceptical of the non-proliferation regime in general: in his eyes the IAEA was just an agency designed to prevent non-nuclear countries from obtaining quality nuclear technology; the NPT bound their hands while making the nuclear-weapon states' commitments vague and non-binding. His suspicions about the cynical nature of the enterprise were (to his mind) confirmed when the nuclear powers secretly met in London in 1975 to form a nuclear suppliers club (the London Club – later called the Nuclear Suppliers Group) to limit the global supply of nuclear technology.

Etemad viewed the club as being in total contradiction to the NPT's Article IV. It also confirmed his suspicions about the nuclear-weapon states' desires to stifle the spread of technology to their non-nuclear counterparts. He was determined to have his say and got his chance in mid-1975 when US Secretary of State Cyrus Vance flew to Tehran to discuss nuclear co-operation. The two men met at the US Embassy and it was clear that Vance was uncomfortable with the whole situation and he vainly tried to convince Etemad that the policy would not affect Iran. But Etemad was not convinced and decided to fight it by organizing an international conference in response. The 'International Conference on the Transfer of Nuclear Technology' was held in Shiraz and Persepolis in April 1977. Over four days of talks the participants almost unanimously expressed their opposition to any restriction on the transfer of nuclear technology. Even industry representatives from nuclear supplier countries (no doubt fearing a shrinking of the market) joined in the condemnation.[18]

As Iran's energy establishment was becoming increasingly disgruntled, the Shah continued to show the West that Iran would not be any trouble. At the very first NPT review conference in 1970 Iran had abstained from the disquiet voiced by other modernizing nations over the treaty's inequity, specifically the nuclear-weapon states' perceived failure to fulfil their perceived disarmament commitments under Article VI of the treaty. Senior Iranian officials had expressed misgivings, but they were private grumblings and, mindful of the Shah's public stance, only articulated 'sotto voce'.[19] These issues divide the two worlds today; of the eight review conferences held since the NPT's entry into force in 1970, only four – 1975, 1985, 2000 and 2010 – have produced 'consensus' final declarations.[20]

The NPT cleaves the nuclear world in two. There *are* sides to choose. The Shah's nuclear programme enabled him to take part in relevant international forums and the accompanying nuclear debate enabled him to show which side of a Manichean debate his country was on. In the nuclear realm clashes are (thus far) rhetorical and the Shah was able to ally Iran linguistically with the West, adopting similar registers of form and tone in his public statements, and in so doing to circumvent the central diplomatic clash between the nuclear countries (and their allies) and the developing world, non-nuclear countries. So there was a marked absence of any grumbling about the iniquity of the NPT, the IAEA or nuclear governance in general – that key signifier of a modernizing country's diplomatic posture.

The Shah's wish to ally with the West went beyond the rhetorical into the political; he almost always ensured that Iran voted with the West at non-proliferation forums, subordinating informed policy decisions on a case by case basis to a greater, and more nebulous, obsession. At an IAEA General Conference in 1977, following clashes between South Africa and developing world countries, Etemad was called to cast Iran's vote; he called the Shah, who told him to vote as the developed countries did. It was a familiar instruction to Etemad and he knew what it meant: in the international arena he had to leave aside Iranian grievances and frustrations. As the Shah told him more than once: they had to *act* like a Western country.[21]

THE SHAH CONSIDERS WEAPONS ...

The official position was clear and Iran had signed the NPT. But then so would North Korea, which eventually went nuclear. More to the point, the nature of the Shah's ambitions would suggest a desire for the bomb and, in fact, he did break from the official line and voice weapons desires at certain points in his reign. The question is why. Various (and often different) pressures – be they security or prestige or whatever – push a country towards getting a bomb and they are always instructive as to the country in question. Israel, for example, believed it had a clear security need to develop a nuclear deterrent; for France, prestige factored more.

From a security point of view, two factors are preeminent. The first is to counter an existent nuclear threat, which Iran certainly faced with the USSR, its perennial foreign policy problem. The Shah constantly railed against the Russians, repeating his belief that the 1917 Russian Revolution had, if anything, only increased their imperialism.[22] Moreover, the nature of the Cold War world meant that Iran, now so firmly allied with one superpower, could not avoid the enmity of the other, and Moscow, through its use of Iran's communist Tudeh Party and a stream of propaganda from Russian radio, invested great effort in trying to undermine the Shah's rule. But the Shah's interest in nuclear weapons was never envisaged as a nuclear deterrent to counter the Soviet threat. In fact, in April 1975, he declared the idea of Iran having nuclear weapons to counter any Russian nuclear threat 'ridiculous': 'How many do you think it would take to count against the Russians?' he asked rhetorically, 'or the United States? How much would they cost?'[23]

The second reason countries proliferate is if they feel a security threat from the proliferation of one of their rivals; states always look to each other in these matters. China, for example, developed the bomb largely in response to the threat of US attack at the end of the Korean War and again during the Taiwan Straits crisis during the 1950s. As they say: proliferation begets proliferation. The so-called 'Snowball Effect' was a real concern to the US State Department, which had long worried about a possible proliferation chain across the modernizing world (and undertook periodic assessments of the likelihood of proliferation in the region).[24] While the Shah maintained a public rejection of nuclear weapons, he became more publicly aspirant after India's 1974 test. No longer content with merely showing compliance with the NPT, he questioned its norms and made his dissatisfaction with the new status quo clear. So-called 'Peaceful Nuclear Explosions' like the one India had just carried out were impermissible under the NPT, and, therefore, for Iran. Delhi, it seemed, had benefited by staying out.[25]

Shortly after the Indian test the French news weekly *Les Informations* asked the Shah if Iran might also seek a bomb. His response was unequivocal: 'without any doubt, and sooner than one would think'. The Iranian Embassy in Paris immediately (and feverishly) denied the statement, accusing the press of fabricating it 'out of whole cloth without any foundation',[26] while Iranian Information Minister Gholam Kianpour described it as a 'complete falsehood' (and actually claimed the Shah had said Iran was 'not thinking of having such weapons').[27] But it stands as probably the first publicly declared Iranian nuclear weapons ambition. A month later, when the Shah was again asked about nuclear weapons, he replied that 'Pakistan and India ... talking about nuclear strength' might force Iran to reconsider its options.[28]

A fear of those around him was no surprise. Notwithstanding its problematic relations with the Great Powers, Iran suffered (and suffers) from a perennial 'foreign policy problem'; it lives in a 'rough neighbourhood'. During the 1970s the India-Pakistan problem and the fate of Baluchistan and Pakistan's territorial integrity, particularly since the 1971 Indo-Pakistan war, were of considerable concern, and relations between Tehran and New Delhi were strained. The Shah had promised to come to Pakistan's aid if it were attacked and there was a real chance that Iran might get dragged into a regional war. The Indian test ignited fears that Pakistan would seek to reciprocate with its own bomb and cause a proliferation chain that might force Tehran to go nuclear too, if only to match India psychologically, or deter it strategically.[29]

But the Shah never actually vocalized a concern over a chain of proliferation *per se*; clearly he watched his rivals' actions carefully, but security wasn't at the heart of his concerns as prestige arose once more. All the advantages of a civil nuclear power programme – technological advancement, the display of advancement and modernity – are applicable to nuclear weapons. But weapons can bring added benefits to a state's international standing in general. For a modernizing country seeking more independence and self-respect they can bring an added prestige that is highly desirable – especially for a ruler like the Shah. First of all, there is a prestige to merely having a bomb. Nuclear weapons, like civilian programmes, can be a symbol, albeit a more potent one, of a modern state, and a more effective display of national capability than improved education. What is more, nuclear tests are irrevocably 'public events': when they happen everyone knows it. They are the *symbolism* of power. For a country like Iran that had significant difficulties in building up its national capability, due to a lack of adequate infrastructure, such grand gestures might provide a shortcut to a highly desirable status, as well as suiting the Shah's predilection for the dramatic and conspicuous over the slow and steady.

Then there are the political benefits. When France got the bomb, received wisdom held that it was in direct response to the existent Soviet nuclear threat. But many other European states such as Sweden, for whom the threat was (at least) as great as it was to France, did not proliferate. A more complete reason perhaps emerges with an understanding of what the bomb meant, psychologically and therefore symbolically, to the French. There was undoubtedly pride in the achievement, but the bomb altered its self-perceived global standing in a way that a merely civilian programme (which it already had) could not. As French President, Charles de Gaulle told Eisenhower in 1959 that a France without world responsibility would be 'unworthy of herself, especially in the eyes of Frenchmen'. It was for that very reason, he continued, that 'she intends to provide herself with an atomic armament. Only in this way can our defence and foreign policy be independent, which we prize above everything else.'[30] A statement that could just as easily have been uttered by Mohammad Reza Shah himself.

The question of precedent was, as ever, also important. To many in the region it was no coincidence that, five months after India's test, Kissinger journeyed to New Delhi and established the joint Indian-US commission on nuclear energy. The equation of international influence and nuclear weapons was (and is) heightened by the bitter observation that all permanent members of the Security Council are nuclear-weapon states. What a nuclear weapon could offer in terms of status seemed almost designed for Pahlavi Iran, particularly in the final, post-1973 phase of the Shah's reign when he could strut the regional stage unencumbered by financial restraint.[31] The Shah planned to make Iran the fifth Great Power.[32] Nothing would get in his way and nothing would threaten Iran's self-perceived rightful position of predominance. The actions of neighbouring states might, therefore, be a threat on more than just a security level.

In September 1975 *The New York Times* interviewed the Shah and asked him if he wanted nuclear weapons. His response was as illuminating as it was blunt: 'I am not really thinking of nuclear arms', he replied, '[b]ut if 20 or 30 *ridiculous little countries* are going to develop nuclear weapons, then I may have to revise my policies. Even Libya is talking about trying to manufacture atomic weapons' (emphasis my own).[33] He reiterated his thinking a few weeks later, telling the press that he didn't want nuclear weapons but if '*small states* begin building [them] then Iran might have to reconsider its policy' (emphasis my own).[34] The prospect of 'little' states acquiring nuclear weapons was not a security threat; it was an affront to Iranian pride. A civil programme showed Iran's technological capacity. If things changed militarily, nuclear weapons would provide not a deterrent, but the necessary prestige to maintain commensurate status with the Pahlavi vision – to assuage its own sense of itself.

... BUT ULTIMATELY REFRAINS

Under the circumstances, nuclear weapons seemed not so much logical as inevitable; and as the Shah's occasionally voiced weapons desires showed, the impulse for a bomb was certainly there. By the mid-1970s, his power was at its zenith. The Nixon Doctrine combined with the Shah's leadership of OPEC and his huge military capabilities had given him the international recognition he craved. The removal of Mossadegh and then Zahedi had rid him not only of opposition but also of anyone capable of standing up to him, and his ego had grown in proportion to Iran's geopolitical standing. Only a few years earlier, in 1971, he had marked 2,500 years of (supposed) Iranian monarchy with the most expensive party in history. Food, cutlery and waiters were flown in from France, while hundreds of red Mercedes-Benz ferried guests to and from their custom-built luxury tents amid the ruins of Persepolis. Designed to celebrate Iran's pre-Islamic past, it was perhaps the defining moment of royal hubris. The British Embassy described the party as a good idea marred by 'excess', suffering, like so many other things, at the hands of the Shah's 'megalomania' while a still largely unknown (to the West) cleric called Ayatollah Khomeini described it as the 'Devil's Festival'.[35]

None of this was lost on Etemad, who knew from the beginning that, regardless of the NPT, the issue of nuclear weapons would have to be addressed; the question was what approach to take. He had begun meeting regularly with the Shah shortly after they founded the AEOI but didn't feel he could immediately ask him outright if he wanted a bomb. Even if he did, he wasn't sure he would get a straight answer; the Shah might want weapons but not say so and it would be left to him to decipher his boss's true intentions. So he devised a plan. The Shah always wanted direct involvement in the programme, which was a problem. Nuclear power is so technical that Etemad feared the Shah might not understand what he was being told and be left unable to make informed decisions – there needed to be a common language between them to avoid misunderstanding. So he decided to teach his boss about nuclear power.

Over the next six months the Shah underwent a crash course in nuclear physics; the 'lessons' were based on a typical university nuclear science syllabus, albeit a truncated one. He started with the basics – what an atom and a molecule were – and went from there. The two men met twice a week, generally for about two to three hours in the Shah's office at Sa'dabad. Sitting around his mahogany desk cluttered with gold pens and bejewelled letter openers (of which it seemed the Shah was especially fond) they would go through diagrams of the fuel cycle and its various processes. The Shah particularly liked this aspect of nuclear power; he could see its possibilities. Occasionally they would stroll in the palace gardens while Etemad fired questions on neutrons at him. The lessons were a success. Etemad pushed his boss and would gently berate him if he made what he considered to be an inexcusable error, which the Shah would invariably acknowledge. Only once, after the Shah had finished a clearly unpleasant phone call to one of his security chiefs, did he snap back. The 'course' continued for about six months. The Shah was keen to learn, and at the end of each session Etemad would hand him some papers and ask him to take a look if he had the time, which he did. He always did his homework.[36]

As time passed, the bond between the two men strengthened, and one afternoon in late 1975 Etemad finally felt he was in a position to ask. They had just finished discussing the process of fission for the third time, and he had begun gathering up the papers spread across the desk. He had decided before the 'lesson' on a direct approach, which was what he now took. 'Your Majesty', he said. 'We have been meeting for six months now; you understand everything. So now I have to ask: do you want nuclear weapons?' He had been blunt and, as the Shah paused, he feared he might have gone too far. 'Let's talk', the Shah replied. Etemad then set out the dilemma as a simple choice: if nuclear energy was the goal then the programme would go one way; if it were weapons it would go another. They talked for over two hours while the Shah outlined his national vision: Iran's position in the Middle East, in the Indian Ocean, the country's strengths and its weaknesses, and the role of nuclear weapons in relation to all of this. Two concerns dictated his thinking. The first was Iran's conventional weapons capabilities. As ever, once the Shah started to talk about anything military, he changed; palpable excitement entered his voice. His armed forces, he told Etemad, were the brightest feather in the peacock's plume; Iran's 'destiny' required it to maintain a military force commensurate with its international (and historical) standing, and, as Iran's ruler, he was determined to make sure that it did.[37]

Certainly, these desires dictated government policy. More prosaic factors such as the need to effectively repress any dissent in the country also factored, but, as time passed, more and more arms were needed for the Shah's globally integrated foreign policy. Iran had joined CENTO in 1955, which gave the Shah his own 'mini-NATO' from which to implement the global and regional role he saw for his country (although he only gained the confidence to really act on this in the mid-1970s when he was rich and felt politically secure). Military buildup was rapid and proceeded from a modest base: in 1966 Iran's military budget was $225 million; by 1975 it had grown to around $10 billion. In the space of almost seven years, the number of helicopters increased from 25 to over 700 in inventory or on order, and its navy had grown to be the dominant local power in the Persian Gulf.[38]

According to a 1976 Senate Foreign Relations Committee report, the USA now sold more arms to Iran than to any other country.[39] The quality of equipment bought was also high: the numerical advantage, for example, that Iraq possessed in terms of combat aircraft was offset by Iran's ability to deliver over twice the ordinance tonnage of Iraq and Saudi Arabia combined. By the late 1970s, Iran could be declared the dominant military power in the Persian Gulf, on land, on sea and in the air.[40] In the latter stages of Pahlavi rule, Iran's military capabilities were becoming comparable to some Western countries', and by the end of the 1970s analysts projected that the Iranian Air Force would have more fighter planes than any NATO country except the USA.[41]

What this meant, the Shah told Etemad that day, was that Iran had no immediate need for nuclear capability. States generally seek to develop nuclear weapons when they face a significant security threat that cannot be met through alternative means.[42] The strength of this alternative means, the Shah argued, rendered nuclear weapons superfluous. For the time being Iran was strong enough. It could defend its interests in the region and its neighbours respected it. He saw no security or, critically, status problem. Only a couple of months earlier in April 1975 he had told the *Washington Post* that the idea of Iran having nuclear weapons was 'ridiculous'. 'Only a few silly fools believe it,' he said. 'The best guarantee that I do not want nuclear weapons is the programme I have launched in conventional weapons. I want to be able to take care of anything by non-nuclear means.'[43]

Such was Iran's superiority in conventional weaponry, he continued, that nuclear weapons might actually be a disadvantage. Going for a bomb might hurt Iran's efforts to get international assistance with its civil programme, and, more importantly, as long as there were no nuclear arms in the area, Iran would remain the preeminent military power not only of the Persian Gulf, but most of the Middle East and the Indian Ocean as well. Iran was a superpower in a mini-unipolar world; the introduction of nuclear weapons – that great 'equalizer' – would neuter this.

But he had a further concern that he now outlined, leaning back and toying, rather nervously, Etemad noticed, with a Montblanc fountain pen: the USA. Despite strong relations between the two countries, the Shah always became uneasy when discussing Washington and it slowly dawned on Etemad that while his boss wanted to emulate the Americans, and while he respected them, he didn't like them. In fact, he feared them. Any move towards a bomb, he told Etemad, would also destroy the relations he had worked so hard to build and that had come at such a domestic political cost. On that day more than 35 years ago, the Shah articulated what would be a perennial truth: that throughout the meandering 60-year history of the nuclear programme from 'Atoms for Peace' to Obama's White House today, the USA has remained the single most important factor in deciding whether Iran goes nuclear or not.

In the first place Washington provided something very simple: a security guarantee. This was a staple of the Cold War and post-Cold War world and it works very simply: in an unforgiving world 'weak' (non-nuclear) countries do what they can to survive. One way is to ally with a nuclear power that promises to retaliate on their behalf if they are attacked – thus functions the system of extended deterrence. The US security guarantee was not infallible, but it did factor in the calculations of states like Australia and Japan[44] and certainly impacted on Iran. The USA had been Tehran's official security guarantor since the 5 March 1959 bilateral co-operation agreement in which both countries undertook to maintain their collective security and to resist aggression, direct or indirect, and the Shah made clear the importance of this, particularly given the Soviet threat:

> The present world is confronted with a problem of some countries possessing nuclear weapons and some not. We are among those who

do not possess nuclear weapons, so the friendship of a country such as the United States with its arsenal of nuclear weapons . . . is absolutely vital.[45]

Second, and more important, was Washington's unprecedented fear of proliferation: 'We never', wrote a US official in 1953, 'had any of this hysterical fear about any nation until atomic weapons appeared on the scene and we knew that others had solved the secret.'[46] The Americans were especially worried about the possible introduction of nuclear weapons into the Middle East, with officials determined to maintain the closest possible consultation on all matters that could affect such an eventuality.[47] Iran's broader relationship with Washington was one of dependence – an asymmetric one. Washington was confident that the Shah knew this and that he would act accordingly; and so it proved.[48]

The relationship was so important to Iran because it was one based on security, which had a meaning above and beyond the merely military because of the idiosyncratic way in which the Shah viewed security. From early in his reign he believed Iran suffered from an 'inadequate freedom of action in world politics', undoubtedly caused by not only its economic and political backwardness, but also the country's 'insecurity'.[49] Security, he argued in *Mission for My Country*, was the 'first essential for advancement . . . Freedom-loving peoples forget – but the Communist powers never forget – that most of the world's economically underdeveloped countries are also militarily underdeveloped.'[50] If Iran needed to modernize for greater autonomy then it logically needed security, and Washington was a guarantor of the entire Pahlavi project. The Shah was determined not to risk the relationship through the acquisition of a bomb he felt was of little immediate use anyway.

It all seemed settled. The Shah had monologued at Etemad for the last half hour of their meeting, and his position seemed considered and, importantly, certain. But then he leaned across his desk and introduced a caveat: this, he said, was his decision as things stood now. But if things changed for any reason, particularly if anyone else in the region got nuclear weapons and Iran's security was threatened, they would sit down and reconsider. Etemad now understood that they had arrived at the Shah's true feelings, which he naturally accepted. But he was uneasy; he knew that if anything changed, as head of the AEOI, the final responsibility would be with him to deliver. So he told his King that if the policy was to go for nuclear weapons he had to understand that it couldn't happen overnight, which the Shah accepted. Still, knowing just how much work was involved, he needed unambiguous clarification: was it possible, he asked, that in, say, ten years he might well want a nuclear bomb? The Shah looked at him, and, after a self-consciously dramatic pause, replied, in English: 'Why not?'

Security did then ultimately factor into the Shah's longer-term thinking, but it is important to understand its particular quality. The thought of 'little' states acquiring a bomb had affronted his sense of pride – keeping up would be necessary to maintain Iranian prestige. And a similar impulse partly fuelled his longer-term security concerns. For the Shah, as for the Islamic Republic that would follow him, and indeed for Iranians in general, the separation between national prestige and security is blurred. The Shah's first-hand experience of his country's implosion in the face of the 1941 British and Russian invasion had convinced him of the need for Iran to be militarily strong: security was necessary to ensure it would never be so used again. But the experience – only the latest in many Iranian capitulations – was also deeply shameful. A militarily strong Iran, possibly with a nuclear bomb, also therefore carried within it an implicit prestige that was more keenly felt by Iran than most countries. In the eyes of Iranians of whatever political persuasion, the country's large size, its location and its energy reserves would always make it a target for others. This needed to be resisted; and if Iran was strong it would also be proud.

As he left the Shah's office and walked down the long corridor, Etemad thought about what he needed to do in light of what had just occurred, which did not take long. He knew he would have to expand the AEOI's research and development activities to encompass not only peaceful nuclear applications but also potential military ones too. He couldn't afford to wait ten years for the Shah to come to him one day and say they needed the bomb only to be told it would take another ten years. He returned to the AEOI offices later that day and at the following day's morning conference (without mentioning his discussion) told his staff to pursue every avenue of nuclear research. While no actual weaponization work took place, every time an employee came to him with a research proposal he sanctioned it. Money was no object and he was uncomfortably aware of just how long research took to reach fruition, in some cases 20 years. Everything was tried, and in 1976 Etemad signed a contract for the development of a pilot plant for laser enrichment – a small laser enrichment programme would continue over the coming years.[51] The country would have access to all nuclear technologies. It would be prepared.

Interestingly, as no actual work on a nuclear bomb took place there was no need for the AEOI to work clandestinely. Weaponization is a complex area, not least because there is a significant difference between the process of weaponization itself (developing the technology to create a nuclear bomb such as a warhead) and the more general processes for creating a nuclear bomb, such as plutonium-producing reactors or uranium enrichment, which are vital for civil purposes for manufacturing nuclear fuel and also have military applications (to create the Highly Enriched Uranium (HEU) or plutonium necessary as a raw material for a nuclear bomb). Nothing in the NPT prohibits any nuclear process not directly related to weaponization; in fact, the NPT only prohibits acquisition of weapons or control of weapons. Everything else is allowed: weapon-components, fissile material, missiles for delivery and so on. Anything which is not explicitly forbidden is allowed. This makes it considerably harder to ascertain for sure if a state is developing a bomb (especially given that most of the relevant technology is 'dual use'). Set against this is of course Article IV of the treaty, which provides for the 'inalienable right' of the non-nuclear states to develop any peaceful nuclear energy for peaceful purposes 'without discrimination'.

This often creates tensions. Despite the IAEA safeguards regime of inspections, which theoretically provides a neutral means of monitoring adherence to the NPT's non-proliferation obligations, unless deception or bad faith can be proved, suspicion may, in certain instances, be a subjective judgement dependent on other factors: the country's reputation, its behaviour in other areas, international perception of its leaders, even its relations with the superpowers. In essence, it can often be largely political. The same uranium-enrichment programme in the hands of, for example, Denmark, will not be of concern, but may be considered a danger if operated by Iran. The reasons for this – a state's 'rogue' behaviour in other areas, for example – may be perfectly valid, but it often sees groups of countries pressuring the IAEA to more intrusively scrutinize that country's programme even if the Agency has pronounced itself satisfied on a technical level. The state in question then, with some justification, complains that its case has become political rather than purely technical (as it theoretically should be).

A CHANGED WORLD AND A CLASH OF FRIENDS

It was, in fact, the worst time for Iran to be expanding its nuclear programme. Only a year earlier, in May 1974, Dixie Lee Ray, Head of the US Atomic Energy Commission, had come to Tehran for a series of meetings on US–Iranian nuclear co-operation. One morning Etemad received an invitation for a lunch meeting at the US Embassy in Tehran with Ray and some US officials over from Washington. After a heavy meal the group retired to the gardens to discuss nuclear co-operation when a messenger came in and handed a note to the US Ambassador, Richard Helms, who read the note and then passed it to Ray, who also read it and passed it on to a colleague. It was then passed to Etemad to read the news that India had just conducted a nuclear explosion. He was shocked and looked up expectantly at his hosts, none of whom showed any surprise at all.[52]

Despite the Americans' apparent languor, India's nuclear test shattered the uneasy equilibrium that had existed after China's test in 1964, and, in the words of the CIA, probably initiated a second phase of nuclear proliferation.[53] The 'peaceful' nature of many developing world nuclear programmes now came under scrutiny, with significant repercussions for any country wanting to acquire nuclear technology. India's programme, like Iran's, was dependent on technological assistance from the West and the underground explosion had been possible only through the use of plutonium in a reactor provided by Canada – officially for peaceful purposes only. The test vocalized the West's unspoken fear since the beginnings of 'Atoms for Peace' that the NPT's Article IV, which legitimized the sale of 'dual-use' civil nuclear facilities able to produce weapons-grade materials provided they were placed under IAEA inspections, could be used to divert technological assistance towards the production of a nuclear explosive.

The previous years had seen growing technological capabilities across the developing world, due largely to increased nuclear links between European nuclear suppliers and developing countries for the supply of technology that could bring the nuclear weapons option closer to many developing countries. Nowhere was this concern more acute than with oil-rich Iran. Despite the lack of US surprise at the news, the White House – even with the Shah's friend Nixon in residence – became progressively more worried about possible Iranian proliferation. Washington's lucrative arms trade with Iran meant it would accede to pretty much any of the Shah's requests for arms, but it always stressed 'the very important exception' of any nuclear weapons capability.[54] Commercial imperatives were repeatedly subordinated to non-proliferation goals, and at all times the supply of nuclear technology and materials was conditional. The early nuclear co-operation that Iran had enjoyed gave way to a hardening of the US position towards its own 1957 bilateral agreement with Iran, and quibbling and caveats became the norm.

This was due largely to the scale of the Shah's more general ambitions – his huge military spending, love of sophisticated technology and of course the projected scope of the programme. As the oil money poured in, the sums became staggering. From the fiscal years 1975 to 1976 alone, the AEOI's budget soared from $30.8 million to over $1 billion.[55] More than this, the facilities planned – as many as 20 1,000 MW reactors to be operational by the end of the 1980s – would theoretically produce enough plutonium to build hundreds of nuclear weapons a year if, critically, Iran were also able to obtain plutonium reprocessing technology.[56]

Reprocessing is the chemical operation that separates useful fuel for recycling from nuclear waste.[57] Used fuel rods from the power plant have their metallic outer casing stripped away before being dissolved in hot nitric acid, which produces, among other things, about one per cent plutonium.[58] The Shah's programme was based entirely on power plants – it had no uranium-enrichment programme and, therefore, no uranium path to a bomb. A plutonium bomb was the only option and, what was worse, it was well suited to a country that might want to pursue a clandestine weapons programme because a reprocessing plant can easily be hidden in an innocuous building. Moreover, only about 4 kg of plutonium is needed to make a bomb, and to produce 12 kg of plutonium per year only a relatively small reprocessing facility would be needed.

The AEOI had, however, chosen light-water reactors for the programme, and while it is possible to use the plutonium produced in this type of reactor for nuclear weapons, it is very difficult (it contains the isotope Pu-240 which fissions spontaneously and leads to premature detonation). But Washington (especially when the Carter Administration came to power) was against the reprocessing of spent fuel in any form on general policy grounds (there was also of course the 'thin edge of the wedge' argument). It was also possible that if reprocessing of Iran's light-water reactor fuel were allowed, then Iran (or indeed any country) could buy a CANDU reactor from Canada, which would enable it to reprocess the fuel in a suitable manner. Either way, Washington was worried.

In what was to become a common attack, diplomats considered the Shah's plans for so many reactors to be premature considering Iran's huge oil resources. Suspicion was compounded because Iran's electrical consumption in the mid–late 1970s was only 14,000 MW, which meant that projected nuclear power production far exceeded any realistic demand. Set against that, annual plutonium production from the planned 23,000 MW Iranian nuclear programme could produce 600–700 warheads. The State Department was worried, not least because if the Shah's dictatorship collapsed, domestic dissidents or foreign terrorists might be able to seize nuclear material stored in Iran to make a bomb. Even if this did not occur, 'an aggressive successor to the Shah' might wish to use a bomb to complete Iran's domination of the region.[59]

CIA analysts also suggested that given the Shah's 'ambition to make Iran a power to be reckoned with', Iran's declared peaceful policy could change (which in light of his discussion with Etemad was correct).[60] If he were still on the throne in the 1980s, and Iran had a vibrant nuclear power industry and all the facilities necessary to make nuclear weapons, and if other countries had proceeded with nuclear weapons development, the agency had no doubt that Iran would 'follow suit'.[61] Conversely, without reprocessing technologies Iran's reactors were not a proliferation threat and Washington was adamant that it would not allow Iran, with its plans to build up to 20 reactors (which it had the money to do), to acquire a plutonium reprocessing plant. Some form of confrontation was now unavoidable.

A state that has mastered the entire fuel cycle has, more or less, achieved nuclear independence, which is of huge importance for national sovereignty in many parts of the developing world and to Iran in particular. The prestige that ownership of such technology brings is considerable. But there is also a more practical consideration. As long as a developing country depends on an industrialized trading partner (and usually a Western one at that), it relies on the technological largesse of its 'patron'. In 1975 Argentina had come to an agreement to buy a 600 MW CANDU reactor from

Canada only to then be forced to renegotiate financial terms and accept more stringent anti-proliferation conditions or face cancellation of the deal.[62] The avoidance of this type of technological dependence in such a politically volatile field is obviously desirable, especially for those with a sensitivity to being 'dictated to by foreigners'.

Washington had initially not allowed any US company to build nuclear power plants in Iran – leaving the grateful French and Germans to take the early contracts. By June 1974, it had finally agreed to sell Iran nuclear reactors by inserting some bilateral controls in addition to the standard IAEA international safeguards. The now imperial Shah was torn between his desire to please Washington and an assertion of what he believed were his natural rights, so he agreed to consider some of the safeguards as long as Iran were treated no differently to the USA's previous nuclear customers. But pressure was now increasing and, despite his boldness, the Shah's priority remained to try to avoid overly antagonizing Washington; whenever disagreement arose he tried to compromise.

Later that year, for example, Dixie Lee Ray spearheaded a new American non-proliferation initiative to establish regional uranium enrichment for the entire Middle East under international control, which Washington hoped would preclude the need for individual Middle Eastern states to enrich uranium domestically. Relations with Iran (which was reluctant to cede ground on what it considered to be an issue of its national sovereignty) had strained accordingly and talks on multi-billion-dollar nuclear co-operation between the two nations stalled. Seeing tension mounting on an increasing number of nuclear fronts, and not wishing to damage US relations, the Shah simply backed down, declaring that he had no intention of constructing a reprocessing facility.[63] At all times dealings with the Americans were conducted with the utmost sensitivity and respect for protocol. When Iran sought to reprocess US spent fuel it was at pains to stress that it would make a 'good faith' effort to establish a multinational reprocessing plant in return.[64]

But things got worse with Nixon's resignation. The incoming Gerald Ford was under conflicting pressures, with some in Congress alarmed by Iran's burgeoning nuclear programme, while US nuclear suppliers, seeing their French and German counterparts taking all the Iranian contracts, made their dissatisfaction equally plain. White House officials also knew that, given the Shah's personal interest in the programme, US policy would be important to overall US–Iran relations. Iran was still a valued source of oil and an ally in a hugely volatile region, and at a private dinner on 21 October 1975 Ford asked Ardeshir Zahedi, now (very) happily ensconced as Iran's Ambassador in Washington, to tell him 'candidly' if there was any misunderstanding between the two nations.[65] Despite his climbdown on the reprocessing facility, the Shah still argued that Iran should be allowed to pursue a wide range of nuclear technologies.

The USA was also now concerned about a possible Iranian move to a bomb through the alternative uranium route – namely, a uranium-enrichment programme on Iranian soil. Charges that Iran was pursuing covert enrichment activities began to surface (although they did not ascend to official IAEA charges until 2005). Western media also began to report that Iran was working on the first two stages of the fuel cycle: uranium mining and conversion. South Africa, it was rumoured, had agreed to supply $700 million of yellowcake (processed uranium ore that is converted into UF_6 to be enriched in centrifuges) per year to Iran in return for help in financing an enrichment plant in South Africa.[66]

The problem of course is that the fuel cycle also theoretically provides the indigenous means to build nuclear weapons: in this instance, the uranium path to a bomb. And while possession of an indigenous fuel cycle does not by any means indicate the presence of a nuclear weapons programme, if a state has the capability to enrich uranium to levels required for civil usage to power civil reactors – that is, LEU (which is any enrichment up from 0.7 per cent – natural uranium – to 20 per cent) – it theoretically has the technological capability to make HEU (anything above 20 per cent) to weapons-grade levels (around 80 per cent, though

93 per cent is preferred by weapons manufacturers). And here lies the dilemma: the USA and other nuclear-weapon states were (and are) desperate to prevent indigenous uranium enrichment in the developing world, but, once again, the NPT's Article IV, which allows for all forms of nuclear technology, meant that some non-nuclear countries (like Iran) felt aggrieved at this perceived failure by the nuclear-weapon states to fulfil their part of the NPT's bargain, especially since they showed no signs of moving towards disarmament.

Nonetheless, uranium enrichment had now joined reprocessing in US concerns, and Lee Ray's idea for regional fuel centres under international control in the Middle East, which would preclude the need for countries like Iran to enrich indigenously for nuclear fuel, took hold. But the AEOI was resistant to the idea, and several meetings with the Americans took place without progress. Growing frustrated, in early 1976 Washington sent Henry Kissinger to Tehran to meet with Etemad personally. During a meeting at the AEOI, Kissinger asked him why Iran was repeatedly refusing to co-operate. Etemad had always argued that Iran had the right to enrich uranium indigenously to help it master the fuel cycle under the NPT's Article IV, which allowed for the 'inalienable right' of all parties to pursue all forms of nuclear research 'without discrimination'. He believed that US attempts to prevent this were an infringement of Iranian sovereignty, but this argument had gone nowhere with the Americans and he now realized a change of approach might be necessary. So he asked Kissinger to envisage, not as Secretary of State but in his capacity as a Harvard Professor of International Relations, the likely outcome of a joint fuel programme that involved co-operation between Iraq, Pakistan, Egypt – would they be able to agree on anything? Surely it just wouldn't work? Kissinger pondered this for a minute before admitting it was unlikely to succeed and the AEOI heard no more about it.

But problems persisted, and they always concerned key stages of the fuel cycle. The Americans demanded a 'right of prior consent' clause that stated that the AEOI had to run all nuclear activities past Washington first, and seek US approval for whatever it wished to do with the spent fuel (which, after reprocessing, could be used to manufacture a bomb) produced in any reactor Washington would sell Iran. This was unacceptable to Etemad, who considered it an outrageous infringement on national sovereignty. But Washington would not budge either, and throughout the 1970s it sent endless delegations to Tehran to try to get the AEOI to accept the 'right of prior consent' amendment to the bilateral agreement the countries had signed in the 1950s.

The AEOI often faced the same problems they had with the French during the Framatome deal, as the Americans tried to bypass the AEOI and speak directly to the Shah in the hope that pressure could be more effectively applied at the political level. The Iranian response was the same, too. One afternoon in late 1975, shortly after President Gerald Ford had replaced Nixon, a US delegation met with the Shah at Sa'dabad to deliver a personal letter from Ford. It was the first order of business and the Shah read the letter in front of his guests, before politely discussing some generalities with them. As soon as the delegation left, however, he called Etemad and told him to come to the palace whereupon he showed him the letter, which requested, once again, that Iran forgo reprocessing of spent fuel. Etemad's reaction was unsurprisingly unfavourable and he went into the office next door to prepare an answer. Fifteen minutes later he returned and handed his brief but pointed refusal to the Shah who read it and then politely presented it to the disappointed Americans later that day.[67]

Matters only got worse with Jimmy Carter's inauguration in 1977 – the worst possible thing that could have happened at the worst possible time. The Shah was at the height of his power: an isolated figure living in a formal court (which he had always insisted be modelled along Western lines). Not only would no Iranian official dare contradict him, but foreign ambassadors also often 'cringed' at his responses to official presentations that displeased him. Only a couple of years previously, US Vice President Nelson Rockefeller had compared the Shah to Alexander the Great, urging him spend a couple of years in Washington in order to teach the Americans 'how to run a country'.[68] Since 1975, the Shah had also been on what the CIA called his 'lending binge', giving away billions to countries in need, including, in what must have been a thrilling gift, the mighty Britain. Never had he felt more secure, and less inclined to face dissent.

But Carter was determined to be tough on proliferation. Proposed US co-operation almost immediately fell 'prey to legal complications' when Iran's continuing wish to reprocess plutonium and other elements from spent fuel extracted from its reactors forced Congress to invoke section 123 of the US Atomic Energy Act 1954 (which states that a country wishing to conclude a deal for nuclear material, equipment or components from the USA must commit itself to adhering to US-mandated nuclear non-proliferation norms).[69] Again, the Shah backed down and agreed that any reprocessing plant would be subject to international control. Privately, he was furious. He had liked Nixon but he just couldn't stomach Carter. He often couldn't even bring himself to utter Carter's name, instead referring to him as 'this man'. AEOI staff resented Carter, too, believing that Washington had been happy to assist the programme in its early stages, assuming it would be a good source of income from which it would derive the lion's share, but began to backtrack once it expanded into a life of its own.[70]

For its part, Washington's concerns over Iran's programme had evolved from suspicion into disbelief of the Shah's supposedly benign intentions. On 18 June 1977, William Sullivan arrived in Tehran to present his credentials to the Shah as Washington's new Ambassador to Iran. During their meeting, the Shah told Sullivan that he was ready to resume nuclear negotiations and expressed hope that the long-anticipated US reactors would be forthcoming. Sullivan said nothing and later cabled Washington to explain that he had deliberately not followed up on the Shah's observations because, knowing that the State Department needed clarity on the Shah's nuclear intentions, he wanted the Iranians to 'put all their cards on the table' before any further discussion. Nonetheless, the Shah's 'specific disavowal of interest in reprocessing plant' that Sullivan cabled back met with a sceptical response from a wag at ISA's Iran desk, who drew a little picture of a bull next to the words.[71]

At the official level Carter was determined to continue good relations with Iran, and on New Year's Eve 1977/1978 toasted the Shah at a state dinner in Tehran, calling Iran 'an island of stability' in the troubled Middle East. But at the same time he worked to create an even more restrictive nuclear export policy. His Non-Proliferation Act of 1978 created a set of new conditions for countries seeking US nuclear technology, which the AEOI viewed as overly onerous (though most countries did not complain too much) and only made things between the two countries more tense. Etemad resisted almost every US attempt to (as he saw it) interfere in the programme. He did not want to make decisions that would affect things 15 years down the line for the next generation of Iranians; and he argued repeatedly with Dixie Lee Ray, categorically refusing to accept conditions on Iran's right to the fuel cycle. The two sides had gone round in circles for years without any movement on either reprocessing or enrichment. It was wearying.

In the summer of 1978, Etemad heard that a US delegation was coming to Tehran with instructions to reach a 'positive conclusion'. Sitting in his office at the end of the day shortly before he was due to attend a dinner engagement, he greeted the news miserably. He just didn't have it in him to go through one more round of interminable negotiations on the same subject; no resolution was possible because he wasn't going to agree on any text that limited Iran's freedom of action. He decided not to attend the meeting and instead summoned two of his colleagues into the office and told them to go on his behalf. As a last attempt at a solution he told them that if the Americans continued to insist on the 'right of prior consent' clause that obliged Iran to run all nuclear activities past Washington first, they should concede to a clause granting Iran 'most favoured nation' status in nuclear dealings with the USA. The negotiations dragged on for two days until the Iranians came back to Etemad and said the Americans had agreed. Of course it would have to be secret, and no information about the deal would be recorded in open documents. But, finally, they had agreed.

* * *

Washington's fears over Iran's programme became considerable as the 1970s wore on, but it is important to note that they centred on Iran's future intentions or its future capabilities – and US actions were always preventative measures. The programme itself caused little alarm. Most pertinently, the Shah chose light-water reactors as a basis of his programme, the type least conducive to weapons uses. When combined with the lack of any indigenous weapons-grade material producing technology such as uranium enrichment (all enrichment under the Eurodif project was done in France) or plutonium processing, Iran's choice of nuclear technology (and its acceptance of IAEA safeguards on all facilities) was as reassuring as it could be.[72] Regardless of any weapons desires he may or may not have had, the Shah did not allow these to shape the nuclear programme itself. Added to this, all the projected Iranian nuclear installations (notably Bushehr) were 'turnkey' projects controlled and staffed significantly, or in some cases almost entirely, by foreign contractors. As an NPT signatory any proliferation would therefore have to be covert, and almost impossible without the complicity of large numbers of foreign personnel who, with no political or nationalist interest in Iran, had no reason to help and keep quiet about it. Quite simply, even if the Shah were desperate to acquire nuclear weapons, the possibility was at least a decade away. He could afford to be more circumspect and put off difficult decisions that were a long way off.

But much of this was largely a choice. The Shah could have gone further down the weapons route – certainly many of his contemporaries did, most of whom lacked his oil wealth. More than anything else, restraint characterized the Shah's programme, and his reasons for this restraint are the fullest expression of its nature, purpose and ultimate meaning to Pahlavi Iran. If a state rejects nuclear weapons it usually has a particular set of reasons for doing so that say a lot about its view of itself and its place in the world. Japan, for example, has a large and sophisticated nuclear programme but totally rejects nuclear weapons because of its experience as the world's only victim of an atomic bomb. Its programme has a specific technological purpose (to create energy to power Japan) but it also has a wider meaning. With its considerable technological capability, its huge economic wealth and global political status (not to mention its very real proliferation incentive in the form of neighbouring, nuclear-armed China), Japanese restraint is a choice, a choice that carries within it an explicit rejection of the *idea* of nuclear weapons. Nuclear programmes are often a statement of identity, and what they mean to their owners, beyond the practical, is what will direct their purpose. Their purpose, in turn, performs the function of a mirror, reflecting back onto the state its own nature.

The Shah's restraint shows that while the programme's technological goals were important to him, they would always be subordinate to its symbolic, political purpose. Israel, for example, which also relied on good relations with the USA, and which faced similar US opposition to any nuclear weapons drive (and, moreover, at the time it 'went nuclear' in the 1960s, did not enjoy as strong a relationship with Washington as the Shah), nonetheless proliferated. On a fundamental level, Jerusalem's programme meant nothing more to it than security (indeed, it remains officially secret); it was a technological means to an end, and the possibility of Western opprobrium was a risk worth taking. For the Shah, the programme was always an almanac of the Pahlavi narrative – its most extreme manifestation. Even its legitimate economic benefits were subsumed into a greater, more nebulous display of modernity. And on its most practical level even the preservation of oil reserves and desire for national advancement was subordinated to the need to cement relations with the West – both commercially and diplomatically.

Because prestige relies on reputation, it relies on the perceptions of others. So what brings prestige will depend on whom you want to impress and what their values are: it is audience-specific. In the early 1960s, Canada was asked to put US nuclear weapons on its aircraft and missiles, which would have raised its estimation in NATO circles, but lowered it among the Non-Aligned Movement, which saw the move as yet another example of US imperialism (Canada subsequently refused). In 1974 India's nuclear test earned it the respect of the modernizing world but the displeasure of the West. The Canadians immediately ended all nuclear assistance to Delhi, and the USA slowed shipments of enriched uranium fuel to its Tarapur Atomic Power Station, which disrupted performance severely – a price the Indians gladly paid. For the Shah, desperate to maintain relations with the West, restraint gained him the most prestige from the audience he most wanted it from; he preferred to garner the moral legitimacy and political capital he derived among his Western allies by holding back.

Such ideas were energized by the NPT – perceived as the brainchild of the West – which established a set of values or 'norms' to which the Shah could publicly adhere and show the world what kind of state his Iran was. Many years later, Ukraine would be born as an independent state from Russia with a nuclear arsenal inherited from the USSR already within its borders. Kiev had a genuine security need for a nuclear deterrent to protect itself from irredentist Russian designs, which had not disappeared with the breakup of the USSR. Yet after some initial uncertainty, the country made the decision to eliminate its nuclear arsenal. Ukraine acceded to the NPT as a non-nuclear state in the early 1990s as a way of separating itself from the USSR. The NPT had created a world in which the most recent examples of new or potential nuclear states were pariah or 'rogue states' such as North Korea and Iraq. This was hardly a nuclear club whose new members would receive international prestige, and during the debate in Kiev, numerous pro-NPT Ukrainian officials insisted that renunciation of nuclear weapons was the best route to enhance Ukraine's international standing. Without the NPT, keeping its nuclear arsenal would have made Ukraine like France; with it, Ukraine was Pakistan or Iraq or North Korea. Twenty years earlier, the Shah knew who he would rather be.

CHAPTER 5

SLOW DECLINE, QUICK FALL: THE END OF THE SHAH'S PROGRAMME

On the afternoon of 16 January 1979, just over a year after Jimmy Carter had described his country as an island of stability in the Middle East, Mohammad Reza Pahlavi stood, like his father had done almost 40 years before him, bereft and about to flee Iran. In the Royal Pavilion of Tehran airport he said goodbye to the only two men that had come to see him off: his Prime Minister-designate, Shapour Bakhtiyar, and General Abdolali Badrei, commander of his imperial guards. Five crates of his belongings had already been loaded onto another plane: the only fruits of his long reign (along with sizable amounts of cash in European and American bank accounts). Taking Bakhtiyar's head in his hands, he told him that he was placing Iran into his care, and God's.

Over the previous years he had cursed everyone from communists to 'foreign agents' for his rapidly waning power. A testament to his total misunderstanding of the reality, brought about by years of listening to sycophants, was that even in exile he blamed not Ayatollah Khomeini and the clergy, but these forces for his fall. In early September 1978, a crowd of 50,000 had marched through Tehran protesting his rule. Almost all the demonstrators were middle class – teachers, students, professionals – but the Mullahs led it, and its slogan was 'Freedom, Independence and Islamic government'. The people marched and then, *en masse*, they prayed. Even then, the Shah failed to see that popular dissent, albeit political in character, was being channelled by the clergy. Deluded by a rising GNP, rapid modernization, and his international 'statesmanship', he just could not believe that the people for whom he thought he had done everything could be so ungrateful. But while he had attained unchallenged control of the state he had neglected to create at least a believable veneer of democracy to legitimize his rule. His reliance on relations with the West always made him vulnerable to domestic attack, and it played its part in his end. His decision in 1977 to bow to Carter's pressures to liberalize when he was at his most vulnerable (and therefore needed to be at his most autocratic to keep control) allowed a civil society to re-emerge, and with it the opposition that overthrew him.

Even his apparent successes – his modernization and mass industrialization – were largely overheated, lopsided and often superficial. By the late 1970s many Iranians had acquired refrigerators, washing machines and televisions but found that the electricity shut down for eight hours a day, rendering them unusable. They could afford to order a car, but with production insufficient to meet demand they couldn't have one, and the streets were choked with the cars already on them. Many rural towns were literally 'semi-modernized', with electricity and cars running through one half of the town, while the other half resembled a hamlet from the Middle Ages. In this sense the nuclear programme was perhaps the most developed expression of the Shah's doomed modernization, and like his reign it failed. As his rule crumbled in the face of popular unrest his nuclear programme became vulnerable to attack, synonymous as it was with Pahlavi corruption and waste. The frequent power cuts in the mid-1970s were seen as indicative of government ineptitude, and contributed to increasing criticism of the monarchy allowed by a relaxing of dictatorial behaviour, which, in July 1977, unseated the 13-year-old Hoveida government.

That same year problems mounted for the nuclear programme and the AEOI when Hoveida's successor, Jamshid Amouzegar, sponsored a review of the organization, alleging that it had not fully assessed or reported 'the growing costs and risks' involved in the 'substantial' Iranian commitment to nuclear power.[1] In concert with Bijan Mossavar-Rahmani, energy correspondent for the newspaper *Kayhan International*, he raised concerns about the programme's cost and practicability. The review concluded that the limited availability of uranium and political restrictions upon its use forced Iran to depend upon a 'small group of highly politicized and commercially aggressive suppliers'.[2] Mossavar-Rahmani also deemed nuclear power too expensive: with predicted costs of over $3,000/kW being three times greater than AEOI cost estimates for Bushehr.[3]

The AEOI naturally denied the charges – claiming per kilowatt costs were less than $1,000, excluding infrastructure costs – but the criticisms chimed with popular sentiment and Amouzegar decided to transfer responsibility for the planning, construction and operation of the reactors to the energy ministry. The AEOI could do little in response; the nuclear programme was almost entirely dependent upon its primary advocate, the Shah. No significant political pressure groups with a vested interest in the nuclear project's continuance existed to defend it. His gradual weakening was accompanied by Hoveida's resignation and then that of Etemad after charges of mismanagement and corruption[4] and deprived the programme of its few important supporters in government aside from the Shah himself. The programme enjoyed no wide-scale popular support because the nature of one-man rule often discouraged public awareness of key issues (public opinion would have no effect so why seek it?). Even MPs in the Majlis didn't dare criticize the programme.[5] The new climate was summed up by Etemad's replacement, former AEOI Vice President Dr Ahmad Sotudehnia, who declared that 'there will be some place for atomic energy, but whether it will be 23,000 MW I cannot say'.[6]

Under Pahlavi rule, nationalism became a cult of monarchy from which the people were largely disenfranchised. Ideas of national prestige and modernization were contaminated by association with the Shah and could not be used to harness popular support. Most striking in the Shah's nuclear programme was that it contained none of the overt populism that would characterize the programme under the Islamic republic, and, despite the genuine benefits it could bring Iran, the Shah was not able to use the programme to the same rhetorical effect as today's regime: to garner support for the regime on nationalist grounds. At the very end of his reign, as the government struggled to survive, retreating on many of its unpopular policies, it is notable that funding to the nuclear programme was heavily cut. With no real public advocacy either for or against nuclear power in general, the programme itself came to be viewed as just another totem of royal profligacy.

Towards the end of his reign the Shah became ill with the cancer that would eventually kill him. Etemad still saw him often, though the tone and content of the meetings had changed. It was clear that the Shah couldn't cope – he was not a man for a crisis. Some days when they met he was in very bad shape – he seemed lost, in fact. But he retained his belief in Iran's need for modernization, and for nuclear energy, to the end. As Etemad watched things fall apart he believed that his country had become a victim of its own success. In his eyes, the desire for revolution that swelled across Iran stemmed from the popular dissatisfaction brought about by the rapid rate of the country's development, which had brought a commensurate increase in popular expectations. When these went unfulfilled the results were inevitable. This wounded the Shah more than anything else. He just could not understand it: 'Why are they like this?' he complained to Etemad. 'We're doing so much for the country. They just don't understand.'

THE SHAH'S NUCLEAR PROGRAMME: AN ASSESSMENT

The nuclear programme was the Shah's 'man to the moon'. It was not a pragmatic vision and it failed on pragmatic grounds. The economic benefits the government used to justify the programme were valid – there was a genuine argument for nuclear power. But they were always less important than the wider, more ideological, ambitions of the Pahlavi project, to which the programme, as the most complete expression of an Iran vaulting to modernity, was integral. It is what 'modernity' represented to the Shah – technological advancement and, critically, Westernization – that is so instructive. While nuclear power was viewed across the developing world as a conduit to modernity, it was typically Pahlavi to view modernity and Westernization as synonymous.

From the Shah's first utterances, nuclear power was intertwined with notions of national pride and progress: normal desires for a developing country that were magnified by his personal ambitions. But his wish for greater independence and national self-respect was undertaken not through the defiance of many of his developing world contemporaries, but by donning the clothes of his Western role models. This is what differentiated his nuclear posture from other contemporary modernizing states and what most shaped it. Indicative of these motives was the country's official name – The Empire of Iran – a title that carried within it an implicit rejection of anti- (or even post-) colonialism. As oil revenues swelled both Iran's coffers and the Shah's ego, he decided that as the Middle East had experienced many controlling forces before, he would be the latest. Even when he told Etemad that possible proliferation of neighbouring states (which would both affront Iranian pride and risk it falling behind militarily) might prompt Iran to choose the nuclear option, security and pride could not be divorced. No one was more aware of Iran's comparative historical weaknesses in the face of others than the Shah. If the country could become the regional policeman, it

87

would compensate for a century of shameful defeats and Iran would no longer be a target.

Once all of this is understood, the hyper-projects and financial excess of his reign are more easily seen as what they were: symptoms of a modernizing state's attempt to find a place for itself in the world, which, in this instance, meant an Iranian identity commensurate with the Pahlavi ideal. The nuclear programme was merely one more (perhaps the ultimate) symptom of his paradoxical need to escape the Western oppressor while simultaneously being drawn to him. But the means of escape was imitation, and the two impulses fused together, often in the Shah's language, as he pronounced on both the greatness and the uniqueness of Iran while simultaneously expressing a deep fascination with the West and the technology it represented. In this sense the Shah was right: his reign was deeply revolutionary, in many ways no less so than the Islamic Republic that was to come, although its manifestation was markedly different.

But it is by considering what ultimately held the Shah back from getting the bomb – so odd in the circumstances – that the true nature and purpose of his programme can most clearly be seen. The huge buildup of his armed forces following the 1973 oil boom; the Iranian fleet dominating the Persian Gulf; the party in the desert ('the most sumptuous in history'); the joy of mass industrialization, which was complemented by international statesmanship; the suggested campaign to get the Shah the Nobel Prize ('If they beg us, we might accept,' he said. 'They give it to anyone these days.');[7] the lending binge and Royal 'magnanimity'; the endless palaces and yachts and cars and jewels ... and yet he held back from what could have been the brightest feather in the Peacock's plume. He showed restraint, when in almost all other areas he showed none.

Restraint allowed him to showcase his similarity to the West: on a technological level, and, perhaps most importantly, on a political level. He exploited the developed–developing world nuclear divide by coming firmly down on the 'Western side'. Admittedly, he clashed with the USA over Iran's right to the full range of nuclear technologies, but he did so after signing up to the very treaty that made it so hard to exercise those rights. The NPT was, in the end, one more way in which he could win Western favour and show the West that Iran was a similar kind of state. That Iran was also exactly the kind of threshold state – genuinely capable of going nuclear – that the NPT most affected, only makes his action more odd and shows just how much less important the programme's technological potential was when compared with its political purpose. It is a heavy irony that his reign ended through revolution since no one used the discourse of revolution more than he did. He was a revolutionary monarch who would bring democracy and modernity (and in so doing legitimize himself and his dynasty) to Iran, and nothing was more revolutionary than nuclear power, which only ten years before it came to Iran had changed the world forever. Nuclear programmes are often a statement of identity, and the Shah used his programme to both create and then exemplify the identity of his Iran: modern and Western, and defined above all else by progress. And it failed.

CHAPTER 6

CHILDREN OF THE REVOLUTION: A YEAR OF CHAOS – 1979

On 1 February 1979 Mohsen Sazegara stood onboard an Air France Boeing 747 to Tehran counting heads for the fourth time. Sazegara had been one of Ayatollah Khomeini's aids for several years; he had helped organize opposition to the Shah and then joined Khomeini in Paris, where they now were, waiting to take off. More than anyone, Khomeini had brought down the Shah. Originally an obscure cleric from Qom, he had made his name in 1963 by publicly denouncing the land reforms of the White Revolution and, a year later, accusing the Shah of submission to America and Israel. In November 1964 he was arrested and exiled to Turkey before moving on to Najaf in Iraq, where he spent the next 14 years formulating his theory of Islamic governance and later preaching against the Shah on cassette tapes smuggled into Iran and disseminated across the country. In September 1978, by now the spiritual and intellectual leader of the revolution, he was expelled from Iraq at Tehran's request, and settled on the outskirts of Paris, where he was joined by other revolutionaries to prepare for the Shah's imminent fall and his return to Iran.[1]

Now, after years of struggle, it was happening. As the *de facto* press officer, Sazegara had issued plane tickets for the 450 journalists hoping to witness Khomeini's return and the birth of a revolution, but Prime Minister Bakhtiyar's last-minute announcement that he wouldn't allow the plane to land in Tehran was causing problems. Worried officials had reduced passenger numbers in case extra fuel were needed to fly on to Turkey and the journalists who could not board were arguing, in some cases almost right up until the doors shut. In the air the atmosphere was febrile: half celebratory, half fearful. Khomeini himself was impassive. ABC reporter Peter Jennings asked him what he felt on returning to Iran. 'Hich ehsâsi nadâram', he answered, with the calm expected of an Imam. 'I feel nothing.'

The plane landed at Mehrabad airport. As it sat on the runway Sazegara looked through the window and saw air force guards surround the plane, and in the distance Ayatollah Pasandideh, Khomeini's elder brother, was among the waiting dignitaries. Stairs were connected to the plane and Sazegara scurried down them to organize things for the journalists that would follow him; he was the first person onto Iranian soil. All around him flashbulbs started exploding – for a second he thought the army was firing on them. Upon landing people had started bickering about who would help the Ayatollah down from the plane – he was almost 80. Finally, to avoid showing favouritism, Khomeini had asked the French pilot to aid him. Sazegara looked up and saw Khomeini being helped slowly down the steps. 'We've done it', he thought. 'The Ayatollah has come.'

After pushing its way through the shoving, prodding mass of journalists (and dodging the assembled dignitaries waiting to greet them) the revolutionary party left the airport for the 4 km drive to Behesht Zahra cemetery, where Khomeini would make his victory speech to the masses. Sitting in a minibus behind the Ayatollah's 4 × 4, Sazegara gawped at the throngs lining the streets to watch the entourage: among the crowds he could see the old left-wing activists – the godless communists – holding up large banners

welcoming Khomeini, which made him smile. Khomeini's car had
been forced through the crowds, but the rest were at a standstill.
Assured that the Ayatollah had sufficient numbers with him, Sazegara got out and took a cab to his parents' house. All his family
except his father had gone to see Khomeini. None of them knew
he had been on the plane.

Approximately three miles across town in North Tehran, Dary-
oush Homayoun, the Shah's former Minister of Information, sat
in the communal room of Jamshidabad military prison watching TV. He watched stairs wheeled over to the plane, the door
open and then not Khomeini, but a little man in a suit scam-
per down the steps. He could see him gesturing at the thicket
of journalists bristling with cameras and microphones. And then
the Ayatollah appeared. There was a feeling of awe among the
prisoners, almost all of them former government officials. But
there was also the sense of total loss – for both them and the
country. They feared what Khomeini would do, and what was
coming.[2]

* * *

1979. The revolution changed everything. The Shah's overthrow
destroyed a monarchic tradition that had lasted centuries, and
transformed the country from an autocratic, pro-Western kingdom to an isolationist, Islamic and populist republic under Ayatollah Ruhollah Khomeini's clerical rule. The gradual return to
public life of the veil and beard signalled to the watching world,
and it *was* watching, just how different things would be. The new
government, set up on 4 February and (ostensibly) led by Prime
Minister Mehdi Bazargan, had two immediate goals: to distance
itself from the reviled Shah and to implement the nascent state's
new ideological principles. This in and of itself was a confusing
task. Ideology was to become the Islamic Republic's flag – short-
hand for its very existence to the watching world. But what exactly that ideology was is more complex. Khomeini brought a new
ideological framework to Iranian political life, the *Velayat-e faqih*,

which prescribed supervision over government by those best equipped to interpret God's will, the religious jurists, or Mullahs, like him. It would be a gradual process, but change had arrived on a Boeing 747, and the world knew it.[3]

The revolutionaries began to overhaul government, which would subsequently become quasi-dictatorial, with an unelected leader at its head, and quasi-democratic, with elections and a written constitution at its heart. While Khomeini eventually became the 'Supreme Leader' and undoubtedly the final arbiter on affairs of state, decision-making became more diffuse, spread throughout seemingly endless bodies, and no single authority existed in quite the way it had under the Shah. The immediate effect on the programme was that nobody knew what to do with it; certainly, nobody knew where it stood in relation to the new regime's principles, and the 'official' position on the programme during its first year was confused and contradictory. The Hostage Crisis and then the Iran–Iraq war threw the country into disarray and alienated it on the world stage. Quite simply, other things were important. As, of course, was ideology, though what that was even the revolutionaries were struggling to decide.

During the revolution, crowds had walked through the streets carrying banners of Mossadegh, chanting 'Margh-bar Amrika' ('Death to America') and denouncing Western decadence. The 1953 coup, already iconic in the national consciousness, was reduced to a simple homily about the perfidious role of (mainly) Western powers in Iran: the Shah's Western 'subservience' had emasculated the country. The revolutionaries' reassertion of Iranian nationalism carried within it an implicit desire to preserve Islamic, Iranian identity in the face of Western influence: a resistance to what was called *Gharbzadegi* (literally: 'West-struckness'), or *Westoxification*. The term was a staple of the revolutionary lexicon, first coined by Ahmad Fardid, a Tehran University professor in the 1940s, but popularized by the (ironically) secular Marxist writer and social critic, Jalal Al-e Ahmad, in his 1962 book, *Occidentosis: A Plague from the West*.

Khomeini had publicly embraced Al-e Ahmad's message as early as 1971, claiming that Western influence was 'penetrating to the depths' of towns and villages throughout the Muslim world, displacing Qur'anic culture and recruiting Iranian youth en masse 'to the service of foreigners and imperialists'.[4] Critically, Al-e Ahmad had argued that *Westoxification* infected its subjects with so severe an identification with the West that its enthralling effects became a product of their own selves, 'hypnotizing' them into believing they wanted what the West offered and convincing them that they needed to mimic it in order to progress – the very definition, his critics charged, of the Shah's rule. Iran had bowed before Western corporations and imported a Western mode of life into the country with disastrous results. The influence of *Westoxification* would be immediately felt in the revolutionary government, and its nuclear programme.

For the Shah the world really was a stage, and its international institutions the opportunity for him to play upon it. The Islamic Republic conversely viewed the world as essentially hostile, its institutions mere 'tools' of Western hegemony and Iran the only true non-aligned country with a duty to help oppressed Muslims and oppressed nations. 'We will not play the policeman of the Persian Gulf', said Khomeini with disdainful reference to the Shah's foreign policy, two weeks before he returned to Iran.[5] His worldview was conspiratorial and it was binary: Manichean in tone, Islamic in expression, Third Worldist and historical in construction and not nuanced. Good versus evil; the oppressor (*Mustakbarin*) versus the downtrodden (*Mostazafin*); the realm of peace and belief (*Dar al-Islam*) versus the realm of war and disbelief (*Dar al-Harb*) and truth and justice (*Haq va Adalat*) versus falsehood (*Batel*). In a Cold War world further sundered by the struggle between the USSR and USA, in which communism battled capitalism, Iran was the only 'true' independent state. Never again would it look to the 'godless East' or 'the tyrannic [*sic*] blasphemous West, instead it would look skywards, to God'.[6]

THE NUCLEAR PROGRAMME: THE OFFICIAL POSITION

Nothing of course was more 'Western' than the nuclear programme, which was based on Western technology bought from Western countries and built by thousands of Western contractors. Added to this was its huge cost – and it was widely seen as a symptom of royal excess. Political pressure to do something about it – for the Islamic Republic to live up to its own rhetoric – was huge. Inside the AEOI, Reza Khazaneh, who had stayed in Iran to continue heading up the Isfahan Nuclear Technology Centre, already suspected what was coming. He had already watched events on the streets with alarm and, just days after the revolution, Abbas Taj, the new Minister of Energy, made the revolutionary government's policy ominously clear when he visited the AEOI and told its staff that everything they had done had been a waste of money.[7] On 10 March 1979, just over a month after Khomeini returned to Iran, things became clearer still when Fereydun Sahabi was appointed Under Secretary at the Ministry of Energy and Head of the AEOI.

Sahabi was the archetype of the new 'revolutionary man' that now began to fill government. His father, Yadollah Sahabi, was Minister for Implementation of Revolutionary Affairs in Bazargan's revolutionary government and only a month earlier, on 12 February, Khomeini had appointed his brother Ezzatollah to the Council of Islamic Revolution. As a geologist with no nuclear training, he was also totally unqualified for the job – another characteristic of the 'new' Iran as the well connected and ideologically 'sound' were preferred to the suitable. Sahabi met with senior AEOI staff soon after his appointment. He was clearly upset that some of them (like Khazaneh) hadn't been a part of the revolutionary movement but refrained from overt criticism, most likely because he needed their expertise in an area about which he knew nothing.

Nonetheless, Sahabi immediately made his presence felt. A week after his appointment, he gave an interview to *Keyhan* in which he bemoaned soaring costs that he claimed were never predicted when the programme was started. This tallied with the Islamic Republic's desire to immediately distance itself from the financial irresponsibility perceived to be among the previous regime's worst characteristics. Specifically, he claimed that the cost of Bushehr had nearly doubled to $7 billion and the budget was out of control – typical of the Shah's rule.[8] The new frugality chimed with political expediency as the government now promised farmers farm-to-market roads instead of nuclear power plants and massive arms purchases. Both Sahabi and AEOI executive Mansour Ruhi also expressed safety concerns and claimed that Iran's lack of expertise, especially given the potential dangers of nuclear power plants, meant that it was not a propitious time for them.[9] The regime seemed determined to delegitimize the programme on any grounds and thereby dismantle the deposed Shah's grandiose development plans. Given the genuine economic case for nuclear power, for both electricity and longer-term goals such as the preservation of oil reserves, it was clear that governmental determination was about more than purely practical concerns.

On 11 April 1979 Sahabi announced that the programme as a whole was under serious review because it was reliant on 'help from abroad which would bind us economically and industrially to those countries'.[10] Later in the same month he announced further cutbacks, declaring that the AEOI had created 'a consumer market in Iran for the industrial products of other countries', and that, critically, in future 'no foreign manpower would be utilized' by the AEOI.[11] Certain rhetorical tropes characteristic of the Islamic Republic's ideological stance were emerging: notably, that the programme now provided a 'consumer market' for foreign interests. All the Sahabis had a socialistic bent to their economic outlook, which clearly influenced the AEOI's initial nuclear policy here (just as left-wing ideas had influenced the revolutionaries).

But more pertinently, while the revolution's Islamist elements had not yet attained total control of government (Bazargan, for

example, still wanted to retain relations with the West) the declaration of an end to 'foreign manpower' explicitly conformed to
the tenets of *Westoxification* and nascent Khomeinism. Certainly
Khomeini's overarching influence was clear. One of the first pri-
orities for an Islamic government, he said in January 1979, would
be to review all the commercial contracts the Shah's regime
had made with foreign companies.[12] Sahabi then announced
that henceforth the AEOI's 'essential mission' would be to
'enhance the country's knowledge of nuclear energy with a view to
achieving self-sufficiency'.[13] No longer a banner of Iran's global
inclusiveness, the *raison d'être* of the nuclear programme had transformed completely.

Rapid and drastic scaleback was now the goal. In early June
1979, Reza Amrollahi, one of the AEOI's directors, asked
Khazaneh to accompany him (along with two Tehran University
professors) to Bushehr to view the installations and see if they
could be used for anything else. Amrollahi was also against a nuclear programme in Iran and the group flew to Bushehr, staying
there for several days while they inspected the installations and
equipment that had been shipped there before the revolution.
Much to Amrollahi's disappointment it was clear that the plant
and equipment could not be used for other purposes. Bushehr
would have to stay.[14] Sure enough, a few days later Sahabi declared that apart from Bushehr all other nuclear power projects
would be cancelled.

In the revolution's aftermath, Washington had ceased its supply
of HEU to Iran, which, in turn, cancelled its agreement with the
Eurodif consortium, demanding full repayment of its $1 billion
loan for the construction of the Tricastin plant. On 2 June 1979,
co-operation with Kraftwerk on the two Bushehr nuclear reactors broke down with the Iranian authorities' refusal to extend
the work permits of the 200 German workers there past 21 June.
Preparations were made to put the project back in indigenous
hands and it seemed doubtful that construction would proceed
at all.[15] At the official level, the government emphasized its right
to make unilateral decisions. Nobody would push Iran around

anymore. On 10 April 1979 it cancelled construction of the two proposed Framatome power plants at Darkhovin[16] and two months later, on 17 July 1979, Sahabi also told state radio that Bushehr's fate depended on the government's 'final decision'; contractors were no longer being paid.[17]

Understandably, all of this did nothing to improve Iran's foreign relations. The programme was built around a nexus of interlocking contracts with Western partners and the inevitable duly happened: on 31 July 1979 Kraftwerk formally terminated its contract to build the Bushehr power plant, citing Iranian debts to the company of $450 million.[18] At this stage the first reactor was around 80 per cent complete, the second reactor 45–70 per cent complete, while 90 per cent of the parts had been shipped.[19] A theatrically outraged Sahabi protested that the cancellation of the contract had inflicted financial damage on Iran amounting to DM 5,877 million; he demanded compensation and, in early 1980, Iran and Kraftwerk began litigation in Geneva.[20] Eurodif had also taken Iran to the International Chamber of Commerce Arbitration Court in Paris and on 24 October 1979 the court ordered a freeze on all Iranian assets in the company and ruled that repayment of Iran's $1 billion loan to Eurodif be suspended.[21] The programme had now become mired in legal wrangling and its major developments now took place in court, where nothing much happened either.

After a year of turmoil the revolutionaries had finally arrived, almost piecemeal, at an overall official position. On 17 June 1980 at a meeting between Hasan Abbaspur, Minister of Energy (accompanied by Sahabi) and the new (and first) President Abulhassan Bani-Sadr (who had replaced the more accommodating Barzagan) discussions were held concerning the nation's energy needs, universal government support for the official suspension of large parts of the programme was agreed, and it was collectively declared that:

> The construction of these reactors, started by the former regime *on the basis of colonialist and imposed treaties*, was harmful for the country from the economic, political and technical points of view, and *was*

a cause of greater dependence on imperialist countries. These contracts were stopped after the victory of the revolution.[22] (Emphasis my own)

The nuclear programme was now officially viewed as the continuation of colonialism by other means. The atom was not merely too expensive, it was ideologically unclean. Only the previous month, Khomeini had declared that he wanted 'no Westoxification' in Iran.[23] The dissident writer Jalal Al-e Ahmad had critiqued Western technology (and by implication Western 'civilization' itself) by, among other things, labelling the decline of traditional Iranian industries such as carpet-weaving due to competition from more modern Western technologies as Western 'economic and existential victories over the East'.[24] His very language was now pointedly echoed by AEOI and government officials.

Westoxification had also given Khomeini part of his justification for the *velayat-e Faqih*, and its influence began to be felt in all areas of life. Women who worked as secretaries and interpreters for foreign newsmen had been warned to stop wearing Western dress, and foreign cigarettes had even been banned (although a Tehrani supplier claimed he could manufacture Iranian cigarettes to taste just like Winstons). As far as the revolutionaries were concerned, the Shah's rule had comprehensively demonstrated that the average Iranian citizen was incapable of defending himself from its influence, so they would have to do it.[25] The new regime needed to guard against any Western infiltration and the nuclear programme, clearly a 'Trojan horse' for such influence, had to be carefully policed, which is what Sahabi and others had done since their arrival, and which now reached its logical conclusion. Classic anti-imperialist impulses were obviously present, but the strength of more idiosyncratic influences was clear from the tenor of complaint. Modernizing–modern world clashes in the nuclear realm generally centred on perceived 'imperialist' denial of technology to modernizing states. Here Iran decried Western co-operation; far from being denied technology and expertise, it rejected it.

Even at this early stage, however, there was a clear ideological severance between construction of the plants themselves and nuclear research. Perhaps mindful of the constitutional injunction to direct all resources to 'strengthening the spirit of enquiry ... in all areas of science' (not to mention Al-e Ahmad's emphasis on the nationalization of industry for independence and 'self-sufficiency'), research that offered the possibility of scientific advancement, did not require Western expertise and could be undertaken with Iranian nationals was permissible. Sahabi stressed that work would continue in the field of nuclear research, particularly in prospecting and extracting uranium. Pragmatism also played a role in the decision: Mansour Ruhi knew that uranium was one of the natural resources Iran possessed that could be sold abroad if it was not used indigenously.[26]

This was the programme's one hope, and what Khazaneh was counting on. Never a 'true believer', he was disappointed though unsurprised by all that had happened. He had many meetings with Sahabi in which they argued over the programme's future, and whenever they talked it struck Khazaneh that his new boss's lack of knowledge about nuclear issues coupled with his total commitment to shutting down the programme could only mean his wish was political. Sahabi was naturally of the opinion that construction on Isfahan Nuclear Technology Centre (which was still ongoing) should cease. But Khazaneh pointed to its indigenous educational and research benefits and managed to change his mind. In fact, he convinced Sahabi to reappoint him director of the centre and allow him to transfer a temporary laboratory in Tehran – along with around 300–400 people – to the Isfahan Nuclear Technology Centre, where they continued nuclear research, though now of course without French help.

Nonetheless, in the space of just over a year, a programme that had absorbed increasing revenue and enjoyed increasing prominence in the latter stages of Pahlavi rule was, on a practical level, dead. It was a tumultuous time for Tehran. Political infighting was endemic, coercive social changes painful and nuclear decision-making mirrored the wider picture as the energy establishment struggled, in a chaotic political situation, to synthesize the State's ideological imperatives while dealing with a great white elephant that represented a considerable financial outlay and had a significant although rudimentary structure in place, but that was now ideologically impermissible. Even apparently practical criticisms, such as cost, appeared almost rhetorical: a means by which to attack the Shah, rather than a considered analysis of the balance sheet. It is notable that government reaction was one of outright rejection, with no suggestion of any possible continuation with adjusted, more modest goals.

Nuclear power is always more a statement of national identity than a mere technological undertaking. In largely rejecting nuclear power, the revolutionary government rejected what it believed the nuclear programme symbolized *politically* to Iran: an embodiment of Pahlavi ambition. In essence, it rejected a particular form of statehood. Much of the criticism against the Shah was that he had been a lackey of imperial powers and Iran was 'enslaved', dictated to by foreigners. Now defiant and self-sufficient, the Islamic Republic had abandoned the Shah's imitation of the West and embarked upon a new strategy of confrontation and recalcitrance; a new means by which to achieve some long-desired independence.

CHAPTER 7

RESTART ALL ALONE – 1980–9

The first year of revolutionary government had been disastrous for the AEOI. Reza Khazaneh and his colleagues were now unsure what direction what was left of the programme would take (if indeed there was programme) or if they would even have jobs for much longer. Some of those that had been among the most vocally critical of nuclear power were having second thoughts. In the final Pahlavi years the AEOI had consumed a larger and larger budget and grown in political influence. Now its staff realized that by publicly criticizing the programme they had jeopardized their jobs and possibly helped to kill the goose that had been laying golden eggs with such impunity for so long. But the atmosphere outside the organization was starting to change. While God may be adept at guiding Islamic jurists, he cannot, alas, run a state or power its factories; at least not directly. Severe electricity shortages that had strafed the country for years made finding a reliable (and therefore new) power source a priority. Iran's population had grown from 35 to 43 million over the previous five years and the government now needed to increase the supply of energy in general and nuclear power was on the table once again.

President Abulhassan Bani-Sadr had initially opposed the project on practical grounds – cost – and he would sanction its restart for the same reasons. One morning in early 1980, after he had spent almost two hours in a meeting on Tehran's road system, Sahabi came to him with the director of Iran's central bank to arbitrate on a dispute the two men were having about restarting the programme, which Sahabi was now in favour of doing. He argued that the country's need for energy required it to investigate nuclear power once again, while the banker, knowing just how much it would all cost, was protesting that there wasn't enough money to even contemplate such a course. Even before the meeting Bani-Sadr had begun to question the wisdom of cancelling the programme. He was convinced that so much money had been spent, and that they had come so far, that it was worth mastering the technology; and he told the crestfallen man just as much.[1] Nuclear power was about to make a comeback, but not under Sahabi, who, despite his change of heart, was dismissed shortly after the meeting. Reza Amrollahi, an AEOI director and, more pertinently, a nuclear scientist (with a Master's degree from Texas A&M University and a French PhD), was chosen to replace him.

But the regime had problems. Next door in Iraq, Saddam Hussein had watched the revolutionary chaos unfold and decided that now was the time to attack Iran and settle some longstanding grievances, namely to 'reclaim' Iraqi territory following several border disputes. Given Iraq's own Shi'i majority, he also feared that Iranian threats to export its Shi'i revolution could destabilize the country. On 22 September 1980 Iraqi planes and tanks invaded Iran without warning and began what would be an eight-year war that devastated both sides. Iran, meanwhile, was also bickering in court with its nuclear partners. By late 1981 Kraftwerk had filed financial claims against it at the International Chamber of Commerce, and demanded some $700 million for breach of contract and outstanding payments. In response, Amrollahi claimed $600–700 million from Kraftwerk for equipment allegedly paid for and not delivered.[2] But at least there was dialogue between the parties. Tehran needed a solution, which was in itself a problem; its previous anti-nuclear stance had been so adamant that the government couldn't contradict it too egregiously without a loss of face. So Amrollahi settled on a traditional political formula of weasel words and, in early 1982, while announcing the programme's restart, stressed that Iran did not wish 'to repeat the massive import of foreign technology embarked upon by the late Shah' (who had died in Egypt in July 1980), and that things would 'go very slowly'.[3]

This *volte face* was not easy for the regime, and its advocates faced continuing opposition in the Majlis and in the press on cost and viability.[4] Those in government that supported the programme's restart were forced to act delicately to maintain as much rhetorical orthodoxy as possible in order to appease the more conservative elements of government, who still denounced all forms of Western collaboration. Nonetheless, by June 1982 ongoing legal disputes between Iran and Kraftwerk reached a preliminary agreement at arbitration in Geneva. Iran claimed that Kraftwerk was legally bound to complete the reactors but it had sent Kraftwerk a fax unilaterally cancelling the contract and this was rejected.[5] Instead, Kraftwerk was ordered to deliver some 35,000 tonnes of parts and equipment that had been withheld since 1979. It complied by shipping 28,000 tonnes of merchandise, including reactor parts from the Italian company, Ansaldo. The remaining 7,000 tonnes were stored in Italy, Germany and Scandinavia, while they awaited German government export approvals, and Kraftwerk declared that only it could supply the critical reactor assemblies.[6]

It was a far from perfect ruling, but, nonetheless, claims of losses from both sides for the construction of one of the two reactors at Bushehr were, in principle, settled. That same month, Iran formally agreed to have Kraftwerk complete the reactor, and engineers returned to the site later that year. At the official level, this apparent reversal of policy was justified by the need to gain 'native expertise'.[7] Thus, by rhetorical sleight, ideas of indigenous capability and self-reliance – key components in the new national aspiration – were now used to justify not the programme's abandonment but its restart. No mention was made of the legitimate economic energy case. The regime was still not prepared to treat such a politicized issue as a mere commercial enterprise with a concomitant cost-benefit analysis (although this was creeping in).

Tehran also made moves to reconcile with its other major nuclear partner, France. In February 1980, Andre Giraud, the French Industry Minister, had announced that France would not refund the $1 billion Iran had put into the Eurodif consortium[8] while Iran (seeing conspiracy everywhere) in turn accused the French government of forcing the French courts to impound its assets.[9] Iranian–French relations were especially acrimonious as Iranian fugitives, including the now deposed ex-President Bani-Sadr and Massoud Rajavi, leader of the leftist, proto-Islamist Mujahideen-Khalq (who had both escaped on the same hijacked plane), had found sanctuary in Paris. Tehran Radio accused President François Mitterrand of dishonouring France by giving refuge to 'airplane thieves' and 'pirates'.[10] What was worse, France was arming Iraq in its war against Iran. But it is a testament to a growing (relative) strain of realism that while acrimonious public exchanges between the two countries continued, private efforts were made to find a solution. While Mitterrand refused to supply Iran with any of the enriched uranium produced by the Eurodif plant at Tricastin, agreement was reached in mid-1982 on the issue of materials (although not on repayment of the $1 billion). Thirty-five thousand tonnes of equipment and half of the required amount of fuel for the reactors would be given to the AEOI.[11]

Reconciliation with France and West Germany was positive but was undercut by the far more serious collapse of relations with Washington. Throughout the revolution and its aftermath anti-US feeling had fuelled instances of vandalism and widespread chanting of anti-US slogans and demonstrations. Washington, for its part, was desperate to maintain the friendship of its Gulf ally, and had sent National Security Advisor Zbigniew Brzezinski to meet several times with Bazargan, and for a while it seemed as if some semblance of a relationship could be salvaged. But then Carter allowed the Shah (who was ill with cancer) into the USA for medical treatment, prompting a group of students calling themselves the Muslim Student Followers of the Imam's Line to storm the US Embassy in Tehran on 4 November 1979 and take the helpless diplomats inside hostage for 444 days. While most likely in the dark before the fact, Khomeini gave the hostage taking *a posteriori* approval. The kidnapping of diplomats violated all international norms of diplomacy, enraged the USA, weakened moderates such as Bazargan and strengthened the Islamists, who believed that the hostage taking was payback for the years the USA had supposedly spent plotting against Iran. 'You have no right to complain,' a hostage taker told one of his protesting American captives. 'You took our whole country hostage in 1953.'[12]

The Islamic Republic raised its flag to the world with the Hostage Crisis, which destroyed any hope of good relations between Tehran and Washington and nationally humiliated Carter. Images of blindfolded Americans and the burned corpses of US soldiers from the April 1980 failed rescue, *Operation Eagle Claw*, now embodied the Islamic Republic to the watching world. Carter himself described the act as unprecedented in 600 years of recorded diplomatic history and froze Iranian assets abroad, imposed economic and military sanctions on Iran, made moves to isolate it diplomatically, supported anti-Khomeini forces, and began strengthening Saudi Arabia and befriending Iraq as counterweights to Iran in the Persian Gulf.[13] He also ended all nuclear assistance to Iran.

This was a problem because Iran needed nuclear partners beyond Kraftwerk if it were to move forward. The hostages were finally released just hours after Carter left office in January 1981, but the situation only worsened with new US President Ronald Reagan. It was now an American article of faith that any possibility of doing business with the Islamic Republic had been destroyed by the Hostage Crisis,[14] and in September the following year the White House announced a tightening of export controls, naming

Iran as one of 63 countries to which the transfer of nuclear materials would be scrutinized more thoroughly.[15] Iran, meanwhile, continued to try to bring itself back within the international nuclear fold and informed the IAEA of plans to build a reactor powered by indigenous uranium at the Isfahan Nuclear Technology Centre (with yellowcake bought from South Africa and imported in 1981).[16] The IAEA inspected the facilities in early 1983, and under its Technical Assistance Programme agreed to assist Iran in various areas, but US pressure forced the Agency to terminate assistance until a 'further review'.

And it only got worse as the 1980s progressed. Iran was fighting for its life in the Iran–Iraq war and saw the majority of its human and financial capital channelled into the country's defence. Iraq's strategic bombing of Iranian cities, chiefly Tehran, and Iran's subsequent retaliation, began the so-called 'War of the Cities', causing huge destruction and loss of life on both sides. Internationally, the government found itself almost totally isolated after the Hostage Crisis. Indeed, at the initial Security Council meeting to discuss Iraq's invasion, Britain's Ambassador to the UN, Sir Anthony Parsons, had witnessed the Council members less willing to condemn Iraq's invasion (and possibly avert the war) than they might otherwise have been had Iran not been in such international disgrace due to the hostage taking.[17] Tehran now reaped the consequences of its earlier behaviour, but the decision to restart had to be pursued, and in 1984 allocation was made in the national budget for nuclear power, and the completion of Bushehr in particular.[18]

BREAKDOWN IN WESTERN COLLABORATION

The successful 1982 arbitration agreement between Iran and Kraftwerk meant that, in theory, dispute no longer prevented collaboration between the two parties, but the announcement that work was to restart had been premature.[19] Iran had no contract and could not legally compel Kraftwerk, which was now reluctant to work on Bushehr as the war intensified, to do anything. In early

1984 it agreed to deliver components as per the agreement, but talks had continued for so long that some of the original agreements were now out of date. And more problems were to come. In February 1984 Kraftwerk surveyed Bushehr and decided it would only complete the plant when the war ended. The following year, under continual Iranian pressure, Kraftwerk sent another team to visit the site to assess the feasibility of undertaking any work at all, but it arrived at the same conclusion.[20] The plant had now been subject to no fewer than three Iraqi attacks, the dome on the reactor was badly damaged and much of the supporting infrastructure destroyed.[21] In late 1986 disputes spread to the delivery of components as Kraftwerk declined even to ship necessary parts to Iran while the war continued.[22] Despite repeated Iranian requests, it refused to work on the plant throughout the war. In fact, construction never resumed; West German co-operation had ended.

Iran's announcement of an agreement over Eurodif had also proved premature and relations with France underwent similar disintegration. The diffuse nature of Iran's numerous governmental bodies and power centres that were, moreover, often disorganized and at odds with each other, combined with the often intemperate rhetoric of their spokesman, meant that as well as hyperbole, premature triumphalism often characterized official statements. Despite reaching an agreement with Eurodif over the delivery of materials, Iran's outstanding $1 billion loan continued to be a source of tension and Tehran now tried new 'diplomatic' strategies. Since 1979 the country had forged stronger links with militant Shi'i minorities in the Middle East. The 1982 Israeli invasion of Lebanon had proved a blessing by enabling the Islamic Republic to gain a foothold in the country through the Shi'i militant group Hezbollah that had emerged to resist the Israelis. This new Iranian aggressiveness reached its apotheosis in the October 1983 bombing of the US barracks in Beirut, which killed 299 American and French serviceman. Many suspected the attack bore Iranian fingerprints and it forced the USA to withdraw from Lebanon just a few months later.

Proxy militant groups, it seemed, could be useful to Tehran. In December 1986, after years of haggling, agreement was finally reached between France's Finance Minister Jean-Bernard Raimond and Iranian Foreign Minister Ali Akbar Velayati over the $1 billion loan made by Iran to Eurodif, with France agreeing to an initial instalment payment of $330 million.[23] Importantly, the settlement was seen as a part of Prime Minister Jacques Chirac's attempt to elicit Iranian help in securing the release of seven French hostages held in Lebanon by Muslim extremists beholden to Tehran, further establishing the synonymy between Iran and terrorism in Western eyes.[24] In the end, legal wrangling continued throughout the 1980s and it was only in 1991 that an agreement was finally reached on Eurodif. France refunded more than $1 billion with Iran remaining a shareholder of the company via Sofidif, a Franco–Iranian consortium, with no right to any of the uranium produced at the Tricastin plant (for fear it might be used for a bomb). After all the legal wrangling neither German nor French collaboration produced anything of real substance after the revolution.

'WE ARE ALONE'

Despite its difficulties being largely self-inflicted, Iran took this all to heart: as far as it was concerned, its foreign partners had abandoned it, like the rest of the world. The intensifying of the Iran–Iraq War in the mid-1980s saw Iraq bomb Bushehr, and Iranian officials now used the IAEA as a platform to complain about Iran's treatment and the iniquities of the world in general. Informed by Khomeini's conspiratorial worldview, all international bodies were seen as tools of Western hegemony, a *Weltanschauung* that, in its own eyes, had been confirmed by experience.[25] A mere three days after the first air strike on 24 March 1984, Amrollahi wrote to the IAEA, claiming that the attack had demonstrated Iraq's 'complete disregard for all internationally accepted codes of conduct'.[26] And that was before Iran got angry. In April 1984 the Agency's failure to act in the wake of the Iraqi attacks prompted

Ali Akbar Velayati, then Iran's Foreign Minister, to declare that such 'inaction' demonstrated:[27]

> The harsh reality that an august international body such as the IAEA is either totally impotent in observing and/or implementing its own adopted resolutions or else, and here more disturbingly, is strongly biased in its dealings with the relevant affairs of its various member states.

Velayati then demanded to know why the IAEA allowed itself to become 'a mere tool in political power games?'[28] Such language, almost adolescent in its anger, was not the established speech of Western international diplomacy that the Shah had tried so hard to mimic; and it now characterized Iran's relations with the world and served to justify Western beliefs about Iranian irrationality (which obviously didn't help Tehran's efforts to acquire nuclear technology). A world that failed to act was doubly damned in Iranian eyes as the damage suffered was from a 'decadent regime ... fully equipped with war material, donated by the powers of the east and the west'.[29] Given the lack of commensurate action, the IAEA was not merely biased but, inevitably, part of a wider international conspiracy:[30]

> The response of the IAEA, or rather the lack thereof, to the repeated military attacks of Iraq on Bushehr Nuclear Power Plant leads to the conclusion that such aggressions have created an inconvenient non-conformity between the atrocities of the aggressive regimes which are supported by the powers of the east and/or the west on the one hand and the internationally adopted resolutions or codes of conduct on the other.

In this vein, Iran *blamed* the IAEA, now portrayed as little more than a mouthpiece of the Great Powers, for a third Iraqi attack: 'Confident of the immunity from IAEA [sic] and, therefore, armed with the tacit support of superpowers', Velayati thundered, 'the Ba'athist regime of Iraq attacked for the third time the site of Bushehr Nuclear Power Plant on 4 March 1985'.[31] He went on to hold IAEA Director General Hans Blix personally 'responsible for rendering the International Atomic Energy Agency impotent in enforcing its own resolutions' and actually 'encouraging acts of aggression'.[32] Holding the IAEA tacitly responsible for Iraqi inaction was followed, perhaps inevitably, on 17 November 1987, with demands that the 'IAEA . . . take immediate appropriate measures in order to prevent any further threat or attack' as Iran now tried to enlist the IAEA's help in its war against Iraq.[33]

All of this, however, raised a fundamental point. Throughout its litany of complaints, Iranian criticism of Iraq was almost entirely couched in terms of its violation of international regulations. The attacks, for example, proved that the 'criminal rulers in Baghdad' had 'found another way of violating the most common norms of political conduct'.[34] They were also 'a clear violation of Agency General Conference Resolution GC (XXIX)/RES/444'.[35] While railing against the system, Iran still viewed violations of its rules as transgression, and it is instructive that it constantly sought recourse to and remedy from international institutions, even if after a while the argument was merely rhetorical. In 1982, when Iran was in legal dispute with foreign contractors, it could confidently declare that 'we think we have a good case' – a statement only possible with a presupposing belief in the validity of legal norms.[36]

Thus, for all the rhetoric about the iniquity of international institutions, at no point was there any suggestion that the system itself was inherently wrong *as a system*. It merely perceived it to be unfairly weighted against the developing world due to pervasive Western influence, and its criticism was almost exclusively moral (if everyone just behaved better things would be all right). As the nuclear programme had once been emblematic of a modern Western state, what emerged now was the defiance of a modernizing state overtly confronting the system that denied it justice. Little had changed as far as Iran was concerned: the great colonial powers, now nuclear-armed, oppressed the Third World, restricting its freedom through the buildup of arsenals and support of surrogate powers. The Iranian quest for autonomy now took the form of rhetorical steadfastness in the face of 'victimization'. But, importantly, the system was not rejected; the struggle was for greater independence *within* it.

THE BIRTH OF NUCLEAR NATIONALISM

Without nuclear partners and with the trauma of the Iran–Iraq war and (so Iran believed) an unfair world, the programme faced even greater difficulties – which, perhaps counter-intuitively, only strengthened Tehran's will to progress. On 6 November 1985, *Kayhan International* invited Iranian nuclear scientists living abroad to attend a conference from 14–19 March 1986, offering to pay all expenses incurred.[37] If the world would not help then more 'self-sufficiency' was the answer: it was time to bring Iran's scientific base (much of which had fled during the revolution) home. On 29 October 1986, Ali Akbar Hashemi Rafsanjani, then Chairman of the Iranian Parliament, addressed an international AEOI-sponsored seminar on civilian nuclear energy programmes at the Caspian Sea resort of Ramsar. Nuclear energy was now high on the political agenda and leading government officials, including the Prime Minister Mir-Hossein Mousavi (who would later become an opponent of the regime after the 2009 elections and *de facto* leader of the Green Movement), Education Minister Mohammad Ali Najafi and Amrollahi, also attended. Rafsanjani urged the gathered scientists to return home and work on the nuclear programme to serve their country at this difficult time. At a similar gathering on 29 October 1988, Rafsanjani again urged 150 Iranian nuclear scientists to return to Iran, repeating private appeals issued over the past three years. 'If you do not serve Iran,' he exhorted, 'whom will you serve?'[38]

Working on the nuclear programme was now a national service; and in the space of a few years it had transformed from an anathema to a patriotic duty. The emergence of nationalism to harness support for the programme (and by proxy the government) was totally new. It was first created and then bolstered by the abandonment (in Iran's eyes) of foreign contractors, many of whom had absconded with Iranian money, the international community's mute response to Iraq's invasion and subsequent use of chemical weapons, as well as tacit US and near universal Arab support of Iraq during the war, all of which conformed to pre-existent prejudice. Khomeini's Manichean worldview again mingled with traditional Iranian phobias, both now apparently confirmed by experience. And the lesson was stark: Iran could trust only Iran.

What is, therefore, also clear is the changed quality of the emergent nationalism; the nuclear programme now exemplified Iran's strength in the face of adversity. As Amrollahi had said on more than one occasion:

> Despite the problems resulting from the war imposed by the Iraqi regime, the puppet of Zionist imperialism, which invaded and occupied our country and killed thousands of our people, there have been remarkable improvements in the scientific and industrial fields in our country.[39]

The programme was now an integral part of how the Islamic Republic defined itself in the modern world. When he wrote *Westoxification*, Jalal Al-e Ahmad had decried the values and culture promulgated by the 'Western machine' (loosely speaking, Western civilization) while simultaneously advocating an engagement with the technology that furthered Westernization. Iranians, he argued, had to use this technology for their own gain – only by harnessing it could Iran negotiate the modern world (which was a product of the 'Western Machine'), but on its own Iranian and Islamic terms; Iranians would have to become participants rather than bystanders in their modernization. In this sense, far from contradicting the Islamic Republic's early ideological stance there was also an imperative for Tehran to push on with nuclear power. Its initial rejection of the nuclear programme had been viewed as yet another example of an anti-modernism reflected in its anti-Western rhetoric (not least because the West is generally seen as a metonym for modernity). This 'anti-modernism' was characterized by a regression to the past and now collided with Western democratic liberalism. What the Islamic Republic now began to do was embrace, through its nuclear programme, its alternative conception of modernity.

Both the Shah and the Islamic Republic sought greater independence for Iran in the world, but the Shah attempted this through his desire to embrace it as an equal but similar *kind* of state – Western and modern. The Islamic Republic, with its essentially hostile view of the world, saw it as a means of forcing the West to accept its self-declared 'otherness', but on an equal footing. The nuclear programme had once again become a symbol for Iran, but this time it was not something a modern 'Western' state had to have to be modern and Western, but something a modernizing state had to have to be palpably non-Western and defiant. Now that Westernization was no longer a political goal, indeed was rejected, status was not gained but lost by close relations with the West. The very fact of having a programme was an almost implicit rejection of the US and held a commensurate (albeit different kind of) prestige. Like the soldiers on the Iraqi battlefield it had become a symbol of a nation's refusal to be beaten.

* * *

But while Iran was re-embracing the programme on an ideological level, Washington was doing what it could to combat the perceived threat from the Islamic Republic on a practical level. The 1984 US *Operation Staunch* stemmed weapons supplies to Iran and its biggest problem remained a hostile White House. But Iran was learning and, Great Satan or not, between 1984 and 1986, despite mutually belligerent rhetoric from Tehran and Washington, moderates like Velayati, who argued that having relations with the USA was not the same as accepting its hegemony, explored the possibility of secret conciliation.[40] The timing was propitious. Cold War tensions had lessened with the advent of Gorbachev and *Perestroika* and *Glasnost*, and Washington now focused more attention on the Middle East.

Secret talks were held between the two countries, and progress appeared to have been made only to be undone when Mehdi Hashemi, a cleric and head of the Office for the Export of the Islamic Revolution (and close relative of Ayatollah Montazeri), leaked details of the talks to the Syrian newspaper *Al-Shi'ra* in late 1986. The revelation of the so-called 'Iran-Contra' affair (in which it emerged that Washington had, despite its own embargo, secretly facilitated the sale of arms to Iran to help secure the release of US hostages held by Iranian proxy groups) became a global scandal. The Hostage Crisis had brought down the Carter Administration; Iran-Contra almost brought down Reagan's Administration (as well as reducing its flexibility to deal with Iran because of the bad publicity). Several US officials were indicted and imprisoned, while the Democrats used the scandal to attack their Republican rivals (as the Republicans had attacked Carter during the Hostage Crisis); again Iran entered US domestic politics as the ultimate bogeyman. Both Democrats and Republicans had now been burned by Iran, which was subsequently to occupy a particular place in the American psyche. The scandal also weakened the 'moderate' faction within Iran and strengthened the radicals, who were fundamentally opposed to any relations with the Great Satan. It was a disaster for Iranian–US relations, the effects of which are still felt today.

With the USA now both unwilling and unable to reach any diplomatic accommodation, Iran intensified its search for nuclear partners. The modernizing world was the destination as Iran looked towards Africa, South America, Asia and the Eastern Bloc.[41] Circumstances (Western rejection) and ideology (Khomeinism) – especially following Iran-Contra and the 'vindication' of the radicals, who had always argued that negotiations with the West were doomed – made such countries the only real choice left. Over the next few years Iran explored co-operation with various modernizing countries including Argentina, Pakistan, India and China, all the while struggling with US non-proliferation efforts to pressure (often successfully) any nuclear partner into reducing or ending assistance to the AEOI.[42]

In terms of tangible progress, the late 1980s were no more fruitful than the previous five years. But they were a turning point politically for Iran, and on a more practical level the programme was partially responsible for reconfiguring Tehran's international relations through a re-ordering of its commercial and (necessarily in the nuclear realm) political partners. Tentative communications with Pakistan began to grow, and Iran also focused strongly on China. It was doubly damned: first by its own revolutionary self, and now by association. Western media began to speculate about potential weapons ambitions. Even the left-leaning US magazine *The Nation* argued that nuclear proliferation in the Middle East was likely to increase over the coming decade because new supplier states, such as Argentina, Brazil and India, which were not party to the NPT, might be willing to sell sensitive facilities to 'suspect states' such as Iran.[43]

CHAPTER 8

IRAN'S ISLAMIC BOMB? NUCLEAR WEAPONS UNDER THE ISLAMIC REPUBLIC

One afternoon in the early 1980s, Ali Asghar Soltanieh, then serving his first term as Iran's Ambassador to the IAEA, listened to his country's Supreme Leader, Ayatollah Khomeini, issue a *fatwa* against nuclear weapons, decreeing them 'un-Islamic'. Shortly after, he had the *fatwa* translated, published as a Christmas card, and sent to his fellow diplomats in Vienna: Merry Christmas from the Islamic Republic.[1] While endemic political infighting and lack of governmental experience in the Islamic Republic's early years might have precluded a consistent position on civil nuclear energy, Tehran was consistent in its attitude towards nuclear weapons. Officially, it continued the Shah's line and categorically rejected the bomb. Ideology played its part here, too. As with the Shah, the government was keen to stress the programme's peaceful nature – especially now Iran was at odds with the West – and whenever any foreign collaboration was suggested, the AEOI was keen to stress it was 'peaceful'.[2]

Peaceful protestations are of course never enough and, as ever, the reasons for rejecting the bomb are important. Under both the

Shah and the Islamic Republic, the intent – public rejection of nuclear arms – was identical, but the reasoning was almost entirely different, representing the antithetical nature of the two regimes. The Shah rejected nuclear weapons on the largely practical grounds that they were a danger to both Iran and the world; that, anyway, Iran would not be able to compete with superpower arsenals; and that his conventional forces were adequate enough. In essence, he rejected them for geopolitical reasons. For the Islamic Republic the reasons were characteristically more nuanced and contained within them central building blocks of the state's worldview.

At 10:30 am on 29 October 1986 Hassan Mashhadi Ghahvechi, the Iranian representative at the UN, stood up before the 41st session of General Assembly in New York to outline comprehensively the Islamic Republic's official attitude to nuclear weapons.[3] He began with a castigation of the 'insane' Cold War arms race that threatened 'all mankind' – an uncontroversial opinion, widely espoused by even the nuclear-weapon states themselves. What made the threat so potent, however, was 'its objectives of domination'. It was a race to expand superpower 'spheres of influence', which made the threat greater than the 'mere' destructive potential of nuclear weapons, and created a world where 'the big powers' became increasingly dominant at the expense of 'the oppressed nations'. Beyond Iran's international obligations as an NPT signatory there was an immediate ideological conception of nuclear weapons – allied as they were with the 'imperial' superpowers.

Warming to his theme, Ghahvechi then outlined the Islamic Republic's views on theories of deterrence, which were naturally subsumed into the broader conceptual rubric of the Islamic Republic. Deterrence was accordingly mere hokum (justification for the 'expansion of spheres of influence') and the prevailing theory of war in the mid–late twentieth century merely a cover for Western expansionism. Disarmament was, then, a process that contributed to 'decolonization', while the arms race was 'the hegemonistic approach'.[4] As the weapons of the powerful, nukes were, in fact, symbolic of colonialism; the primeval impulse of strong against weak, synonymous with the arrogant oppressor (*Mustakbarin*) against the downtrodden (*Mostazafin*), and the Islamic Republic had an ideological obligation to oppose them. Ghahvechi further argued that the link, 'between disarmament and development' was 'a well-established reality', completely reversing previously held Iranian views on nuclear power and weapons. For the Shah, nuclear power was seen as the vanguard of modernity; even nuclear weapons were associated with strength and leadership – something Iran might need to stop it 'falling behind'. For the Islamic Republic, viewing weapons as part of a broader scheme of Western oppression, they became, at the official level at least, antithetical to Iranian development.

The Islamic Republic's view on nuclear weapons was spelled out unambiguously, and there was nothing Islamic about it. It was the language of the Sandinistas and Fidel Castro or later of Hugo Chávez. It was also consistent. Throughout the 1980s Iran voted consistently for disarmament measures, urged greater 'bilateral nuclear negotiations' between the nuclear and non-nuclear countries, and urged the introduction of a comprehensive nuclear test-ban treaty (which it signed but to date has not ratified). It had, in fact, extended the official Pahlavi stance of non-proliferation to the developing world stance of disarmament (in November 1982, for example, it voted for a draft UN resolution prohibiting the manufacture of WMDs).[5] By the end of the 1980s Iran had voted for over 20 disarmament initiatives as political behaviour matched rhetoric to align with the developing world; the country also voted many times in favour of legislation on anti-colonialism and apartheid.[6]

But nothing is ever simple with the Islamic Republic. The political divide between the developed and developing world in the nuclear sphere now found Iran firmly in the developing world camp. The result was a seemingly contradictory stance in which its fondness for anti-nuclear resolutions was not matched by a corresponding attitude to all non-proliferation treaties, which, as far as Tehran was concerned, were the product of a world in thrall to the superpowers. It almost immediately refused to sign the Convention on the Physical Protection of Nuclear Materials when it opened for signature on 3 March 1980. Essentially uncontroversial, the treaty was designed to prevent unlawful use of nuclear material, while acknowledging the right of all states to develop nuclear energy for peaceful purposes.[7] While Iran had clearly become sensitive to any perceived signs of discrimination in the non-proliferation regime, it is hard to escape the impression of a certain defiance on principle here (not to mention a possible reluctance to accept the Convention's transparency measures).[8]

More worryingly (as far as the USA was concerned), a public disavowal of the bomb did not necessarily mean that a state was not working covertly on one, and the mid-1980s marked the beginning of Western suspicion that would eventually evolve into today's impasse. While the Islamic Republic disavowed the Shah's notions of Iranian grandeur, it certainly aspired to a leadership role in the Middle East. Obtaining a nuclear weapon might give Iran a 'prestige' to which the modernizing world was sensitive and, failing this, it certainly had other reasons to go nuclear. Diplomatically isolated, at loggerheads with the world's most powerful nation, at war with an enemy that, moreover, was said to be building its own nuclear capability until nuclear-armed Israel destroyed the Iraqi reactor at Osirak in 1981 (though Saddam's capability to manufacture nuclear weapons was in doubt), not to mention the longstanding problem of India and Pakistan, Iran had very real security worries.[9] States had gone nuclear for less.

There was much discussion of a bomb at senior levels of government throughout the 1980s. During the revolution's early days, Ayatollah Beheshti told Iranian scientist Fereydun Fesharaki that it was his duty to build the atomic bomb for the Islamic Republic. 'Our civilization is in danger and we have to have it,' he said.[10] A few years later, in April 1984, then President of Iran (and future Supreme Leader), Ali Khamenei, met with senior political and security officials at the Presidential Palace in Tehran, at which the men discussed the nuclear programme. According to Khamenei a nuclear deterrent was the only way to secure the 'very essence of the Islamic Revolution from the schemes of its enemies, especially the United States and Israel, and to prepare it for the emergence of Imam Mehdi'. Khamenei further declared that a nuclear arsenal would serve Iran as a 'deterrent in the hands of God's soldiers'.[11]

Some years later, in February 1987, Khamenei reportedly made a speech to the AEOI in which he demanded a 'tireless effort' to obtain 'atomic energy . . . now', in order to 'let our enemies know that we can defend ourselves'.[12] These sources are not in official Iranian records and are, therefore, unverifiable, but with the war against Iraq taking its toll thoughts increasingly turned to the ultimate deterrent. In the last year of the war, Rafsanjani wrote to General Mohsen Rezai, then commander of the Revolutionary Guards, asking what he believed was needed to win it. Writing in the aftermath of an Iraqi chemical weapons attack, Rezai replied that Iran would need 300 new fighter bombers, 2,500 tanks, 300 attack helicopters and several laser-guided missiles capable of carrying nuclear warheads. It was an official plea to one of the highest authorites in Iran, and it was, in part, the knowledge that Iran could never get this equipment that forced Khomeini, very reluctantly, to agree to a ceasefire.[13]

If the politicians were increasingly considering the nuclear option, things were certainly changing inside the AEOI. Apart from some research activities carried out at the Tehran Research Reactor and some temporary laboratories at the Isfahan Nuclear Technology Centre, Iran's civil programme had officially stalled as collaboration ended and war with Iraq began. Its only real nuclear facility of note, Bushehr, had been repeatedly bombed and the AEOI had certainly declared no other nuclear activities involving either the production of plutonium or the enrichment of uranium to the IAEA. As far as the nuclear fuel cycle went, Iran had made a start on the first stage – the mining of uranium – under the Shah (ideologically permissible as it exploited indigenous reserves), and reports surfaced that it had supplemented these with uranium from abroad – notably from South Africa and Namibia – but the subsequent stages appeared as distant as ever.

The truth was rather different. The second stage of the nuclear fuel cycle is conversion – when the uranium ore that has been mined from the earth and ground into a fine powder to make yellowcake (Uranium Oxide) is sent to a UCF to be 'converted' into UF_6 ready to be enriched to make nuclear fuel.[14] In 1977 Iran had received depleted uranium and uranium conversion technology from an entity in China. Depleted uranium was not covered by the early version of the NPT safeguards Iran had signed (and Iran only declared it in 1998 when the material was de-exempted) but nothing much was done until a few years later.[15] In 1981 at both the Tehran Nuclear Research Centre and at the Isfahan Nuclear Technology Centre Iran began laboratory and bench scale experiments to produce the materials important to uranium conversion – without declaring this to the IAEA. Critically, these experiments went on for over a decade and Iran only decided to stop domestic research and development on UF_6 in 1993, in expectation of help from China with the construction of a uranium-enrichment plant and a uranium conversion plant.[16]

On stage three of the nuclear fuel cycle – uranium enrichment – things were very different indeed. As far as the world was concerned Iran had run out of nuclear partners; but it had one more than anyone thought: Pakistani metallurgist Abdul Qadir (AQ) Khan.[17] Khan created the biggest network of illicit nuclear materials the world has ever seen; NPT loopholes (namely, that European suppliers could sell dual-use components without any commitment that they were used solely for civil purposes or placed under IAEA safeguards) and espionage enabled it. In the late 1970s Khan was employed at a subsidiary of the Dutch nuclear firm URENCO and was able to illegally copy European gas centrifuge designs, which Pakistan then used to follow South Africa's example and buy the individual parts for a gas centrifuge plant on the open market to produce HEU with the centrifuges it had built from the stolen designs. China then provided Islamabad with a weapons blueprint (possibly in exchange for Pakistani help on centrifuge work), and ten years later Pakistan had the bomb. Once achieved, the Khan network moved into the proliferation of technology and began to sell nuclear technology, for cash to North Korea, and for cash and some form of quasi-solidarity to fellow Muslim countries, including Libya and Iran. It was perhaps the ultimate modernizing world defiance.

At this stage Iran's remedial programme obviously centred on power plants – albeit the unfinished one at Bushehr – as well as some necessary supporting infrastructure at the Isfahan Nuclear Technology Centre and the Tehran Research Centre (construction of another support facility – the Karaj Nuclear Research Centre for Medicine and Agriculture – would begin in 1986). But apart from the basic conversion technology it had received from an entity in China it was unable to acquire other nuclear fuel cycle facilities or technology, least of all enrichment technology.[18] Enriching uranium is not only a usual means of producing nuclear fuel to power nuclear reactors but also a usual means of producing a nuclear weapon, and if Iran wanted weapons capability then, from a security point of view, an enrichment programme was the logical choice. Only a few years earlier Israel had struck the Iraqi nuclear reactor at Osirak and in so doing ostentatiously demonstrated the vulnerability of single above-ground installation; centrifuge systems, which could be placed underground, would be easier to protect.

Whether or not it was for a nuclear weapon, the Iranian leadership decided it wanted an indigenous uranium-enrichment capability in the form of a gas centrifuge programme, and in 1985 the AEOI began its efforts with a search of available technical literature.[19] But it lacked both the experience of running centrifuge programmes or any blueprints or designs to build them, so the decision was taken to source these on the black market. This decision came from Amrollahi himself and, moreover, had the backing of Iran's Prime Minister, Mir-Hossein Mousavi: a centrifuge programme was clearly a political as well as a technical consideration.[20] With a PhD in plasma physics from Case Western Reserve University in Cleveland, Masud Naraghi, head of the Plasma Physics Department at Tehran Nuclear Research Centre, was given the job of sourcing the necessary components.

He had worked in the USA (even on some projects for NASA) and, crucially, had contacts internationally. While Naraghi did not know for sure why Iran wanted enrichment technology – the decision was made above his head at the political level – he knew that military use was a possible reason.[21]

The Khan network was his first port of call. German firm Leybold-Heraeus had a reputation as a firm that a country like Iran could do business with – largely thanks to its previous exploitation of lax export regulations to sell vacuumed centrifuges to Khan, either by claiming they were 'dual use' or by shipping them to places like Dubai that had almost nonexistent import regulations. Naraghi bought various parts straight off Leybold's catalogue (which he combined with purchases from other European companies) and eventually met Gotthard Lerch, an engineer at Leybold, and Khan's business partner. Lerch presented him with a sample list of what would later become an official offer for a centrifuge system (which included a blueprint of a centrifuge and a document for a cascade of 12) that could not have been made without Khan's close involvement.[22] In late 1986 or early 1987 Naraghi met Lerch and a colleague, Heinz Mebus, in Switzerland where they offered him a complete gas centrifuge plant, which included delivery of a disassembled sample P-1 (so-called because they were used in Pakistan's nuclear programme) centrifuge machine complete with drawings, descriptions and specifications, along with the equipment to turn the resulting HEU into metal bomb components.[23] The offer was relayed to Amrollahi in Tehran, who in turn passed its details on to Prime Minister Mir-Hossein Mousavi in a communication on 28 February 1987, urging that the activities 'be treated fully confidentially'.[24] A few days later, on 5 March, Mousavi approved the deal.

Naraghi then travelled to Dubai to meet with Lerch and some German colleagues, as well as Pakistanis S. Mohammed Farooq from the Khan Laboratories and his nephew and assistant B.S.A. Niazi. It was clear to Naraghi that the package of drawings was incomplete and that, from their format, they came from Khan.[25] But the deal was done, and Iran paid between $5 and $10 million for specifications and manufacturing instructions for a gas centrifuge programme, which compensated for its own lack of indigenous technology and expertise in the area.[26] When the network was exposed in December 2003 Khan claimed that the technology would not have allowed Iran to enrich uranium because the documents referred to old technology dating from the 1970s. But with the know-how in place Naraghi returned to Europe and over the next few years acquired, piecemeal, the various items necessary for a centrifuge programme. By the late 1990s improved regulation of the international nuclear market meant Iranian efforts tailed off.[27] In the end Iran bought few items from the Khan network – what it got was the start it needed.

In 1987, Iran duly began the first phase of research and development based on the Pakistani P-1 design centrifuge specifications it had received (which lasted until 1993). Various factors, mainly financial constraints, meant that the AEOI only put three researchers on the project.[28] The goal at this initial stage was to understand the behaviour of centrifuges and their assembly, and to try to indigenously produce components. The AEOI conducted this research alone, without the support of Iranian universities or the Physics Research Centre, which might have indicated a desire to keep the enrichment side of the programme as secret as possible (in keeping with Amrollahi's exhortation to Mir-Hossein Mousavi). Iran faced technical problems with some of the relevant technology but made no attempts to contact the Khan network for support.[29] Nonetheless, Khan squats at the centre of Iran's enrichment programme. The P-1 centrifuges that form its basis came directly from his network; without him it would not be the sophisticated programme it is today.[30]

THE WEAPONS DIMENSION: AN ANALYSIS

Iran was, to say the least, less than forthcoming about its nuclear activities during the 1980s. The question that faces the historian is whether its undeclared, or, perhaps more properly, covert, activities were part of a concerted drive towards a bomb. It is inconceivable that the possibility of weapons did not cross Tehran's mind, and it is even logical in the circumstances that it would. The problem in assessing any possible weapons drive is that the manufacture of a nuclear bomb involves general nuclear processes like plutonium production or uranium enrichment that also have civil uses, as well the more specific processes of weaponization such as the necessary detonators and development of missile delivery systems. Without definite proof of the latter, it is difficult even for the IAEA to ascertain a weapons intent.[31]

Iran's activities during this time did not constitute a 'smoking gun'; and its explanation to the IAEA (made almost 20 years later) that its nuclear collaboration had yielded nothing due to external political pressures leaving it no choice but to work indigenously and covertly does carry weight.[32] But Bushehr was a ruin, so why the need to make nuclear fuel at this stage? Logic would dictate first building a reactor, or at the very least having a construction project in place for that reactor. The war was draining Iran's financial resources, and spending millions of dollars on nuclear fuel for reactors that did not exist was financially unsound and totally illogical. But if a bomb was the goal, then an enrichment programme – able to be hidden (and well protected) underground – made perfect sense. Especially since no one would now sell nuclear reactors to Iran, so the plutonium path to the bomb that had so worried the Americans with the Shah's programme was closed to the AEOI. The pursuit of a nuclear capability with a potential military application – even if only to keep the option open – makes more sense. The closer Iran got to the ability to enrich uranium, the closer it got to a bomb that it might one day well need. Taken together, Iran's considerable security concerns, the reported statements of regime officials and, most damningly, the scope and nature of its undeclared activities render the claim that all enrichment-related efforts were solely civil in intent, with no thought of the military applications, improbable to a degree that borders on the impossible.

But none of Iran's undeclared activities were known at the time; and it would take almost two decades for the Khan network to be exposed (though intelligence services most likely knew of it before). Yet speculation and accusation against Iran was endemic, and appeared to affect even reputable publications such as *Jane's Weekly*, which, in 1984, declared that 'Ayatollah Ruhollah Khomeini's nuclear bomb' was 'entering its final stages', a claim which, to be fair, is only 28 years premature and counting.[33] Certainly the IAEA never expressed concerns. Rather, there seemed to be general agreement on Iran's *lack* of any nuclear capability. Iran had gone from an oil-rich state where nuclear power was a high priority for the Shah to a diffuse, politically fragmented state, in the midst of a war absorbing the majority of its resources, led by a government that had initially abandoned its nuclear programme. Despite Tehran's covert efforts to acquire enrichment technology, short of buying a bomb 'off the shelf' there was simply no way it could obtain a nuclear deterrent.

Despite this, speculation was tenfold what it had been under the Shah, and so was political action against the programme. And one has to return to the central relationship – Iran and the USA, Protagonist and Antagonist – to understand why. The Hostage Crisis had split the two countries politically, but the wider conceptual communicative breakdown was perhaps more damaging. For Iran, the crisis was merely part of a greater revolutionary process, so in the popular revolutionary conception the break in diplomatic relations between the two countries had nothing to do with its own behaviour in the hostage taking, and everything to do with Washington's unwillingness to accept Iran's Islamic Revolution. For Washington the embassy seizure was the cause of the collapse in relations – the beginning of an era characterized by a rogue Iran that could not be trusted, least of all with nuclear technology, which given its dual-use nature meant in almost all its forms.

In 1984 the State Department urged a worldwide ban on the sale of nuclear materials to the Islamic Republic:[34]

> The United States will not consent to the transfer of U.S.-origin nuclear equipment, material or technology to Iran, either directly or through third countries, where such consent is legally required [. . .] In addition, we have asked other nuclear suppliers not to engage

in nuclear cooperation with Iran, especially while the Iran–Iraq war continues.

However, *in the very same document* it continued:

> We believe it would take at least two to three years to complete construction of the reactors at Bushehr [...] those reactors are light water power reactors ... not particularly well-suited for a weapons programme [...] In addition, we have no evidence of Iranian construction of other facilities that would be necessary to separate plutonium from spent reactor fuel.

The State Department wanted to deny nuclear technology to a state it admitted was incapable of posing a genuine proliferation risk. Velayati, in turn, described efforts to stifle aid to Iran's nuclear programme on proliferation grounds as 'malicious actions that are not supported by any evidence from the IAEA or any impartial observer'.[35]

What had now emerged was what might usefully be termed the politicization of proliferation. In 1984, US Senator John Glenn claimed the world was 'drifting passively towards nuclear disaster' and called for a blanket ban on all nuclear materials exports to countries with developing nuclear programmes. In the absence of any real reasons for this policy, he merely invoked the image of a world in which 'Khadafy of Libya and the Ayatollah Khomeini of Iran have nuclear weapons; a world in which unstable fanatical leaders can start a world war. And we will face state-supported nuclear terrorism.'[36] The reaction from Tehran was depressingly predictable: the USA was motivated not by any basis in fact but by the desire to slander the Islamic Republic for its own imperialist ends.

The USA had begun to view Iran (just as Iran viewed it) ideologically. Despite the absence of any formal relations, the two countries retained a real presence in each other's political life.[37] The Hostage Crisis and the Iran-Contra affair had made Iran a lacuna in Washington's worldview; once official relations were broken off, the two countries had no direct means of communication, a problem accentuated by the communicative or cultural 'gap' that now existed between them. (Washington, for example, had been genuinely perplexed by Iran's inability to 'play by the rules' of international diplomacy during the Hostage Crisis.[38]) Neither side could adequately understand the other, yet each remained omnipresent in the other's imagination – symbolic images of demonization that would draw the battle lines for the coming clash between Iran and the West. On the one hand, the 'Great Satan' (in itself, a semantic tool by which Khomeini Islamized Marxist rhetoric against global capitalism); on the other, the 'Mad Mullahs'.[39]

'NEVER AGAIN'

The years between 1979 and the end of the Iran–Iraq war were formative for the Islamic Republic: it was born, attacked and forced to fight to survive. The single biggest influence onIran Iranian policy will always be Iran itself: perennial determinants – geographical location, religion, ethnicity – always remain. But the Islamic Republic, in the huge political and social rupture it represented, was also in many ways a new type of state. Its various ideological, religious and nationalistic motifs created an idiosyncratic worldview that collided with harsh experience to create a 'new' Iranian political identity that was, at the end of the war, complete. In 1988, Velayati spelled out the Iranian worldview in his response to UN Resolution 582, which called on both Iran and Iraq to end the war (and which Iran, with great misgivings, was eventually to accept):

> Almost all the decisions of the security council, under the influence of some Arab states and certain influential members of the council, were not made as instruments of suppressing the Iraqi aggression or forcing the aggressor immediately to withdraw its forces from our territories, but as instruments of pressurizing the Islamic Republic of Iran to concede to the aggressor.

History showed that Iran did not 'surrender' to this pressure. A singular lesson was therefore imprinted onto the Iranian psyche, articulated succinctly by Velayati: 'For the liberation of their territories and to bring justice to the aggressor,' he pronounced, 'the Muslim people of Iran could count only their own efforts and sacrifices and not on the international organization allegedly entrusted with the maintenance of international peace and security.' The Iran–Iraq war maintains a stranglehold on the Iranian psyche. Billboards honouring the war dead dot Iranian cities and line the country's motorways, and its memory is a perennial of Iranian culture. In 1988, in a speech reflecting on the Iran–Iraq war, Ali Akbar Rafsanjani (then-speaker of the Iranian parliament and commander-in-chief of Iran's armed forces) declared:

> With regard to chemical, bacteriological, and radiological weapons training, it was made very clear during the war that these weapons are very decisive. It was also made clear that the moral teachings of the world are not very effective when war reaches a serious stage and the world does not respect its own resolutions and closes its eyes to the violations and all the aggressions which are committed in the battlefield. *We should fully equip ourselves both in the offensive and defensive use of chemical, bacteriological, and radiological weapons.* From now on you should make use of the opportunity and perform this task.[40] (Emphasis my own)

This speech was probably the Islamic Republic's first public statement calling for nuclear weapons. It was a mandate for the acquisition of these weapons and it spelled out why exactly they were needed. Rafsanjani's reasons consisted of the emotive – the world's hypocrisy and iniquity – and the pragmatic – the effectiveness of such weapons in the face of this iniquity. But most critically, when Iranian weapons desires did finally arise, they did so because of security concerns, but concerns that were bolstered by and subsumed into Iran's overarching narrative of victimization. Iran had taken all of the events of the previous ten years and synthesized them into an ongoing narrative of the self. The sense of abandonment and betrayal had combined with the imperatives of Khomeini's thought (informed by historical experience, Shi'i theology and the political writings of Jalal Al-e Ahmad and others) to 'create' a new Iranian identity with which the Islamic Republic would face the world, but on its own terms.

CHAPTER 9

RESTART FOR REAL: THE PROGRAMME GOES LIVE – 1989–2002

By 1989, eight years of war had imprinted itself onto the Tehran cityscape, and into the national consciousness. Charred tenements and tangled steel ruins dotted the capital, while Iranian society was only just coming to terms with the tens of thousands of new martyrs that had been minted on the battlefields. Tehran had also experienced ten years of government, and had learned from its years of hardship to emerge somewhat more reflective and with much (though by no means all) of its initial revolutionary fervour burned away. A new wave of politicians – including many war veterans – now staffed government and questioned the wisdom of many of the regime's actions, which had exacerbated Iran's isolation, and, therefore, its suffering. This new generation found its voice with the election of Rafsanjani to the presidency in August 1989. Pragmatic and commercially minded (his administration would see a steady influx of US goods into the Iranian market), his initial moves to amalgamate the Prime Minister and President positions to streamline government and bureaucracy were indicative of a new strain of comparative realism that entered policy. Khomeini's death in June 1989 also saw the elevation of mid-ranking cleric Ali Khamenei (who in fact lacked the necessary religious qualifications) to Supreme Leader.

Rafsanjani had supported nuclear research since his days as Speaker of the Parliament, and his first post-war reconstruction and development plan, Iran's continuing shortage of electricity and the rapid growth of the country's population were three reasons for Iran to push ahead with the nuclear programme immediately. On 9 October 1990 Rafsanjani chaired an AEOI extraordinary meeting at which he reactivated the Shah's custom and appointed the AEOI chief, Reza Amrollahi, as one of Iran's Vice Presidents in order to emphasize the programme's importance to Iran's future.[1] The immediate effect of all this was the programme's 'normalization' as it became an official part of Iran's 'restructure and rebuilding'. In mid-1990, in one of the many arbitrary Iranian deadlines that has plagued the programme since its birth, the AEOI decided that by 2005 up to 20 per cent of Iran's energy would be produced by nuclear electric power and ten power plants would be built over the next decade.[2]

In 1980, the Islamic Republic had justified the programme's restart on ideological grounds (the need for 'native expertise' and so forth). Now that the energy establishment could view it as a technical concern in and of itself, it underwent an internal depoliticization (though it retained all the symbolic importance of a national nuclear programme and was certainly not depoliticized internationally) and the economic case for nuclear power returned. At a press conference in Vienna, Amrollahi pointed out that two- to three-hour power cuts were a regular occurrence in Iran and that nuclear electricity would rectify this by supplying about 10–20 per cent of Iran's energy needs.[3] The attendant educational and scientific improvement that Etemad and the Shah had argued a nuclear programme would bring was now also pursued rigorously.

In February 1990, Iran's Speaker of the Parliament, Mehdi Karroubi (who had replaced Rafsanjani and who later became a dissident candidate in the 2009 Iranian elections), inaugurated the Jabir bin al-Hayyan laboratory for the teaching of nuclear technology and in early 1992 the AEOI inaugurated the country's first Master's degree course in nuclear engineering, admitting the first batch of 30 graduates to the course later that year. But most telling was the return of the idea that a civil nuclear programme itself brought a country prestige (as opposed to by virtue of being a symbol of defiance), the apotheosis of the Shah's beliefs. Iran was a great nation; it needed great things. While inaugurating yet another new research laboratory in Tehran, Rafsanjani told his audience that a nuclear programme was something without which no country could 'find its real standing in the world'.[4]

Since the 1980s Rafsanjani's efforts to tempt Iranian scientists abroad back home had met with mixed success. Those that had fled had a perhaps rather obvious tendency to dislike the regime and were certainly not inclined to return when it was at war. But with the war's end and the election of a (comparatively) moderate leader it seemed to many expats that the country was rumbling towards some form of stability. With a lack of viable political opposition abroad or at home, the end of the Mullahs remained unlikely, and for many Rafsanjani was the best they were likely to get. For scientists like Reza Khazaneh, who had headed up the Isfahan Nuclear Technology Centre, had US qualifications, was just the type of man in demand, and who still had property in Iran, it was time to go back.

Khazaneh had left Iran in 1981. He had watched the war begin, all 444 days of the Hostage Crisis and the country's descent into war and he knew it was time to go. He also knew Amrollahi wouldn't let him, so one Thursday morning he simply packed his bags without telling anyone at work, took his family and fled to France, where he found a job with the French nuclear company Framatome in Paris. Amrollahi had not held a grudge and contacted him a couple of times in the 1980s, once even going to see him while on AEOI business in Paris to try to convince him to return, without success. He now tried again, eager to get things moving, and in particular to finish Bushehr. Khazaneh's

Framatome experience was needed and Amrollahi urged him to return home and work on the programme. This time it worked, and in 1992 Khazaneh agreed.

When Khazaneh flew back to Tehran in March 1992, Amrollahi was well established as Vice President and AEOI chief. Khazaneh became one of his official advisors and the two men worked closely together. The immediate problem was clear: the severe state of relations with the West – especially the USA, which was determined to smother the nascent programme. Amrollahi's plan was to build on the co-operation the AEOI had undertaken with other modernizing nuclear states in the 1980s. Argentina was a logical choice because it had a large programme of its own but once again US pressure forced Buenos Aires to cancel any proposed nuclear assistance.[5] Iran was again forced yet further afield for help and over the following years the AEOI signed agreements with countries like Mexico, while Amrollahi even visited Indonesia for nuclear talks. But in truth these countries could offer little; Washington had stymied almost all meaningful nuclear co-operation.

This really bothered Amrollahi; as far as he was concerned it was discrimination pure and simple. The NPT was an unfair treaty, and the IAEA's 'promotional' role had been sacrificed to its safeguards role. Moreover, contrary to the belief of 'the politicians' who ran the industry, he, straight-faced (conveniently forgetting India), claimed this was especially unfair because no developing country had managed to divert civil nuclear material towards military applications.[6] Khazaneh and Amrollahi spent hours discussing the problem: they desperately needed co-operation with suitable countries; the indigenous route was simply not viable. Two criteria were essential: (1) countries should have sufficient nuclear know-how; and (2) should be able to withstand US pressure. This was an understandably small field and in the end Amrollahi came up with two candidates: China and the USSR. Both were global powers with a seat on the UN Security Council and little love for the USA. Both, moreover, needed the money and might be persuaded to help.

From the outset, Rafsanjani's Administration was at pains to assure the world that the 'normalized' Islamic Republic was open for business – within ideological limits of course. In early 1991 Amrollahi went on Tehran radio to announce that, with the exception of the USA, Israel and the 'racist South African regime', the AEOI would undertake nuclear co-operation with any country. Rather pointedly (if not redundantly) he added that China was 'not excluded from this'.[7] He was in reality sending a signal. In the absence of co-operation with the West – always the preferred option – China was the first choice. Russia's nuclear industry was in turmoil after Chernobyl (the clean-up involved 500,000 workers and around 18 billion rubles and crippled the Soviet economy) and the country was in a transitional phase under President Boris Yeltsin. China had been involved in Iran's civil nuclear programme since 1985 when, among other things, it had agreed to train Iranian nuclear technicians under a secret nuclear co-operation agreement. It was the logical first choice.

But it would be difficult. Only the year before, on 21 January 1990, Iran's Minister of Defence, Ali Akbar Torkan, and China's Deputy Director of the Commission on Science, Technology, and Industry for National Defence had signed a ten-year agreement to construct a 27 MW plutonium-production plant at the Isfahan Nuclear Technology Centre. They had also begun discussions for the construction of a UCF there (the Centre had officially opened on 15 March 1990).[8] But in the face of what it viewed as an unsavoury nuclear partnership between the two countries the US State Department expressed concerns that any civil dual-use equipment sold to Iran could be diverted to military applications, especially since a proposed reactor of that size was capable of producing a weapon's worth of plutonium a year (North Korea's plutonium-production reactor would be of about this size).[9] Despite this, discussions also began over the proposed sale of two 300 MW pressurized water reactors to be built at a site called Esteghlal, adjacent to Bushehr.

Washington was unhappy with the proposed deal and with Bill Clinton's election the following year the US position towards

Tehran calcified into hostility. Clinton arrived with tough talk on rogue states in general (and Iran in particular); and the threat of WMDs, sponsorship of terrorism and opposition to the Arab–Israeli peace process now defined Iran in American eyes. The appointment of Warren Christopher, a veteran of the tortuous Hostage Crisis negotiations, as Secretary of State only increased already widespread institutional antipathy towards the Islamic Republic. In May 1995, the Esteghlal contract was signed and Iran made a down payment of between $800 and $900 million to Beijing for construction to begin. It was a lot of money and Amrollahi was eager to see quick results.[10] But despite being permissible under the NPT, Washington considered it unacceptable for the Chinese to sell nuclear technology to the 'militant' Iranian government.[11] Christopher took a personal interest in preventing the deal and, after several meetings with Chinese Foreign Minister Qian Qichen, the latter finally agreed to cancel the contract (which Washington had made an informal condition of certifying the 1985 US–China Nuclear Cooperation Agreement, which authorized the export of US nuclear technology and equipment to China) at a September meeting at New York's Waldorf Astoria Hotel.

Iran, however, gamely continued negotiations with China, and by 1997 China was its most important nuclear trading partner, selling Tehran over $60 million worth of equipment per year (although Iranian scientists were disappointed with the quality of some of the equipment), and the weight of Washington's concerns had reached a critical mass.[12] The negotiations for the Chinese-built UCF at the Isfahan Nuclear Technology Centre that had begun in 1991 had reached agreement in 1995, which meant that Tehran would soon be one step closer to being able to produce nuclear fuel, and two subsequent years of discussions appeared to be bringing the reality close. It was too much for Washington, which made its views known to Beijing in the most forceful terms, and on 30 October 1997, in a confidential letter to new US Secretary of State Madeleine Albright, Qian Qichen pledged that China would complete existing areas of co-operation but provide no new nuclear assistance to Iran. The undertaking was made official at a 29 October 1997 press briefing, at which US National Security Advisor Sandy Berger announced that Washington had received assurances from Beijing that it would not engage in any new nuclear co-operation with Iran.

BUSHEHR AND THE RUSSIANS

Bushehr, as Iran's most advanced facility – albeit a ruined one – remained top of the AEOI agenda. The question was who would finish it. Amazingly, Iran still tried to claim that Kraftwerk was legally bound to complete the reactors, which was met with another refusal from the German firm. Added to this, the German Foreign Office in Bonn – now worried about instability in the Gulf with the US invasion of Iraq – expressly prohibited Kraftwerk from involvement in the project. Iran was stuck; so it got creative, and in February 1990 signed a protocol for Associated Enterprises of Spain to build the Bushehr reactors with assistance from Kraftwerk, which hoped to circumvent German law by getting Spain to be the main contractor.[13] But this also failed and in July Kraftwerk was again forced to formally refuse to complete work on the Bushehr reactors.

In Iran's eyes the West German government had not only prevented co-operation with Kraftwerk to complete Bushehr, but now prevented co-operation with Spain too, and the German government came under attack from the conservative press in Iran, with *Kayhan* in particular castigating Bonn.[14] The problem was political (Kraftwerk wanted to complete the plants and presumably pocket the cash now the war had ended) and in February 1991 the Iranian Foreign Minister, Ali Akbar Velayati, personally gave the German Environment Minister, Klaus Topfer, a tour of Bushehr to no avail.[15] The reliability of the West was at an all time low in Iranian eyes. Iran again threatened to sue Kraftwerk (whose refusal, it claimed, only meant that it would 'lose out') but its frustration with what it perceived as the abandonment of contracts only made it more determined. At the 1990 35th IAEA general session in Vienna, Amrollahi told the gathered diplomats that Iran would complete Bushehr 'through any means possible', even if it meant purchasing and re-ordering the project's withheld spare parts.[16]

Throughout the negotiations with Kraftwerk, Amrollahi had taken care to explore alternative ways of completing Bushehr including possible co-operation with South Korea, Argentina and China (which had refused). Iran had also begun negotiations with what would become its primary nuclear partner, the USSR – a difficult choice, and indicative of the will to progress. Russia had been Iran's primary foreign policy problem for over a century but the 1953 coup had transferred Iranian suspicions away from the historic Anglo-Russian axis towards Washington, and after the revolution Tehran had looked to Moscow for leverage against the USA.[17] In June 1989 Rafsanjani had gone on an official visit to Moscow to conclude a bilateral long-term economic, scientific and technical co-operation agreement (valid to the year 2000) that would form the basis of nuclear co-operation between the two countries for the next 20 years.

The USSR was a definite second (or third or even fourth) choice for Iran; historical enmity aside, both Khazaneh and Amrollahi had huge reservations over Moscow's technological capability. At the same 1990 IAEA General Conference in Vienna, Amrollahi explained that the tentative discussions Iran had begun with the USSR on Bushehr, which had inevitably begun to attract international concern, were simply the 'logical consequence' of West Germany's 'unacceptable attitude' since the revolution.[18] For its part, Moscow knew that working with Iran would anger Washington, but each country needed the other. Iran needed Russia for technology and expertise and Russia (as it was now called following the dissolution of the Soviet Union in December 1991) needed Iran's money. In 1992 they signed a long-term agreement on the 'Peaceful Uses of Atomic Energy'. To assuage Washington's concerns, Russian President Boris Yeltsin (who had replaced Gorbachev in December 1991) initiated a 'two-track' policy of dealing with Iran, while discussing Washington's security concerns over any proposed co-operation.[19]

Tentative negotiations continued over the next couple of years (while Russian engineers conducted feasibility studies at Bushehr) and in September 1994 the Ministry of Atomic Energy for the Russian Federation (Minatom) and the AEOI finally agreed on the scope of work required to complete one of the two unfinished Bushehr reactors (Bushehr-1). With considerable optimism Michael Ryzhov, Minatom's director of international relations, declared that the plant could be finished in five years. Despite its oft-repeated desire for 'native expertise', the Islamic Republic, like the Shah, ideally wanted new turnkey VVER units from Minatom, rather than have it finish the existing units, as ideological constraints melted in the heat of the desire to get the reactor finished. The Iranians were pleased. Only a few months earlier Amrollahi had gone on national TV and outlined in full Iran's need for Bushehr (which, to be fair, the AEOI had been trying to restart for a decade). Given that the reactor was 80 per cent complete, and (at the current rate) more than $10 billion had been spent, it was, he said, the 'sane' thing to do.[20]

The financial details had yet to be finalized, though, and there was a problem with parts. Few of the major system components had been installed, and many were in Italy awaiting shipment to Iran, which the USA, inevitably, would not allow.[21] At a UN Conference on Disarmament in Geneva that month, Iran berated Western states for a failure to engage in nuclear commerce as required by the NPT's Article IV. Western diplomats, meanwhile, privately referred to the Iranian side as 'murderers' and – in a reference to Iran's Ambassador to the conference, Kia Tabatabaee, who had been involved in the Hostage Crisis – as 'hostage takers'.[22] As in Tehran, factionalism played its part in US policy, which was created by 'hardliners on the Iran Desk' at the State Department now headed by Warren Christopher and driven by 'post-hostage crisis paranoia'.[23] The antipathy on both sides was as clear and as divisive as ever.

But this time Iran had found a partner sufficiently willing (or desperate) to stay the course; and in January 1995, Viktor Mikhailov, Russia's Minister of Atomic Energy, arrived in Tehran to sign the deal, which was valued at around $800 million.[24] Under its terms, Russia would build a nuclear plant with one VVER-1000 water-cooled reactor over four years, with the possibility of another generating unit of the same capacity in the future. The reactor would be under IAEA safeguards and capable of producing up to 180 kg/year of plutonium from its spent fuel, which could be used to manufacture around 30 bombs, but would be returned to Russia to allay any proliferation fears. Moscow also undertook to provide a 30–50 MW thermal light-water research reactor, as well as 2,000 tonnes of natural uranium, and training for about 15 Iranian nuclear scientists per year. The controversy over the deal was clear from the defensive and justificatory nature of the Kremlin broadcast that announced it, which stressed that Russia had only signed the deal after first offering to undertake the project jointly with West Germany (which was refused). The broadcast also stressed that Iran was an NPT signatory, and that co-operation did not violate international law.[25] Inside the AEOI, people rejoiced. The directors surrounded Amrollahi, laughing at all the difficulties they had overcome to get there; the celebrations were interrupted only by Amrollahi's occasional disappearances as he took several congratulatory phone calls, including one from Rafsanjani himself.

But the deal drew criticism. Under a secret protocol to the contract's Article 6 were several items that Russia promised to supply – plutonium-production reactors, a gas centrifuge plant and what appeared to be a nuclear weapons test shaft (which, the USA charged, effectively transferred nuclear weapons technology to Iran) – that caused alarm. Clinton's election promises of tough action on rogue states and executive orders targeting the Islamic Republic had seemingly failed and Republican opponents back home trumpeted Bushehr as a 'defeat' for the administration. But this was not totally fair. Only a few months after the contract had been signed – at a barely cordial May 1995 summit – Yeltsin assured Clinton that Russia would not go forward with the centrifuge plant (the light-water research reactor was also cancelled) and, moreover, subsequently admitted that, while the agreement had contained 'components of civilian and military nuclear energy', Russia had now excluded 'the military component' from the contract.

After a hiatus of almost 16 years Bushehr was under way. It became quickly apparent that its completion deadline was hopeful to say the least. Russian engineers faced immediate difficulties in adjusting their technology to the infrastructure already in place, which Khazaneh had known would happen and believed Moscow should have too and not promised such an early completion date. But a deal was a deal. From its inception the programme's official goal was the creation of a nuclear-powered electrical grid; it still had nothing remotely approaching this, but Iran was up and running again, in theory at least.

AGHAZADEH AND A CHANGING AEOI: ACCELERATION FROM THE TOP

Officially, the next 18 months were quiet: work finally got under way on Bushehr while co-operation with China petered out. Serious political changes were coming, however. On 23 May 1997, a largely unknown, reformist-minded cleric called Mohammad Khatami was elected President of Iran with a landslide 70 per cent of the vote. Like Rafsanjani, Khatami wanted to improve relations with the West, which he believed were hindered by a 'bulky wall of mistrust'; and he added to his predecessor's pragmatism a more reformist spirit that manifested itself domestically with a more pluralist press and internationally with a proffered olive branch to the USA. In a January 1998 CNN interview he categorically rejected terrorism, expressed qualified regret over the 1979 Hostage Crisis, pointed to similarities between Iran and the USA and offered a 'Dialogue Between Civilizations'.[26] It was a gamble for Khatami and Washington's announcement that it was ready for formal talks was unfortunately prefaced by a long list of conditions that simultaneously enraged Iranian hardliners and confirmed their expectations. As usual, the two countries danced together, always entwined but constantly out of step; despite Khatami's efforts, the nuclear programme would continue to operate in the same international climate as before.

Internally, things would be very different. On 27 August, just a few weeks after he had officially taken up his post in early August, a series of meetings between Khatami and senior government officials irrevocably changed the AEOI and its nuclear programme. After 16 years in charge Amrollahi was replaced with Iran's former Oil Minister, Gholamreza Aghazadeh. Amrollahi was close to Rafsanjani and as long as Rafsanjani remained in place, so would he. There was, nonetheless, surprise in the organization when he was replaced so swiftly – especially since he was also close to the newly elected Khatami. In fact, the move was controversial. Amrollahi was a nuclear-trained scientist (with a Master's degree from Texas A&M University and a French PhD) while Aghazadeh, though trained as an engineer, and with proven administrative capabilities, had no background whatsoever in nuclear energy. He was, however, close to Khamenei (he had been one of Khamenei's 'men' in Prime Minister Mir-Hossein Mousavi's cabinet in the 1980s). Many within the organization believed it was a political appointment, which its speed only appeared to confirm.

Civil servants, including senior AEOI staff, never publicly back one candidate over another. But Amrollahi was from Yazd, a town southeast of Isfahan, just like Khatami, and the two men knew each other well. A week before the elections Amrollahi took some colleagues with him to Bushehr to inspect Russian work on the power plant. After the visit, Amrollahi asked them to accompany him to a nearby mosque where, after the usual prayers, he made a short speech. In a bizarre deviation from protocol he praised Khatami, describing him as an excellent candidate for the presidency. It was clear he personally liked the man and wanted him to win. But just after Khatami was elected he was sacked. Nobody, least of all Amrollahi, could understand why Khatami, of all people, had removed him. The two men met and Khatami was apologetic. He told him that he hadn't wanted to get rid of him but the order had come from above – from the Supreme Leader Ayatollah Khamenei – the one man he couldn't refuse.[27]

Amrollahi was bitter; he believed that his contribution over many years had been disregarded and complained to many of his colleagues. He continued to come into the AEOI to supervise work in his cherished fusion technology lab, but Aghazadeh didn't like it, and had it stopped pretty quickly. Aghazadeh was the ultimate political appointment. Khamenei was sick of the slow pace of nuclear progress and wanted to press on. He believed that Amrollahi – eager to maintain good Western relations – lacked the necessary backbone to do this; Aghazadeh did not. He had run the oil industry under hugely difficult circumstances during the war, and developed a reputation for being able to get things done quickly, which was what was now needed. Khamenei was anti-Western by temperament, had little concern for mollifying Washington and was eager to push for the development of nuclear technologies, whether controversial or not.[28]

Aghazadeh took immediate, extensive (and intensive) briefings from AEOI staff, and one Tuesday morning met with Khazaneh in his office. He asked Khazaneh the most basic questions about nuclear energy and, at times, appeared to not fully understand the answers. What struck Khazaneh most was the man's determination (that clearly stemmed from political pressure at the highest levels) to move quickly. With the obvious obstacles it faced, the programme had not sufficiently progressed; billions of dollars had been spent with little result. Top priority, publicly at least, was to complete Bushehr, which, even though the contract had finally been signed, was going nowhere. In fact, now that co-operation with most other nuclear countries was impossible, especially since China had ruled itself out of any more nuclear co-operation (though it retained strong trade links with Iran), broader nuclear co-operation with Russia was the goal.

AGHAZADEH AND THE RUSSIANS

The Bushehr project had faced domestic criticism since the revolution, which had never gone away. There was nothing much the anti-Bushehr faction could do because the Russian deal had been signed with Rafsanjani's (and presumably Khamenei's) blessing. The arrival of a new President, however, raised the possibility of a change of policy. In June, just days after Khatami's election, opponents in the Majlis had mobilized to attack the Bushehr deal, and Amrollahi, as its most vocal proponent, became the target of parliamentary attack. MPs argued that details of the deal had still not been clarified: Minatom's projected cost of $800 million for completion of the reactors had been greeted with a scepticism born of experience, and Aghazadeh's AEOI was now challenged to explain how the reactors could be installed for such a suspiciously low price. Without an itemized breakdown of cost, they argued, the price was more likely to be around $1.5 billion.[29] It was decided that funds would only be handed over incrementally (a first tranche of 418,000 million Rials – $140 million – was released that October) for the completion of the plant. Some in the Majlis also argued – as they had almost 20 years before – that Bushehr would be unsafe.

Frustration played a large part in all of this as well – to many in the Majlis, Bushehr represented everything that was wrong with the programme itself. Some 25 years after the project had begun the plant still stood uncompleted. Two years after the new deal had been signed, components for basic elements such as the reactor steam supply system still had not been delivered due to a contractual dispute (Minatom insisted on payment in cash, while Iran argued to pay for equipment via trade). It was Kraftwerk all over again. Despite this, Aghazadeh announced that once Bushehr was completed Iran would buy more reactors from Russia and, in February 1998, that Bushehr would become a total 'turnkey' project in order to speed things up. Three months later, in a pointed show of unity, Aghazadeh met new Minatom head, Yevgeny Adamov (who had replaced Viktor Mikhailov in January of that year), in Moscow and declared that despite all the delays Iran was satisfied with Bushehr's progress and he saw no obstacles to the project's completion.[30]

For his part, Adamov rejected continuing US criticism and vowed to contest any attempts to hinder co-operation under international law. The fact was, Russia needed the money. Nuclear technology was one of its most successful exports and was seen as critical for its economy. Moscow, Adamov vowed, would continue all nuclear co-operation with Iran because to cancel co-operation would be tantamount to the support of sanctions, and Russia objected to sanctions on principle (a statement that would become of huge significance in the coming nuclear clash between Iran and the West).[31] But despite blooming relations between the two countries, the project was still a shambles. In November 1998 Aghazadeh claimed that the plant would be ready in 52 months, the Deputy Minister of the Russian Atomic Energy Ministry claimed it would take ten years to finish, while Russia's Foreign Ministry said the first phase of the reactor would be completed in May 2003.

Events elsewhere also proved unpropitious. 1998 was another landmark year in nuclear history. Both India and Pakistan conducted nuclear tests, which, as India's 1974 test had done almost 25 years before, highlighted the dangers of developing world proliferation through the diversion of internationally supplied 'peaceful' technology. On 29 July, President Clinton had signed an executive order barring US aid to seven Russian firms accused of selling weapons technology to Iran, and the following month the US House of Representatives cut US funding for the IAEA by the exact amount that the Agency was assisting Iran with the construction of Bushehr.[32] Tehran claimed that the move defied all logic in light of Washington's continued support of Tel Aviv, with its purported 200 nuclear weapons. More pertinently, the move sparked opposition from the IAEA, which claimed the move would not influence its policy; that all its member states were satisfied with the peaceful nuclear co-operation with Iran; and that it would continue to support all peaceful use of nuclear energy in the world.[33]

For probably the first time since the Shah, Iran had an official nuclear ally. When Washington accused Tehran of nuclear weapons ambitions – especially in relation to Bushehr – Moscow now leapt to its defence; it had no choice, not to do so would be to face guilt by association or, worse, implied complicity. Moreover, Washington had backed Moscow into a corner, forcing it into ever more defensive positions (and making it angrier). In January 1999 the USA imposed sanctions on three more Russian companies supposedly aiding Iran's nuclear weapons and ballistic missile programmes, to which Moscow responded, days later, by announcing that it would increase the number of staff working on Bushehr to 1,000.[34]

The political duel between Washington and Moscow continued to intensify and on 11 May 2000, in response to the US Congress's passage of the Iran Non-Proliferation Act, which imposed yet more sanctions on Russian companies suspected of supplying Iran with nuclear technology, new Russian President Vladimir Putin pointedly changed a 1992 presidential decree ('On Controlling the Export of Nuclear Materials, Equipment and Technologies from the Russian Federation') to allow for a much broader export of Russian nuclear technology and materials.[35] More co-operation also meant more money for the Russian treasury – and in an illuminating statement Adamov said that US efforts to prevent co-operation with Iran should be viewed as a desire to deprive Russian factories of orders.[36]

Despite their unity in the face of external pressures, Tehran and Moscow continued to squabble over the quality of Russian work on Bushehr. In early 2001, Putin himself had to step in and reassure Khatami that delays came from technical problems due to the sluggishness of some of Russia's partners, which would be corrected. Days later, Moscow admitted what Khazaneh had known from the beginning – that Russian promises under the original contract had been unrealistic. Late 2002 (the latest completion date) was unrealistic; six years would be needed.[37] Still, a nuclear partner was a nuclear partner; Iran had no one else, and, for almost the first time since the revolution, Washington had been resisted.

CHAPTER 10

PROLOGUE TO THE NUCLEAR CLASH - 1989-97

Reza Amrollahi had never liked hills. He liked mountains even less. As he scrambled up various (and to his mind identical) rock-strewn paths, he wondered how the latest fission experiments were getting on and wished he were back home eating *Qormeh sabzi* instead of running around mountains like a teenager. He finally arrived at the tract of unused land that had been identified: it was, he had to admit, promising. It was about 100 km northwest of Tehran, not too far from the AEOI, but not too close either. As he had just experienced so arduously, the mountainous terrain made it difficult to access – it was pretty much impossible by car or foot (that made him laugh); in fact, you needed a helicopter to get there. There was no chance of anyone stumbling on it accidentally; it was well out of public view, perfect for the 'sensitive' nuclear installations he had in mind. When he got back to his office he ordered the purchase of the site and the construction of some temporary buildings: a dormitory, a conference hall and similar facilities. He was careful; the site had to be kept well away from IAEA inspectors in view of what was going to be built there.

* * *

The end of the Iran–Iraq war and then Rafsanjani's 1989 election to the presidency had allowed Iran to finally move forward with its civil nuclear programme. Unfortunately for the AEOI, its accompanying controversy also moved forward, and began to evolve into the form it would eventually take today. The 1980s had seen the emergence of the 'nuclear debate' as Iran and the West (mainly, at this stage, the USA) had lined up against one another, each with a dogmatic construction of the other. But the Iran–Iraq war had precluded any real progress and the nuclear clash was merely the birth of US fears of a country it now deemed suspect in the extreme. Now, as the civil programme began to progress and Iran had sought, and found, nuclear partners, international concern heightened and Rafsanjani's presidency marked the change from mutual suspicion to sustained diplomatic confrontation over Iran's nuclear programme.

When Rafsanjani declared the civil programme back on track in 1989, he had also sought to address growing international concerns about a possible covert weapons programme by reassuring the world that everything would be above board. A few weeks after Amrollahi's mountain hike, in late October 1990, AEOI staff were informed that IAEA Director General Hans Blix would be visiting, which would be a real chance to showcase the 'new' AEOI – everything should be done to ensure success. Offices were tidied, equipment cleaned and put on display. In early November, Blix duly arrived in Tehran. After a tour around some of the facilities, he praised Iran's 'sincere co-operation' with the IAEA while Rafsanjani praised the Agency's non-proliferation efforts. As the new President, Rafsanjani also (no doubt forgetting his own previous exhortations on the subject) re-emphasized Iran's need for atomic power and reiterated the official rejection of nuclear weapons.[1] The overall line, as Amrollahi would state repeatedly, remained the same: nuclear weapons still threatened the world; disarmament was still the solution. Iran's nuclear programme was for 'peaceful use'. Its application was for electricity, agriculture and medicine, and, continuing the Shah's altruistic bent, it would be employed to 'serve human welfare'.[2]

But things had changed. Stressing that the mere signing of an agreement banning the use of nuclear weapons was not enough, Rafsanjani declared:

> In view of ... Iraq's use of chemical weapons in the war against Iran, it has been proved that whenever the vital interests of countries are threatened, they will not obey international regulations. The Islamic Republic of Iran, which is a system based on ideological and ethical principles, will, of course, abide by its commitments; but that is not true of all countries.

As a victim of WMDs itself, the Islamic Republic now had both an almost unique moral authority to pronounce on their dangers and an added reason that the world should believe its peaceful protestations. Just as the Shah had pointed to his prompt compliance with nuclear treaties as evidence of his sincerity, so the Islamic Republic used its suffering (which, in its eyes, almost equalled Japan's) in a similar rhetorical bent. Moreover, given that other countries did not share such 'morality', the urgency with which the world had to rid itself of nuclear weapons was even greater.

The problem was that if Iran's list of peaceful protestations was interminable, its litany of extreme statements and threats to Israel and the USA was endless. The elevation of the middle-ranking cleric Ali Khamenei to Supreme Leader in June 1989 brought little change in foreign policy, and only a year into his reign he threatened that Iran might join its Iraqi enemy in jihad against the Great Satan (which was threatening Iraq in response to Saddam's invasion of Kuwait earlier that year).[3] Khamenei also more than once hinted darkly that the road to 'righteousness' lay through Tel Aviv, prompting more Western fears that Middle East peace could go up in a 'mushroom cloud'.[4] While these sorts of statements stemmed more from the perception of Israel as an imperialist American proxy than any genuine ideological animus against Tel Aviv, it was foolish to utter them with a nuclear programme becoming so internationally alarming. Iran's actions were not reassuring either; Khomeini's February 1989 *fatwa*, for example, that called on all Muslims to kill the

British novelist Salman Rushdie for supposedly insulting the prophet Mohammad with his novel *The Satanic Verses*, was seen as further proof that Iran was, at its highest level, irrational and homicidal.

These wider political clashes were critical because the debate over Iran's nuclear programme is framed by organizing principles on both sides that must be understood. Its elemental shapes (namely, the two 'sides' – Iran and the West – that comprised it) had emerged during the 1980s. Now that Iran could focus on its programme, Washington no longer needed Senator John Glenn to invoke dire possibilities; it could and did point to (true) rumours that Iran had illicitly tried to acquire nuclear materials and technologies, as well as to the inherent dangers of its nuclear relations, especially with China and Russia. The dual-use nature of nuclear technology meant that almost any activity could arouse suspicion, especially if you were looking for it, which, with the Mullahs in power, Washington was. All the upheaval of the previous years had settled in the manner of sediment on a riverbed and both sides were ready to clash. The programme was now a battle of competing narratives formed by each side's respective view of the other: murderous, irrational Iran versus the perfidious and imperialist West. Practically, Washington tried everything to stop Iran getting nuclear technology while Iran tried everything to get around this. A rhetorical battle was on: the US and its allies versus Iran, which now had to justify and defend the programme at every turn.

Iran's primary means of defending the programme had always been its own, inherently limited, peaceful protestations. What it now needed was independent confirmation of these, which could only come from the IAEA. The Shah had not been at odds with the West, and during the Iran–Iraq war progress was so minimal (and the AQ Khan connection had escaped the Agency's notice) that the IAEA had little to inspect, and its relations with Iran largely consisted of being berated for not doing enough to stop Iraqi air strikes on Bushehr and lectured on the general unfairness of life. Now that almost all Tehran's nuclear dealings were controversial, the IAEA's role as nuclear 'policeman' became central. Each 'side' needed it (or rather its findings) to support its own case and, in what would become a staple of the nuclear clash, to press into service for its own cause.

No inspection the IAEA made or report it wrote on Iran would now be free of international repercussions – even on such ostensibly straightforward activities as uranium mining. In September 1989, Amrollahi had announced the discovery of uranium deposits near the town of Saghand, in the eastern province of Yazd, and at ten other areas across Iran. As work progressed, reports inevitably surfaced (in February 1992) that Iran was developing an unsafeguarded supply of uranium that could be used for a bomb.[5] Amrollahi duly invited IAEA Deputy Director General John Jennekens to inspect Saghand and five other sites under suspicion. At the end of the trip, Jennekens pronounced himself satisfied and thanked the AEOI for its 'sincere and truthful' cooperation. But this 'cursory visit' did not satisfy Western intelligence agencies, which claimed that the inspection team failed to visit all the mines, or to ask to be shown other locations near Saghand where a milling plant was rumoured to be located. French intelligence sources believed Jennekens had been 'duped'.

The pattern was clear: on the Western side, criticism of the Agency's efficacy; on the Iranian side, an IAEA (which had morphed from a tool of imperial powers to an esteemed international body) keen to be 'impartial and even handed', even though 'the Western media engage[d] in all sorts of propaganda against its findings'.[6] The Agency was trapped. Even more so because the inspection process was limited: the IAEA was only ever a guest in Iran and the decision on what inspectors could see and when ultimately lay with the AEOI. In October–November 1993, for example, the IAEA inspected three nuclear research centres at Tehran, Isfahan and Karaj and reported that everything inspected was consistent with peaceful nuclear activities. But the inspection teams were not given full access to all ongoing activities nor to soil and particle samples at the sites, and Western critics inevitably – and fairly – questioned the findings.[7] Nonetheless, the IAEA made numerous inspections up to 2002 and generally pronounced itself satisfied (which Iran would erroneously claim meant the programme as a whole had been exonerated). Tehran had an ally of sorts.

With the IAEA (in Tehran's eyes) satisfied, increasing suspicion meant only one thing: Iran was being victimized. So it went on the offensive. In the 1980s the programme had suffered from US export controls, but because things were largely at a standstill, tangible interference was limited. Now that both the desire and opportunity to proceed were present and Tehran found itself blocked at every turn, its default emotions of anger and injustice were joined by frustration. Iran's response was concerted, intense and self-defeating. In late 1991, in an editorial titled 'The Big Lie', the newspaper *Abrar* claimed Western allegations about a nuclear weapons programme were designed to discredit Tehran because it resisted the US plot to strengthen Israel, which was (naturally) part of a wider plot against the developing world.[8] Iran's programme was a symbol of modernizing world defiance and affronted Washington by its very existence. As Rafsanjani told bellowing crowds on War Memorial day in September 1994, the large US military presence in the Gulf following the 1991 Gulf War only provided further 'evidence' of Washington's goal of 'global domination'.[9] While much of this sort of rhetoric was for domestic consumption, the conspiracy had now reached fantasy levels. Only two months earlier Sadegh Ayatollahi, Iran's representative to the IAEA, had gone on Tehran radio to claim that 'Western propaganda' was the result of the CIA's need to create an enemy to save itself from 'bankruptcy' following the Soviet Union's collapse.[10]

Then there was Israel's nuclear weapons capability – the biggest open secret in international politics and, like Tel Aviv's refusal to sign the NPT, something Washington patently ignored. 'We demand,' said Amrollahi on Iranian TV in February 1995, 'an even-handed and impartial attitude ... towards Israel, which says that it neither accepts the NPT nor is prepared to allow the IAEA to inspect its facilities.'[11] In response to these attacks, and to Iran's belligerent rhetoric, Israel now began to describe Iran's nuclear programme as an 'existential threat'. Israeli officials publicly stated that if the programme was not stopped, they would be forced to consider attacking its facilities, as they had Iraq's in 1981. 'When we look at the future and ask ourselves what is the biggest problem we will face in the next decade,' said an Israeli military official in 1995, 'Iran's nuclear bomb is at the top of the list.'[12]

Iran's diplomatic nuclear posture was now complete, and whenever clashes occurred these guiding principles would inform its behaviour. The NPT calls for meetings of its signatories every five years to review the progress of its goals, which include nuclear disarmament, the non-nuclear states' main grievance. The 1995 NPT Review and Extension Conference was seminal because it would decide how the Treaty was to be extended: for one period, for a rolling set of periods, indefinitely or not at all. The industrialized states (including several non-nuclear states) wanted to pass an indefinite extension for which they needed their developing world non-nuclear counterparts for a sufficient majority, which allowed the latter a newfound leverage. In the months leading up to the conference Tehran made it known that it was considering leaving the treaty due to difficulties in acquiring nuclear technology from the West despite meeting its NPT commitments. Thus far it had remained within, but it was an increasingly difficult case to make, particularly given that North Korea had recently threatened to withdraw from the NPT, only for – in what many saw as a bribe – Washington to convince it to freeze its plutonium-production programme in exchange for oil, economic co-operation and the construction of two modern light-water nuclear power plants. Why, argued Tehran, shouldn't it just do the same?

Frustration boiled over in Geneva in September 1994 at the third session of the Preparatory Committee for the conference. In what would become a familiar diplomatic phalanx, the Iranian delegation, supported by the Non-Aligned Movement, objected that Tehran had not sufficiently benefited from Article IV, and

Amrollahi requested that the UN Secretariat prepare a background report on Article IV's implementation as the NPT infringed the sovereignty of the non-nuclear countries. With the Non-Aligned Movement behind it, Iran was the *uber*-non-nuclear state. Well aware of what it conceived to be its 'inalienable rights' (a term that would come to feature heavily in Tehran's diplomatic lexicon), it would fight in the developing world's nuclear corner against the nuclear state 'oppressor'.

And why, Iranians diplomats wondered aloud, should Tehran agree to an indefinite extension of the treaty when Washington didn't even believe in the NPT? It was, after all, not Iran but the USA that did not fulfil its commitments. If it did it would not have put nuclear arms at the disposal of the 'regime occupying Jerusalem' (in fact, the USA has never provided any nuclear weapons co-operation to Israel). Israel, moreover, in 'total and utmost shamelessness', rejected the NPT while Washington defended it on the one hand and sent a delegation to Cairo to convince the Egyptians to sign the treaty on the other.[13] With its rhetorical posture finalized, Iran now began to hone its diplomatic strategy, a key ingredient of which was brinkmanship. The conference convened in New York from 17 April to 12 May 1995, and on its very last day, at a session that lasted until late into the evening, agreement was reached for the Treaty to 'continue in force indefinitely' and to link this extension to a set of Principles and Objectives for Nuclear Disarmament.[14] Iran went along with the indefinite extension in the end. But the point, it believed, had been made.

THE DEBATE: AN ASSESSMENT

The 1980s had seen the two 'sides' formed, now they clashed rhetorically – the precursor to the grand diplomatic clash that would blossom so publicly over the next decade. But how justified were global concerns at this stage? The necessary starting point must be what was known. In a May 1998 assessment of Iran's nuclear programme to Congress, US Military Analyst Michael Eisenstadt conceded that Tehran had done little more than amass some nuclear material and equipment, and certainly had yet to build, as the North Koreans had, a reactor that could be used to develop weapons. 'Iran's known nuclear technology base,' he reported, 'is at present rather rudimentary, although it is building an extensive civilian nuclear infrastructure that could serve as a stepping stone to a weapons program.'[15] The statement outlines succinctly the problems faced by both contemporary analysts and the historian. It consists of two clauses of fact – 'is rather rudimentary' and 'building an extensive civilian nuclear infrastructure' – followed by an assertion or, more correctly and instructively, a fear – 'could serve as a stepping stone to a weapons program'. The problem was not what Iran had but what it 'might have' or 'might want'; the concern was largely a series of conditionals.

Of particular concern to Eisenstadt were Iran's efforts to acquire reactors, power plants and fuel cycle-related facilities; and its apparent investigation of various enrichment techniques (gas centrifuge enrichment in particular), as evidenced not by the as-yet unsubstantiated Khan connection but by its known dealings with China and Russia. That was the technological state of affairs. But the debate was and is framed within a political not a technical context. According to Eisenstadt all of this pointed to a:

> clear Iranian strategy [to] ... build up its civilian nuclear infrastructure while avoiding activities that would clearly violate its NPT commitments, using its new contacts in Russia and China to gain experience, expertise, and dual-use technology that could assist in creating a military program.

In and of itself the argument may be valid, but again the problem is plain: until the final clause, which is conjecture, this is not necessarily abnormal behaviour for a state with a civilian nuclear programme (though 20 of 30 states with nuclear power do not seek to produce their own enriched fuel). It is the resulting ontological leap from statements of a buildup of civilian infrastructure and desire to stay within the NPT to the idea of a 'clear' strategy for a military programme, when the issue was anything but, that is instructive. Especially since Eisenstadt then acknowledged that Iran's programme faced a number of 'formidable obstacles'. Iran faced a Catch-22. Dual-use technology meant that any move it made to acquire technology could or would be viewed with suspicion. The suspicion was, to a great degree, political: if Switzerland had the same programme it would not have raised alarm, or at least not to the same degree.

Again, this was not unreasonable. In April 1997, a German court had found members of the Iranian government, including Supreme Leader Ayatollah Khamenei and other senior officials, guilty for the 1992 assassination of four Kurdish dissidents shot in the Mykonos restaurant in Berlin. Tehran's militant regime was an increasing sponsor of terrorism (most recently the 1994 Israeli Embassy bombing in Buenos Aires), diplomatically irrational (though perfectly capable of barbarous pragmatism if required) and rhetorically aggressive, all of which gave genuine cause for alarm – especially since the 1990s saw North Korea threaten the NPT's viability and the collapse of the USSR (the 'gift from heaven' Khomeini had promised) raise fears of smuggling networks of plutonium and enriched uranium in the former Soviet states.

Since almost the beginning of the Islamic Republic the programme had been subject to alarmist predictions about an imminent weapons capability. Examples are too numerous to list but an example from January 1995 is illustrative of the wider problem: according to US and Israeli sources, 'the date by which Iran will have nuclear weapons', was 'no longer 10 years from now . . . If the Iranians maintain this intensive effort to get everything they need, they could have all their components in two years . . . If Iran is not interrupted in this program by some foreign power, it will have the device in more or less five years.'[16] Time, of course, has palpably disproved this claim. Some of the speculation was most likely deliberate fear-mongering among the diplomatic and intelligence community to increase political pressure on their political masters and on Iran. Nonetheless, it fuelled Iranian protestations that accusations against the programme were baseless and did little for the credibility of international attacks in general.

Alarmism was often joined by the downright erroneous, often made worse by the certainty of the claims. And it is not as if the accusations were mild. In March 1992 Paul Muenstermann, the Vice President of the German Federal Intelligence Service (BND), claimed that 'two or three nuclear warheads' (and accompanying medium-range nuclear delivery systems) missing from Kazakhstan were now in Iranian hands, only for Kazakh deputy Ozhas Suleymanov to say, three months later, that the warheads had been found at Semipalatinsk (which in itself does not instil huge confidence in international nuclear safety).[17] The concern here is again totally understandable, and so is the belief that warheads missing from a former Soviet state in need of cash (at a time when Iran's relationship with Russia was blooming) might be transferred to Tehran. But the degree of alarm and false accusations only made discovering the truth of any weapons programme more difficult instead of less.

THE REALITY: UNDECLARED ACTIVITIES AND THE FUEL CYCLE

While much of the speculation was overblown, Iran made steady progress in its covert pursuit of the full nuclear fuel cycle throughout the early to mid-1990s. The first stage – the extraction of uranium ore to produce yellowcake – was publicly pursued at Saghand and other declared sites. Iran also tried to pursue the second stage of the fuel cycle – the conversion of yellowcake into UF_6 – with China, only for Washington to step in and veto co-operation. And US suspicion of Chinese–Iranian nuclear relations was, it seems, justified. In 1991 China secretly exported natural uranium to Iran (though uranium ore is not covered by NPT safeguard agreements and Iran did not necessarily need to report its import from China; China certainly had no need to report it), which was subsequently used in experiments to test parts of the uranium conversion process at locations not reported to the Agency.[18] A few years later, under the 1995 agreement in which China had agreed to provide a UCF to the AEOI, Iran received documents relating to the conversion process as well as engineering designs for the plant itself, which it retained when the contract was cancelled under US pressure in 1997. These allowed Iran to complete indigenously the detailed design and manufacturing of the equipment necessary for the UCF, and construction on it began (secretly) in the late 1990s.[19] Throughout this time Iran also carried out a wide range of research and development in other more complex conversion processes using nuclear material at the Jabr Ibn Hayan Multipurpose Laboratories and at the Tehran Nuclear Research Centre (which it repeatedly denied until 2003).[20] Critically, the plant was also extended to include a process line for uranium metal production because the AEOI intended to carry out enrichment of UF_6 domestically, up to five per cent, for civil purposes.[21]

More worryingly, Iran's enrichment programme now entered its second phase. From the basis of Naraghi's efforts in the mid-1980s, limited research and development was undertaken on centrifuges and the enrichment process, although Iran continued to experience problems with producing components for P-1 centrifuges and actually manufacturing reliable P-1 centrifuges. In 1993 the Khan network (supposedly on its own initiative) approached Iran with another offer of enrichment technology, and between March 1994 and 1996 Iran took delivery of two shipments containing design drawings – apparently duplicate sets for the P-1 centrifuge design – along with components for 500 P-1 centrifuges from the Khan network.[22] But the P-1 centrifuge components remained of poor quality, and, at a 1996 meeting in Dubai, the Khan network, by way of compensation, provided Iran with a full set of general P-2 centrifuge drawings.[23]

Despite receipt of the P-2, Iran did not yet have the technical and scientific capabilities to master centrifuge manufacturing and claimed that 'a shortage in professional resources' led to no work beginning on the P-2 until 2002.[24] At any rate, the gas centrifuge R&D testing that had begun at the TNRC in 1988 continued there until 1995, when the activities were moved to a workshop of the Kalaye Electric Company (a Tehran company belonging to the AEOI). Iran was getting closer to the ability to begin testing centrifuges, from which it might feasibly be able to enrich uranium to make a nuclear bomb. Suitable places for a hidden centrifuge plant now began to be considered, and certain, very senior, members of the organization found themselves scouting for sites in the unlikeliest of locations.

Of more immediate, and, public concern was Iran's missile programme. Any drive towards a bomb necessarily involves the capability to deliver one. The Iran–Iraq war had taught Iran the value of missiles, and since the mid-1980s it had steadily pursued greater capabilities in this area. With the usual problems of a lack of materials, human capital, technological expertise and funding, Iran's ability to manufacture sophisticated weapons domestically had thus far eluded it, but suspicions now grew that assistance from Russia, China and North Korea with equipment (including guidance systems) and materials might change this. Iran could already produce Scud missiles domestically, and now began to build two hybrid liquid-fuel systems with substantial help from Russia: the Shehab-3, based on the North Korean Nodong-1 (expected to have a range of 1,300 km) and the Shehab-4, based on the Soviet SS-4 (expected to have a range of 2,000 km). In 1997, Iran conducted six to eight static ground tests of the motor for the Shehab-3, which leaked intelligence estimates calculated would make its first test flight within 1–2 years, and the Shehab-4 its maiden flight within about 3–4 years, at which point Turkey, Egypt and Israel would all be in range of Iranian missiles. 'Through the Holy Koran, God promised believers the power to defeat all their enemies,' Khomeini had proclaimed before his death. 'This power might not arrive in my lifetime, but I promise you it will come, and in the form of thunderbolts.'[25] There was little doubt over what form these thunderbolts would take. Ballistic missiles combined with nuclear capability in the hands of what many believed was a fanatical regime was disconcerting, to say the least.

* * *

A WEAPONS PROGRAMME?

As ever, accurate assessments of whether all this pointed to a clear weapons programme are difficult due to the overlap between civil and weapons technologies. But Iran was clearly acting in bad faith. The official line remained peaceful, but this was matched by neither Iran's threatening rhetoric nor, frankly, its high military spending. Moreover, the security need for a nuclear weapon that had been present from the Islamic Republic's birth had only increased with time. The war had taught Tehran two things. First was the devastation of WMDs. Early in the war, Iraqi aircraft dropped mustard gas and tabun bombs to horrific effect; official figures estimate that they were responsible for approximately five per cent of all Iranian casualties from a total of around 188,000 killed. Much of the civilian population in bordering towns was also contaminated, and many of their descendents (and those of war veterans themselves) have developed blood, lung and skin complications.

The second was the futility of trusting in either the international arms agreements or the Western-controlled international community. Rafsanjani had cited this as a reason for Iran to acquire WMDs in his speech at the end of the war. Khomeini and Jalal Al-e Ahmad had been bolstered by blood and gas. Its 'rough neighbourhood problem' had worsened with Saddam's invasion of Kuwait, his suspected WMD programme (reactivated with greater vigour after Osirak's destruction), and an increasingly alarmed Israel.[26] In mid-1992, Ata'ollah Mohajerani, Deputy President of Iran, had reportedly called for an Iranian nuclear weapons capability so that the Muslim world's capability could match Tel Aviv.[27] Perhaps most serious of all for Iran, the collapse of the USSR had allowed Washington to flex its considerable military muscle in the Middle East. The 1991 Gulf War had showed Iran not only what Saddam was capable of, but what Washington could and would do in the region. In the words of Velayati, then deputy speaker of the Majlis and the secretary of the Supreme National Security Council, in a 1994 speech in Tehran:[28]

As a result of the military presence of the United States in the Persian Gulf, and with a fleet equipped with nuclear weapons at that, and because of the presence of nuclear weapons in neighbouring countries, the Islamic Republic of Iran has more reason than most to be worried in this respect.

A year later at a September 1995 conference in commemoration of the bombing of Hiroshima and Nagasaki, Hassan Mashadi – a senior Iranian arms control adviser – stated unequivocally that Iran was 'keeping its nuclear options open'.[29] Iran's tough security environment and the threat it felt from the US fleet in the Middle East, and from Israel, were reasons, he argued, to pursue nuclear research. While he did not think that Iran wanted nuclear weapons, nor would it renounce the option – especially if its survival were at stake. The Shah's programme was most clearly understood in its ultimate restraint. A restraint shown because it was in the end a symbolic programme, a central trope in the Shah's grand narrative of Pahlavi Iran. Meanwhile, his counterparts India and Israel went nuclear, caring little for international opprobrium because their programmes were designed for the attainment of a clear security goal.

Getting a nuclear deterrent now made sense for many in Iran. It could never hope to compete with the USA in a conventional weapons battle. Its only response thus far to US hegemony had been to cause trouble through the use of terrorist proxies (as it had done, for example, in the 1983 US marine barracks in Beirut). But this was like a flea biting an elephant. Another war with Iraq would be devastating; even if a post-Kuwait invasion Saddam was in disgrace and unlikely to receive the support he had before, no one, Tehran was convinced, would come to Iran's aid. The ballistic missiles Iran was developing were needed to deter an Israeli attack on Iranian nuclear facilities or other military assets, but nuclear weapons provided the most comfort: as ever, pride and security meshed to (possibly) drive policy. The Islamic Republic had defined itself on the need to protect Iran from a hostile world that had ill used it for almost two centuries. The country would always be a target for more powerful nations, but the shameful capitulations of history would be consigned to history if Iran possessed the necessary means to defend itself. 'You cannot expect a nation with legitimate security concerns to sit idly by in the face of a threat,' Mashadi said. 'If you tell them not to go nuclear, then what option do you leave open for them?'

CHAPTER 11

AGHAZADEH'S MISSION: ACCELERATION – 1997–2002

Reza Khazaneh watched Gholamreza Aghazadeh with interest during the early days of his new boss's tenure at the AEOI. He was clearly a man in a hurry. The change in the organization's atmosphere from the more lackadaisical reign of Amrollahi, a scientist by profession and temperament, was palpable. He wanted to know everything and he wanted to know it now. Staff grumbled at this 'oil man' lecturing them on the AEOI's shortcomings. A parvenu with little knowledge and even fewer manners was the general consensus. But everyone knew he was Khamenei's man; and that the order for his appointment had come down from the very top. Some of the staff were too frightened to talk politics around him – just in case. Some just feared for their jobs; they had all seen Amrollahi tossed aside after over a decade in charge – Aghazadeh had even stopped him coming back into the building. Things, he was fond of repeating, are going to change.

When Aghazadeh joined the AEOI it quickly became clear to the Iran-watchers that now filled the intelligence agencies of most Western capitals that the government wanted to speed the programme up. What was less known was that it also wanted a change of direction; and this, it became abundantly clear to the AEOI staff, meant the aggressive pursuit of the production of heavy water and uranium enrichment, both legitimate means of making nuclear fuel, and also paths to a nuclear bomb. Under Amrollahi, there had been discussions about the possibility of building a 40 MW heavy-water reactor in the town of Arak in western Iran. The designs for Arak had been completed but left untouched because Amrollahi, fearful of further jeopardizing Iran's international relations, refused to give the go ahead for construction. He knew that to begin work on the reactor would cause international consternation because Iran had no need for heavy water, and heavy-water reactors, especially 40 MW ones, are a type well suited to producing the plutonium used in nuclear weapons. (The following year Pakistan would test a nuclear bomb built from plutonium produced in a 40 MW heavy-water reactor.) But Aghazadeh had no such qualms, and as soon as he arrived he gave the green light for work to start.

Soon after settling in and a few days after their first, preliminary meeting, Aghazadeh called Khazaneh into his office. The discussion flitted across several topics before Aghazadeh asked what it was clear he wanted to ask – about Khazaneh's experience. He was particularly interested in Khazaneh's time in Paris working for Framatome. Aghazadeh told him he was about to take a fact-finding trip to Paris and that he wanted him to come along. They would go and meet French nuclear companies that Iran had worked with before the revolution, and ask them to co-operate once more. It was agreed that Aghazadeh would leave first with an AEOI lawyer who spoke French, and Khazaneh (who had to finish some work) would join them a couple of days later, which he did.

When he arrived in Paris it was clear that no expense had been spared. The three men were booked into the Hotel Crillon, and over dinner in the restaurant that evening Aghazadeh told them he wanted to see as many nuclear technologies in action as he possibly could in the few days they had. The following morning they met two representatives from Framatome (in which Khazaneh still had shares) and the men briefed them on their work in France and around the world. Aghazadeh asked them if they might be willing to build nuclear power plants in Iran, to which they replied that, naturally, they would be delighted to prepare a proposal for the AEOI, but they would have to contact the Foreign Ministry to see if they would be allowed to proceed. In reality it was a perfunctory exercise. Everyone in the room knew it would be impossible to get permission. The Iranians then went to Eurodif (in which Iran still retained a ten per cent share but since the revolution had been unable to benefit from its enrichment services) and sat in on a board meeting that yielded little of substance. It was clear that Aghazadeh had no interest in corporate affairs and only attended out of politeness. He was eager to see as much of the scientific side of things as possible and, namely, Eurodif's enrichment plant in Tricastin, not far from Lyon. The men duly visited the plant and inspected the four 900 MW reactors which supplied the electrical energy necessary to run the plant. But the diffusion plant, they were told, was under maintenance and access to it prohibited, much to Aghazadeh's disappointment.

Aghazadeh was determined to view as many stages of the fuel cycle in action as possible: he wanted to know everything about indigenously producing uranium. The next stage of the trip was a visit to the Cogema fuel fabrication plant (a subsidiary of French nuclear firm CEA), which produced the nuclear fuel for power plants in France (as well as exporting it to many European countries). The men had two more meetings back in Paris: with Cogema about nuclear fuel and with Technicatome about the possible transfer of nuclear technology to Iran. On both occasions the men were told the same thing: that the French were ready to cooperate with them if their government gave the green light. What struck Khazaneh – not for the first time – was how eager Aghazadeh, who knew literally nothing about nuclear technology when he took over the AEOI only weeks before, was to progress. The extensive expert briefings he had taken when he joined had been time well spent and he was now able to ask questions about the fuel cycle and, specifically, what Iran would need, and would need to do, to progress as quickly as possible.

On the plane home Khazaneh could see that the trip had markedly affected his boss, who asked him constant questions about the manufacture of nuclear fuel. The Tricastin visit in particular left a deep impression on him. Back at the AEOI, Aghazadeh called Khazaneh into his office shortly after they had returned from Paris and with characteristic bluntness told him that he wanted the AEOI to start enriching uranium to make its own nuclear fuel. He knew Khazaneh had written a book on the production of nuclear fuel, and asked him to take charge of the project. Khazaneh was taken aback. 'For what?' he asked. 'Why do we need to produce nuclear fuel?' 'For research reactors and power plants', Aghazadeh replied. This made no sense to Khazaneh. Nuclear fuel production is so complex that the world-leading nuclear companies had only managed to do it successfully after several years of struggle. Post-war and still almost bankrupt, with a remedial programme and a serious lack of expertise, Iran simply lacked the know-how to do it properly, and he argued that it was not in the country's interest to try. Rather, the best way for Iran to produce nuclear fuel, he argued, would be to buy a license from a company in one of the countries that had the technology (at this time the USA, UK, France or Germany), and produce the fuel under that license as South Korea had done. '*Agha*', he said, using the Persian term of respect. 'Let's do it this way, it makes much more sense.' But Aghazadeh's reply was simple: 'We are going to do this by ourselves.'

Khazaneh was no longer in tune with the AEOI orthodoxy. That was the last meeting he had with his boss, who told him that if he didn't want to take responsibility for the project, he should find work in another part of the organization. Khazaneh went to see one of the AEOI Vice Presidents, responsible for nuclear safety, and, several days later, he transferred departments.[1]

The real objectives of the 'new' nuclear programme under Aghazadeh's AEOI were now clear to everyone in the organization. First was to get Bushehr built: it had gone on for so long that it was almost a matter of pride to finish it now. Second was to start a uranium-enrichment programme – which required the production of the UF_6 originally received from China and then produced in Isfahan, and that would ultimately be sent to Natanz for enrichment with the centrifuges received from Khan and tested at Kalaye Electric. This was now the programme's real technological goal. Third was the construction of the Arak heavy-water plant, and the fuel factory in Isfahan that would produce its fuel. Khazaneh and many of his AEOI colleagues realized that Iran was going down a path they did not like. Their goal had been to build nuclear power plants so that Iran could benefit from nuclear energy. This was something else entirely.[2]

Aghazadeh was true to his word. Thus far, only limited human resources had been devoted to the enrichment programme. In mid-1998 the AEOI moved more people onto the programme and additional theoretical and experimental studies were initiated at the Amir Khabir University.[3] Later that year the AEOI began to assemble and test the Khan-acquired P-1 centrifuges at a pilot enrichment facility at the Kalaye Electric Company workshop where Chinese-sourced UF_6 gas was fed into a centrifuge for the first time a year later, in 1999.[4] Between 1999 and 2002, the AEOI conducted covert tests on these few assembled centrifuges at Kalaye Electric in clear violation of Iran's IAEA safeguards obligations (which states that the IAEA must be informed within 90 days of fissile material being introduced into nuclear facilities).

But this was only the beginning; the AEOI needed a bigger area in which to test the centrifuges – and to properly start enrichment. With this in mind, the decision was made to go ahead with larger-scale research and development and eventually with an enrichment plant. Several locations at Hashtgerd Karaj, Natanz and Isfahan were considered before Natanz was selected as the site for the enrichment plant. In 2001, Iran covertly began construction of two facilities there: the smaller scale pilot fuel enrichment plant, which planned to have some 1,000 centrifuges; and the large scale commercial fuel enrichment plant, which planned to eventually house over 50,000 P-1 centrifuges. In 2002, the AEOI began to feed nuclear material into a number of centrifuges (in up to 19 machines) and procurement activities were intensified as vacuum equipment as well as special raw materials such as maraging steel and high strength aluminium were acquired from abroad.[5] That year Iran also finally began to make tentative steps on the P-2 centrifuges it had received from Pakistan in 1996, and between 2002 and 2003 a contracting company briefly carried out some research work on a modified P-2 design, which involved the purchase of some magnets suitable for the P-2 centrifuge design and some additional inquiries regarding magnets.

All this had a cost, however. After Khazaneh moved into nuclear safety, one of his tasks was to advise on the Bushehr power plant, in particular Russian construction work (which continued to disappoint). Safety checks on a power plant are generally conducted in concert with an external body – in this case the IAEA – and Khazaneh wanted to create an Iranian technological support unit for the programme's power plants, a kind of centralized research centre to deal with all power plant-related issues not concerned with the plant's actual operation. A technological backup for the programme was critical because whenever a fault occurred Iran had to rely on the Russians to fix it, which rarely yielded fruitful results. In fact, it just added to delays in completing the reactor. But Aghazadeh was so focused on the pursuit of uranium enrichment and building the heavy-water reactor at Arak that a technological backup remained only an idea. Had the project been given the necessary support, Khazaneh was sure the Bushehr plant would have been finished far more quickly. But it was typical of Aghazadeh's management, which saw many nuclear energy programmes cut back and denied vital support at the expense of uranium enrichment.

Aghazadeh's arrival marked the programme's change from a largely rudderless project that centred on the uncompleted reactors at Bushehr combined with a hotchpotch of varying research-related activities to more sinister moves towards illicit centrifuge procurement. AEOI policy changed, at the highest political levels, to privilege the indigenous production of the fuel cycle, and this period marked the beginning of the programme that causes so much international concern today. As Khazaneh and so many within the AEOI knew from experience, Iran's options were severely limited. International pressure repeatedly prevented Iranian collaboration on conversion and enrichment facilities which, had it been allowed, would presumably have occurred in the public eye and therefore been subject to inspections. Historical objectivity requires a concession to the argument that much of Iran's illicit nuclear work was 'pushed underground' and Iran was forced to become 'self-sufficient' to produce its own nuclear fuel. But at the same time, why was the decision to pursue such technology made at the political level? It simply wasn't needed; and when a country that does not yet have any nuclear power plants goes after enrichment and plutonium production through heavy-water reactors – the two ways of making nuclear weapons – something is amiss.

* * *

Aghazadeh (or perhaps more correctly Khamenei) changed the AEOI. The arrival of George W. Bush's neoconservative administration in 2000 changed Washington. Tehran had faced bellicose US rhetoric for years – but this was different; the USA now wanted 'regime change' in Iran. Previous US threats against Iran had been met with almost perfunctory hyperbolic threats of 'flames' and 'lightning bolts' (their effect to a degree neutered by their own foolishness), as if both the 'Mad Mullahs' and 'Great Satan' knew their respective roles and continued, almost mechanistically, to play out a 20-year pantomime. US threats now brought a more considered Iranian response born of a genuine fear of what Iran might do in the now (in its eyes) very real event of a US or Israeli attack. And genuine fear bred genuine thought. On 26 August 2000 on Iranian TV, Iranian Defence Minister Ali

Shamkhani addressed the existent threats to Iran and the nature of its possible response:[6]

> We have neighbors who, due to international competition, have gained nuclear weapons ... We have no other alternatives but to defend ourselves in view of these developments. Although we are not trying to obtain non-conventional weapons, we must, however, be able to protect ourselves against such threats.

The statement was notable for its absence of emotionally charged language or hyperbole, merely expressing awareness of the serious disequilibrium of power between two states drawing ever closer to conflict and the need to address this. It also, of course, worried the CIA (and cast doubt on Iran's peaceful nuclear protestations), which pointed to Tehran's spending of $1.2 billion on the Shahab missile, capable of carrying a one-ton warhead 1,200 km.[7] Israeli intelligence meanwhile revised its previous estimate of a likely Iran nuclear weapons capability from five to seven years to two to three years.[8]

Then came 9/11: the events of that tragic September day are so familiar as to make their retelling redundant. Iran's response, however, was significant. The 'Mad Mullahs' from Khatami himself to the Mayor of Tehran displayed a hitherto unseen public empathy (and sympathy) with the USA, while thousands of Iranians demonstrated on the streets against terrorism. The terrorists were Sunnis from the USA's ally Saudi Arabia, and as Washington sought redress through the UN, Khatami was able to convince hardliners that to assist the coalition against Afghanistan was in Iran's interests. Of key relevance to the ever important subject of Iranian pride was that Washington now needed Iran (as evidenced by its participation in the formation of the Post-Taliban government at the 2001 Bonn conference), and the relationship would be a (more) equal one. During the subsequent October 2001 US-led invasion of Afghanistan, Iran played an important if discreet role in affairs – arming the Northern alliance, extraditing al-Qaeda members to Pakistan and Saudi Arabia, as well as briefing Western intelligence agencies on al-Qaeda activities. Tehran

even pledged direct help – promising to search for any American
pilot shot down over their territory. Its reward for all this came,
a few months later, in President George W. Bush's now famous
2002 State of the Union address:[9]

> Iran aggressively pursues these weapons [WMDs] and exports terror
> ... States like these, and their terrorist allies, constitute an axis of
> evil, arming to threaten the peace of the world. By seeking weapons
> of mass destruction, these regimes pose a grave and growing danger.
> They could provide these arms to terrorists ... They could attack
> our allies or attempt to blackmail the United States. In any of these
> cases, the price of indifference would be catastrophic.

This was a serious blow to Khatami in his internal battle with
hardliners who argued that the Great Satan was pernicious and
should never have been trusted. More pertinently, it was clear
that Iran now faced an American regime in a self-declared War
on Terror that divided the world into good versus evil, right versus wrong. The Islamic Republic's binary worldview, here at least,
had met its equal. A new policy of counter-proliferation and the
pre-emptive use of military and covert force before enemies had
acquired WMDs was announced in the egregious *National Security Strategy of the United States of America* of September 2002 that
enshrined a mode of diplomatic expression and policy that miti-
gated against compromise or nuance. Both sides were now totally
committed and ready to clash.

PART II

THE GREATER GAME: THE IRANIAN NUCLEAR CRISIS – 2002–12

CHAPTER 12

CRISIS – 2002–3

At around three in the morning on 13 August 2002 in the high humidity of a Washington summer, Alireza Jafarzadeh got a phone call from Europe. Jafarzadeh was the press officer for the Iranian opposition group, the People's Mujahedin of Iran (PMOI or MKO), and he was half asleep. The MKO is a militant Iranian opposition group dedicated to the Islamic Republic's overthrow. It was founded in 1965 as a left-wing, anti-Shah guerrilla group that became the shock troops of the revolution in 1978–9, before promptly falling out with Khomeini following the Shah's overthrow. Many of its members were arrested and executed while others managed to flee, some to Iraq, where they mounted attacks against Iranian forces during the Iran–Iraq war. Several countries, including the USA, list the MKO as a terrorist organization, and even beyond this it has a questionable reputation as a narrow, dogmatist organization whose members are slavish devotees of the leadership. Much of the group's intelligence on the Islamic Republic had been proved exaggerated or on occasion simply false, but this time the information it would provide was both accurate and explosive. And with Iraq in the Security Council (and soon to be invaded) as the Bush Administration turned its attention to 'rogue' states with suspected WMDs, the timing could not have been worse for Iran.

Despite his slumber, Jafarzadeh instantly recognized the voice at the other end of the line: a member of the Paris-based Iranian parliament in exile, who told him that information had come to light about Iran's nuclear programme. Exactly what could not be said over the phone but he should look at some information, analyse it and put together a press conference to release it. Jafarzadeh got the information that night and spent the next seven hours painstakingly translating the documents, Persian dictionary in hand due to the sheer number of scientific words it contained. He finished at around 9 am and put out a terse press release announcing a press conference for the following day at Washington's Willard Hotel. Then he got some sleep.[1]

14 August 2002 was a hot day. When Jafarzadeh got to the hotel he was sweating. He was worried there might not be a big turnout – he needn't have; as he entered the room he counted cameras from 13 different TV stations as well as reporters from all the major newspapers and news agencies. He then proceeded to publicly expose the full details of the uranium-enrichment site at Natanz and the construction of the heavy-water plant at Arak, which, once operational, would be capable of producing plutonium. Neither of these activities is illegal *per se*, as Article IV of the NPT sets out the 'inalienable right' of all State Parties to develop, research and produce nuclear energy for peaceful purposes. But Tehran was obliged by a 1974 comprehensive Safeguards Agreement with the IAEA to be transparent about all its nuclear facilities (although Iran was only required to declare the existence of any facilities six months prior to feeding nuclear fuel into them). As Jafarzadeh outlined the findings he sensed the atmosphere in the room thicken. Even the lackadaisical cameramen leaning on their tripods stiffened and intensified their gaze along with their focus. Jafarzadeh had the exact location of the Natanz and Arak sites, the coordinates of the buildings, their size, the range of activities going on. Everything. The conference ignited international uproar; the nuclear crisis had begun.

* * *

In Vienna, the IAEA's Deputy Director General for Safeguards, Olli Heinonen, was flustered. It was mid-August, the IAEA Director General, Mohamed ElBaradei, was on holiday in Egypt, and Heinonen was acting head of the Agency in his boss's absence. The revelations were not a total surprise. The Agency suspected that Iran may have received nuclear material it had not reported, and also that undeclared activities had taken place; critically, it knew about Natanz, but Heinonen was surprised at its size. He had also seen information on construction of the Arak heavy-water production plant, but was unsure how it all fitted together because he was unaware of the heavy-water reactor's existence. Quite simply, the Agency was unaware of the magnitude of Iran's nuclear activities. It was clear that Tehran had serious questions to answer, and the first thing Heinonen did after he read the press release was to call ElBaradei, who told him to get in contact with the Iranians.[2] During a frantic afternoon he called Iran's Ambassador to the IAEA, Ali Akbar Salehi, to inform him that information had come to light that required an explanation, and then wrote him a one-page letter to officially request further information and access to the sites. As all the relevant Iranians would be in Vienna for the September IAEA Conference in a few weeks, ElBaradei and Heinonen decided that it would be best to have the first substantial discussions then. Neither man suspected the issue would continue for the next decade.

At the September Conference, ElBaradei duly asked Gholamreza Aghazadeh to confirm whether, as reported, Iran was building a large underground nuclear-related facility at Natanz and a heavy-water production plant at Arak, which Aghazadeh did. Aghazadeh also claimed that there was no legal obligation to declare either facility until they were closer to completion, then provided information on Iran's intentions to further develop its nuclear fuel cycle and agreed to an IAEA inspection of the two sites later in the year.[3] The revelations had caused an international furore and the IAEA was keen to visit the sites as soon as possible, so an inspection was scheduled for the following month. In fact, it would take almost six months until the IAEA was finally allowed access in February 2003, much to the frustration of the European and American IAEA Board members. They didn't blame the IAEA because everyone knew the Agency was trying its best to gain access; rather, they believed that the Iranians were deliberately delaying, failing to issue the invitation they had promised ElBaradei. Diplomatic consensus was that they were likely still working on Natanz; specifically, that they wanted time to complete construction of the centrifuge assembly and facility's outer shell. Satellite imagery showed earth being poured onto the roof, most likely to reduce the risk of damage from any possible aerial bombardment.[4]

On 21–22 February 2003 the IAEA finally inspected the sites. Heinonen went to Natanz with ElBaradei and Pierre Goldschmidt, the IAEA Deputy Director (and his direct boss). Aghazadeh was there to meet the group when they entered Natanz. After some preliminary formalities, he took them to the exhibition hall, where it became palpably clear that the Iranians had rigorously prepared for the inspection. They had dismantled all the centrifuges and put their components on display, complete with manufacturing and testing instructions; all 92 components of the IR-1 centrifuge (that, to the trained eye, was clearly the Pakistani P-1 centrifuge) were laid out for their inspection. Heinonen had to admit: it was nicely done. Aghazadeh told the team that all the centrifuge work was indigenous, using services and information available from open sources, but Heinonen, as a scientist looking at just how far the Iranians had come, doubted that this was true.

The by now increasingly sceptical team also asked to inspect the Kalaye Electric Company in light of Agency information on the undeclared (and as yet unproved) testing of centrifuges and uranium enrichment that had taken place there during the 1990s. The Iranians refused to show them the workshop, arguing that they were not obliged to do so until Iran signed the Additional Protocol to its IAEA Safeguards Agreement (which allows the IAEA, among other things, greater inspection powers to increase its ability to detect undeclared nuclear activities). Instead, the team were assured that nothing in connection with its centrifuge enrichment development programme involving the use of nuclear material had taken place, either at Kalaye Electric or at any other location in Iran – clearly untrue – and were then taken to the company's offices, which were obviously of little relevance.[5] The inspectors returned from Iran dissatisfied. They concluded that the uranium-enrichment plant in Natanz and heavy-water production plant in Arak were on a larger scale and much closer to completion than previously thought. The IAEA Secretariat informed its Board of Governors that Iran had for almost two decades concealed nuclear material and a considerable number of nuclear activities and was, therefore, in breach of its Safeguards Agreement.

Iran's covert nuclear activities were beginning to see daylight. In a May 2003 letter Iran officially informed the Agency of its uranium-enrichment programme, which was described as including two new facilities located at Natanz, namely a pilot fuel enrichment plant nearing completion of construction, and a large commercial-scale fuel enrichment plant also under construction; its intention to construct its 40 MW heavy-water research reactor at Arak (IR-40); and its plan to begin construction of a fuel manufacturing plant at Isfahan. In essence, Iran publicly admitted that it was pursuing the indigenous nuclear fuel cycle. More pertinently, of course, uranium enrichment (at Natanz) and plutonium production (at Arak) are the two paths to producing nuclear weapons.

The following month in the June 2003 IAEA report (the first since the inspection), the IAEA officially published all its findings, and while ElBaradei stopped short of accusing Iran of wanting to build nuclear weapons, he concluded (unsurprisingly) that it had failed to meet its safeguards obligations.[6] Matters then got more serious. Under IAEA pressure Iran agreed to let the inspectors visit the Kalaye Electric workshop, and Heinonen and the others returned that June. They found, unsurprisingly, the type of normal workshop one would expect in a private company that had no connection to the AEOI and had certainly undertaken no centrifuge development work. But the team were allowed to take environmental samples, and when the results came back in August contamination of the equipment by uranium particles was discovered, which could only mean the presence of nuclear material there.

* * *

All of this had been greeted with considerable satisfaction in Washington. US Deputy Secretary of State, Richard Armitage, was with Under Secretary for Arms Control and International Security Affairs at the US State Department, John Bolton, when the news of the February findings first came through: 'We got 'em,' he joyously told his colleague. Like the IAEA, both Armitage and Bolton already knew much of what had been publicly revealed; but they were delighted that the IAEA, the UN's 'revered' watchdog, and not those 'unilateralist cowboys' in the Bush Administration (who were suffering a credibility problem in the run-up to the Iraq war, especially when claiming a country was developing WMDs) had revealed Iran's deception.[7] The revelations had, moreover, coincided with a summer 2002 visit by Israeli Prime Minister Ariel Sharon to Washington at which Sharon bluntly told Bush that Iran posed an existential threat to the State of Israel. The meeting energized the US President on Iran, and from that day onwards he repeatedly referred to the dangers of an Iranian nuclear holocaust on Israel and promised to do all he could to prevent it.[8] Iran now began to dominate his international fears, and he later told British Prime Minister Tony Blair that Iran was the 'big enchilada' in the War on Terror. Bolton believed that on a fundamental level both the President and the Vice President, Dick Cheney, calculated that the USA would have to overthrow the Iranian regime.

In Tehran, the Iranians were scared. The Islamic Republic had fought a war of words over its programme for over 20 years only to see Washington and Tel Aviv seemingly proved right before a global audience. The Iranians claimed they would have publicized their activities, both to their own people and to the IAEA, at the appropriate time, but 'international spies', traitorous AEOI employees, and 'the treachery of the [MKO]' (who wanted to 'hand over' Iran's national advancement to its enemies) prevented them.[9]

180

Spring 2003 was a worrying time for the Islamic Republic. The Bush Administration had just made good on its threats of regime change against one member of the Axis of Evil and smashed Iraq; with Iran's dossier now at the IAEA it could well go to the Security Council for the inevitable to follow.

The Iranians had to formulate a position, do so quickly and ensure it was effective. Most immediately, if they were to defend the programme (as opposed to, say, scrap it as Libya would soon do) what exactly would they defend? Almost 30 years after the AEOI's founding, what did the nuclear programme mean to Iran? Political expediency was necessary but certain fundamental principles would frame all policy, preeminent of which was the *prima facie* belief that the nuclear programme was integral to Iran's future; it would not be abandoned. As ever, policy was framed by Iranian perceptions of history – namely, the overarching problem between Iran and the West:[10]

> The authority of the Islamic regime, its national security and the unification of all its territories, have not at any given time during these past twenty-seven years been supported or even recognised by [the West] in any realistic manner . . . the determination of this great nation to ensure its stability . . . and to seek independence and justice has never been and never will be welcomed by the West . . . At no stage after the victory of the Islamic Revolution has the relationship between Iran and the West become normalised.

In the Islamic Republic's eyes its nuclear programme was a symptom of this; targeted from its beginnings by the USA and Europe, who abrogated contracts to cheat Iran of both promised technology and money to 'keep Iran down' in the best traditions of Western imperialism. The Shah's reasoning, outlined over 30 years ago, still stood. The need to diversify its energy, the associated benefits in science and technology, and the status commensurate with its own as a great power were why Iran would continue with its programme:

> The deprivation forced upon Iran by the West in the field of peaceful nuclear activities has never been acceptable to the Islamic Republic

of Iran. It has been clear to us that with the gradual decrease of hydrocarbon resources, nuclear energy will play an important role in the upcoming decades for the provision of fuel as the third source of energy after oil and gas. Therefore, the provision, protection and improvement of the nation's abilities on the nuclear stage came to be considered a necessity and despite extensive international limitations this course was seriously and continuously followed.

Its nuclear history was, characteristically, reduced to a single aphorism: a national need faced an international obstacle. Bushehr in particular highlighted this trend: under three consecutive US Presidents, the prevention of its construction 'dominated' Russian–American relations (while Europe also 'followed the US example'). What this meant was that there was no other option for Iran but to produce nuclear technology, to the best of its ability, 'within its own borders'.[11] Historical experience fused with the classic wants of a modernizing state and found its nuclear expression in the need for the indigenous fuel cycle:

> The clash between the Islamic Republic of Iran and the western world will never be resolved until Iran's ability in various political, economic, scientific and technological arenas reaches an equal comparable to that of the West's and a just relationship [between us and them] becomes inevitable.

The belief in Iran's need to face the world from a position of strength drove nuclear policy; the situation was now dangerous but this only made the need for strength more critical, from which the achievement of the indigenous nuclear fuel cycle could not be divorced. To compromise would mean to compromise on the regime's existence itself, which was self-evidently unacceptable.

* * *

Tensions were high in June 2003 in the tight circle of diplomats that composed the IAEA Board. All agreed to work through the Agency, and that Iran had to suspend uranium enrichment, which meant the next opportunity for any substantive action on the nuclear file would be the September 2003 Board Meeting. On one side, the Americans argued hard for Iran to be found in non-compliance with its Safeguards Agreement and reported to the Security Council; on the other, the Director General, the Non-Aligned Movement and most of the European countries wanted more time to discover exactly what had gone on in Iran. At this stage, London shared Washington's belief that the appropriate reaction to the Director General's June 2003 report would be to pass a board resolution finding Iran guilty of non-compliance and report this to the Security Council to impose whatever legally binding resolution it deemed appropriate. The strength of a non-compliance resolution is that it takes punitive sanction from the IAEA to the UN Security Council where its five Permanent Members exercise far more decision-making power than at the IAEA Board, where each is merely one of 35 countries (with no right to veto). But they were outnumbered, and Peter Jenkins, the UK's Ambassador to the IAEA, was forced to send an unwelcome communication to London telling his bosses that it would be impossible to get consensus for finding Iran non-compliant, though British policy would change within a matter of weeks.

What is clear (and important) is that from the outset serious, structural divisions existed between Europe and the USA. These arose for two reasons. The first was a *prima facie* belief in certain US quarters that Iran was unquestionably seeking a nuclear bomb; US Under Secretary for Arms Control and International Security Affairs, John Bolton, headed this faction. In Bolton's eyes, each new revelation made it plainer that the civil programme was merely cover for a military one. He mistrusted the IAEA and ElBaradei in particular, whom he viewed as the worst kind of international bureaucrat. Here they all were, faced with one of the greatest threats to the non-proliferation regime in contemporary history, while the IAEA's own Director General couldn't appreciate the severity of the threat. ElBaradei, he believed, never wanted Iran to go to the Security Council because he wanted to keep power with the IAEA and avoid a repeat of Iraq. He had a problem with governments (he thought he was above them); he was, frankly, a pain in the neck.[12]

The second reason is more interesting and points to the conceptual difference in diplomatic approaches between the USA and 'Old Europe'. From the beginning, Bolton believed that the Europeans had no real plan to deal with the Iranian programme and merely wished to prove that the problem could be resolved differently to Iraq and to avoid the use of military force. Taking matters from the IAEA and, ergo, from European negotiations, and giving it to the Security Council, they saw, in effect, as an admission that the diplomatic route had failed. As he saw it, they were invested in the diplomatic process in and of itself – in means rather than ends – and simply not prepared to take the necessary steps to prevent Iran from attaining nuclear weapons. Only substantive pressure, he argued, would make the Iranians take notice, and the fundamental problem with the European policy was the lack of anything behind it. Despite the talk of carrots and sticks, there were only ever carrots. Equally, the Europeans believed Bolton was fundamentally misguided, and US diplomacy too aggressive and ultimately counterproductive – it was as much a cultural as a political clash. According to Peter Jenkins:[13]

> Ambassador Bolton always tended to overestimate the value of sticks. In dealing with Iranians, he failed to understand that the Iranians are proud people who have broad backs, and on the whole they don't react well to sticks, and they're rather good at just hunkering down and enduring these outrageous blows and waiting for things to get better ... this was a fundamental source of disagreement between the Europeans and Ambassador Bolton; we believed we were much more likely to make progress towards the goal that we actually shared with Ambassador Bolton through persuasive diplomacy than through coercion.

The policy, Jenkins believed, was all the worse because it just played into Iranian hands:[14]

> ... their sense of being victims of the West would be re-enforced and it would give their leaders a pretext to call for sacrifices from the Iranian people ... There's a very long history of first British and then more recently American interference in Iranian affairs, which

has conditioned them to expect the worst from us, and so when we deploy sticks we merely confirm all those atavistic reservations about the Anglo-Americans.

These arguments had little effect on Bolton and it was clear to the Europeans that he now heavily influenced State Department policy and a collision was inevitable. The transatlantic disagreement that began as the June discussions spilled over into the end of July duly curdled into opposition in early September when, shortly before the IAEA Board Meeting, Jenkins received an email from London telling him he was no longer to join the USA in arguing for a non-compliance resolution. The diplomatic forces had subtly realigned and now all the Europeans were on one side, with the USA (often with Canada, Japan and Australia) on the other. Jenkins's brief was now to work for the Director General's recommendation – a resolution requesting suspension of uranium enrichment and giving the Iranians two months to increase co-operation with the Agency. Pressure would be applied with the caveat that the resolution should make clear that a failure to supply the required information would likely see the UK join the USA in pressing for a non-compliance resolution at the next Board Meeting in November.

Interestingly, no one on the European side doubted that Iran had been seriously non-compliant and should technically have been reported to New York. But a European policy had emerged based on the calculation that more would be gained by holding the *threat* of Security Council referral over Iran than actual referral itself, a seemingly curious train of logic guided by the belief that the latter option would merely prompt Iran to end co-operation with the agency and make discovering the truth more difficult. Nonetheless, when Bolton heard this he was unimpressed. He found the argument completely illogical because it privileged inaction over action. But Jenkins believed it was the correct decision. In the summer of 2003 the US invasion of Iraq was a military success (the disaster of the 'peace' was yet to come). Tehran desperately wanted to avoid referral, fearing that, once on the agenda there, authorization for military action might follow, and it would be next. Around this time, Jenkins spoke to his Iranian counterpart, Salehi, and it was clear to him that Salehi was genuinely frightened about the possibility of an American invasion.[15]

The IAEA published its latest report on Iran just before the September Board Meeting, which, in forensic detail, outlined everything that had been discovered since the crisis began: that Iran's centrifuges were the Khan P-1 model; that plans for a centrifuge enrichment programme began in 1985 not 1997 as the Iranians claimed; that the plans and drawings for these (acquired through Masud Naraghi's dealing with the Khan network) had been in their possession since 1988; that they had secretly imported UF_6 from China in 1991 (though China's name was not mentioned); that traces of HEU had been found on equipment at Kalaye Electric; that the Agency had faced huge problems gaining access to Kalaye Electric and that, when they did, it was obvious that changes designed to camouflage activities had been made; and that uranium had been enriched there and not declared.[16]

What more, Bolton wondered, did the Europeans want? He knew a resolution calling for Iran's immediate Security Council referral would be rejected so he wanted one that created a 'trigger mechanism' making referral almost automatic if Iran failed to comply with whatever resolution was passed. He faced immediate problems with his colleague, the US Ambassador to the IAEA, Ken Brill, who wanted to compromise along European lines, so he appealed to his boss, Deputy Secretary of State, Richard Armitage. Due to the six-hour time difference between Washington and Vienna the three men had a 6:45 am conference call. Armitage was in Washington, Bolton in his car going to a breakfast speech, and Brill in his office in Vienna. Much to Bolton's surprise, Armitage sided with him: if there was no chance of Security Council referral, the resolution passed should be as strong as possible and the men agreed to press for the 'trigger'.[17]

The Americans were united but now faced the wider problem of the developing–developed nuclear divide in all its diplomatic force. Seeing 'one of their own' attacked by the 'hypocritical' nuclear states, the Non-Aligned Movement mobilized on Iran's behalf. Led by South Africa's IAEA Ambassador, Abdul Samad Minty, the group complained about the NPT's perpetually troublesome Article IV. Minty argued that if it were established through Iran's case that an NPT signatory could not exercise its Article IV rights, how could the other non-nuclear states be sure they wouldn't suffer the same fate if the West deemed it appropriate? And it didn't matter how many times the Europeans told him that Iran was a special case – a country that had concealed its activities from the Agency for 18 years and so forfeited international confidence – they remained resolved and forced the Europeans to put language like 'voluntary' and 'non-legally binding' into the resolution.

At the Board Meeting the South Africans began proceedings by actually tabling a rival 'softer' resolution. If it was a diplomatic ploy designed to dilute the European resolution, it worked: the Europeans convinced ElBaradei, who enjoyed good relations with Minty, to persuade the South African to drop his resolution in exchange for yet more flexibility. A resolution was agreed on: a time-limited suspension of all further uranium-enrichment activities, including the introduction of further nuclear material into Natanz (a definition that would become crucial after the Tehran Agreement). The Europeans also conceded that the resolution would be tabled by Japan (it was late at night in a very stuffy room filled with emotional people). But on the last day the Europeans had to make one final concession: this time, pressure came from the other side. The Americans, true to their decision, insisted the language be as robust as possible and that the resolution allow for 'definitive' conclusions, and therefore action, on 'non-compliance' at the November Board, which, in practice, meant further action along Security Council referral lines. The Iranians, their Non-Aligned Movement allies and, crucially, Iran's nuclear partner, Russia, wanted 'definitive' struck out, and Brill came under intense pressure to drop the word or face a vote.

He called Armitage and Bolton, and Armitage told him to stand firm (if they would not get the language they initially wanted, they would not allow the resolution to be so weak as to be laughable). So Brill refused and called their bluff; he won, and on 12 September 2003 the resolution was passed by consensus. Iran was serving a two-year term on the IAEA Board at the time (ten members of the Board are permanent; the others are elected for two-year terms) and Salehi walked out of the room before the resolution was passed. Tehran later reproached him for not having called a vote, but it was a clever move on his part because Iran would have been the only one to vote against.[18] After the conference call with Brill, Bolton and Armitage awaited the outcome of the negotiations. When word came back, they were at a meeting of National Security Council deputies and everybody broke into applause; they were amazed they had actually won a diplomatic victory.

The September Board was a microcosm for the wider nuclear clash in its precise adumbration of the constellation of forces that would affect its course. On one side Iran, China and Russia and the Non-Aligned Movement; on the other the Americans with the Europeans leaning towards them but remaining, more or less, in the middle. And of course, all of this was played out within and energized by a developed–developing nuclear world that re-entrenched positions on both sides; and that Iran would use for its own diplomatic ends. It set the pattern for the next decade, though no one then knew it.

INSIDE TEHRAN

The Americans might have thought their victory slight, but the Board resolution was taken very seriously in Tehran. As far as the Iranians were concerned, the Shahrivar 1382 (September 2003) resolution threatened national security and turned the situation into a crisis. The view in Tehran was that Washington believed it had won 'a great and easy victory' in Iraq and that, using a 'false excuse' of 'so-called nuclear weapons', Iran was now its next target.[19] Jenkins was right: the Iranians were scared. Thus far the AEOI and Foreign Ministry had handled the crisis but in mid-October, after a meeting of regime leaders including Khatami (who was reeling from repeated domestic, political defeats) and Khamenei, it was decided to transfer responsibility for handling the crisis to the National Security Council led by Hasan Rowhani, who took control of the nuclear file. He faced an immediate problem: the media furore surrounding the crisis, not only internationally but within Iran, had polarized the internal debate on the nuclear programme. 'It seems,' he dryly remarked, 'that we have nothing else to do but be preoccupied with the nuclear issue all day and all night.' In part, this was due to 'partisan and factional motives and interests' in Iran as two sides had emerged within government (and the country) that now complicated the situation.[20]

More 'moderate' opinion held that Iran should accede to 'America's requests' and halt the nuclear programme in order to avoid Western reprisals. Libya's decision in December 2003 to voluntarily reveal and then give up its nuclear programme in exchange for normalization of relations and other benefits would subsequently be used to support the logic of this view.[21] In August, Khamenei had declared Iran fundamentally opposed to WMDs, forbidden as they were by Iran's Islamic principles, which was cited by those who favoured a more flexible approach to negotiations.[22] Among these 'nuclear moderates' was the editor of the newspaper *Entekhab*, who urged Iran to stay in the NPT at all costs, because to leave would validate Washington's 'absurd' allegations about Iran's nuclear weapons ambitions.[23] In the Majlis, Foreign Minister Kamal Kharrazi stressed that the use of WMDs was *haram*, forbidden by Islam.[24]

Those of more hardline opinion favoured direct confrontation. Iran, they argued, should ignore the IAEA and press ahead – possibly even with nuclear weapons. The West would quickly fold and, as with North Korea, 'bribe' it to stay in the NPT. The only sensible national security policy was one based on the most atavistic elements of Khomeini's worldview. International institutions and diplomacy were symptoms of an inequitable world, and a farce – self-reliance was the only option. The USA clearly

wanted to overthrow the regime and since the first Gulf War in
1991 had a huge military presence in the Middle East, with military bases in Saudi Arabia and the UAE (not to mention the fifth
Fleet in the Gulf), all within easy striking distance. 2001's *Operation Enduring Freedom* saw huge numbers of American troops
gathered on the country's eastern border in Afghanistan, while
Saddam's recent overthrow may have removed a pressing Iranian
security concern, but saw yet more US troops amassed now on its
western border. With US forces also in the CIS republics, notably
Uzbekistan and Tajikistan, Iran was encircled by the USA on its
own continent. A bitter joke did the rounds in Tehran: 'There are
just two countries in the world that have only the USA as their
neighbour: the other one is Canada.' No one needed remind-
ing of the dangers of US meddling in Iran; it would have to be
prepared.

Then there was the question of precedent. Following the 9/11
attacks America had invaded Afghanistan to destroy the Taliban –
a regime that had harboured and supported al-Qaeda. But
Islamabad had also harboured and supported al-Qaeda, and was a
longstanding sponsor of terrorism, a dictatorship with a dismal
human rights record that had also spawned the AQ Khan network.
(Over two years after the invasion in April 2004, Washington's
Ambassador to Kabul, Zalmay Khalilzad, would claim that the
Taliban and other terrorist organizations continued to operate
from the country.) Despite all its help in Afghanistan, Iran was de-
clared a triumvir in the Axis of Evil while Secretary of State Colin
Powell described Pakistan as a major ally in the Global War on
Terror. Now Washington had just smashed an Iraq that turned
out not to have WMDs. Many in Tehran had concluded that the
White House treated nuclear states differently.

In September, just after the Board resolution, the Secretary of
the Guardian Council, Ayatollah Ahmad Jannati, had urged Iran
to withdraw from the NPT[25] while several conservative newspapers, such as *Resalat*, publicly opposed Iranian adoption of the
Additional Protocol, which, in their eyes, Iran had signed under
Western pressure, and which, moreover, was another way into

Iran for Western spies.[26] Iran should increase its defence budget and, with a threatening Israel, build a nuclear deterrent. The regime ensured that the crisis was playing out on the streets, too. The programme was a totem of Iranian pride once more, and AEOI promotional videos showed nuclear installations intercut with blooming flowers and snow-capped mountains while a voice-over cooed that Iran was a 'country of intelligent people'.[27]

The Shah's vision had returned in full but was given an added thrust by the more politically adept Islamic Republic: the nuclear programme was a symbol of Iranian achievement, which was why Washington wanted to destroy it. As one Iranian official noted, US pressure had 'unified the people in wanting nuclear technology, even more because the US says we can't have it'.[28] As ever, public opinion was crucial to Iran's internal nuclear debate (perhaps indicative of the regime's concerns over its legitimacy). As Rowhani would later say in a September 2005 speech to the Supreme Cultural Revolution Council, a critical reason to delay Iran's referral to the Security Council was that time was needed to 'justify' the government's 'position' as completely as possible to the people. The government, he argued, had to 'cool down and lower the intensity of our propaganda'. 'Whatever we do,' he concluded, 'we must have the support of the public.'[29] Thus far, this had not been a problem. Indeed, the regime had managed to turn the crisis into a national cause. In the streets grafittied slogans vowed to fight the 'American threat', while posters declared that 'we are not interested in wars, but we will defend our land'.[30] The constant bellicose rhetoric that had emanated from Washington ever since Bush's arrival, by triggering the nationalist impulse, served to push a young and vibrant population, many of whom loathed the Mullahs, into the arms of a regime increasingly fearful of its own country's demographics.

ROWHANI'S PLAN

Rowhani rejected both sides. Iran was not ready for a major confrontation but nor would it give up all its hard-won benefits at the first sign of Western pressure. Instead, he came up with a five-step plan. First (and most important) was to keep the crisis under control and to deter threats against the country; second, to preserve the existing nuclear facilities; third, to actually improve and strengthen Iran's existing nuclear capabilities; fourth, to ensure the country's legal position under IAEA statute and international law was as strong as it could be; and fifth, a somewhat more nebulous desire, to transform the 'existing threats into opportunities'.[31] Urgency was needed for the first stage because mere passive acceptance of Iran's 'supposed mistake or crime' could well result in Iran's dossier being passed to the Security Council, from where, as with Iraq, the Council would pass a resolution calling for military intervention and Washington would have accomplished what Tehran believed to be its aim of the last 25 years: the regime's end.[32]

The plan would be based on 'prudence' and 'comprehensive planning'. It was dual-track: preparation for any possible confrontation combined with protection of the nuclear facilities. But the crisis offered something else: in the sustained engagement that would be required for its resolution was the possibility, if handled correctly, of the normalization of Iran's international standing. Iran would first deal with the legalities of its position (something likely to receive a receptive ear post-Iraq, especially among the Non-Aligned Movement and ElBaradei) and co-operate with the IAEA through an agreement to implement the Additional Protocol. Political resolution through 'deliberation with influential countries in the international arena' would also be sought.[33]

Rowhani then systematically considered Iran's possible allies. The USA was a paradox. It was evidently the main complainant against Iran, and its capacity, both in its power to confront or to find resolution, was unmatched; the question was whether to engage or not? Senior figures discussed the issue and decided that Washington was only interested in 'forcing Iran to surrender' – so Iran wouldn't. As ever, history was inescapable and the possibility of engagement was also dismissed because the lessons of Iran's past experiences with the USA meant that it was unlikely to bring favourable results. Russia was a logical ally. It was Iran's premier (pretty much only) nuclear partner and had a vested financial interest in not seeing the programme shut down and preventing Iran from being taken to the Security Council. But Tehran doubted Russia's capability to influence the situation (which would actually prove unfair) for the same reasons. Who would listen to arguments so clearly borne from self-interest? And it was no match for the USA anyway; moreover, Moscow did not approve of Iran's desire to master the fuel cycle and indigenous fuel production. Nor for that matter, Rowhani believed, did China, which, with hundreds of billions of dollars in US trade, would not jeopardize its relationship with the USA for Iran's sake.[34]

The Non-Aligned Movement were good allies but lacked the political strength to confront Washington, while Europe clearly didn't want Iran to acquire nuclear capabilities and was obviously not a real option. There was, of course, the traditionally useful IAEA, and while ElBaradei was, Rowhani acceded, an Arab, he did not seem to be anti-Iranian (though he had his limitations). He was a politician before anything else, and obviously concerned with his and his institution's position; and his aides were Europeans.[35] And, besides, as the supposed arbiter of the crisis, the Agency could never be an overt ally. There were, frankly, no good options, but the deterioration in relations between Europe and the USA over the Iraq war, as well as developing world solidarity, provided an opportunity for a strategy. Pretty much everyone was against further Iranian nuclear progress, but they had their differences, too, which had been so recently illustrated at the September Board, and which Iran would exploit.

THE ROAD TO TEHRAN

The strategy was a prescient one. If the Americans thought the September Board was bad, things would only get worse as diplomatic disagreement evolved into parallel diplomatic strategies. A frequent USA–UK conduit on the nuclear file was between US Secretary of State Colin Powell and British Foreign Secretary

Jack Straw. In mid-August, a few weeks before the September Board, Straw, together with his German and French counterparts (Joschka Fischer and Dominique de Villepin) had written a letter to the Iranians (which had prompted London's change of instructions to Jenkins) with a simple proposal: if Iran abandoned enrichment, the Europeans were ready to offer a number of things (a perfect example of Bolton's despised 'carrot'). When the letter was first mooted, the ministers discussed what should be requested – limited enrichment or a total abandonment – so while the ministers spelt out their desire for co-operation, they insisted, at the USA's request, on abandonment of enrichment – a so-called 'zero centrifuge' formula.[36]

In early October, a short time after the September Board, Bolton heard via a phone call from Powell that, following the letter, all three Foreign Ministers were about to go to Tehran, which he considered a bad idea. Powell and Bolton had taken to calling the three EU Foreign Ministers the Three Tenors, and Bolton told Powell they would inevitably fail to dissuade the Iranians from proceeding with their nuclear programme, but completely undercut their multilateral strategy. Powell told him he didn't think it was a great idea either, but, nonetheless, he didn't tell the Three Tenors not to go – perhaps, he told Bolton, it would just come to nothing. A few days later, Bolton was at a breakfast at The Royal Yacht Club in Knightsbridge, London, with a British diplomat who told him that Straw was determined to see the European effort with Iran through. So Bolton called Powell and Powell called Straw to tell him Bolton was in London and suggested the two speak, which Straw did not want to do. Rather, he reassured Powell that he was not going off to Tehran to give things away.[37]

Meanwhile in Tehran, François Nicoullaud, France's Ambassador to Iran, was charged with organizing the visit, a task that had caused him nothing but problems from the beginning. First was the problem of de Villepin, and his renowned impatience. When Nicoullaud first received a telegram from him back in August asking his thoughts on the proposed trip, de Villepin had insisted on a quick, formal answer from the Iranians and suggested that the

Foreign Ministers come personally to Iran to get it. But Nicoullaud was worried that premature action would result in failure of the mission and that, as Ambassador, it might be blamed on him. It is diplomatically embarrassing for an Ambassador to have his minister travel somewhere and have negotiations collapse (which is why the minutia of negotiations are usually completed by civil servants beforehand). He sent his boss a cable warning him of the risks, recommending that the ministers delay coming until after the September IAEA Board Meeting (when they would have a better idea of how things stood) and asking him to first send a political director to try to strike the deal beforehand. De Villepin agreed.

Then there was the problem of the Iranians. The three Foreign Ministers had written the letter with the intention that their respective Ambassadors personally present it to Iran's Foreign Minister, Kamal Kharrazi. Nicoullaud was on vacation in France at the time and had to return to Iran, only to discover that Kharrazi was refusing to see them; Khatami was preparing his own letter to the Europeans and wanted to send that first. The Ambassadors went through a dull pantomime of repeated requests for an appointment over four or five days until they were finally told that a mid-ranking civil servant would receive them. They refused. The Iranians were worried that the letter contained an ultimatum or something that might embarrass them and kept asking what was in it, saying that if they were told its contents a meeting might be possible. The Ambassadors refused: 'That's not the way diplomacy works,' they said. Finally, Nicoullaud spoke to Kharrazi's nephew, Sadegh Kharrazi, his opposite number in Paris and a relative of Khamenei (and his confidante on foreign affairs), and told him that there was nothing in the letter to worry about, which finally resulted in the desired appointment and the letter's delivery.

THE BIRTH OF THE EU-3

The Iranians debated whether to accept the overture and invite the three Foreign Ministers to Tehran. In the end, it was decided that the IAEA had such a deep knowledge of Iran's nuclear activities (which were now too difficult to conceal) that the best course of action would be to try to resolve the problem quickly.[38] In early October the British, French and German political directors duly arrived in Tehran to meet with the Iranians. The trip was the first step towards what became the Tehran Agreement and was when the so-called EU-3 – France, Britain, Germany, the three countries that would now take the lead in negotiations – was born. It was in many ways an arbitrary choice and there was jealousy in European circles. Why not Italy or Spain? It came about purely because de Villepin believed that France should not go it alone and, as the three traditional European powerhouses, the UK and Germany seemed the logical partners.[39]

Nicoullaud accompanied the political directors to the meeting, where they met with the Spokesman for the Supreme National Security Council, Hossein Mousavian; as well as Javad Zarif, Iran's UN Ambassador; Cyrus Nasseri, head of the nuclear negotiating team; and Sadegh Kharrazi. (Rowhani considered the discussions beneath his level, although they had a formal meeting with him at the end.) Stanislas de Laboulaye, the French political director, did most of the talking, and John Sawyers from Britain was tough and on top of the brief, but the meetings were unsuccessful. On the eve of the ministers' arrival a text had been produced but without a common declaration, full of qualifications and caveats. Nicoullaud's worst fears had been confirmed: his minister would come to Iran without a deal in place.

The ministers duly arrived in mid-October, three or four weeks before the November IAEA Board Meeting. It was not entirely logical to pre-empt the meeting – it created some tensions with ElBaradei, and it was a risk – but de Villepin was philosophical: he told Nicoullaud that if they failed they would have demonstrated a diplomatically useful willingness to try, and if they succeeded, even better. The meeting took place on 21 October 2003 inside Sa'dabad, the Shah's old palace in north Tehran. Sa'dabad is a large complex that overlooks the city. Surrounding the main palace is a series of smaller palaces or pavilions that originally housed the Shah's family, and the meeting was scheduled to take place in one of these. The ministers were initially received by President Khatami and Foreign Minister Kamal Kharrazi in one pavilion before moving on to another for negotiations with Rowhani and his team.

Everyone knew that Washington wanted to drag Iran to the Security Council and that, if nothing was agreed, the USA would most likely present a draft resolution to this effect at the November Board, which created a useful pressure on both sides to reach an agreement. Rowhani was especially nervous. He had battled hardliners (who objected to negotiations on principle) to get the meeting to go ahead, and opened with a long and boring speech, clearly more designed to calm himself than to welcome the ministers, which everybody ignored.[40] Naturally, the discussions focused on enrichment. The Europeans could have mentioned any number of issues – reprocessing, heavy-water production at Arak, possible weaponization – but calculated that it was better to stick to the critical issue. Their room for diplomatic manoeuvre was restricted due to the USA's insistence on the zero centrifuge 'formula' – total abandonment of enrichment, with 'zero' centrifuges spinning.[41] As the initiative's architect, de Villepin played a leading role; he spoke first in the meetings and the other ministers instinctively looked to him throughout very tense negotiations that for a long time threatened to go nowhere. The initial stalemate at one point prompted Joschka Fischer to almost storm out. He was uncomfortable with the negotiations in themselves because, as a member of Germany's Green Party, he was party-bound to ideologically oppose nuclear power, and feared the domestic criticism he might take for even being there; he reminded everyone, repeatedly, that he was anti-nuclear before he was anything else.

There was deadlock. Just as their political directors had been unable to strike a deal, neither could the ministers, and what occurred was that rarest of diplomatic sights: ministers sat together in a room while they negotiated the minutia of an agreement, arguing over commas and parentheses, striking out clauses and then reinserting them. The Iranians wanted to limit suspension to the actual action of enrichment, which is obtained by introducing gasified uranium (UF_6) into centrifuges that spin at supersonic speed to concentrate the percentage of the fissile isotope U-235; the Europeans wanted it limited to producing the UF_6 feed material in the first place. The Iranians would just not agree on the zero centrifuge formula. The Europeans then discussed possible Iranian guarantees that the programme would not be diverted to military use. But again, the only objective guarantee that the Europeans could accept was the zero centrifuge formula. The timing of suspension was also at issue, with the Foreign Ministers arguing for total suspension while negotiations on the overall nuclear file took place, to which the Iranians would also not accede. The whole process was redundant and circuitous. Throughout all this Rowhani remained very nervous – it was clear his political future was on the line.

After almost two fruitless hours, he requested a pause in negotiations, which all sides used as an opportunity to call home. Rowhani made a call, too, almost certainly, the Europeans assumed, to the Supreme Leader,[42] who must have told him to do as he saw fit because when Rowhani returned he made an announcement: he told the room he was taking a huge, personal risk as he had no instructions to this effect but that he accepted the principle of suspension while negotiations on the overall nuclear file took place.[43] The negotiations, he was adamant, must not last too long. The meeting ended with an agreement, to universal relief (though nothing had yet been signed), that Iran would suspend uranium enrichment for the length of negotiations; again Rowhani emphasized that these should move fast and last no more than a few months. No agreement on the 'zero centrifuge' formula was possible; the subsequent declaration merely made reference to 'enrichment and other matters' and declared that definition of the scope of the suspension would be left to the IAEA (a diplomatic swerve to allow for an agreement). ElBaradei was furious when he heard. Defining the scope of enrichment is complex: the limit is more or less where one wants, so it is a political not a technical choice and it placed a political responsibility on the IAEA, but he agreed nonetheless – what else could he do? The meeting finally finished and everyone made their way to a neighbouring pavilion where a gaggle of Iranian journalists waited impatiently. Rowhani was clearly desperate to reassure the press that Iran had not wilted under Western pressure. The first thing the Iranian journalists asked was how long the suspension would last, to which he quickly replied that it wouldn't be long – a few months at the most. A crowd of Basij had gathered outside the palace to shout slogans in protest at the deal, which thoroughly embarrassed the Iranian diplomats. More problematically, the crowd was stopping the Europeans from leaving. They were now stuck behind the palace gates; de Villepin couldn't find his driver in the melee and became even more impatient than usual. After about 20 minutes, the driver finally appeared but they still couldn't go anywhere because the Basij outside made it difficult to move, which prompted Nicoullaud to go outside and ask them what was wrong; they were quite pleasant and explained their opposition to negotiations on principle. The French party then insisted the guards open the gates and got through the crowds to make their way to the airport.

* * *

As per the initial accord reached in Tehran, the Iranians committed themselves to suspending the enrichment of uranium, as defined by the IAEA, and the reprocessing of spent fuel to produce plutonium. They also committed themselves to enhancing access to the nuclear programme for IAEA inspectors and to resolving all outstanding issues, or at least to answering all outstanding questions. In return, the Europeans explicitly agreed to recognize Iran's nuclear rights and to discuss ways it could provide 'satisfactory assurances' regarding its nuclear power programme (after which Iran would gain easier access to nuclear technology) and committed themselves to ensuring that Iranian non-compliance was not reported to the Security Council.[44]

On the face of it, the agreement was a diplomatic coup. The EU-3 got the suspension of enrichment it needed, albeit not with the exact formula it wanted. On 18 December 2003 Iran signed the Additional Protocol and agreed to act as if it were in force, making the required reports to the IAEA and allowing the required access by IAEA inspectors, pending its ratification by the Majlis. The Iranians were also happy: that the agreement had started with a European overture gave them hope that compromise was possible. As they saw it, the trip and subsequent agreement were a simple bargain: the guarantee of Tehran's security in exchange for halting the nuclear fuel cycle and signing the Additional Protocol; they had got 'clean' quickly. The Iranians acknowledged that talks were difficult and felt they had secured a 'victory' (always important for national pride) because a voluntary and temporary suspension was agreed upon instead of a permanent suspension.[45] Critically, the Iranians believed the Tehran Agreement was merely the first step in building trust between the two sides. Above all, though, there was relief that the initial danger had passed. The crisis had been averted and the first stage of Rowhani's plan accomplished.[46]

In the Iranians' satisfaction can be found the agreement's undoing. The length of suspension was never properly addressed – a deliberate diplomatic fudge to allow for a compromise. To Iran suspension may only have been temporary to allow for broader nuclear negotiations to progress, but for the Europeans, who had got what they wanted, there was no hurry to reach another agreement. They naively hoped that Tehran would just forget about enrichment. But the Iranians were always impatient, constantly asking the Ambassadors when they would next meet to discuss the matter.[47] And there was also the deeper problem that the Europeans could offer nothing of real note to Iran as long as Washington maintained its arsenal of unilateral sanctions on the Islamic Republic. Even when trade did not directly fall within the ambit of US sanctions, European interests in US markets meant that no firm would risk upsetting Washington. Structurally, negotiations were most likely doomed because the USA and Iran's continuing refusal to speak meant there was no one who could offer Iran any genuine incentives to make it dramatically alter its nuclear policy, and the wider problem of Iran and the USA still remained unresolved.

This first phase of nuclear negotiations saw not only a (limited) vindication of European strategy, but also highlighted the EU-3's limitations as a diplomatic force in itself. Beginning with the 2002 revelations, the Director General and his inspectors were able to uncover a mass of detailed information about Iranian nuclear activities going back 18 years. The subsequent ability of the Europeans to play on very real Iranian fears in the wake of the USA's comprehensive military defeat of Iraq was instrumental to the seeming diplomatic success of the Tehran Agreement. The Iranians suspended enrichment and allowed the Agency exceptional access to Iranian nuclear facilities not required under their standard safeguards agreement. But once this was achieved the Europeans' ability to build on their success was limited (as the following years would make clear).

CHAPTER 13

FROM TEHRAN TO PARIS
AND BEYOND – 2003–5

As far as Rowhani was concerned, things were going well. The EU-3 kept their side of the Tehran Agreement and Iran escaped the Security Council; but by Iranian calculations the USA, always the principle concern, was angry: its 'plans had failed', and it believed the 'simple' European delegation to Tehran had been cheated, which only increased its desire for confrontation.[1] 2004 started badly for Iran. At the end of 2003 (on 19 December) Muammar Gaddafi, who had witnessed the fall of Saddam with alarm, announced that Libya had a secret WMD programme, which it would now dismantle and allow the IAEA access to all its nuclear facilities. Libya had also dealt with AQ Khan, and a by-product of Gaddafi's move was the public exposure of the Khan network, which prompted Pakistan to (ostensibly) investigate Khan.

Days later, Malaysian police announced the discovery of evidence that Khan's network had sold Iran $3 million worth of nuclear centrifuge parts, and in February 2004, the IAEA confirmed that Iran had indeed acquired P-2 (second generation) centrifuges from Khan in the mid-1990s.[2] Both the Agency and several member states raised the point that Iran had not declared this information either in October or at the November Board (where it was supposed to have made a full disclosure of everything).[3] In response, Iran argued that its enrichment programme at Natanz was based on the P-1 design (and the IAEA was informed of the research and development on the P-1 design during the inspectors' 2002 visit to Natanz) so it had no reason to include the centrifuges in its October 2003 declaration. On 23 February, IAEA inspectors discovered yet more undisclosed research in Iran – namely, experiments with Polonium-210 (used in the production of nuclear weapons). Again, Iran was forced to acknowledge the charge but pointed to polonium's possible use in power generation and claimed, irrelevantly, that the experiments had occurred 'some time ago'.

On 25 February ElBaradei circulated his latest report on Iran. Beginning with his usual desire to stress the positive, he described the P-2 centrifuge discovery as a 'setback', expressed the (rather desperate) hope that it would be Iran's last oversight as regards disclosure and suggested that a 'comprehensive' suspension of centrifuge manufacturing and assembly would be a good confidence-building measure.[4] US Ambassador to the IAEA Ken Brill's immediate response was that the report 'proved' Iran's October 2003 declaration to the IAEA was neither correct nor complete, that Iran's nuclear efforts were clearly geared to the development of nuclear weapons, and again called for Iran's Security Council Referral.[5]

Brill was technically correct, but there was still no appetite among the European and Non-Aligned Movement Board members to pursue this course of action. As far as the Europeans were concerned, the diplomatic game – to ensure Iran maintained suspension – remained unchanged. For their part, the Iranians still stressed that suspension was temporary and at their discretion – the abandonment of the indigenous fuel cycle was still politically and ideologically impermissible. In February 2004, John Sawers, Director General for Political Affairs at Britain's Foreign Office, visited the IAEA to meet with Mohammad Reza Alborzi and Javad

Zarif, Iran's UN Ambassadors, and Cyrus Nasseri, head of Iran's nuclear negotiating team. At the meeting, Jenkins was asked to take the floor and outline the European position on the length of Iranian suspension. As per his reading of the Tehran Agreement, he assumed, and said, that suspension should last until all outstanding questions were resolved which, being familiar with the Agency's methodology, likely meant three or four years. Zarif exploded with rage.[6]

Three weeks later, at a meeting in Brussels, however, the Europeans were able to get the Iranians to officially agree to widen the definition of suspension to suspension of the assembly and testing of centrifuges and suspension of the domestic manufacture of centrifuge components (to the extent possible without abrogating existing contracts) in return for a vague promise of European support in exchange for Iran's continuing good behaviour. It was a small diplomatic coup and the Europeans repeatedly tried to buy more Iranian concessions by offering economic and technological incentives in exchange for permanent suspension, but the Iranians were totally uninterested. What they wanted was to resume enrichment.

Matters were to intensify when, on 8 March, the IAEA Board met for the first time since the new revelations. ElBaradei spoke (for him) in harsh terms and criticized Iran's questionable record of declaration to which Iran tepidly responded that its October 2003 declaration was never intended to present a 'full picture' of past nuclear activities, a clearly disingenuous statement: even Rowhani had acknowledged that the Tehran Agreement rested on Iran coming clean. And it got worse. Two days into the Board, the traces of uranium detected the previous year on centrifuges at Natanz were revealed to include some centrifuges enriched to 90 per cent (HEU) – weapons-grade levels.[7] Iran argued that traces were already on the centrifuges when Iran had imported them from Pakistan, which was subsequently proved true the following year, but at this stage it looked as though Iran had HEU.

All of this gave the Americans their chance. The Europeans had not considered it necessary to table a resolution at the Board because they had just got the Iranians to widen the definition of suspension. They failed to foresee that the Americans (supported by Japan, Canada and Australia) would take the opportunity to table a resolution of their own, drafted, like the September 2003 resolution, to create a trigger, which would result in the long-desired Security Council referral for any further Iranian breaches. The Europeans moved as swiftly as they could to tone the resolution down, which was not difficult because the vast majority of board members still supported them, but they could not totally oppose it. The Iranians were angry with them, but it was, frankly, a balancing act: to side outright with Iran and the Non-Aligned Movement against their four closest allies was unthinkable.

Now Iran was unhappy. Within the country, hardliners stoked popular resentment. The conservative newspaper *Jomhuri-ye Islami* argued that continued relations with the Agency were pointless,[8] and that Iran now had no choice but to withdraw from the NPT given its double standards: citing dissatisfaction of the treaty's iniquities and, of course, Israel's nuclear arsenal.[9] The conservative-dominated seventh Majlis passed a bill supporting the resumption of enrichment (though the final decision would obviously remain with Khamenei).[10] Majlis Deputy Ala'eddin Borujerdi exemplified the government's mood from the Majlis floor and declared that Iran should not allow international pressure to violate its 'rights'.[11] Hossein Shari'atmadari, editor of another conservative newspaper, *Keyhan*, proposed that Iran issue a three-month ultimatum to the IAEA to take Iran's case off the agenda, resume reprocessing and even leave the NPT. If the IAEA sent Iran to the UN, Iran should leave the Agency.[12] The AEOI, meanwhile, resorted to what would become a familiar diplomatic tactic – banning inspectors from its nuclear sites – and just after the Board Meeting Iran announced a postponement of IAEA inspections due to 'administrative draw downs' with the approaching Iranian New Year on 21 March.[13]

Bolton was by now apoplectic. In London that spring, Jenkins witnessed a conversation between the Political Director of Britain's Foreign Office, John Sawers, and Bolton at which Bolton yet again argued that Iran's nuclear file should be immediately passed from the IAEA to the Security Council. But it seemed that, as ever, he was unable to explain why specifically (given his seeming mistrust of international institutions) such a course of action would be of use. Jenkins subsequently learnt that Bolton believed it would simply demonstrate the Security Council's ineffectiveness and clear the way for Washington (and anyone who wanted join them) to take more effective action, which meant military action.

* * *

Meanwhile, Tehran was taking careful note of the intensifying pressure. A cognitive dissonance between the Europeans and Iranians over suspension had existed since the Tehran Agreement, which in Iranian eyes was only the first step towards wider negotiations and only ever temporary. Moreover, as Rowhani would later tell the Supreme Cultural Revolution Council, Iran had suspended only what was mastered already and he now implemented phase two of his plan (the consolidation of existing facilities) by continuing to work on other nuclear activities throughout negotiations.[14] In fact, he had actually ordered the acceleration of other nuclear activities – just in case. The Arak heavy-water plant was never under suspension and its construction continued apace, as did work on the UCF at Isfahan for the production of UF_6 (through its conversion from yellowcake – the second stage of the fuel cycle), which Iran completed in July. Also a priority for the AEOI was to build the minimum number of centrifuges necessary to begin enrichment (while refraining from actual enrichment itself as per the Tehran Agreement). Once this was achieved, when the inevitable decision was taken to resume, Iran could continue to produce enriched fuel should the nuclear facilities come under military attack. Rowhani was creating facts on the ground: the West would have to understand that halting Iran's nuclear progress was impossible; the only realistic solution to the impasse was a balanced and mutually acceptable deal.[15]

THE PARIS AGREEMENT

By now events had pushed even the tortuous diplomatic process into some form of evolution and the September 2004 IAEA Board passed a resolution that contained, if not Security Council referral, its threat.[16] It was a struggle as the Non-Aligned Movement mobilized on Iran's behalf once more, but after a lot of negotiations a resolution was passed. If things did not improve, ElBaradei was requested to present a 'comprehensive' report at the November Board – a phrase that meant he would remind the Board of all Iran's past breaches, which would more than likely be strong enough for Security Council referral. It was not the 'trigger' the Americans wanted but, finally, a clear diplomatic message.

Iran's vulnerability was now at its height, something the Europeans intended to exploit. The goal was now to get Iran to widen the definition of enrichment and to stop work on the production of feed material for the enrichment process (the stage before actual enrichment). Unable to resist political pressure from all sides, the Iranians were, once more, brought to the table in early November 2005, this time at the Quai d'Orsay in Paris. The first day of negotiations was a disaster; nothing could be agreed on and by midnight everyone was exhausted. The biggest service Jenkins rendered to the Europeans that day was to go to John Sawers when the Iranians had proposed some characteristically tricky wording and tell him that his brain was no longer working, that the situation was getting dangerous and that they should break off and reconvene tomorrow. Over breakfast the following morning at the residence of the British Ambassador, Sir John Holmes, they came up with what they considered more appropriate wording relating to the scope and duration of suspension; the remainder of the text they agreed on Sunday.

But nothing is ever simple in this saga. Back in Vienna, on the Friday that the agreement was due to be signed, Jenkins was in his office at the IAEA with his French and German counterparts, applying the finishing touches for its adoption later that afternoon when, to his horror, he learned that the Iranians were arguing with the IAEA Secretariat that under the terms of the agreement they should be allowed to hold back 20 sets of centrifuge components for research and development purposes. This was clearly absurd. There was nothing to that effect in the agreement but nonetheless the Ambassadors told the Chairman of the Board of Governors to hold off consideration of their Draft Resolution until Monday. A fraught Saturday morning was then spent with the Iranian delegation at their hotel, trying to convince them that they were departing from what had been agreed in Paris.[17]

Unsurprisingly, it turned out that this new caveat was little more than a negotiating ploy. The Iranians were ready to drop their insistence on the 20 sets of centrifuges if the Europeans were prepared to drop the need for suspension to avoid Security Council referral. Jenkins refused to give way; and he warned the delegation that if they reneged on their Paris commitments the Europeans would table a totally different resolution calling for Security Council referral. The Iranians remained defiant: 'Do your worst,' Iran's UN Ambassador, Javad Zarif, told him. Jenkins called his bluff. It was a difficult decision because each Ambassador knew his respective minister was delighted an agreement had been reached and would not welcome its collapse. But, they, too, were defiant. Jenkins then spent a nervous 24 hours before the phone call came through from the Iranians; they had backed down. On Sunday evening Jenkins and John Sawers celebrated with a jolly champagne-fuelled meal at the residence of the French Ambassador, Patrick Villemur. On Monday (15 November 2004) the resolution was duly passed and the Paris Agreement was officially signed in Tehran by Nicoullaud, and the other EU-3 Ambassadors and Zarif in Vienna.[18]

* * *

In the Paris Agreement, Tehran reaffirmed it would not seek nuclear weapons, committed to full co-operation and transparency in its dealings with the IAEA and agreed to prolong its suspension of all enrichment-related and reprocessing activities. In turn, the EU-3 pledged to 'begin negotiations, with a view to reaching a mutually acceptable agreement on long-term arrangements'. Importantly, as well as providing 'objective [Iranian] guarantees that Iran's nuclear program is exclusively for peaceful purposes', the agreement was meant to provide firm guarantees on nuclear, technological and economic co-operation and firm commitments on 'security issues' from the West.

But, again, a major diplomatic 'coup' contained the seeds for future conflict. The Paris Agreement, just as the Tehran Agreement before it, was meant as a precursor to negotiations on a mutually acceptable long-term arrangement, and also side-stepped the core of the dispute: Iran's asserted right to enrich. To maintain Iranian face (always a central concern), the EU-3 recognized the suspension as a 'voluntary confidence-building measure'. Throughout the negotiations, Iran stressed its desire to resume uranium conversion and requested that the IAEA remove the seals at the Isfahan facility in preparation. Rowhani was clear to Khatami on what the Agreement did and did not mean:[19]

> Contrary to public belief, the Paris Agreement is not the end of this process but in fact the beginning of the real discussions to reach an agreement. Because Iran had completed its structural capacities regarding the fuel cycle, the possibility of suspending the enrichment process for a period of a few months without creating major problems for the fuel production programme was possible. Europe agreed to normalise the situation at the Agency in order to prepare the ground for comprehensive discussions in a calm and balanced environment.

The Paris Agreement did, however, mark the starting point of the fifth stage of Rowhani's plan – the need to transform crises to opportunities; indeed, it exemplified it:

> [T]he Europeans are obliged to give decisive guarantees in the political, economic, security and technological arenas. This signifies the normalisation and the betterment of relations ... because finally, the only real and long-term guarantee for both sides besides confidence, trust and assurance regarding one another's aims and actions is to increase and improve the relationship and Europe's support [for example] of Iran's membership in the WTO.

First was the benefit of engagement itself. The Islamic Republic, Rowhani pointed out, had not experienced many previous negotiations with the West, and certainly, since the Hostage Crisis and Iran–Iraq war, never any with this 'degree of gravity';[20] and, he concluded, they had been carried off successfully, both politically and technically.[21] Moreover, engagement was critical because Rowhani understood, on a fundamental level, that only resolution of the wider problem between Iran and the West could solve the nuclear crisis permanently. The Paris Agreement was the first step, and it was especially promising for Tehran because discussions encompassed wider issues of Iranian concern such as the MKO (the Iranian opposition group that had started the crisis back in 2002) and its possible recognition as a terrorist organization 'like al-Qaeda'. Such discussions, he believed, were positive.[22]

But he remained realistic; détente would not happen any time soon. Referral remained uppermost in his mind, and to have delayed the Security Council was, he pointed out, a considerable achievement: Iran was now far more technologically prepared than the previous year, and he calculated that if and when it came it was better to be referred due to the failure of negotiations with the EU-3 than by IAEA resolution.[23] He was also frustrated. The 'whole dynamic' of the crisis would change if they could just somehow manage to complete the fuel cycle; the West would have no choice but to accept it. And, finally, there was regret, too. Everything would have been so much easier had they just announced their plans from the very beginning, instead of delaying. ('We have not lied,' he would later tell the Supreme Cultural Revolution Council. '. . . in all cases, we have told them the truth. But in some cases, we may not have disclosed information in a timely manner.'[24]) In the end, however, he was not hopeful on the possibility of avoiding sanctions: 'We don't trust the Europeans,' he told the Council, and 'unfortunately they don't trust us either.'[25]

BUSH'S SECOND TERM: THE COMING OF RICE AND BURNS

Despite Rowhani's pessimism, events appeared to be recalibrating in Iran's favour. On 20 January 2005, George W. Bush began his second term in office with several personnel changes. Bush's National Security Advisor, Condoleezza Rice, replaced Colin Powell as Secretary of State, and Nick Burns, the US Permanent Representative to NATO, was preferred as Under Secretary of State for Political affairs, over the more conservative Senior Director for Proliferation Strategy, Counterproliferation and Homeland Defence, Robert Joseph. To the increasingly glum John Bolton, the choice of political director rather than nonproliferation director was an immediate sign of things to come.

Burns, like many in the Bush Administration, was convinced that Iran's nuclear programme would be one of the Administration's great international challenges. As he and Rice travelled across the continent it struck them that at each European capital they visited Iran was the first topic of discussion and the first question at each press conference. Their tour coincided with President Bush's post-inauguration 'fence mending' trip to Europe, in which he encountered much of the same. Both Gerhard Schroeder and Jacques Chirac told the President that the Europeans needed US support for negotiations with Iran. Washington alone had the power to apply suitable pressure on the Islamic Republic to move the political process forward. The Americans now had to finally decide (they had refused the chance in 2003 and 2004) whether to support the European negotiations or not.

Bush and Rice discussed the problem. It was a difficult situation. Both were part of an administration in a self-declared War on Terror and both were well aware that Tehran repressed its own people, was a violator of human rights and funded most of the terrorist groups in the Middle East. Nor did either think Iran's programme was benign. One of the most interesting things that Burns ever experienced in government was that he never met a diplomat or official (from any country) who doubted that Iran was seeking a nuclear weapons capability. It was a given in international politics.[26] But pervasive anxiety that a nuclear Iran would change the balance of power negatively against the West and the moderate Arab world could not be ignored. Bush's first term had been full of talk of regime change without result and

211

there was a strong belief that the use of military force was fraught with difficulties. The regime was strong; it wasn't going to disappear overnight, and Washington was already engaged in wars in Afghanistan and Iraq; a third war in the greater Middle East was seen as too much for any country to bear. Moreover, Washington's three closest European allies were now telling them that US support for the process was crucial. The logic for a change of tack was overwhelming: 30 years of not talking had achieved nothing.[27]

The decision was made to support the European negotiations and to seek to work, with Europe, towards eventual negotiations in which they ultimately might take part. Rice made Burns point man on the negotiations and asked him to make it his top priority as soon as he was sworn into office in March 2005. Diplomacy over war was the simple rationale behind the decision taken in those early months of 2005 but it did not eliminate the military option for Washington. As a matter of statecraft and strategy, Burns and Rice believed it imperative to leave the threat of force, very publicly, on the table. If negotiations were to take place, Iran needed to be serious, for which it needed an awareness of the possible consequences of its actions. Burns had a clear strategy in mind: to tell the Iranians they had two paths. One path offered them Western co-operation that amounted even to civil nuclear aid, all incorporated within a possible US offer to negotiate directly and bilaterally with Iran for the first time in 30 years. If Iran chose not to grasp this opportunity, the other path was strong sanctions and the possible use of military force. Washington would make clear that it judged Iranian acquisition of a nuclear weapons capability to be so detrimental to its interests and so potentially destructive to peace in the wider world that despite the problems in Iraq and Afghanistan it would consider that option.[28]

That two-path strategy became the template for possible nuclear negotiations with Iran – in essence, the Americans now formalized the 'carrot and stick' approach that Bolton had so loathed – but Burns felt there was something more at stake than just the nuclear file. As a career diplomat he considered Iran to be the most unusual relationship Washington had with any country in the world, and he could not attribute this simply to the bad blood between the countries. Washington had a liaison office in Havana, Cuba, despite famously bad relations with Fidel Castro, and it had maintained embassies throughout the entire Cold War in both Moscow and Beijing. American diplomats had even talked on several important occasions to the North Koreans.

Burns saw an extraordinarily icy relationship between two countries completely opposed to each other in the greater Middle East, the tinderbox of world politics. He considered it irresponsible for the USA to even think about the use of military force against a country with which it had had no contact for three decades: diplomacy had to be exhausted first. And if the USA tried diplomacy and failed, it would actually be better off. Washington would have much greater international credibility to turn to Russia and China and the Arab Governments, say it had tried, and urge them to support the toughest possible sanctions against Tehran.

Diplomatically, the change was almost immediate. Within weeks of Rice's arrival at the State Department, Jenkins attended the March IAEA Board. He was immediately struck by a change in American tone that he never quite understood. It was as if while Rice was at the White House she was determined to make life impossible for the State Department, and once she was at the State Department she was suddenly the embodiment of sweet reason. John Bolton's simultaneous move away from State to the UN created an almost 'new' Washington that to someone not privy to the internal US discussions was baffling. When it came to the American turn to make an intervention on the Iranian issue, it was much more dispassionate and measured than any Jenkins had heard over the previous two years. Moreover, the head of the American Delegation, who had been positively icy when he had tried to talk to her the previous November, had suddenly become much friendlier.

* * *

The singular tragedy of 30 years of Iranian–US relations is timing. As Washington seemed to be overcoming its longstanding antipathy, the Iranians were finally getting fed up. The EU-3 had continued negotiations into mid-2005 in Paris, London and Geneva only for Iran to reject any offer that did not address enrichment. In March 2005 in Paris the Iranians put forward an informal proposal that would allow them to resume uranium enrichment within a matter of months. The proposal was for a four-phased approach which, in its second, key, phase, called for the 'assembly, installation and testing' of 3,000 centrifuges in Natanz. In return, they were ready to offer what some on the European side regarded as several rather useful, confidence-building and additional safeguard measures – these included a permanent onsite inspector presence and a written promise that Iran would never seek to withdraw from the NPT. But the Europeans remained determined to prevent any continuation of the Iranian enrichment programme. Jenkins and his counterparts promised to go away and think about it. But he suspected the Iranians realized that the answer was 'no'.[29]

The USA, meanwhile, had decided to begin to try to engage and now needed to announce this decision and get things moving. On 30 May 2005, Rice called John Bolton (newly installed as Washington's UN Ambassador) into her office in Washington: 'John,' she said, 'You're not going to like this.' She proceeded to inform him of the change to the US–Iran policy, which Bolton took to be at 'the behest' of the Europeans and their complaints that Washington's unwillingness to sit down with Iran was preventing a resolution of the crisis. Rice told him exactly what had been decided: that Washington was now prepared to sit down along with the Europeans and have direct discussions with Iran so long as they ceased their uranium-enrichment programme.[30]

Bolton was sceptical about the change of tack. In particular, he was dismayed by the offer to actually sit at the negotiating table with Iran. Bolton didn't think a US presence or absence would make the slightest bit of difference because there was never any doubt in anybody's mind that the EU-3 were speaking for the USA. But Rice had made her decision and it would be announced the very next day at a press conference. He was disappointed but not surprised. As far as he was concerned it was consistent with the change she had made at the very beginning of her tenure as Secretary of State, to explicitly endorse the European position, something that, for all his faults, Powell had never done.[31]

That evening Rice invited Bolton together with National Security Advisor Steve Hadley, Nick Burns and Senior Director for Proliferation Strategy, Counterproliferation and Homeland Defence Robert Joseph to a dinner at the Aqua Royal restaurant in the Watergate Hotel in Washington DC, where she kept an apartment. The purpose of the dinner was to decide which conservative journalists Joseph and Bolton would call to pitch the new policy. Bolton didn't want to do it but he was being told not asked; and so, in silent protest at yet another 'carrot' without an attendant 'stick', he ordered carrot soup. Only Joseph got the joke.

After dinner, Bolton returned to New York. One of his responsibilities was to meet with Iran's Ambassador to the UN, Javad Zarif, to give him a copy of the speech that Rice would deliver to announce the change in policy. He called up the Iranian Embassy and asked the Ambassador for a meeting. The two men agreed to meet but, in a possible taste of the difficulties to come, after checking with Tehran, Zarif pulled out. So Bolton called again and told him that he had instructions to deliver the speech to him while Zarif clearly had instructions not to meet with him. What would they do? After a little more palaver, they decided that Bolton would messenger the text of Secretary Rice's speech over to the Iranian mission to the UN. But Zarif insisted on an explicit agreement that they made clear they had not actually met, which Bolton guessed Zarif needed more than he did.[32] The USA was now officially on board. And together with EU-3 it opted to wait for the June 2005 presidential election, gambling on a victory for former President Hashemi Rafsanjani, a man with a reputation for pragmatism and, importantly, the devil they knew.

CHAPTER 14

ENTER AHMADINEJAD: REVERSING INTO THE FUTURE – 2002–5

Almost double was the margin by which the Mayor of Tehran, Mahmoud Ahmadinejad, defeated Hashemi Rafsanjani in the June 2005 presidential elections. Ahmadinejad, then an international unknown, made his name as a populist and conservative Mayor of Tehran. A blacksmith's son from the dusty village of Aradan in northern Iran, he was four when his father changed the family name from 'Sabourjian' or 'Sabaghian' (from the root 'Sabor', Persian for thread painter, a luminously rural – read low class – name) to avoid discrimination when the family moved to the capital. 'Ahmadinejad' ('from the race of Ahmad' – one of Mohammad's names) was chosen to show the family's piety. Rural, working class, devout: Ahmadinejad is a man of the early revolution. To emphasize his pious credentials he held his first cabinet meeting as President at the Imam Reza shrine at Mashhad, one of Shi'i Islam's holiest sites.

During a populist election campaign based on Islamic and revolutionary principles, Ahmadinejad targeted religious conservatives and the poor; ironically enough, his campaign slogan 'It's possible and we can do it' would find an echo in the jangling vacuity of Barack Obama's 'yes we can'. He ran on an anti-corruption platform, promising to put Iran's oil revenues on people's dinner tables. Crucial to nuclear policy was his overarching international posture. He was the only presidential candidate who spoke out against future relations with the USA, accused the UN of bias against the Islamic world and defended the nuclear programme, claiming 'arrogant powers' wanted to limit Iran's industrial and technological development. With Rice and Burns now at the State Department it was also catastrophically ill-timed. His election caused consternation among the Europeans; the Iranians quickly assured them that their nuclear policy would remain unchanged. In a private letter, Rohani urged EU-3 officials to keep negotiations moving by accepting the first phase of Iran's March 2005 proposal: a resumption of uranium conversion activities under IAEA surveillance at Isfahan.

While Ahmadinejad settled in, things moved forward. The Iranians, frustrated at the lack of progress after nearly two years of suspension, were in no mood to continue along what they considered to be an increasingly fruitless path. Negotiations broke down in early August 2005 with Tehran's frustration at the Europeans' refusal to respond to some new Iranian initiatives, which, while they were good confidence-building measures, involved a resumption of enrichment (even if only its early stages). When, on 8 August 2005, the Iranians announced that they would resume production of feed material for the enrichment process, and asked the IAEA to remove the seals from the Isfahan plant (where the feed material was produced) and restart uranium conversion activities, there was no going back. The change in policy had nothing to do with Ahmadinejad; Khamenei had just lost patience and, despite giving Rowhani his blessing (not to mention protecting him from hardliner attack), decided that Iran should no longer compromise on enrichment.[1] The Iranians rejected the EU-3 package even before Ahmadinejad was inaugurated, and Rowhani made it plain that as far as he was concerned European inflexibility was behind the decision:[2]

We even suggested entrusting the IAEA with the task of devising a formula of objective guarantees for the resumption of enrichment activities in Iran ... But it is clear that negotiations are not proceeding as called for in the Paris agreement because your side has continued to refrain from responding substantively to our proposals, in whole or even in part, or to present your views on objective guarantees for the exercise of Iran's rights under the Treaty without discrimination.

The EU-3 attempted to clarify their position in an extensive document distributed on 9 August in which they recognized and agreed to support Iran's right to develop a civilian nuclear power programme, but Iran's leadership described the proposal as an insult for which the EU-3 should apologize.[3] Some more exchanges made it clear that the Iranians weren't going to back down, and a swift exchange of emails between Jenkins, his two colleagues and their respective ministries resulted in an agreement to, finally, find Iran in non-compliance.

Perhaps mindful of the problems that were about to arise with the resumption of uranium enrichment (or, more cynically, with the new President), Iran began something of a PR offensive. On 10 August 2005, in a statement to an emergency IAEA meeting, Iranian nuclear negotiator Cyrus Naseri read a statement to the IAEA Board of Governors which outlined the supposed religious prohibition on nuclear weapons:[4]

> The Leader of the Islamic Republic of Iran, Ayatollah Ali Khamenei has issued the fatwa that the production, stockpiling, and use of nuclear weapons are forbidden under Islam and that the Islamic Republic of Iran shall never acquire these weapons. President Mahmoud Ahmadinejad, who took office just recently, in his inaugural address reiterated that his government is against weapons of mass destruction and will only pursue nuclear activities in the peaceful domain.

Khamenei appeared to have issued the *fatwa* at Friday prayers in September 2004.[5] But only a few weeks later, in November 2004, Iranian legislator Hojatoleslam Mohammad Taqi Rahbar claimed that the *fatwa* was 'not expedient', because Iran was in a region of proliferators and further claimed that there were no 'Shari'a or legal restrictions on having such [nuclear] weapons as a deterrent'.[6] Certainly, the *fatwa* was a change from Khamenei's reported comments at the 1984 meeting. Either way, Iran was preparing for what was coming, and the Paris Agreement was now officially dead.

* * *

Iran's abrogation of the Paris Agreement marked the end of the third phase of nuclear negotiations. In the end, Iran suspended enrichment for two years and, from its point of view, received nothing in return. The Europeans got a two-year delay in Iranian enrichment but the longer-term consequences of the Tehran and Paris Agreements must be seen as negative. They forever killed the idea of suspension in Iranian minds, and those more 'moderate' figures within the establishment who advocated co-operation would forever have the agreements thrown back at them by the hardliners: we suspended once and it brought us nothing, they would repeatedly argue. What the Europeans seemingly never understood was the centrality of Khamenei to the agreements. He had personally backed Rowhani's decision to suspend, shielding him from hardliner accusations of backtracking or *sazesh* (a very loaded term in Persian). Just as he had appointed Aghazadeh in 1997, sick at the slow pace of technological progress, Khamenei was always the prime decision-maker on nuclear policy. His natural anti-Western instincts meant that any suspension was always going to be fragile – and the perceived lack of reciprocity from the Europeans only confirmed his prejudices about the folly of trusting the West.

But there is a second, perhaps more negative, result of the agreements. On 30 September, just over a month after Iran requested that the seals be broken at Natanz, Rowhani made a speech to the Supreme Cultural Revolution Council during which he made clear that his plan to deal with the crisis had always been based on the belief that referral to the Security Council was inevitable.

Such a belief may have stemmed from a Khomeinist worldview of all international institutions as inherently untrustworthy, but it does cast the two-year suspension in a slightly different light. If referral was inevitable then Tehran did gain something from the agreements: it delayed the inevitable by two years. When this is considered in the context of Rowhani's assertion that Iran only suspended what it had mastered already and that, moreover, during the suspension it made great progress on various nuclear activities in preparation for the resumption of enrichment, then Iran gained quite considerably. In mid-2005 Rowhani also submitted a report to Khatami that, he argued, vindicated his nuclear policy:

> In the last six years ... the valuable work of the National Atomic Agency as well as the genius and the efforts of the country's scientists have gradually reached a level that has *forced* the World to believe in Iran's nuclear capabilities. Today Iran is the possessor of indigenous nuclear technology that derives its existence from its people and belongs to the people. And because it is indigenous, it cannot be taken away ...

Iran, he claimed, had forced the West to take its capabilities seriously, and it is the question of capabilities that becomes the issue. Rowhani mentioned nuclear weapons only once in his speech to the council – in relation to Iran's mastering of the fuel cycle. In what must be regarded as a critical statement, he explained that the only thing (as he saw it) that stood between mastering enrichment technology to civil levels and enriching to weapons-grade level uranium (the difference between enriching to 3.5 per cent and to above 80 per cent, which is technologically minimal) is a political decision to make that transition.[7] Iran had spent two years pushing on with all nuclear activities not covered by its suspension agreements and (as the following months would make clear) was now approaching the ability to master the civil nuclear fuel cycle. Obviously, enriching to weapons-grade levels to try to build a bomb would be impossible without throwing the IAEA inspectors out of Iran and obtaining the necessary weaponization technology, but Iranian thinking here was instructive, and worrying.

In his book *gharbzadegi* (*Westoxification*) Jalal Al-e Ahmad had argued that just as Iranians had to be vigilant about the pernicious effects of *Westoxification* so they should understand the values of the West and, more importantly, appropriate its technologies for their own benefit. This is how Iran would make its journey into modernity, but on its own terms: preserving its Islamic, Iranian identity and forcing the world to accept it for what it was. Forty years later, Rowhani told Khatami that Iran had done just that.

THE NEW PRESIDENT

Ahmadinejad's first act in the nuclear sphere was to appoint conservative Ali Larijani to replace Rowhani, whom he deemed responsible for conducting 'frightened' negotiations with the Europeans, as Secretary of the Supreme National Security Council and chief nuclear negotiator. A 'popular and fundamentalist government', he declared the day after his election, would quickly change the situation in favour of Iran; it certainly changed its negotiating stance. Rowhani and his team were interested in both achieving the fuel cycle and avoiding Security Council referral. As far as the Europeans could tell, the new team consisted of people concerned with the fuel cycle alone.[8]

The Europeans wanted the IAEA Board to meet in early September but the Russians suggested they first have a ministerial week in New York for the UN General Assembly to get to know Ahmadinejad (who had been sworn in on 6 August) and speak to Iranian officials. Russia would now be needed to pass tougher action on Iran, so the Europeans and Americans agreed. It was a disaster. Straw met Ahmadinejad and the two did not get on; there was tension everywhere and the mood was accordingly sombre as the world's diplomats filed into the UN building in New York on 18 September to hear Ahmadinejad introduce himself, comprehensively, as Iran's new President in his first speech to the General Assembly. No doubt to the inward despair of the listening Europeans, it became clear that Khomeinism at its most atavistic would now underpin all nuclear negotiations. The world where 'arrogant' powers bullied others, the West's role in the 1953 coup and Iraq's Western-supplied use of WMDs against Iran during the 1980–8 Iran–Iraq war would be the prism that would inform Iranian policy. And no one should be in doubt as to Iran's position as regards the fuel cycle at the heart of the world's concerns:[9]

> ... peaceful use of nuclear energy without possession of nuclear fuel cycle is an empty proposition. Nuclear power plants can indeed lead to total dependence of countries and peoples if they need to rely for their fuel on coercive powers ... The history of dependence on oil in oil-rich countries under domination is an experiment that no independent country is willing to repeat. Those hegemonic powers, who consider scientific and technological progress of independent and free nations as a challenge to their monopoly ... have misrepresented Iran's healthy and fully safeguarded technological endeavors in the nuclear field as pursuit of nuclear weapons. This is nothing but a propaganda ploy.

Ahmadinejad also played to the developing world and attacked the NPT, namely the failure of Article IV to deliver on its stated goal and the inherent problem of dual-use technology:

> How can one talk about human rights and at the same time blatantly deny many the inalienable right to have access to science and technology with applications in medicine, industry and energy and through force and intimidation hinder their progress and development? Can nations be deprived of scientific and technological progress through the threat of use of force and based on mere allegations of possibility of military diversion?

He then reaffirmed the religious prohibition on nuclear weapons; Iran's readiness to engage in 'serious partnership' on its uranium-enrichment programme; and that, in keeping with Iran's 'inalienable right' to the nuclear fuel cycle, 'co-operation' with the

IAEA would continue. Policy would be formulated with the historical lesson that nuclear fuel-delivery contracts were unreliable and Iran therefore considered it reasonable to receive objective guarantees for its uranium-enrichment programme. Diplomatic crassness then morphed into the gratuitously offensive; turning to 9/11, he wondered how it was that the USA's huge intelligence gathering and security organizations failed to prevent such an extensive operation.

Ahmadinejad's speech so disgusted the Europeans that any residual reluctance over Iran's Security Council referral evaporated. But ElBaradei desperately wanted to avoid referral, and the run-up to the September 2005 Board was complicated by his determination to try to prevent it if he could. Whenever he was asked for his opinion in private conversations, he would make clear that by his analysis no good would come of sending Iran to the Security Council. It was clear that Iraq weighed heavily on him; he did not want another country referred to the Security Council on suspicion of developing WMDs.[10] His efforts meant that the European side had to work doubly hard to persuade waverers, mainly the Non-Aligned Movement, that Security Council referral was the right thing to do.

Now Russia and China began to get involved. While there was no sanctions threat, both were content to let pressure build on Iran to answer outstanding questions, but referral was a different thing altogether. Both had expressed early misgivings at the prospect of sanctions, and, while neither could actually block a Resolution (all that was needed was the support of 18 members – a majority – of the IAEA Board), the Europeans wanted to pass the Resolution by consensus. The proposed Resolution would make clear that Iranian non-compliance was viewed as a 'threat to peace and security' and should therefore be considered under chapter 7 of the UN Charter, which can result in the authorization of military action; and given the Iraq precedent, they wanted unanimity. Although the Russians tried to avert this, they knew, in their heart of hearts, that it was inevitable. The Iranians had been seriously non-compliant since 2003 and the only reason this had not been reported was because of their willingness to suspend. Now that it was no longer an option, the deal was off, and the Russians were nothing if not realists, and pessimistic ones at that.

Moscow had until then largely avoided direct involvement in negotiations, having little faith in their success (particularly without US participation) and preferring to maintain good relations with both sides.[11] In fact, thus far both Russia and China's main contribution to negotiations had been somewhat dubious. The Europeans naturally had to show them all draft resolutions for their comments, which always came back with lots of changes. Eventually the Europeans realized what was happening: they would give the Russians and Chinese a draft, which they would then show to Iranians, who would ask for offending words and passages to be deleted, which the Chinese and Russians would come back with as their own.[12]

Now the Russians realized that things were escalating, which didn't benefit anyone. Joining forces with developing world stalwarts of Brazil, India and South Africa, they spent the best part of five days in Vienna trying to persuade the Iranians to accept a formula that would have allayed international concerns and averted referral. The process, it seemed, was a struggle. Jenkins enjoyed good relations with his Russian colleague whose lugubrious face and manner belied a sharp wit (and who, unlike his Chinese counterpart, was teaseable) and the two met after the negotiations. He told Jenkins that the five days had been among the hardest in his diplomatic career – and he'd negotiated with the North Koreans. Jenkins asked him why he thought the Iranians were so difficult. The problem with these guys, he was told, is that they take their orders from Allah. The Russian was a great chess player and set out to him his analysis of the situation as a chess game: the way things stood, he said, they were playing for a draw in the hope that their adversary would make a mistake.[13]

The September Board started with a European resolution of Iranian non-compliance. Rice and Burns, though eager to support negotiations, were pleased that action had been taken, or so they thought. In practice, the Europeans made them wait another six months. Mid week, they introduced a change into the resolution to hold off from reporting the non-compliance finding to allow Iran time to influence the report's timing and content. While evoking the possibility of Security Council action, the resolution stopped short of setting a concrete time-frame for any such action (Russia abstained). Unfortunately, Iran's response to the resolution – as it would increasingly become – was more defiance. Only five days later, on 29 September, the Majlis passed a draft law that suspended the Additional Protocol until Iran's right to 'use atomic energy for peaceful purposes' was acknowledged.

Now the Russians were really concerned, and in October 2005 put forward a proposal to solve the enrichment impasse, similar to the Shah's Eurodif deal. Iran would not enrich uranium on its soil; instead, it would be allowed a large financial stake in a Russia-based enrichment facility from which it would import enriched fuel. London, Paris, Berlin and even Washington all approved and encouraged the Russians, who worked very hard at it over several weekends of negotiations between Russian Deputy Foreign Minister, Sergei Kisliak, and Larijani in Moscow that extended into February 2006. In the end, Iran refused to sacrifice 'self-sufficiency' and Hamid Reza Asefi, an Iranian Foreign Ministry spokesman, told the Russians that Iran would never give up its research and development programme.[14]

WEAPONIZATION?

And it was about to get worse. The dual-use nature of nuclear technology makes assessing whether a state is going for a bomb complex enough, but matters are even more problematic because there is a little understood but significant difference between the overall process of developing a nuclear weapon, which includes broader areas such as uranium enrichment (that also have civil uses), and the more specific process of weaponization (obtaining the necessary technology to create a nuclear bomb). Even when Iran admitted to buying illicit centrifuges from the Khan network, it could argue that it merely wanted to enrich uranium to create nuclear fuel and was being denied this technology on the open market – it was not only a step to a bomb.

But Iran had raised concerns the previous year when IAEA inspectors discovered evidence of Iranian experiments with the production of Polonium-210, which could be used for military purposes.[15] And on 18 November 2005, ElBaradei submitted a report to the Board citing documents from the late 1970s to late 1980s acquired from the Khan network on how to enrich to weapons-grade uranium and chemically convert this into metal components for use in nuclear weapons. Among the documents was a 15-page document on the casting and machining of enriched uranium metal into hemispheres (components of nuclear weapons), which was identical to one Iran had shown to the IAEA.[16] It was a fluke. The Iranians had shown it to an inspector by mistake; they claimed that they never requested the document, that Khan must have included it by mistake along with the P-1 centrifuge documentation sold to Naraghi in 1987, and that they had never used it. Some of the developing world countries believed (or said they believed) them; the Europeans raised their eyebrows.[17] All their experts confirmed that the 'hemispheres' document could only be of use to detonate a bomb. The outstanding issue was whether Iran received the entire collection of documents and if so, like Libya, it also received the nuclear-weapon designs contained in them. There was, many argued, no logical reason to think it had not. Bolton, in particular, argued that the report proved Iran was going for nuclear weapons and repeatedly pointed out that there was simply no other explanation for the data that the IAEA itself had accumulated.[18]

THE BIRTH OF THE P5+1

It was all very worrying. On 10 January 2006 Iranian officials broke the IAEA seals on the centrifuges at Natanz, gave them to IAEA inspectors and announced that it would resume research and development activities at the plant. Tehran had crossed the

EU/US redline. The decision to resume nuclear work did not violate Iran's Safeguards Agreement, but it was inconsistent with the IAEA's request that it re-establish suspension of all enrichment and reprocessing-related activity, and as a political statement it was clear. Burns and Rice had always known this was possible but considered it an outrageous refutation of everything the UN stood for, by a UN member state. There was also considerable anger across European capitals. A sense of resolve spread across the coalition that Iran be made to pay: tough sanctions would be passed.[19]

Burns and Rice decided that now was the time to get more involved and to work internationally with the Security Council as well as Germany to apply substantial diplomatic and economic pressure on Tehran. At the end of January 2006 the pair went to London for what turned out to be a marathon meeting of Foreign Ministers hosted by Jack Straw at the Foreign Secretary's residence at Carlton Gardens. The meeting lasted until two in the morning. Arguments, principally between Rice and Russian Foreign Minister Sergei Lavrov, dominated the evening. Burns and Rice kept repeating the same point: the need for the Security Council members not to let Iran get away with a wilful violation of everything the UN stood for.[20]

The meeting, though fractious, finally resulted in an agreement among the six Foreign Ministers to unite. January 2006 was a momentous time in the nuclear crisis because it reordered the coalition trying to prevent Iran from becoming a nuclear-weapons power into its most powerful expression: the P5+1 (the five Security Council powers + Germany). Burns thought the alignment of Britain, France, Germany and the USA throughout 2005 had been adequate, but he calculated that the addition of Russia and China would show Iran that driving a wedge between Russia and China and Europe and the USA would be more difficult. (In this he was correct, and the coalition proved strong enough to push through several Security Council resolutions against Iran over the following years.)

The results were immediate. On 4 February 2006, the IAEA Board expressed 'serious concern' over Iran's nuclear ambitions, as well as the 'absence of confidence that Iran's nuclear program is exclusively for peaceful purposes', and finally referred Iran to the Security Council with the resolution passing 27 votes to 3. In yet another effort to gain time for last-minute diplomacy – and to ensure Russian and Chinese support – the resolution postponed Security Council consideration for a month to allow for renewed deliberation by the Board in early March. The Europeans were delighted because they got 27 positive votes instead of 22 (the three who voted against – Cuba, Syria and Venezuela – they believed required no comment). They considered it a powerful message to the Iranians, who had miscalculated if they believed that the Non-Aligned Movement was not persuadable. In response, Tehran immediately announced it would resume uranium enrichment and halt application of the Additional Protocol, thus disallowing IAEA surprise inspections and inspections of non-declared sites. On 14 February, Iran said it had begun small-scale uranium enrichment.

The broader coalition, now comprised of these six countries, still faced problems, the main one being that the road to sanctions had started at a time China was becoming Iran's principle trade partner and the European governments were decreasing their trade. Russia was of course already a nuclear partner of Iran on the Bushehr plant and a leading exporter of arms to the country. The Americans suspected that Russia and China had a fairly cynical approach to the whole process – paying lip service to international effort to stop the Iranians, voting for sanctions resolutions – after much cajoling – while effectively undercutting the European and American effort with trade links and arms deals.

THE 1 JUNE 2006 OFFER

By the spring of 2006 it had become clear to both Burns and Rice that despite Washington's increased support of negotiations, its lack of actual contact with Iran meant that it would forever remain 'outside of the room'. Rice was adamant that it was time to sit down with Iran, specifically that she, as Secretary of State, be at the table with the Iranians in order to give diplomacy a chance. Again, it was not an easy decision. A group met at Rice's apartment at the Watergate Hotel in mid-May to talk it out over dinner. By the end of the evening the great majority of people thought it was the right thing to do, but most importantly Bush and Rice had decided that the USA would speak to Iran face-to-face.[21]

At a joint press conference on 1 June in Vienna, Burns and Rice offered direct, bilateral negotiations to the Iranian government for the first time in almost 30 years – with the important caveat that it suspend enrichment and permit more intrusive international inspections to resume. They had every expectation that Iran would accept. Both Burns and Rice publicly stated that the USA would meet Iran any place, at any time, and that US Secretary of State Condoleezza Rice herself would personally be present to sit down with the Iranian leadership.

Iran's Foreign Minister, Manouchehr Mottaki (who had replaced Kamal Kharazi on 24 August 2005), replied that Iran was ready to accept the US offer but rejected the condition that it first suspend enrichment.[22] The truth was that, as ever, Iranian diplomacy was hamstrung by internal conflict. While a hardline now predominated, Tehran's endemic factionalism had not evaporated but, with such a divisive President, only increased. There was general consensus on Iran's right to pursue a nuclear programme, but disagreement on how negotiations should be handled.[23] There were broadly two camps. The first, grouped around the Supreme Leader and Ahmadinejad, favoured an uncompromising pursuit of continued uranium enrichment regardless of the political cost. Its members had a deep suspicion of the West, which they considered to be in decline – a prognosis that the Iraq war had only validated. Critically, their continuing ability to avoid sanctions with the help of Russia and China had convinced them that they simply needed to continue as they were.[24]

The second camp, while operating within the same ideological framework, believed there was something to be gained from a degree of co-operation. Somewhat ironically (given that he had replaced Rowhani because his views supposedly tallied more closely with Ahmadinejad's) it was primarily grouped around Ali Larijani who, while adamant on Iran's 'inalienable right to a nuclear fuel cycle', also judged that diplomacy should not be abandoned – a point he had articulated comprehensively in an interview on Iranian TV the previous year. 'We have a right to nuclear technology,' he had argued. But, he had also pointed out, 'a country's survival depends on its political and diplomatic ties. You can't live in isolation ... the new government must pursue the national demand for nuclear technology, but must make use of all diplomatic tools as well.'[25]

The question was whether he would be allowed to make use of these tools. Despite the US offer, matters were complicated on both sides and there were still no official channels of communication between the two (with the Swiss continuing to act as intermediary). Washington still needed the Europeans. Beginning in June 2006, Javier Solana, the EU's Foreign Policy Chief, acting on behalf of the USA, Europe, Russia and China, began a series of conversations with Larijani in which he offered him US negotiations several times throughout June and July 2006.

The offer of direct talks was domestically problematic for Iran. The regime's anti-Western (and in particular anti-US) posture was critical to its political legitimacy, which descended directly from its supposed struggle to uphold the values of the revolution in a hostile world; and there was no struggle without the Great Satan. Bush's anti-Iranian rhetoric had always been a political boon: it allowed the regime to distract from its oppression and economic incompetence (though not by any means completely) and turn Iran's own nuclear misbehaviour into a national struggle against a self-avowed enemy. People otherwise unfavourable to the government rallied to its cause on nationalistic grounds; Iranians might not like Tehran, but they would fight if it were attacked. But Ahmadinejad could not say that the Great Satan was only interested in attacking Iran if it wanted to sit down and talk. Larijani could only hint that, provided there was no pressure, Iran might be ready to offer a two-month voluntary suspension, but even this came to nothing, most likely stifled by Ahmadinejad.

Throughout June and July the Iranians repeatedly turned down direct talks. The Americans finally extracted a promise from him to meet at the September 2006 UNGA. Burns and Rice waited in New York for Larijani to arrive.[26] He failed to show.

* * *

While Ahmadinejad rebuffed all offers of dialogue, Iranian scientists continued onwards. In April 2006 Iran successfully enriched uranium to 3.5 per cent (the level required for the nuclear fuel used to power reactors), and Ahmadinejad pronounced Iran a 'nuclear state'.[27] Enrichment to 3.5 per cent carried real significance because the energy needed to enrich uranium from its natural state of 0.7 per cent to 3.5 per cent is around 80 per cent of the energy required to enrich it to around 80 per cent, which is weapons grade (at which point it becomes HEU). In theory, all the Iranians now had to do to create HEU was recycle the 3.5 per cent uranium through the centrifuges at Natanz until it reached the desired levels. Such a step was not without technical difficulties and would be almost impossible without throwing out IAEA inspectors, but Iranian progress was disconcerting.[28] Even more so, when, in an echo of Rowhani's declaration that once a state had mastered civil enrichment the difference between this and enrichment for weapons purposes was merely a political decision, Ahmadinejad declared that Iran's attainment of peaceful nuclear energy could 'change the world equation'. Khamenei stated his case baldly: the Islamic Republic had made its decision, and 'God willing, and with patience and power, it would continue on its path'.[29]

THE FAILURE OF NEGOTIATIONS: SANCTIONS

But the USA had made a decision too. And it took two and a half months of negotiations (from the end of September until early December) to implement it. The P5+1 began talks at the UN in late September 2006; all agreed that Iran had refused to negotiate, had refused the USA's historic offer to sit down and talk, and had, in fact, thrown every overture back at those trying to find a diplomatic solution. Burns and Rice were left with no choice but to go down the alternative path of sanctions. The US delegation argued for the type of tough sanctions that would force Iran to return to the table immediately to avoid any more, but they were met with inevitable Russian and Chinese resistance. It was a difficult situation. On the one hand, Burns wanted to pass tough sanctions; on the other, he wanted to maintain P5+1 unity so that the Iranians knew that they could not be divided now that sanctions were at hand. For this, once again, Russia and China were needed.

Bolton, now Washington's Ambassador to the UN, also took part in the discussions, but he suffered none of Burns's angst because he had given up. He couldn't even begin to count the number of meetings he had had with the P5+1 to try to draft various Security Council resolutions, and as far as he was concerned they were all close to useless because the sanctions adopted would be weak due to the Russians and the Chinese. He was tired of playing, as he saw it, the European game of putting the USA on one side and the Russians and Chinese on the other with the Europeans in the favoured position of the middle. He pushed for tough sanctions, and the Russians and the Chinese for limited sanctions: an interminable pantomime without the entertainment. In the end he let the Europeans negotiate and, in order to stay awake, played Brick Breaker on his BlackBerry.[30]

Nevertheless, on 23 December, an agreement was finally reached. Security Council Resolution 1737 mandated all UN member states 'to prevent the supply, sale or transfer ... of all items, materials, equipment, goods and technology which could contribute to Iran's enrichment-related, reprocessing or heavy-water-related activities or to the development of nuclear weapon delivery systems'. Unless Iran suspended all enrichment activities within 60 days, further sanctions would be considered.[31] The resolution surprised the Iranians. Washington calculated that the Iranians still believed that Russia and China might protect them from sanctions and for this reason the resolution carried a psychological as well as political importance.

It was far from perfect, however. Iran's Sino-Russian strategy still held to a degree. The resolution called for travel sanctions against certain Iranian government officials and for the beginnings of economic sanctions, but little more of real substance. Iran immediately condemned the resolution and criticized the Security Council. Playing to the developing world, Iran's UN Ambassador, Javad Zarif, claimed that the Security Council had punished a developing nation for exercising its 'inalienable rights' and accused it of acting at Israel's behest. The sanctions had also not stopped Iranian enrichment; in fact, they had the reverse effect. Iran pressed on with enrichment throughout the latter part of 2006 and into 2007 and, in response, on 24 March 2007, the Security Council adopted Resolution 1747, imposing additional measures aimed at Iran's nuclear and missile programmes.[32] Nonetheless, by September Natanz was running 1,968 centrifuges and had enriched uranium to 3.7 per cent.[33] In November the IAEA confirmed that Iran now did have around 3,000 operational centrifuges, which was another milestone.[34] Once achieved, the Iranians could theoretically produce enough fissile material to produce one bomb per year. In Washington, more voices labelled diplomacy a failure and urged military strikes against Iran.[35]

THE SECOND IRANIAN REBUFF

Still the Americans tried. In June 2007, just before the G8 Summit in Germany, contacts were made with the Iranians to try, once more, to arrange the long-awaited face-to-face talks. The venue would be the UN General Assembly in New York, and the meeting would be minutely choreographed: simultaneously, Iran would temporarily suspend enrichment and the West would suspend sanctions. The plan was that Larijani would come to New York to the Waldorf Astoria. He would meet with the European, Russian and Chinese Foreign Ministers and would accept from them the basis of negotiations; at that point Secretary Rice would enter the room and sit across the table from him and they would have dinner. New York would give Larijani the chance to win the argument in Iran. He would get rid of the hated sanctions, gain the public respect of world leaders and show that Iran was no longer a pariah state.[36]

The Americans were ready. They had formed a negotiating team, done their research on how best to work with the Iranians, thought through the various elements of the negotiations – their timing, their pace, everything. They were quite looking forward to them. On the Friday before the meeting the Iranians sent word that they were bringing a delegation of 300. And none of them had visas. But Rice said to Burns: let's take away any excuse they have not to come. So he called the embassy in Berne in Switzerland and asked them to stay open the entire weekend and issue all the visas, which they did.[37] But only one Iranian arrived in New York and it was not Larijani but Ahmadinejad. The President, it seemed, had won the argument in Tehran. The plane never took off. The 300 people never left Iran; and Larijani never showed up. Rice and Burns waited in New York thinking maybe he would come tomorrow or the next day or the next week.

Larijani had lost. His comparatively moderate position had seen him clash repeatedly with Ahmadinejad and eventually, on 20 October 2007, he resigned, citing 'unsolvable differences' with the President. Ali Akbar Velayati, now a close adviser to the Supreme Leader, said publicly what many felt privately in Tehran – that it would have been better if the resignation had not taken place. There was recognition in Iran that Ahmadinejad had harmed the country's international standing. When Larijani resigned around 180 of the 290 representatives in the Majlis signed a motion supporting him and implicitly criticizing the President. Saeed Jalili, an ideological ally of the President, was chosen to replace him.

The P5+1 now viewed Iran's behaviour as beyond inflammatory, as well as of substantive concern; and in March 2008 the Security Council passed the third round of sanctions against Iran. Resolution 1803 (4 March 2008) extended asset restrictions and travel bans to additional Iranian individuals and companies deemed to be involved in nuclear work; finally banned the sale of 'dual-use' items; and called on governments to withdraw financial backing from companies trading with Iran and monitor the activities of two Iranian banks.[38]

Each round required many months of difficult, sometimes very angry, negotiations, particularly between the Americans and the Russians. Seeing no alternative, Washington also began to pass unilateral sanctions outside of the Security Council, which, without Russian and Chinese interference, hurt Iran the most. Despite the continuing lack of relations, Washington remained antagonist to the Iranian protagonist. Iran feared the USA; it was the only country with sufficient economic power to maim its economy, and Burns felt a responsibility to use this power to forestall the day that Iran became a nuclear-weapon state.[39] The means was to target individual companies and organizations and, eventually, people. On 17 October 2007, Washington designated part of the Revolutionary Guards a 'supporter of terrorism' and a proliferator of WMDs due to its work on ballistic missiles. It also extended unilateral sanctions on the Guards' commercial activities and on several Iranian banks. The EU froze assets of Iran's largest consumer bank, Bank Melli, and extended visa bans to more Iranians involved in nuclear and missile development.

The British and Americans were convinced of the sanctions' efficacy and Iran's economy did worsen throughout the two and a half years they were imposed.[40] Despite possessing 7 per cent of global oil reserves, Tehran has always failed to distribute oil income effectively enough to combat systemic economic problems. In June 2007 countrywide protests erupted after the government imposed petrol rationing amid fears of a new round of sanctions. The sharp downward spiral of oil prices, a large budget deficit and the global banking crisis converged to ensure that Tehran faced severe financial hardship that was only likely to get worse. Independent US financial sanctions further damaged Iranian economic growth and trade, not least by discouraging European investors from dealing with Iranian banks. But the political impact of this pressure was questionable. Many of the

European institutions, barred from doing business with Iran in dollars, merely switched currencies, which, given the increase in the Euro's value relative to the dollar, actually helped Iran's economy.[41] Then there were Russia and China. Since the first round of sanctions in 2006 China had finalized a gas deal with Iran for $3.6 billion, and Russia announced delivery of more defence systems.[42] Tehran was (and has been) able to anticipate and counter any loss in EU trade by shifting the balance of its economic relations eastwards.[43]

More damningly, on a political level, the sanctions did not reverse Iran's nuclear fuel cycle programme or even halt it. The West was in a difficult position. The sanctions did have an effect but as soon as the P5+1 said so publicly (which was necessary to keep the hardliners who wanted to bomb Iran at bay) it only made the Iranians more determined to prove they weren't,[44] just as the White House's bellicose rhetoric enabled the government to turn an issue of treaty adherence into one of national defiance. Ahmadinejad, true to his populist instincts, used sanctions to rally people to his cause and organized demonstrations, which included frequent chanting in favour of Iran's nuclear rights, at which the President announced that Iran's nuclear programme was 'like a train without brakes'. The emotive was again transmuted into the political, and sanctions became not the result of an international dispute but the latest development in a long, unbroken history of oppression from a hostile world. According to Iran's Ambassador to the IAEA, Ali Asghar Soltanieh, Iran now re-fought its war with Saddam:[45]

> We paid a heavy price during the eight years of Saddam's war. We lost thousands of our loved ones in order to protect the geographical borders of Iran. Now we are protecting the scientific and moral borders of Iran. We won't let anyone interfere with our right to acquire scientific knowledge, our sovereignty and independence. This is much more valuable and it will cost more to defend.

And then there was the anger and defiance of the early republic. No one would push Iran around anymore; the sanctions were the

result of the West's fears of a technologically advanced Iran that
asserted itself and flew the flag for the developing world:[46]

> This kind of language is considered a humiliation to us, the language
> used to animals and therefore whoever is using it is condemned and
> considered uncivilized. This is a colonialist mentality [though] it is
> couched in more modern language, calling it a dual track policy of
> negotiations and sanctions . . . The West has to cope with a strong
> Iran, a country with thousands of years of civilization that is now the
> master of enrichment. I know it is hard for them to understand, to
> digest this, but it is the reality. Iran will never give up this enrich-
> ment technology, at any price.

The regime had, once again, managed to transmute an issue of
compliance with its non-proliferation obligations into one of nationalism and self-determination. To the Iranians in the street,
fed by skilful government propaganda, Washington was trying to
deny them their legitimate right to peaceful nuclear energy in order to 'keep them down', in the best tradition of imperialist behaviour towards the Islamic world. Iranians, now more than ever,
saw nuclear energy as a symbol of their country's independence
and a totem of modernity and progress. Meanwhile, demagogues
in America and Europe painted a picture of 'Atomic Ayatollahs'
desperate to bring nuclear Armageddon. The nuclear crisis was, as
ever, a battleground of competing narratives: on the one hand, of
fanatical, rogue Iran determined to bring nuclear Armageddon;
on the other, of the perfidious, imperialist West determined to
hold back an Islamic nation and block its just advancement.

ENRICHMENT AND WEAPONIZATION?

Nonetheless, Iran now tried to lessen the pressure. On 21 August
2007, Iran and the IAEA had finalized a 'Modalities Agreement'
that listed all the outstanding issues on the programme, which included a uranium mine at Gchine, the alleged experiments with
plutonium and uranium metal, and the use of Polonium-210.
Also at issue were the so-called 'Alleged Studies' – information

contained on a laptop that the USA had acquired in early 2004 from a 'walk-in' source, allegedly proving that Iran had engaged in high-explosives testing, had sought to manufacture 'green salt' (UF_4) and modify the nose cone of its Shahab-3 missile to carry a nuclear warhead – with Iran declaring the documents fakes. In 2005 Washington had shared the contents with intelligence agencies of several allies, and in 2006 the IAEA presented some of the laptop's contents to an audience of international diplomats. (The documents were in electronic form on a computer hard drive and, while print-outs were shared, the hard drive itself was not given to the IAEA.) Under the agreement, Iran committed to addressing the allegations 'upon receiving all related documents' as a goodwill gesture. The Modalities Agreement was supposed to address all these issues, which would allow Iran to be free of weaponization suspicion. A year later, on 22 February 2008, the IAEA reported that it had no evidence of a current, undeclared nuclear programme in Iran, and all of the remaining issues listed in the Modalities Agreement regarding past undeclared nuclear activities had been resolved with the exception of the 'Alleged Studies' issue.[47] It was breathing space, but not much.

THE NON-DIPLOMATIC ALTERNATIVE: MILITARY STRIKES

The failure of sanctions to halt enrichment combined with fears of Iranian weaponization increased calls for military action against the programme. With sanctions seemingly ineffective, Bush's rhetoric heightened, and in summer 2007 he warned that Iran's pursuit of the atomic bomb could lead to a nuclear holocaust, and promised to confront Tehran before it was 'too late'.[48] He also directed the Pentagon to study what would be necessary for a strike 'to stop the bomb clock', at least temporarily.[49] But despite the talk, there were deep misgivings inside the Pentagon about a military strike. US generals believed that with the USA fighting two wars a third would be a huge stretch. And nobody wanted to do it.[50] The truth was, with all the other problems, the USA would most likely not want to get involved; if they did, it would most likely be if Israel took unilateral action.

Meanwhile, Tel Aviv was getting worried. Ahmadinejad's election had understandably hardened Israel's already hawkish position towards the nuclear programme. The new President's descriptions of Israel as a 'tumour' to be 'wiped off the map' and of the Holocaust as a 'myth' caused understandable consternation among the Israelis; Tel Aviv had described Iran's nuclear programme as an existential threat for years, and Ahmadinejad's election only made the perceived threat more immediate. Given the programme's progress, and the failure of diplomacy, Israeli officials argued that the danger had grown, not receded.[51] Israeli Prime Minister Ehud Olmert labelled Ahmadinejad a 'psychopath' who talked like Hitler and assured the Israeli electorate that Iran would never get a nuclear bomb.

Publicly, the Israelis supported diplomacy (the Prime Minister's office would not directly refer to military strikes, merely stating that Israel left 'all options on the table').[52] But there was a belief that sanctions needed to be ramped up dramatically, and some argued for full blockading of Iranian ports in the Gulf and the complete cessation of buying and selling of fuel from and to Iran.[53] Sufficient sanctions required political will and it was believed that the EU-3, the Russians and Chinese and the USA spoke 'different languages'; and the compromises reached on Iran consistently reflected the weakest position, necessary to keep all parties happy.

Talk of a possible strike against Iran's nuclear facilities intensified dramatically. The Israelis did not view the military option as desirable; it was simply the less bad alternative.[54] But there were significant logistical problems. Barring a highly improbable all-out ground invasion, military action would take the form of air strikes, which posed a problem. The Iranians had learned from the 1981 Israeli strike of the Iraqi nuclear reactor at Osirak. The nuclear programme was large, encompassing multiple sites dispersed around the country (Iran had taken the decision to decentralize it on the basis of the Iraqi precedent so that there was no single, decisive target like Osirak). These were well protected, some deep underground, and Israeli intelligence simply couldn't be certain it knew all the locations. Even multiple missions would not destroy all nuclear-related facilities and materials. The Israelis believed that while they might lack the capability to destroy the programme completely, they only needed to destroy a few key facilities to buy time, and they were confident this could be done.[55]

Of more international concern was any possible Iranian response. The Israelis calculated that there was little that Iran could do directly to Israel. It could create trouble via its proxies – Hezbollah in the north and Hamas in the south – but as far as the Israelis were concerned they were already at war with Hamas and Hezbollah.[56] Tehran could launch some missiles against Israel, but so what? They already faced thousands of those from Gaza and the West Bank. The issue was the USA. Realistically, Israel would most likely not attack Iran without US support; and the USA, both with Iran's ability to cause trouble for it in Iraq and with its troops in the Gulf, would bear the brunt of any Iranian retaliation.[57] For their part, the Americans did not think the Israelis were about to attack; though the Israelis claimed they had the capacity to destroy Natanz, their military said they did not.[58] Tel Aviv might be heightening the rhetoric to pressure them but the Americans questioned whether they would launch an attack in the face of strong US objections, and they hadn't been shy about voicing these.

In December 2007, in what was perhaps calculated timing, the United States National Intelligence Council released an unclassified report on Iran's nuclear-weapon intentions and capabilities. Unsurprisingly, the report highlighted the centrifuge plant at Natanz as the danger area for any possible weapons ambitions. It also assessed with 'high confidence' that until fall 2003 Iranian military entities had worked under government direction to develop nuclear weapons; but, critically, it judged with 'high confidence' that in the fall of 2003 Tehran had halted its nuclear-weapons programme. It concluded with 'moderate confidence' that 'Tehran had not restarted its nuclear weapons program as of mid-2007' and with 'moderate-to-high confidence' that Iran did not 'currently have a nuclear weapon'.

The report embarrassed the Bush Administration – only in October, Bush had suggested that a nuclear-armed Iran could lead to 'World War III', and his NSA adviser Stephen Hadley was forced to respond, calling the Intelligence Estimate 'complicated'; several parties in the Israeli and US administrations rejected the findings outright. Even some of the Europeans felt that if it were not inaccurate, it had not been understood, and argued that what it claimed had stopped in 2003 were a pretty narrowly defined set of activities. The problem with the estimate, and the nuclear programme in general, they argued, was that everyone was so terrified by the possibility that they might one day have to take radical action against Iran that they either said there was no problem or no problem that had to be dealt with in the short-term.[59] If that were the case, it worked: the estimate considerably dampened appetite for an attack on Iran.

* * *

Ahmadinejad's first term in office saw steady progress on both paths to a potential bomb – uranium enrichment and (to a lesser degree) plutonium production. Iran was now at an advanced stage in its enrichment programme. From February 2007 to 31 January 2009 it produced 1,010 kg of LEU (nearly enough to manufacture a nuclear device if enriched from 3.5 per cent to c. 93 per cent through Iran's centrifuges).[60] Throughout the programme's history the biggest impediment to a bomb had been its own, considerable, technological limitations but now things were different. Given the enrichment process complexity, Iran would be unlikely to move towards any drive to enrich to HEU without throwing out the inspectors (and thereby leaving the NPT), which it showed no inclination to do.

Progress on Bushehr was also steady during Ahmadinejad's first term. Work continued throughout 2007 and the first nuclear fuel shipment from Russia arrived on 17 December. A few months later, the eighth and final shipment arrived, and in late 2008 several hundred Iranian engineers, trained in Russia, began final preparations in anticipation of the plant's completion. More pertinently, Hasan Rowhani's plan to continue the construction of the IR-40 heavy-water production plant at Arak during Iran's suspension of enrichment had, from an Iranian viewpoint, proved wise. In August 2006, Ahmadinejad inaugurated Arak, which is capable of producing up to 16 tonnes of heavy water per year. The production of heavy water itself does not violate the NPT and, officially, the water will be used to cool a new research reactor under construction; but some worried that Arak had been overlooked because of the focus on Natanz. The stated purpose of Arak is the production of radioactive isotopes for medical and industrial uses, but when fully operational the reactor is estimated to be able to produce about 9 kg of weapons-grade plutonium per year, enough for one or two nuclear weapons – though Iran told the IAEA that it did not intend to build reprocessing facilities to separate plutonium from the reactor.[61] Iran informed the Agency that the plant would likely go online in 2011 (though no one was holding their breath) and that any plutonium from the reactor would not be available before about 2014.

CHAPTER 15

ENTER OBAMA: NUCLEAR DÉTENTE? – 2008–10

Bruce Riedel watched the junior Senator from Illinois win the 2008 US presidential election with satisfaction at things done and excitement at things yet to be done. Barack Obama took the presidential oath of office as the 43rd man to occupy the White House but the first African-American. The change many wanted could not have been more visible. Obama was determined to solve Bush's regional mess and Iran led his foreign policy agenda. Even before his election he demonstrated a sensitivity towards US relations with the Islamic Republic when, during the 2008 Democratic Party nomination campaign, he accused his then rival, Hillary Clinton, of echoing Bush's 'bluster' when she spoke of Washington's ability to 'obliterate' Iran if it used nuclear weapons against Israel. In a January 2009 interview with 'This Week', on US TV network ABC, just over a week before his inauguration, Obama admitted that Iran would be one of his biggest challenges. He outlined a new approach, which included, critically, a willingness to talk with what the previous administration called rogue states.[1]

Obama's overture towards Iran was the result of deliberation throughout his campaign and the transition between his election and inauguration. He was serious. His team of policy advisors on Iran was put in place early on and included Riedel, who had served 29 years with the CIA (including a stint as Special Assistant to the President and Senior Director for Near East Affairs on the National Security Council). All were agreed (as, in fairness, Rice and Burns had been before them) that the Bush Administration's initial refusal to speak to Iran and its castigation of it as part of an Axis of Evil had not worked; even Burns's and Rice's belated *anagnorisis* and subsequent policy of conditional negotiations at the Secretary of State level had been insufficient. Iran was closer to a nuclear weapon at the end of the Bush Administration than at the beginning. A new approach was absolutely essential and that required face-to-face US–Iranian contacts, at the highest level.

Not that any of them had any doubts about Iran's intentions – they all believed that Iran wanted, at the very least, a nuclear-weapons capability. Riedel himself believed that given its 'neighbourhood' any Iranian government, be it the Islamic Republic or a monarchy or a democracy, would seek a nuclear deterrent.[2] The nuclear programme in its present formulation was still unacceptable; the difference was that the team understood, *a posteriori*, that going through the process of engagement and then, possibly, through the process of further sanctions was preferable to incessant threats when trying to build global support to brand Iran's nuclear programme as something impermissible. The change towards the Islamic Republic was practical not ideological.

They were particularly concerned about Iran's nuclear programme because the perceived problem was not just an Iranian nuclear-weapons capability *per se*, but the possible proliferation chain it might create across the world's most volatile region. In 2006–7 about a dozen Gulf Arab states had declared an interest in developing nuclear technology, which was considered a signal from the Arab world that if Iran crossed the threshold they (despite their obvious technical limitations) would too. The wish to negotiate with Iran, or to face it down through sanctions, was a long shot, and the team were fully aware of the possible need to fall back to alternatives like containment, or even that most insidious euphemism, the 'military option', but the diplomatic track should begin with engagement at the highest level. In this sense, the policy was just an extension of Burns's, albeit an important one that required the recalibration of a mindset formed over 30 years.

Riedel and the team also understood the constellation of forces that comprised the nuclear impasse. In the second half of 2008, Riedel had accompanied Obama on a trip he was taking to Israel to reassure American voters that under any administration of his the USA would remain committed to Israel's security, and also to ask the Israeli leadership to give diplomacy with Iran a chance. Tel Aviv's hints of unilateral military action against the nuclear programme were a real problem. Both men thought that an Israeli attack on Iran would be a disaster for the administration. Washington was already trapped in two wars in the Middle East, one in Iraq and one in Afghanistan. It did not need a third. Riedel talked to many senior members of the administration both before and after the election about the possibility of an Israeli strike on Iran, and the vast majority regarded this as one of the worst outcomes for Obama's first administration. Obama's message to the Israelis was to give diplomacy a chance: don't close off my options by launching a unilateral military strike, he told them.[3]

With the promised breathing space from Tel Aviv, the plan could move forward, and the promised change in policy was immediate. On 26 January 2008, in the very first interview he gave as President, to Arab TV channel *al-Arabiyya*, Obama, in an imaginative turn of phrase, told the Islamic Republic that the USA would 'extend a hand' if Tehran would 'unclench [its] fist'. Washington's UN Ambassador Susan Rice later inserted an important, and arguably anachronistic, caveat that Tehran suspend uranium enrichment in line with Security Council demands before it could expect US talks.[4] Obama staked huge political capital on resolution of the Iran problem (for which resolution of the nuclear crisis was crucial) and the size of the task at hand was made immediately clear when Tehran welcomed the move but said the USA should consider its past mistakes. Iran's Foreign Ministry spokesman, Hasan Ghashghavi, turned Obama's imagery back on the President and declared that if anyone had a clenched fist it was Washington. The world, he said, waited to see what was in Obama's open hand.[5]

On 20 March 2009, only two months after taking office, in a video message with Persian subtitles on Nowruz (Iranian New Year), Obama obliged. He reiterated the USA's commitment to diplomacy that addressed the full range of outstanding issues between Washington and Tehran. More important was the act itself: a US President spoke directly to the leadership of the Islamic Republic (thus acknowledging its legitimacy) for the first time in 30 years. Obama then discussed the need for Tehran's nuclear programme to remain for civil usage only (while Khamenei, in his own Nowruz speech, lauded the Islamic Republic's nuclear progress and indicated that he took Obama's approach less than seriously).[6] Just two weeks later, on 8 April 2009, Obama translated words into deeds and the State Department announced that on the 'basis of mutual respect and mutual interest' it would join P5+1 negotiations with Iran as a 'full participant' (quietly dropping the condition that Iran ceased uranium enrichment) and ask the EU High Representative for Common and Security Foreign Policy, Javier Solana, to extend a US invitation to meet with Iran's representatives.[7] The USA would talk to Iran for the first time in over 30 years. A day later Ahmadinejad responded by saying that he welcomed 'honest' talks with Washington.

THE 2009 IRANIAN PRESIDENTIAL ELECTIONS

In Iran, the people were restless, and about to decide if they too wanted change. Ahmadinejad's promises to end corruption and divert oil revenues to the poor had proved as empty as those of his predecessor, Mohammad Khatami, to liberalize Iranian society. With a divisive President, a worsening economy, and increasing international isolation, the election campaign was heated – candidates sparred in fraught TV debates; in the Tehran streets something of a party atmosphere emerged during the run-up to a vote that was intensely followed by the onlooking world. As ever, the Europeans and Americans thought the right result might increase Iran's negotiating flexibility: all they needed was someone to grab Obama's outstretched hand.

As an understandably important part of Iran's national debate, the nuclear programme (and resultant crisis) featured prominently in the Iranian presidential campaign. All the candidates were agreed on the programme's national importance but divided on Ahmadinejad's diplomatic handling of the crisis, which had tried the patience of large sections of the political elite and the country at large. Three rounds of sanctions and Iran's worsening international isolation had exacerbated the problems of an already troubled economy, and with thousands more young people entering a saturated job market each year the problems would only worsen. Ahmadinejad's main threat came from the former Prime Minister, Mir-Hossein Mousavi, who attacked the incumbent's economic policies which had sent inflation skywards and seen oil revenues largely wasted on populist, futile projects. Mousavi argued that Iran needed a policy of détente to work to build international confidence, and indicated a willingness to reciprocate Obama's conciliatory gestures.[8]

As with all the candidates, Mousavi was adamant that Iran would pursue its right to nuclear technology; 'dire consequences' would follow if the country reversed its nuclear drive, which he obviously claimed to be for civil purposes. The programme was not negotiable, but nor was there any need for what he called Ahmadinejad's foreign policy adventurism, a charge echoed even by the other, conservative, challenger, former Revolutionary Guards head Mohammad Rezaee. The most overtly reformist challenger, the cleric Mehdi Karroubi, another politician to base an election campaign on a slogan for 'change', promised to reverse Ahmadinejad's policies and said he wouldn't mind meeting President Barack Obama if it would help the national interest. He, too, supported the nuclear programme, but favoured a greater flexibility on negotiations and suggested that focus might be moved from enrichment onto reactors, which, after all, would provide the electricity that was the programme's supposed goal.[9]

But the more 'moderate' candidates faced difficulties. Ahmadinejad's election, combined with the conservative-dominated seventh Majlis, meant that, since 2005, hardliners and conservatives had dominated both the executive branch and the parliament. Important policy changes on the nuclear issue or US relations would be difficult without the support of the judiciary, parliament and Khamenei himself, and his position was clear. Since 2005, both Ahmadinejad and Khamenei had used the nuclear issue to stigmatize reformists, depicting them as defeatists willing to negotiate away Iran's interests. Despite being ostensibly neutral, Khamenei made these points repeatedly during the election campaign. 'Do not allow those who would throw their hands up and surrender to enemies and defame the Iranian nation's prestige to get into office,' he said in a televised speech in Bijar, in western Iran.[10]

Khamenei had, of course, openly supported Rowhani's decision-making over 2003–5 and his new position was something of a *volte face*. Two years of enrichment suspension had, Khamenei believed, brought nothing thanks to EU-3 prevarication, and this convinced him to follow his anti-Western instincts. As ever his was the final voice that counted. Hardliners like Hamid Reza Taraqi, leader of the Islamic Coalition Society party, now denounced Khatami's reformist government, which had 'surrendered' to Washington by caving in to Western pressure to suspend uranium enrichment (which again was only possible with Khamenei's approval), and hailed Ahmadinejad's defiance. In turn the reformists continued to use the crisis as an example of Ahmadinejad's foolish diplomacy.

But it mattered little. On 12 June 2009, in elections that were patently rigged, Ahmadinejad overwhelmingly 'defeated' Mousavi with 66 per cent of the vote to Mousavi's 33 per cent. Voting patterns were suspicious, with the result announced before some polls had even closed, and which Mousavi refused to accept, forcing a partial recount, which he also lost. Days later, Khamenei himself, supposedly above 'mere' politics, came out publicly to endorse the result. In the following weeks millions took to the streets, swathed in green (the colour of Mousavi's election campaign), to protest the government and the election result; in response, the regime shut down the internet, threw out foreign journalists, killed and imprisoned demonstrators, and generally demonstrated its rogue status. What most struck Western diplomats was the incompetence with which the elections were handled (if not the resulting protests, which were suppressed with barbarous efficiency). They believed the Mullahs had panicked, fearful of a first round Mousavi win.[11] Washington suspected Khamenei might have feared a combination of Obama and Mousavi at a time when the USA was pressing for engagement – which might, in part, have been responsible for the vote rigging.[12]

The elections (or more accurately their aftermath) severely tested Obama's policy of détente. He resisted pressure to condemn Tehran as the regime imprisoned, tortured and murdered its own people or to openly support the opposition 'Green Movement' that coalesced around Mousavi. Again, he displayed historical sensitivity, to the 1953 coup in particular, and while he expressed concern at the violence he stressed that, given the history of US–Iranian relations, interference might be seen as meddling. Within this was sufficient awareness to understand that overt support for the Iranian opposition would undermine their credibility and enable the regime to label them 'imperial agents'. Equally, he refused to start negotiations until the situation was resolved.

Iran's internal balance of power had now changed, with serious consequences for the nuclear impasse. Ahmadinejad's Revolutionary Guard-supported 'victory', combined with the failure of Mousavi, the Green Movement and of more pragmatic players like Rafsanjani, meant almost total hardline control of Iranian politics. Tehran's traditional factionalism, which had always required the accommodation of opposing factions and, as a result, served as a kind of internal political check, was, for the moment, far less of an equalizing force. As the regime's military elite, the Revolutionary Guards control its most sensitive military programmes, including Iran's ballistic missile programme – if a military nuclear programme exists it is under their authority. As the dominant political as well as military force in the Islamic Republic, strategic choices on whether to go for nuclear weapons would likely be decided in line with Revolutionary Guard stated policies to make Iran the regional military power. The March 2009 warning by the Tehran Nuclear Research Centre's head that a nuclear weapon under Revolutionary Guard control would irretrievably alter the domestic balance of power in their favour appeared closer to realization.

* * *

After an explosive start, the summer was quiet. Iran had contained its people, and all sides waited for the G-20 and UN General Assembly in late September 2009. Just weeks before, on 9 September, in response to a mid-September deadline for an Iranian response to the offered talks, Iran presented the P5+1 with a promised package of proposals to resolve the standoff. It was what Washington expected: a lot of hot air and empty rhetoric. Iran agreed to 'constructive' negotiations on a range of issues, including global nuclear disarmament, regional security and the financial crisis, while it mentioned virtually nothing on the nuclear file.[13] The decision was taken in the White House that very day not to dismiss the offer outright in order to keep the channels of communication open, but neither could the White House pretend it was serious; it would become public at some point and the administration needed to retain its credibility.[14]

The Iranian elections had enormously complicated the White House's Iran strategy. Officials believed it less likely that Iran would now come up with a constructive approach to negotiations, but they remained committed to the basic approach of engagement to try to reach a deal. Engagement would remain within a multilateral, P5+1 framework to ramp up pressure and, if need be, to increase Iran's isolation. It would, as ever, be difficult because of the Russians and Chinese, who were quite comfortable with the status quo of neither a deal nor a crisis. White House staff assumed that Tehran had no interest in a genuine deal, although the possibility was not ruled out. One effect of the post-election instability, the Americans calculated, might be an Iranian desire to improve relations with the outside world as a means of stabilizing the regime. Tehran may have quelled the dissent, but it had lost legitimacy: Iranians shouted 'death to the dictator' from Tehran's rooftops as they had under the Shah. There were also signs that it wanted to avoid greater isolation or a further ramping up of sanctions: for the first time in over a year the IAEA was allowed access to Arak. At Natanz around 4,000 centrifuges were up, but the gas was not running and no one was sure why; it might be a political signal that Iran was not going full speed but equally it might be a technical issue (actually it was the beginning of technical difficulties caused by the Stuxnet computer virus). Then again, US officials were aware that it might be simply to head off greater pressure at the UN General Assembly and G-20. Frankly, who knew?[15]

The Americans decided that they would once again propose talks, ideally before the UN, though they suspected (correctly as it turned out) that Iran would refuse to meet before October. By now Washington's goal was simply to slow down Iran's nuclear progress. At the current rate of enrichment, Tehran could soon have enough enriched uranium for several bombs and, if it undertook a crash programme, could 'breakout' within the short to medium term. Washington was still unsure of Iran's intentions; it could well be to have weapons capacity and not a weapon itself, but uppermost in everyone's mind was Israel. Obama's request to Israel for more time had been complicated by the April 2009 election of Benjamin Netanyahu, who was even more unambiguous on the Iran threat than his predecessor, Ehud Olmert. Israeli pressure on Washington was apparent almost immediately, and at a May meeting in Washington between Netanyahu and Obama the former had made Israeli impatience clear. US Secretary of State Hillary Clinton's July statement that Washington

251

would provide 'a defence umbrella' for its allies in the Middle East in the event that Iran developed nuclear weapons was perceived, unhappily, by many Israelis as a tacit acceptance of a nuclear Iran, and only increased Israeli pressure on Washington.

Some clear signal of a slowdown was needed. A 2008 US proposal for a freeze for freeze (a freeze on enrichment in exchange for a freeze on sanctions) followed by suspension and negotiations might have put the emphasis on suspension, but White House staff believed that what mattered was what came next: an opportunity for Iran to regain the international community's confidence. Iran said it wanted to be treated like any other nation; the Americans had some interesting ideas on that which they believed were worth discussing. Washington would publicly put the onus back on them with a straight choice. The end of the September General Assembly in New York was considered the ideal forum: with the P5+1 and the Iranians both there it would offer a period of 'stock-taking' – officials would make clear that US patience was not endless and unless Tehran showed signs of flexibility, pressure would be increased.[16]

CRISIS BEFORE THE UN GENERAL ASSEMBLY: THE FORDOW ENRICHMENT PLANT

But just days before the General Assembly was to meet, Iran informed the IAEA that it had been secretly building a pilot fuel enrichment plant at Fordow near the city of Qom. The announcement caused a perfect if predictable storm; even its revelation was subject to controversy. According to the IAEA, on 21 September 2009, in a letter to the IAEA Director General, the Iranian government informed the Agency of the existence of a previously undeclared uranium-enrichment facility under construction at Fordow near Qom, intended to produce five per cent-enriched uranium.[17] A few days later, on 25 September, Obama revealed its existence to an outraged world in a statement at the G-20 meeting. The intervening days had seen intense diplomacy. Iran did declare Fordow (most likely because they suspected its imminent revelation by an opposition group or Western powers) but without informing the IAEA of its location, its size or when its construction had begun. Western intelligence had known about Fordow for years and debated whether to release the information early to use as leverage or to hold onto it until it was clearly the 'smoking gun' everyone awaited.[18] Western diplomats subsequently informed the IAEA of everything so its inspectors would have the full story. In fact, they were concerned that the Agency would react badly to not having been told before. They told the IAEA before the media, but not by much.

The facility was of serious concern. In subsequent meetings (and correspondence) held in late October, Iran informed the IAEA that the decision to build the plant had been taken in the second half of 2007. It was, Tehran said, being built as a backup to Natanz in response to continuing military threats against the facility from the 'Zionist regime' and Bush Administration. It was both a practical move, so Iran could continue to enrich for civil purposes if Natanz was destroyed, and a political statement, of Iranian steadfastness. According to Iran's Ambassador to the IAEA, Ali Asghar Soltanieh:[19]

> ... this new site at Fordow has a political message: we are saying to the world that even the threat of military attack will not stop enrichment – we have a contingency plan. Enrichment in Iran will not be stopped or suspended at any price. It has not been done by sanctions or resolutions it won't be done by force. If Natanz is attacked, this site will continue enrichment.

This cut little ice. Located in an underground mountain complex near a Revolutionary Guards base, Fordow was widely suspected to be for military use. The White House believed that an enrichment plant containing 3,000 centrifuges could not be a suitable backup for Natanz because 3,000 was an insufficient number of centrifuges to produce regular fuel reloads for civilian nuclear power plants, which require much larger numbers. It was simply too small to be a backup for Natanz and, moreover, it was too big to be a pilot enrichment plant.[20] Conversely, 3,000 centrifuges was a perfect number, if the uranium were enriched through the centrifuges to suitably high levels – 80 per cent or above (though around 93 per cent is preferred by weapons manufacturers) – to produce one nuclear weapon a year. To enrich to these weapons-grade levels at Natanz would be impossible without throwing out the IAEA inspectors, so a covert plant like Fordow was, in theory, perfect. As far as the P5+1 was concerned, Iran had been caught out.

At the end of September, just days after the discovery, the UN convened. France and Britain denounced the site while Obama demanded that Iran open it for inspections within two weeks.[21] No progress on the overall nuclear file was made in New York, and the French in particular (who had taken a much harder line on Iran since Sarkozy's 2007 election) were running out of patience. Paris was convinced that the events of the past three months had clearly not affected Iran's strategic choices and, like the USA, it believed the 9 September Iranian proposal to be a 'smokescreen', designed to slow down the move towards tougher sanctions.[22] Overall, the EU's position was clear – no new concessions. The offer remained the proposal presented to Iran at Geneva the previous year – a 6-week freeze for freeze that would lead to an Iranian renunciation of enrichment. The Americans, meanwhile, were gearing up towards bilateral talks between Iran and the USA in Geneva after the General Assembly that had finally been agreed with Iran. They did not mind France's newfound diplomatic aggression. In fact, they believed it was good that Iran knew their EU allies were impatient and angry at them, though they would have preferred it to have been done in private.[23]

The Russians appeared wholly taken by surprise, and Russian President Dmitry Medvedev could only repeat 'this is very bad' as the Americans briefed him.[24] US officials weren't foolish enough to think it meant a change of Russian approach, but it did put them in an uncomfortable position, forcing them to agree that Iran had been less than honest; the Americans suspected that they would revert to their former position given their relationship with Iran and other calculations. Plus, they knew Medvedev was playing 'good cop' to Putin's bad at the time.[25] China's position was even more problematic: despite Fordow's revelation and Iran's post-election turmoil, Beijing was adamant it would not support increased sanctions against the Islamic Republic.[26] The most important aspect of the affair as far as US officials were concerned was its effect on Iran, which (they believed) had likely made the decision to build Fordow in 2005, some two years after Natanz was discovered, in order to have a hidden facility to covertly produce HEU for nuclear-weapons capability. The plant's discovery had forced Iran to allow in inspectors and thwarted the whole enterprise. The Americans suspected that Iran would do what it did in 2003 after Natanz's discovery: lie low, offer some concessions and hope that, after the pressure had subsided, they could start a 'son of Fordow'.[27] Again, that gave the Americans time, and US intelligence doubted there was another Fordow-like facility in Iran.

US officials were not primarily concerned about the possible production of a bomb through any possible plutonium production at the Arak heavy-water reactor or Bushehr. The main concern was not the number of centrifuges spinning but the 2,200-odd kg of LEU Iran had stockpiled. But they also knew that Iran would have to expel the inspectors to begin the process of enriching this to weapons-grade levels, and if it did so the USA would just bomb Natanz – it was a no-brainer. Their military had told them it could be done, and they doubted Iran would be so foolish.[28] The real problem, as officials saw it, was less Iran's nuclear programme than people's fear of it.[29] If, by the end of the year, they could not show progress in slowing down enrichment or in getting Iran to turn over its uranium stockpile, pressure within the country and from Israel would rise. Already, people were calling Obama naïve.

The plan was to slow the enrichment programme by using the leverage Fordow had given them. They were all for Iran slowing the rate of uranium enrichment, either by not using all 4,000 centrifuges or, at a minimum, a commitment not to expand the number of those they currently used. Ideally the Iranians would export their current stockpile of LEU for enrichment abroad, which would gain roughly two years (the time it would take Iran to replenish its stock). It was a real test of whether Iran was genuinely prepared to make a deal. Only a couple of months earlier (in July 2009), Soltanieh had sent a letter to the IAEA requesting 20 per cent-enriched reactor fuel for the Tehran Research Reactor, which he claimed Iran needed for medical purposes. The Americans saw their chance and immediately began to work with the IAEA and the Russians. With Moscow as intermediary, they proposed that Iran send most of its enriched uranium to Russia, for it to be further enriched to 20 per cent (it was currently enriched at 3.5 per cent). This would then be sent to France for fabrication of the enriched fuel the Tehran Research Reactor required. The Russians delivered the offer and returned with a vague Iranian acceptance. That wasn't good enough: Washington wanted a commitment, and it wanted almost all the LEU. The Russians came back again and said, 'you got it'. When Ahmadinejad began to talk publicly about the Tehran Research Reactor deal later that month, the Americans reasoned he was laying the ground to present Iran's concession as a victory and assumed the agreement would be rubber stamped at the Geneva talks.[30]

Russian support had been crucial. On 17 September – just eight days before the announcement of Fordow – Obama, as part of a 'reset' of relations with Russia, which had deteriorated under Bush, had renounced one of his predecessor's most controversial policies and abandoned a proposed missile defence shield consisting of site missile interceptors and a radar station placed in Poland and the Czech Republic. Ostensibly to deter missiles from Iran and North Korea, the idea had enraged the Russians, who claimed it targeted Moscow's nuclear arsenal. This caused diplomatic tension between Washington and Moscow that (further) slowed Russian co-operation on Iran. Its removal was a typically thoughtful move, and the *quid pro quo* for Russian help on the nuclear file. At the UN General Assembly, Prime Minister Dmitry Medvedev had referred to the Iranian nuclear threat in uncharacteristically forceful terms and even appeared to support the possibility of more sanctions. Now the USA had achieved a possible breakthrough; and the key to it had been the missile defence deal.[31]

THE GENEVA TALKS

The P5+1 met with Iran on a cold morning in Geneva on 1 October 2009. The atmosphere was tense but excited: everyone knew the potential significance of what was coming. The talks began with two hours of preliminary discussions chaired by Solana, who sat between the six P5+1 political directors on one side of the room and the Iranians on the other. The P5+1 offered Iran the same 'freeze for freeze' deal it had in 2008, in which Iran would stop expansion of its enrichment programme for six weeks in exchange for a halt in any sanctions action; during that time the two sides would discuss a full suspension of uranium enrichment in exchange for a package of economic benefits and security guar antees. No one thought Iran would compromise at the meeting, which was essentially just a collection of speeches from all sides. They all knew the key lay in the bilateral talks after the meeting. The Americans clearly couldn't wait for it to be over so they could get the discussions under way.[32]

The following one-and-a-half hour talks between US Under Secretary of State William J Burns and Jalili were seminal. While Iran and the USA had both been present at the 2001 Bonn conference to discuss Post-Taliban Afghanistan, these were the first bilateral, face-to-face talks between the two countries for 30 years. The Americans were working on the (to them obvious) principle that an Iranian commitment to ship its LEU abroad had been agreed. All this was mentioned to Jalili at the P5+1 meeting. He simply nodded. In a later, private conversation, he made Iran's acceptance explicit.[33] The Americans were not necessarily confident that Iran would deliver, but they were confident it had made the commitment. It might try to wriggle out later, but at this stage they calculated that given its internal problems the regime did not want to open up a new front with a united P5+1.

The Americans were right: Ahmadinejad was keen on the deal and shortly after the meeting described it as a great victory; he desperately needed a political triumph to ease the pressure on him after his loss of political legitimacy following the June 2009 elections. He was delighted to be the one that had persuaded the Great Satan to sit down at the negotiating table, but internal Iranian politics intervened: all his political enemies (some of whom would also have welcomed the deal) – Rezaee, Rafsanjani, the Green Movement – lined up to prevent it. Mousavi was especially vocal and accused him of being, of all things, a Western stooge. If his revenge wasn't served cold, it at least had a familiar taste. Iran backtracked and claimed no promise had ever been made.

Was there an Iranian promise? The Europeans and the Americans disagreed here. The British felt 'promise' was perhaps too strong a word, although there was certainly an acceptance of the idea, while the Americans were adamant that they had secured a promise – and they alone had been present with Iran at the bilateral talks after the meeting. But both agreed that for the Iranians to claim (which they subsequently did) that no discussions on this had taken place was ridiculous.[34] The two sides agreed to meet again within a month to discuss wider nuclear issues and the Tehran Research Reactor, and at least three more days of talks at Vienna occurred where Iran agreed to ship around 75 per cent of its LEU to Russia by the end of the year. The EU delegation on the other hand felt that Jalili had neither accepted nor refused – merely said nothing (perhaps their reading of his nod). As far as they were concerned there was no indication of a reversal of Iran's policy of 'self-reliance'.[35] Set against that were the words Solana read out at the end of the discussions – an agreement in principle for the Tehran Research Reactor to be refuelled on the basis of exported fuel to a third country with manufacture of fuel assemblies in another. The wording had been seen and amended by the Iranian negotiators (in between numerous phone calls to and from Tehran) in the garden that very afternoon.[36]

Nonetheless, Soltanieh now claimed that he had merely made a request for fuel for the Tehran Research Reactor back in July, to which, all of a sudden, the Americans had attached conditions: specifically that Iran would have to give an equivalent amount of LEU in return. This was unacceptable because Iran had no guarantee of supply. As ever, the retreat into history was used to bolster the Iranian position as Soltanieh explained that when he was director of the Tehran Research Reactor, just before the revolution, Iran had paid the USA $2 million for reactor fuel. In the aftermath of the Hostage Crisis, the Americans had never delivered the fuel nor returned the money to Iran. How could Iran now be sure it would arrive?

In fact, he went on the offensive. The whole debacle only proved that Iran had a right to indigenous enrichment because it could never be sure of a guaranteed fuel supply. The problem, Soltanieh said, was a deficit of confidence. Naturally, he said, Iran was still co-operative and proposed that when the fuel was delivered Iran would hand over the material. This was the deal on the table, but it would not be there forever.[37] Since the USA had entered negotiations, the Europeans had become impatient with Iran. The Iranian elections and subsequent internal political realignment had only brought the Europeans closer to an increased consciousness of the Iranian threat – despite the 2007 National Intelligence Estimate, Iran had not abandoned its military programme and Fordow was confirmation of this fact. Both the UK and France now favoured a short-term December deadline for tangible Iranian concessions.[38] The risk of a 'transatlantic gap' over Iran's nuclear programme had emerged once more, but this time the EU-3 was certain of Iranian military intentions while Washington believed a final decision may not yet have been taken.

December brought nothing. In fact, Soltanieh declared that if the fuel was not forthcoming the Iranian government might 'unfortunately' decree that Iran would have to make the fuel itself and enrich to 20 per cent to do so. On 8 February 2010, with no deal in place, Iran duly announced that it would do just that. This was Iranian brinkmanship at its best and, timed to coincide with revolution day on 11 February, political cynicism at its worst; it was also an extreme provocation. Iran could not even use any 20 per cent-enriched fuel in the fuel assembly support for the Tehran Research Reactor because it lacked the production line to do this, and it would take several years to acquire it. Added to this, enrichment to 20 per cent involved 90 per cent of the effort required to get to the 93 per cent HEU generally used for weapons-grade uranium.

On 10 February 2010 IAEA inspectors visited the pilot enrichment plant at Natanz where the fuel was to be produced for the Tehran Research Reactor, and were informed that Iran had already begun to feed low-enriched UF_6 into one centrifuge cascade the previous evening and that the facility would begin to produce up to 20 per cent-enriched UF_6 within a few days. Four days later, Iran, in the presence of Agency inspectors, moved approximately 1,950 kg of low-enriched UF_6 from the Natanz fuel enrichment plant to its pilot fuel enrichment plant feed station. Iran then provided the Agency with results indicating enrichment levels of up to 19.8 per cent there between 9 and 11 February 2010.[39] Iran had made good on its word.

Meanwhile, Western diplomats viewed all this with despair. The drive to 20 per cent-enrichment was perceived as two-pronged. First, it was typical of Iran's political posture: perhaps feeling insecure, the Iranians were sending out messages of how powerful and independent they were, while simultaneously signalling their willingness to deal. More worryingly, it was also viewed as yet another cynical step towards nuclear-weapons capability, mainly because without the correct assembly lines the enriched uranium could not be turned into suitable fuel for the reactor, which Iran knew. The problem was a microcosm of the whole crisis: no one could say for sure that there was no practical application for the 20 per cent-enriched fuel because, of course, over time there could be. Iran knew this, too, and its strategy was seen as one of progression by inches – testing the P5+1 to see if anyone would finally say 'enough was enough'. The Israelis would speak of the Iranians turning the single red line that had once existed on Iranian enrichment into a series of thin pink lines. The plan is simple: you push and you push towards your goal. Each time you push through one more (now) pink line (like 20 per cent enrichment), the international community has to decide whether you will 'break out' on the basis of pushing through just one more pink line, to which the answer is usually 'no'. Suddenly you are the other side of the line, and it is too late. Israel believed Iran was not engaged in 'break out' but, like a man negotiating his way through a barbed wire fence, 'crawl out'.[40]

Perhaps sensing that the crawl was working, on 9 April 2010, at a press conference for National Atom Day in Iran, White House Staff watched Ahmadinejad unveil (from behind a curtain no less) a new 'third generation' centrifuge with a reported ability to enrich up to six times faster than the old P-1 centrifuges. Ali Akbar Salehi, who had replaced Aghazadeh as head of the AEOI in July 2009, stated that it could be a year before a cascade of the new centrifuges was available for testing. Assessment of the new centrifuge and its possible effects on the programme were varied. But as a statement of intent – that Iran would continue and even accelerate enrichment (a week later Iran also announced that it intended to start building two new enrichment plants in March 2011) – the political message was clear.

* * *

Both the USA and Europe now felt snubbed and, with Fordow's discovery, deceived. Obama's staff in particular were angry. Their boss's attempts at détente with Iran had become a political liability as Republican opponents in the senate and on the radio denounced him as 'soft', and talk now turned to another round of sanctions. Just over a month later, on 17 May, and seemingly without warning, Iran, Turkey and Brazil announced an agreement (the so-called Tehran Declaration) following trilateral talks in Tehran to resolve the Tehran Research Reactor dispute. Iran agreed to send 1,200 kg of its LEU to Turkey in return for 120 kg of 20 per cent-enriched fuel for the reactor from the Vienna Group (the USA, Russia, France and the IAEA) within a year. Iran would maintain ownership over the LEU in Turkey (and in the event that the declaration's conditions were not met within a year, the material would be returned to Iran). Iran also agreed to notify the IAEA in writing of its deal within seven days of the declaration, which had to be accepted by the Vienna Group. Upon positive response, a written agreement would be made dependent upon a commitment by the Vienna Group to deliver the fuel.

The deal was notable for its participants' diplomatic freelancing. Neither Turkey nor Brazil had a mandate from the IAEA or the P5+1. Turkey understandably wished to avoid trouble on its own borders, and there was an overarching interest for Istanbul to prevent escalation of the nuclear crisis, while the chance to resolve the Iranian nuclear impasse and bolster Turkey's claims to regional leadership was too good an opportunity for Turkish Prime Minister Recep Tayyip Erdogan to miss. Brazil was the more interesting case here. Brazilian President Lula da Silva's personal friendship with Ahmadinejad may have factored, but, as a nuclear threshold state with its own nuclear ambitions, Brazil likely saw Iran as a precedent and for this reason had a vested interest in resolving the issue.

Iranian thinking was more obvious. Ahmadinejad had desperately needed a deal of some sort ever since his political opponents had scotched the deal made with the US at Geneva, and Iran desperately needed to prevent more sanctions. Its economic problems had worsened, and the imminent end of subsidies on basics such as grain and petrol meant an already riled population would face imminent financial hardship. The first anniversary of the 12 June elections and the domestic unrest it would likely bring also approached. The regime needed to diffuse the nuclear situation for a while. Interestingly, it also points to a consistency in Iranian thinking. Back in 2005, Rowhani had outlined the need for more Iranian allies in the nuclear crisis. In particular, he had suggested collaboration with countries like South Africa and Brazil, who were interested in developing their own fuel cycle capabilities. 'We should come up with a formula that these countries can take to the Europeans,' he had argued. 'It should not be just us and the Europeans.'[41] This is what Iran had now done and, as by Iranian calculations (given Iran's dishonesty over Geneva), the West would be made to look unreasonable. Furthermore, critically, when it came to sanctions discussions, Russia and China could say a deal was possible and everyone should return to the negotiating table. The intended message was clear: you can deal with Iran.

Of course, Soltanieh said, the Iranians were not 'happy' with the deal (after all, why should they have to send any of their LEU in exchange for fuel when any other country could just buy it?), but he claimed it demonstrated a genuine desire to find a political settlement. Iran now expected the P5+1 to come to the negotiating table.[42] Alas, the Europeans and Americans saw things differently. Iran had promised to export 1,200 kg of LEU when its total stockpile was around 2,300 kg, so what was on offer was less than half.[43] Moreover, with the current enrichment rate (which might well increase with the new third-generation centrifuge unveiled only a month earlier) it would only take Iran about a year to replace what it had agreed to ship. And as soon as the deal was announced, the Iranian Foreign Ministry had reiterated that Iran would press on with 20 per cent enrichment, so the deal did not even address the fundamental concern.

A day later, the USA, in consultation with the Europeans and, critically, the Russians and Chinese, finalized a draft Security Council Resolution (which Brazil, at this time a non-permanent Security Council member, understandably refused to endorse) that tightened sanctions against Iran. On 9 June 2010 the Security Council adopted Resolution 1929, imposing a fourth round of sanctions (watered down by China and Russia once more) against Iran. These included tougher financial measures and an expanded arms embargo but crucially no oil embargo. Ahmadinejad responded by saying the sanctions were a 'used handkerchief that should be thrown in the dustbin' and 'not capable of hurting Iranians'. And well he might. On 1 July an exasperated Obama also signed into US law new unilateral sanctions against Iran, which aimed to cut off its imports of refined petroleum products such as gasoline and jet fuel as well as limit its access to the international banking system. Without China and Russia to water down sanctions, Washington could target Tehran's (considerable and numerous) weaknesses, which it did.

CHAPTER 16

THE END OF DIPLOMACY? THE NON-DIPLOMATIC ALTERNATIVE – 2010–12

In late 2009, Iranian scientists working at Natanz noticed that centrifuges had started to spin out of control and destroy themselves. It was almost cannibalistic: they seemed to be literally consuming themselves. Problems with centrifuges were nothing new: indeed, problems with nuclear equipment had been a running joke among AEOI nuclear scientists since Khazaneh had first worked on the programme back in the 1970s. Problems had only got worse since Russia had become Iran's primary nuclear partner. Antiquated equipment and malfunctioning parts had made even those hardliners among the scientists long for at least one element of Western 'infiltration' into Iran: working technology. Staff often awaited each new delivery of parts with a resigned forbearance (and some amusement), joking among themselves that Iran's programme had made more strides by attempting to fix flawed parts than by mastering nuclear processes themselves.[1]

But this level of breakage in such a short space of time was unusual. Later that month, staff decommissioned and replaced about

1,000 centrifuges. Even more strange was that examination of all the internal monitoring systems showed the centrifuges spinning normally. After an investigation it became clear that the footage had been doctored. Someone had managed to put a computer malware virus into the computer system at Natanz, which the AEOI head, Ali Akbar Salehi, confirmed on 23 November 2010. The Iranians were enraged. The virus, called Stuxnet, was highly sophisticated and worked by increasing the speed of uranium centrifuges to breaking point for short bursts while it simultaneously fooled the safety monitoring systems. The programme secretly recorded normal operations at the plant then played those readings back to plant operators, so that everything appeared normal while the centrifuges were actually destroying themselves.[2] It was cinematic.

Stuxnet's impact seemed to be huge at the time, but its longer-term effect remains hard to assess. If the goal was destruction of all the centrifuges at Natanz, it failed, but if it was to destroy a more limited number of centrifuges and set back Iranian progress – albeit temporarily – then it succeeded. The virus was almost certainly the result of collaboration between at least two powers. It was so complex that only a major Western power (like the USA) would have the cyber expertise and the nuclear equipment necessary to test the virus. Its delivery – being inserted into an Iranian mainframe with a USB-type device – was hurried, and almost certainly involved co-operation inside the nuclear programme itself, indicating the type of on-the-ground espionage for which Mossad is famed (Iran later claimed to have destroyed a network of ten spies 'linked to the Zionist regime'). Israeli and US officials remained quiet but were clearly pleased. At a December conference, Obama's chief WMD strategist, Gary Samore, dodged a Stuxnet question at a conference on Iran, but declared himself pleased that the Iranians were having trouble, and, with a broad smile, added that the USA and its allies were doing everything they could to complicate things further.[3]

Stuxnet was, if nothing else, a sign of immense diplomatic frustration. Progress had been made with Russia (and to a lesser degree China) following the Fordow revelations and the US commitment to abandon the missile defence shield, and the Europeans had detected a hardening in both countries' attitudes towards the nuclear programme. But the recent round of sanctions proved that both still protected Iran in the Security Council. Also of concern was the transatlantic gap between the Europeans and Americans. Now that Washington had the option of bilateral negotiations with Iran it did not necessarily share the short-term European calendar. But the Europeans feared that a parallel US calendar that Iran might prefer to follow might weaken the coalition and allow Tehran to gain more time. The USA also now risked entering a long dialogue without making progress and being 'used' by Iran as the Europeans had been. The Europeans assessed that Tehran's new priority was to continue its 'divide and progress' strategy to split the international community. Washington's long-awaited entry had brought problems of a new kind.[4]

All of this, of course, suited Iran perfectly. Despite the problems with Stuxnet, Ahmadinejad's policy of defiance appeared vindicated and Iran moved onwards with enrichment, planning eight new units containing 18 centrifuge cascades each at Natanz.[5] Enrichment of uranium up to 20 per cent at the pilot fuel enrichment plant had also started in two interconnected cascades, and in Vienna Soltanieh grinned and proudly brandished a dummy fuel rod that would enable Iran to feed enriched fuel into the Tehran Research Reactor. According to Salehi, Iran had produced 25 kg of 19.75 per cent-enriched uranium since it began the process that February. Even Bushehr was going well, and on 21 August 2010, at a ceremony attended by Russian officials, Iran began loading fuel into its first nuclear power station. According to Sergei Novikov, a spokesman for Russia's state nuclear corporation, Rosatom, it was an 'irreversible step' towards the project's completion.

The IAEA, now with a new Director General, Japanese diplomat Yukiya Amano (who had replaced ElBaradei in December 2009), criticized Iran in stronger terms than ever. At the September 2011 Board Meeting Amano censured Tehran for its

lack of co-operation with the Agency, citing its refusal to comply
with various UN resolutions and its recent decision to ban two inspectors whom Amano characterized as 'experienced and reliable',
from its nuclear facilities. With even the IAEA now becoming
overtly critical, Iran's internal divide over the nuclear crisis grew.
The political fallout from the 2009 elections continued, as did the
programme's evolution from a totem of national unity to political
football, and debates on the nuclear programme became mired in
domestic Iranian politics. In mid-September Rafsanjani addressed
the Assembly of Experts and (without naming him) criticized
Ahmadinejad for failing to take the impact of sanctions seriously.
He warned his audience not to downplay their effects, and while
Iran possessed the capacity to overcome them he doubted it was
being utilized in a proper way. Moreover, the country had never
faced such intense international pressure, which was increasing
each day. Wherever Iran found a loophole, he said, the Western
powers blocked it.[6] It was a clear jibe at Ahmadinejad's diplomatic
mishandling of the nuclear file.

He had a point. UN and (especially) US sanctions now affected
Iran's sales of crude oil, and its shipping, financial and trading
activities, but Ahmadinejad continued to act defiantly. It was an
act that was finding a less receptive public ear, but remained the
official line, and which, at the end of the year, Soltanieh expressed
with his typical idiosyncrasy:[7]

> In Farsi if a taboo is broken then that is it. They have broken the
> taboo by sending the matter to New York and passing resolutions.
> In Farsi – if someone is put in the water it doesn't matter how many
> inches there are there. They think they have put us in the water to
> drown by passing resolutions and sanctions but we don't care how
> many resolutions they pass.

His assessment of Obama, and of his attempts at détente, was even
more pointed:

> He [Obama] has already disappointed everyone in the world, includ-
> ing those in Iran that thought he was opening a new chapter in for-
> eign policy . . . What he is doing on the Iranian nuclear issue is not as

some people thought. There are many reasons for this; one is that island, let's call it an island, the USA is ruled by two kings: Clinton and Obama. So we don't know who is really running the country. On numerous occasions I have noticed that whatever Obama did Clinton and her team just demolish or weaken it. So who is running it?

* * *

2011 started brightly. In his retirement speech at the beginning of January at the weekly government meeting, Meir Dagan, outgoing head of the Israeli secret service, Mossad, said Iran's nuclear programme had run into 'technological difficulties' that could delay a bomb until 2015. 'I did,' he said after 43 years of (not so) public service, 'the best that I could.' Stuxnet had shown those seeking to hinder Iran's nuclear progress the efficacy of 'alternative' means to combat the programme as diplomacy began to yield even less results (if that were possible). Just a week later, in mid-January, another new round of talks between the P5+1 and Iran in Istanbul ended without result. Diplomats presented Iran with a list of steps to build trust in the peaceful nature of the programme, and offered a revamped version of the previous year's fuel swap proposal. Iran refused to even consider the proposals without the lifting of all economic sanctions.[8] Tehran seemed content to let time pass while, technical problems notwithstanding, it crawled ever onwards.

A month later, the IAEA confirmed (as if it were necessary) that, contrary to IAEA Board and Security Council resolutions, Iran continued enrichment. Its LEU stockpile at Natanz now stood at 3,606 kg with an estimated 44 kg of 20 per cent-enriched LEU.[9] Construction of Fordow was still ongoing (Iran had not yet responded to Agency requests for more information on the chronology of the plant's design and construction), and, though no centrifuges had been introduced into the facility, Iran informed the Agency that it would begin feeding nuclear material into the cascades by the summer.[10] In June, new AEOI chief Fereydoon Abbasi-Davani, who had replaced Ali Akbar Salehi in February, announced that Iran would triple its production of 20 per cent-enriched uranium and move it to (the underground) Fordow.

Obama said further sanctions were likely, and a month later Tehran's Foreign Ministry announced the installation of new centrifuges of increased quality and speed (though without naming the facility). A month after that, Iran began to move centrifuges from Natanz to Qom. Nothing, it seemed, would work.

THE ULTIMATE NON-DIPLOMATIC ALTERNATIVE

In August, incoming Mossad chief, Tamir Pardo, inaugurated his reign by having an Iranian nuclear scientist killed. It was the fourth such attack in two years. The victim, Darioush Rezaei, was allegedly involved in developing high-voltage switches, a key component for igniting the explosions needed to trigger a nuclear warhead. The assassination was targeted and it struck, quite literally, at the heart of international concerns. It sent a message. Given the logistical and political problems with military strikes, Mossad now believed that the most effective way to delay Iran's nuclear programme was to strike at those who ran it.[11]

To have a lasting impact – beyond one or two years – the Israelis need to inflict personnel losses on Iranian scientists and engineers. Given Tel Aviv's scepticism over diplomacy and its own history of targeted assassinations (some of which, such as the assassination of Canadian Scientist Gerald Bull, who had been working on a 'supergun' for Saddam Hussein, had been effective), they indicated a new strategy to deal with the nuclear programme – attack, cyber and actual. No Israeli agent would be able to move freely through Tehran, however, and the attacks themselves appeared to be an alliance of Mossad intelligence and training with the use of Iranian MKO operatives on the ground. Both the MKO and Mossad were naturally reticent on the subject, but in March 2012 two senior Obama Administration officials reportedly confirmed that the attacks were carried out by MKO units financed and trained by Mossad. More controversially, reports also surfaced that US intelligence had since 2005 covertly trained MKO units in the Nevada desert – a potentially awkward fact given that the group is linked to the assassination of six US citizens in the 1970s and the State Department has listed it as a foreign terrorist organization since 1997.[12]

With the diplomatic process quadraplegically stalled, 'alternative' solutions increased. On 12 November 2011 a blast ripped through the Alghadir missile base, 25 miles southwest of Tehran. Among the 17 members of Iran's Revolutionary Guard killed was Brigadier General Hassan Moghaddam, the architect of the country's missile programme. Tehran said the explosion was an accident, but it came just days after the IAEA reported that Iran had tested the removal of the conventional high-explosive payload from the warhead of its most advanced ballistic missile, the Shahab-3 and replaced it with a spherical nuclear payload (though this was done before the military programme was supposedly terminated in 2003). Western intelligence sources said more assassinations would follow. There were, apparently, 'more bullets in the magazine'.

And still Iran progressed. By September 2011 it had amassed 4,543 kg of LEU, up from 4,105 kg, and 70.8 kg of 20 per cent-enriched LEU (up from 57.6 kg). Fordow's construction continued (although Iran's vow to start feeding material into the centrifuges by the summer had not been realized).[13] Never had Tehran been more isolated, but it seemed content. That same month Bushehr finally opened. Almost. The plant, 37 years after construction had begun in 1974, started adding electricity to the national grid on 3 September 2011, and the official inauguration was held a week later, attended by senior Russian and Iranian officials. Under the terms of the IAEA-approved Russia–Iran agreement, Russia would be responsible for operating the plant, supplying the nuclear fuel and managing the spent fuel for the next two or three years before passing full control to Iran. Before the plant reached full capacity in November, it would be disconnected from the grid for several weeks to make a number of tests. It has stayed offline ever since.

The world ushered in 2012 with another, unusually competent, killing of an Iranian nuclear scientist. Mostafa Ahmadi Roshan, who worked at Iran's Natanz Enrichment Plant, was driving to work through central Tehran when a passing motorcyclist slapped a magnetic bomb onto his car that killed everyone inside but left the area around the vehicle unscathed. No one, of course, claimed responsibility but, as ever, the Israelis were thought to be responsible – rumours Tel Aviv did nothing to dispel. Iran was predictably (and theatrically) outraged, and a government newspaper intimated that Iran's Revolutionary Guards Corps might retaliate in kind. The previous month, in response to an EU decision to stop oil purchases from Iran, Iran threatened to close the Straits of Hormuz through which 20 per cent of the world's traded oil passes. If it did, Washington said it would reopen them by any means necessary. 'Tit for tat' now seemed inadequate to describe the dangerous escalation of what was arguably the world's gravest global political crisis.

Over the following months, the White House remained cautious, committed to sanctions and (attempted) diplomacy, but came under increasing attack from all sides. Domestically, the primaries for the Republican candidacy to challenge President Obama in the 2012 US presidential elections began to intensify, and Iran once again invaded US politics. With no clear winner emerging after the early primaries, the already internecine contest was particularly elongated and vicious, and an array of potential Republican candidates lined up to accuse the President of being 'soft' on Iran and, by contrast, to assure potential voters how tough they would be on the Islamic Republic in their potential administration. Former Governor of Massachusetts Mitt Romney penned an op-ed in the *Washington Post* in which, in a calculated jibe, he compared Washington's current relationship with Iran to the Hostage Crisis, and described Obama as the most 'feckless' US President since Jimmy Carter.[14]

The White House also came under international pressure from Israel, which had already been heightening its rhetoric against Iran throughout 2011. At a March 2012 meeting at the White House and then the American–Israel Affairs Committee meeting in Washington, Netanyahu made clear once again the gravity of the Iranian threat in Israel's eyes. Declaring that Israel would remain the 'master of its fate', and in a pointed reference to America's refusal to bomb Auschwitz in 1944, he challenged Obama to act against Iran. For his part, while Obama stressed that the bond between the two countries was 'unbreakable', he also stressed that there had been too much 'loose talk' of war with Iran. The meetings were tense as it became clear that Netanyahu had failed to push Washington into a clear commitment to military action against the Islamic Republic if it crossed specified 'red lines'.

Meanwhile, Iran may have been defiant, but it was feeling the pressure. On 23 January 2012, the EU had agreed to embargo Iran's oil (effective from July) and to freeze the assets of its central bank. This prompted Iran to pre-empt the embargo the following month by ceasing sales to Britain and France. (Both countries had already almost eliminated their reliance on Iranian oil – and Europe as a whole had nearly halved its Iranian imports – so the move was mostly symbolic.) In early March, in a direct offer to European Union foreign policy chief Catherine Ashton, Iran suggested further talks, saying the two sides should set 'the date and venue' of the talks as soon as possible so that a solution to the crisis might be found. No one on the Western side felt overly hopeful.

The two sides duly agreed to meet in Istanbul on 14 April – a meeting Obama described as Iran's 'last chance' to lift the threat of military action and increasing sanctions. But the omens were poor. In a 6 April interview on the Majlis website, MP Mesbahi-Moqaddam declared that Iran could manufacture a bomb if it so desired. Echoing Rowhani's point that the difference in enrichment levels was largely a political decision, he reaffirmed Iran's capability to enrich to 20 per cent and that 'the distance from 20 per cent [enrichment] to 75 per cent is very short'. Iran could, in fact, he continued, 'easily achieve over 90 per cent enrichment. [However], even though Iran is scientifically and technologically capable of manufacturing a nuclear weapon, it will never opt for this course'.[15]

As the talks neared, Iran's conservative elements were in full hubristic cry, arguing that the West was in terminal decline, that it was bankrupt and that it was ultimately incapable of imposing its will on Iran. In an 8 April editorial titled 'Lessons from the past for the April talks', the conservative newspaper *Kayhan* argued that there was little reason to take the USA seriously as it had backed down from every position it had taken over the past ten years – a series of 'red lines' on which it had 'capitulat[ed] to Iran's position' on every occasion.[16] Washington was, moreover, 'completely out of options, because it has played all its cards and because the military option is off the table'. Iran should, therefore, enter the talks with an awareness of its own position of strength and without the need to compromise.

As far as *Kayhan* was concerned, Obama, having backed down from all previous demands that Iran completely cease enrichment, was now looking [for] Iran to stop enriching [uranium] to 20 per cent at the Fordow [nuclear plant] and be content with 5 per cent enrichment at Natanz'. The pertinent question, it argued, was what Iran could 'infer from the thrust of the changes in [the American] positions. If we plot [these changes] on a graph, it will show an amazing downward plunge ... The American administration ... always sets large goals, and makes a huge fuss over them, but, once it realizes that they cannot be implemented, quietly adapts ... and replaces them with other, humbler, goals, while continuing to make a fuss'.[17] The USA, it continued, now had 'neither a Military Option Nor an Option of Sanctions'.

But, at least as far as sanctions were concerned, hubris had already met its own nemesis. Frustrated with repeatedly diluted UN sanctions, Washington had adopted a dual strategy of increased targeting of Iran's energy sector (which provides about 80 per cent of government revenues) and attempts to isolate it from the international financial system. The banking sanctions in particular now made it difficult for Tehran to do business in dollars and forced the government to rely on third party institutions of varying reliability to undertake transactions on its behalf. Washington had also pressured Iran's major Asian trade partners – including South Korea, Japan and India – into severing their oil imports to the country while convincing Saudi

Arabia and the UAE to increase oil production to compensate for any decreased flow of Iranian oil.[18] In June 2011, the USA had also imposed sanctions against Iran Air and Tidewater Middle East Co., which is responsible for the majority of Iranian trade. Combined with the effects of decades of internal financial mismanagement accentuated by an end to many state subsidies, Iran's economy was facing a gradual strangulation.

So journalistic bravado was not reflected in political behaviour. In January Tehran had ensured that a meeting with an IAEA delegation to Iran had gone off successfully. Ahmadinejad, desperate for some kind of political success, had welcomed the prospect of restarted talks, as had Salehi, and when the two sides met at Istanbul on 14 April the talks, while yielding nothing substantial, were cautiously hailed as a positive on both sides. Ashton said that there would be future discussions which would be guided by the 'principle of a step-by-step approach and reciprocity'. Meanwhile, Iranian chief nuclear negotiator Saeed Jalili described talks as being based on co-operation and 'very successful'.

Several weeks later, on 23 May, Iran and the P5+1 met once again, this time in Baghdad. After two days of talks a decision was reached: to meet again for yet more talks in Moscow in June. While many in Washington and Tel Aviv were frustrated with the seeming lack of progress on the question of uranium enrichment, the two sides were now engaged in the most sustained period of dialogue for almost three years. From the end of 2009 to the Istanbul talks in April 2012, Iran had made considerable progress on the programme while largely refusing even to meet with the P5+1. Its strategy of stalling diplomacy while continuing enrichment and increasing its stockpiles of LEU had been a success. During 2011, Iran even managed to smash through a technological barrier and enrich to 20 per cent. With things going so well, there was just no reason to negotiate.

But now, it seemed, there was; and the talks began with a P5+1 proposal that would allow Iran to enrich to low levels (far below the 20 per cent at which was currently enriching). Clearly, neither side was ready yet to compromise on its respective red lines. For the P5+1, this was the demand that Iran cease enriching uranium to 20 per cent levels at its Fordow plant, and the need for Tehran to surrender its existing stockpile of LEU. For Iran, it was an end to the sanctions on its oil and banking sectors that had been in place since the end of 2011. During two days of fraught talks, the P5+1 offered to lift only a few peripheral sanctions, on items like Iranian aircraft parts, which Iran greeted with derision, while continuing to argue for its 'inalienable right' to enrich uranium under Article IV of the NPT (which allows states to pursue peaceful nuclear technologies 'without discrimination').

And the Iranians had a point. The P5+1 offered nothing of substance, refusing even to show reciprocity to news earlier in the week that in separate negotiations with the IAEA Iran was close to allowing inspectors greater access to some of its more controversial nuclear sites. While this was likely just another Iranian stalling tactic (showing supposed good faith on a matter of less importance while it stonewalled on the real issues), even IAEA Director General Yukiya Amano had described the possibility of an imminent deal as 'an important development'.

The offer was, however, instructive. Asking Iran to enrich at lower levels than it was currently doing in exchange for a token lifting of peripheral sanctions was to proffer the stick with no attendant carrot. Such a palpably weak offer was always going to be rejected, which indicated that the P5+1 was now confident of two things: that Iran was not currently building a bomb, and that there was time to negotiate before a possible Israeli attack. Moreover, as each day passed Iran's economy weakened even more; its people grew more restless. The days when the Mullahs could sell the programme as a totem of national achievement in the face in western 'imperialism' were long gone – Iranians now cared more about jobs than about centrifuges.

Quite simply: the P5+1 knew that Iranian diplomats were in Baghdad because they needed to be there. For a long time, the Iranians calculated (correctly) that each day without diplomatic movement was one more day of uranium enrichment. Now

Tehran needed some movement, but times had changed. The EU's oil embargo and unprecedented US sanctions on Iran's oil sales would formally come into effect at the beginning of July. At that point, Washington would then move to impose yet more sanctions on Iran's oil exports, with even tougher action to come: why would the P5+1 offer anything of substance now? Rather, they were now content to let the pressure mount on Iran to see just how high a price it was willing to pay for its diplomatic intransigence. For years Western diplomats had vented their frustration at Iranian stalling tactics; now it seemed that the P5+1 were playing Iran at its own game.

It was perhaps then unsurprising that the run-up to the Moscow talks on 18–19 June 2012 was ill-tempered on all sides. In Iran, a few days before the talks began, Jalili told the Majlis that an acknowledgement of Iran's right to enrich was still the key Iranian demand for the talks. There would, he continued, be no suspension of uranium enrichment (still a central P5+1 demand), and claimed Iran would pull out of the talks if they focused solely on the nuclear issue without addressing other concerns such as human rights in Bahrain and piracy in the Persian Gulf. Only after assurances from EU Foreign Policy Chief Cathy Ashton, he continued, had Iran agreed to go ahead with the talks. Jalili then claimed that the West was conducting a colonial war against Iran to keep it from scientific advancement, telling the parliament that the nuclear programme was 'a symbol of our resistance and progress'. The 'West's' opposition to it, he claimed, stemmed from 'fear that the Islamic Republic could serve as a role model for progress and defiance in other countries'.[19]

So the atmosphere was gloomy as diplomats arrived in Moscow. Two days of fraught negotiations followed with both sides as far apart as ever. Ashton reaffirmed demands for Iran to stop enriching uranium to 20 per cent, ship out the existing stock of such material, and shut down the Fordow enrichment facility. Iran still refused to do so but – fearful of mounting pressure (even if this fear wasn't manifested in its official rhetoric) – had for the first time, in Ashton's words, begun to address P5+1 concerns about the nuclear programme directly. There was, however, a long way to go. For his part, Jalili, in Iran's first detailed analysis of the P5+1 proposal, went through a list of objections before inevitably expounding at length about Tehran's grievances with the West dating back to the 1960s. But he also called the talks 'more serious and more realistic' than the earlier rounds in Istanbul and Baghdad and, clearly still eager to keep dialogue going, mooted the possibility that the supply of nuclear fuel from abroad could form part of a deal in the future.[20]

Jalili also warned that the widescale EU and US oil export sanctions coming in on 1 July risked derailing the negotiating process, while US officials remained adamant that there would be no softening of the sanctions against Tehran. As far at the P5+1 saw it, Iran faced the same choice it had faced for the last ten years: the carrot or the stick; more and tougher sanctions or compromise and assistance on a wide array of issues. It was stalemate once more. But, despite Iranian displeasure, the need for engagement remained as sanctions tightened, and talks were kept alive through an agreement of a process for future meetings. There would be more dialogue at least.

Nonetheless, by summer 2012 the situation was depressingly clear. Iran continued with enrichment; the IAEA was increasingly sceptical, and the Europeans and Americans were increasingly concerned but hamstrung by China and Russia in the Security Council. Israel was more belligerent still. The Arab states were terrified and, amid all this, Iran was defiant. Bushehr had finally more or less come online (and would soon go off again) but doubts of the Russian technical capabilities continued and the programme was also said to suffer internal technical problems. No one could be sure. Iran remained internally divided and politically unpredictable. The EU was sanctioning Iranian oil. Iran said such measures would yield nothing. Fifty-seven years on from the birth of nuclear power in Iran, and approaching the tenth anniversary of the crisis, the déjà vu was vertiginous.

* * *

Iran's nuclear programme continues to progress without sign of slowdown. Just as China's Cultural Revolution had no impact on its nuclear programme, Iran's political crisis has not yet affected its nuclear goals, which remain to develop and expand its enrichment capacity, and more besides. The West now faces a strategic programme, more or less on autopilot. Stuxnet may have disrupted centrifuge operation and uranium enrichment, and Israeli assassinations of nuclear scientists may yet complicate things further, but diplomatic pressure has so far been insufficient to change Iranian behaviour. The hardliners that have dominated Tehran from 2005 concluded early on that their strategy was working and just continued. Set against this are wider political pressures that, since the 2009 presidential elections, saw the blossoming of a trend that had begun several years earlier as the nuclear programme evolved from a national totem to a pawn in an internal political struggle. Had Ahmadinejad been able to accept the 2010 Geneva deal he so clearly wanted, the crisis may well have been diffused. So polarized was Iranian politics, and so determined were his opponents to block any deal for which he might get credit, that the national interest suffered. In Ahmadinejad's nuclear hubris may lie his nemesis; his description of the programme as a 'train without brakes' appears accurate. It may yet derail him, and the regime.

Obama's policy had success, even if it failed to achieve the détente he wanted. His unclenched fist slapped the Mullahs in the face by removing their biggest propaganda tool: American enmity. After the elections the Iranian people would no longer be distracted from the regime's incompetence and brutality by the spectre of an external threat, and the Green Movement's challenge to the regime was, in part, encouraged by Washington's attempts to engage. Obama made Ahmadinejad's marginalization, to a large degree self-inflicted, easier. Already in most regards a preposterous figure (with his lick of black hair, flocculent beard and comic malevolence, he is in many ways the corporeal embodiment of the 'Evil Iran' narrative) he now cuts a diminished figure, under attack both nationally and internationally.

Negotiations also did much to boost the credibility of the P5+1 at the expense of the Iranian government. Had the Bush Administration 'revealed' Fordow, it would have likely been met with considerably more scepticism. This time, however, the international community was much more receptive, precisely because of Obama's effort to reach out to the Iranian government. So was the IAEA, whose head at the time – Mohammad ElBaradei – began to speak about Iran in more robust language than ever before. He claimed that Iran's refusal to follow the safeguards requirement (abbreviated as Code 3.1) to report new nuclear facilities at the time a decision is made to build them meant that Iran had operated on 'the wrong side of the law'. But time is now a factor; if Israel continues to threaten Iran's nuclear facilities then there must come a point at which its Israeli leaders live up to their own rhetoric. An imminent change of US President may also signal a hardening of the US position. This points to a wider truth: all the major developments in the programme's history – from its founding to its abandonment and subsequent restart as a symbol of national defiance, and then finally its mutation into the domestic political hand grenade it is today – have been political. It is politics not physics that will dictate the resolution of this crisis, one way or another.

CHAPTER 17

CONCLUSION

This book was an attempt to do what I thought necessary: to begin at the beginning. I believed that to resolve the nuclear crisis a full understanding of the nuclear programme itself was necessary. I hoped that this was possible and expected that this would be found in its history, which is also the history of modern Iran. The programme is one of the country's most overt attempts to negotiate Iran's great crisis – modernity – and it is the vessel that carries within it the various prejudices, beliefs, fears and hopes that together comprise the modern Iranian state. These are what must be addressed in order to find a solution, which will not come through deals over centrifuges but through wider, political solutions that resolve Iran's place in the world.

I argued that Iran's programme has two 'histories' – the evolution of a fairly shambolic project that for the majority of its existence focused on one partially built reactor at Bushehr and some surrounding facilities (within which is a more covert history of undeclared activities), and the 'nuclear debate' – created by organizing principles on both sides that have affected its course for over 50 years. We turn initially to the first: a civil nuclear programme officially designed to create nuclear-powered electricity to preserve Iran's oil reserves. In theory, the argument is economically sound. The Shah's dictum that a barrel of oil was 'too valuable to burn for fuel' was true – Iran has always needed to sell its oil to survive; today the Islamic Republic is just as adamant that it needs to free oil production for export in order to earn foreign exchange. It also argues that new power-generating capacity is needed to meet the rising demand of a population that has been growing for close to a century. At its current growth rate, Tehran says that it needs at least an additional 2,000 MW of electricity each year. If it fails to identify new oil resources within its borders, domestic needs will absorb the country's entire oil production.[1]

But there are significant differences between the Islamic Republic and the Shah's Iran. The Shah was flushed with oil wealth and already implementing plans for a huge programme of up to 20 reactors – enough to supply Iran with nuclear-generated electricity – when the revolution came. The Islamic Republic is in desperate financial difficulties, and while it still talks vaguely about 20 planned reactors, it has spent 30 years struggling to bring a single reactor at Bushehr online. And even when (or more likely if) Bushehr does come online, it will only account for about 2 per cent of Iran's electricity consumption. Most damningly of all, only 17 per cent of the country's electricity is now produced by oil, against 75 per cent from gas, so, despite Tehran's arguments, the amount of oil that nuclear-generated electricity would free for export is questionable. Nuclear power is also more expensive than many other forms of energy generation, such as solar or hydropower, not to mention the huge potential for renewable energies that Tehran seems to have overlooked. When set against its huge financial cost, the nuclear programme has been far from economical for Iran.

The envisaged general advancement in scientific expertise that a nuclear programme would bring has, on the other hand, largely held true. The Russians built Bushehr, but the AEOI has almost finished the Arak plant and with it has gained the ability to indigenously produce heavy water. It also, of course, now has an advanced uranium-enrichment programme. It has a significant base of high quality nuclear scientists and a number of nuclear science programmes throughout the country. The Sharif Institute of Technology is considered the MIT of the Middle East and has benefited from the nuclear programme (as well as the Islamic Republic's general emphasis on science and technology). Perhaps most important of all, Iran has mastered the nuclear fuel cycle and is, from a strictly technical point of view, a nuclear state. Iran is a more scientifically advanced country with its nuclear programme than without.

But at what cost? Sanctions have hurt the country financially and technologically while the programme's political cost has been devastating. And if one were to take an actuarial calculation, it is doubtful that it has been worth it, especially to create nuclear fuel for reactors that do not exist. The slogan of the Islamic Republic was 'Freedom, Independence, Islamic Republic', and in 1979 the AEOI rejected the nuclear programme on the grounds that it was a Trojan Horse for foreign influence – one more 'surrender' to the West. Over 30 years on, has the nuclear programme made Iran more self-sufficient and given it the independence it has craved at least since the 1905 Constitutional Revolution?

The answer is a categorical 'no'. Iran is isolated and in serious danger of military attack from Israel, the Middle East's more powerful military force, and the USA, the world's most powerful state. Tehran's reliance on Russia and China to offset its isolation through trade, protect it in the UN Security Council and supply it with nuclear technology has been crippling. Iran is awash with cheap Chinese goods – of far lower quality than those exported to the West. Meanwhile, Russia continues to 'dictate' to Iran with seeming impunity. In 2007 the two countries signed a contract for Moscow to provide Tehran with at least five S-300 air-defence systems to combat possible airstrikes. Under pressure from fellow Security Council members, Moscow reneged on the deal in late 2011 and merely returned Iran's deposit (without interest). Tehran threatened to sue, but there is little it can do. No other state with suitably advanced military technology to sell will deal with Iran and it cannot afford to alienate Moscow and risk losing its political cover in the Security Council or access to Russian nuclear technology. There has been a greater 'surrender' to foreign powers under the Islamic Republic than there ever was under the Shah (who, at least, received cutting-edge technology from Washington). And all to gain technology that the USA mastered 60 years ago (and even India and Pakistan over 20 years ago) for a reactor that has not yet come online and that will only provide a tiny fraction of the country's energy needs.

Which immediately raises the question: why persist with the programme for so long and at such a cost? Is an Iranian bomb the only logical reason for the programme? The question remains difficult to responsibly answer for sure. Iran has lied to the IAEA for over two decades, but there remains no 'smoking gun' for a weapons programme. Akbar Etemad, Reza Amrollahi and Gholamreza Aghazadeh all tried to co-operate with, variously, the West, the Chinese, the Russians, South America, Eastern Europe and many more. The consistent obstruction that the latter two especially faced from Washington may well, to a degree, have pushed underground post-revolutionary nuclear work on enrichment, reprocessing and conversion (Iran certainly tried to do it publicly first). Certainly, also, the desire for an indigenous fuel cycle is common for countries with a nuclear programme, especially developing countries, and is just as important for a civil programme as for the production of nuclear weapons. Governments dependent upon commercial partners for nuclear technology are always in a weakened position, subject to the whims (and occasional caprice) of their suppliers. For the developing world, nuclear power is both a conduit to advancement and an escape from dependence.

But the decision taken in the mid-1980s and sanctioned at almost the highest political level, by Iran's Prime Minister himself, to pursue a covert enrichment programme during the intensification of a war in which Iran's enemy had used WMDs against it and was (likely) building its own nuclear deterrent indicates, by all tests of logic, a more than purely civil interest in an enrichment programme. Without a reactor to be fuelled, Iran simply had no need for an enrichment programme at all. Even today, Bushehr will be fuelled by Russia. Iranian desires for 'self-sufficiency' notwithstanding, the huge political cost of its enrichment programme (it stands at the centre of global concerns, it *is* the Iranian nuclear crisis) suggests desires that transcend a mere wish for nuclear fuel. Even more worrying is the choice of technology: an enrichment path to a bomb made, and makes, sense on a security level – it can be hidden underground, with centrifuge plants dispersed across the country. In 1985, when the decision was made to commence, the vulnerabilities of a single above-ground reactor had only recently been comprehensively demonstrated by Israel's destruction of the Iraqi reactor at Osirak. Now both the USA and Israel keep the 'military option' on the table when discussing Iran's programme, and threats of possible strikes, both from Benjamin Netanyahu's government and US Republican candidates (one of whom may dictate future US policy), grow each day.

Iran's possible motivations for a bomb make the case for a military dimension even more compelling. The Islamic Republic was born in conflict: with the Shah and, after the Hostage Crisis, with the West. The Iran–Iraq war then taught Iran both the devastating effects of WMDs and that the world would not act to stop their use. The many treaties condemning their use were so many 'pieces of paper'. As far as Tehran was concerned, the war had proved Khomeini right: self-sufficiency was the answer, and it is perfectly conceivable that, to Tehran, this might well be achieved through Iran's own attainment of WMDs. Rafsanjani himself had urged as much at the end of the war. Some years later, Khamenei installed Aghazadeh to preside over an accelerated drive towards enrichment and heavy water, both clear paths to a bomb.

But most serious of all is the clash with Washington: historically, the single most important factor in whether Iran goes 'nuclear' or not. First is the question of the US anti-proliferation stance: even when Washington's great ally the Shah ruled Iran, the USA would not countenance any possible Iranian proliferation – its consistency, and sincerity, on the issue for over 50 years cannot be doubted. Second, and more problematically, is the question of wider relations between the two countries. Over 30 years ago the Hostage Crisis and later the Iran-Contra affair brought Iran into the American psyche. The two countries began to clash politically, and the prospect of military conflict gradually began to grow. The fall of the Berlin Wall in 1989 and the disintegration of the USSR set the USA free. Gulf War One saw the presence of huge numbers of US troops in Saudi Arabia and the UAE, and the US Navy in the Persian Gulf. The 2003 Iraq War found Iran, to all intents, encircled on its own continent by a Bush Administration seemingly decided on 'regime change' in Iran. Even after President Obama's attempted détente, and over 30 years after the Islamic Revolution, the fundamental problem of US–Iranian relations persists.

Iran still invades US politics. It featured heavily during the Republican primaries of early- to mid-2012, which saw the then Republican candidate (and eventual Republican nominee) Mitt Romney ramp up the threat of military action in absolute terms. During a 7 January GOP debate in the run-up to the 10 January New Hampshire primary, Romney set out the choice, as he saw it, facing American voters: 'If we re-elect Barack Obama, Iran will have a nuclear weapon,' he said. 'And if we elect Mitt Romney . . . as the next President, they will not have a nuclear weapon.'[2] Electioneering aside, the assumptions behind the statement are perhaps most illuminating: Iran is an issue on which the American voter is expected to choose his next President. It is a Manichean issue and it is a debate couched in fear. Nothing, it seems, has changed.

Then, of course, there is precedent. The 2003 overthrow of Saddam taught Tehran what Washington would do against states that did not, as it turned out, have nuclear weapons. And it came only two years after Iran watched American troops invade Afghanistan to strike the Taliban for harbouring al-Qaeda, while nuclear-armed Pakistan, which had also harboured al-Qaeda and spawned the AQ Khan network, was welcomed at the White House as a US ally. Libya's decision in December 2003 to voluntarily give up its nuclear programme in exchange for normalization of relations proved (so hardliners in Tehran argued) to be its undoing when NATO planes helped rebels overthrow Gaddafi almost seven years later.

Since the days of the Shah the nuclear programme has been a source of Iranian pride. The Islamic Republic's ideological belief (enshrined in the constitution) of the need to achieve 'self-sufficiency' only accentuates the prestige of having a technologically advanced, indigenous nuclear programme. But for Iran prestige seeps into security: they are two sides of the same coin. As Iran has invaded the American psyche, so too has almost 200 years of foreign meddling invaded the Iranian psyche. The revolutionaries carried images of the overthrown Mossadegh through the streets in 1979, and this image drives Iranian policy to this day. The more Iran is able to defend itself from external threats, the more it redresses the perceived injustices of the past. The stronger it becomes, the prouder it becomes. The need for security is both practical and psychological.

It is all these impulses that make the more obvious elements of weaponization of grave concern. Even leaving aside the controversial 'Alleged Studies' on weaponization (the veracity of which are in doubt) the experiments with metal hemispheres and the possible documentation Iran received from the Khan network on a weapons design point to, at the very least, an interest in nuclear weapons. Then, of course, there are the experiments with Polonium-210, which is used in the production of nuclear weapons. Even the 2007 US National Intelligence Estimate that did so much to dampen appetite for an attack on Iran assessed that Iran had had a covert weapons programme until at least 2003 (and could not say for certain that it had not been restarted). No serious observer can believe that Iran's nuclear-related activities are solely for the purpose of building and maintaining nuclear power plants for civilian uses. There are just too many unanswered questions with military connotations.

An Islamic Republic with even a nuclear-weapons capability would have serious repercussions: for the Iranian people, for the

CONCLUSION

Middle East balance of power, for international relations both re-
gionally and globally, and for the international non-proliferation
regime, not least by triggering a likely chain of proliferation across
the Middle East. The NPT would also likely be dealt a blow from
which it might never recover. Iran has spent half a century telling
the world its programme is peaceful, and if it now 'broke out' into
nuclear-weapons capability it is more than likely that threshold
states such as Brazil would follow its example. The situation is
critical and, given the programme's advanced state today, time is
running out for a diplomatic solution.

The question remains whether or not the decision has been
made to build a bomb, and the answer still cannot be known with
certainty. At the very least, Iran's consistent progress over recent
years in uranium enrichment points to a move to achieve, or to
get close to achieving, the *capability* for a bomb. And this is the answer that this author presents. Iran's technological progress over
the last ten years means it is now in possession of a highly advanced uranium-enrichment programme. This is worrying in the
extreme because, as Hasan Rowhani told the Supreme Cultural
Revolution Council in September 2005, from an Iranian point
of view the only difference between enriching uranium to levels
required for civil purposes (around 3.5 per cent to power nuclear reactors) and to weapons-grade levels (80 per cent or above,
although 93 per cent is considered ideal for weapons purposes)
is the political decision to do so. Iran now has the technological
capability to do it. Only the political decision remains.

A nuclear-weapons capability – by which the state has sur-
mounted all technological obstacles to a bomb without actually
proceeding with the final stages of weaponization (which could
be achieved quickly if the need arose) – has several benefits. Most
potent of these is that it offers all of the political benefits of nuclear
capability – deterrence, prestige, political leverage – without the
political cost – having to leave the NPT, becoming a true pariah
state, totally crippling sanctions. Iran's sense of itself is too great
for it to allow this to happen. It wants more international engagement, not less.

And this offers hope. The programme's political history shows that any desire for a bomb is not the entire story. The crisis has never been about just centrifuges, or if it has they spin within a context. A Manichean conflict sundered by the non-proliferation regime, the divisions between the developing and developed world, and those between the Islamic and Western worlds, have created cultural and ideological assumptions on each side that organize and drive what I have termed the nuclear debate. At the centre of the crisis stands Iran and its attempts to find a place for itself in the modern world.

Nuclear power, in and of itself, strikes a significant register for Iran. It illustrates a developing country's need for all of nuclear power's associated benefits to plug the deficit of prestige it feels in relation to its Western contemporaries. The Persian psyche is cleaved, scarred by past humiliations. It is also bloated with a sense of its own importance. Iranian political rhetoric is filled with pronouncements about its own country's greatness and how this must be recognized by the world. Both the Shah and the Islamic Republic associated nuclear power with ideas of national intellect and advancement – it was and remains a viable shortcut to a desired modernity.

The country is a quasi post-colonial state, still attempting to escape the burden of its 'subservient' recent past, which it has mythologized into a singular lesson of Western perfidy and the virtues of 'self-reliance' and self-respect. Iranian leaders, whether they be the Shah or the Mullahs, like the leaders of other developing countries, have grasped at whatever they can to achieve these goals. In this vein, both the ambition of the Shah's reign and the apparent belligerence of the Islamic Republic are seen for what they are: variant expressions of the same impulse. An impulse made more acute by a deeply held belief that international nuclear governance as enshrined in the NPT has stabilized a system of nuclear division that reflects Western ideological assumptions: a kind of nuclear 'Orientalism' in a world still dominated by colonial oppression that either seeks to keep the developing world 'down' or considers modernizing states incapable of being responsible enough to be trusted with nuclear technology.[3] Ahmadinejad's cries of 'nuclear apartheid' are deliberate and, to the right audience, resonant. The divide remains as strong as ever almost 60 years after the birth of nuclear power and has enabled much of Iran's diplomatic strategy of the past decade.

Over the past ten years Iran has, in fact, played a complex game of brinkmanship involving multifaceted negotiations that it seeks to obstruct and hinder while simultaneously staying within the international fold and, barely, within the pale. Through all its defiant talk it has always expressed a willingness to negotiate – even if only as a stalling tactic. Despite internal debates and the occasional threat, it has shown no signs of withdrawing from the NPT and thereby turning itself into a genuine outcast. In the meantime, it has crept onwards with its programme and entered the diplomatic game of nations more fully than at any time since the coming of the Islamic Revolution.

The nuclear programme is the ultimate expression of modern Iran – evolving alongside the state itself. The Shah needed it to mimic his Western role models – to appropriate their technology to show how modern (read: 'Western') his country was. The programme was his means of negotiating Iran's relationship with a world that had proved so perpetually hostile, and the way he chose to drag his country into modernity. The Islamic Republic initially rejected the programme on the same grounds, but once it came under attack it became a symbol of a defiant modernizing state that overtly confronted the system that denied it justice. Spurred by ideology and Khomeini, the programme became a means of appropriating Western technology to help create an identity for Iran in the modern world, but on its own uniquely Iranian and Islamic terms.

For today's Islamic Republic little has changed, as the great colonial powers, now nuclear-armed, oppress the Third World, restricting freedom through the buildup of arsenals and support of surrogate powers. The Iranian struggle and quest for independence now takes the form of rhetorical steadfastness in the face of 'oppression'. But, importantly, the system is not rejected; the struggle is for greater independence *within* it. Iran does not want to abandon or tear down the international order. It wants its rightful place within that order: Gulf strongman with much to say on global matters (a goal that, although it differs qualitatively, mirrors the Shah's). This has its own problems, of course: the region has much to fear from Iranian ambitions, but it is not totally beyond reason. It is not yet North Korea.

This offers some hope because, above all else, history shows us what the programme was not: a linear project with dogmatically fixed goals, either civilian or military. Rather, antithetical regimes drove it in different directions for different reasons. It is noticeable that throughout much of Iranian history the weapons dimension was often both less developed and of less *concern* than civilian power. This is often misunderstood because there is a failure to grasp what nuclear power itself means to a developing country like Iran that seeks to accommodate itself in the world and uses varying means – of which a nuclear programme is one – to do this. The Islamic Republic is a 'fundamentalist', 'rogue' state, but it is also a modernizing state seeking greater independence and self-respect within the world and using varying means – of which nuclear power is one – to achieve this.

Both the Pahlavi state and the Islamic Republic have tried to forge an identity for themselves in the world. The Shah sought to impose a royal narrative on his state linked with imperial greatness; the Islamic Republic tried to construct a 'biography' of the Islamic 'outsider' treated unjustly yet remaining defiant and resolute. In this sense, the nuclear programme has at its heart perennial drives central to the Iranian state in all its manifestations, and is, in many ways, the exegesis of modern Iran, the *tabula rasa* (blank slate) onto which its evolution has been and continues to be written. Only by understanding this is it clear just how desirable – even beyond any wish for a nuclear weapon – nuclear power has been for Iran under both regimes, although for vastly different reasons; and why throughout the programme's history an energy-rich state facing increasing international political isolation has persisted with a project from which, even today, it derives little benefit. The supreme irony of the nuclear crisis is that Iran's nuclear programme is the ultimate expression of its desire for acceptance (but on its own terms) that is pursued through the one means that will ensure it remains a pariah. Iran continues, nonetheless, because history has taught it that in an unforgiving world this acceptance can only be achieved from a position of strength. How exactly it achieves this desired strength is the question that will irrevocably alter the world we live in, one way or another.

APPENDIX A

STAGES OF THE NUCLEAR FUEL CYCLE

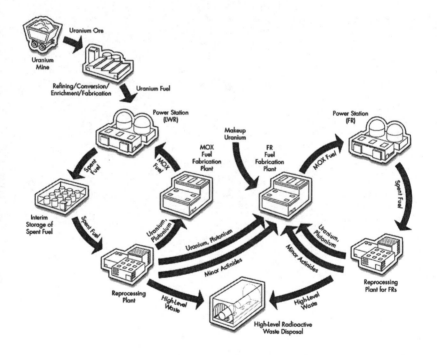

The nuclear fuel cycle uses uranium in different chemical and physical forms. This cycle typically includes the following stages:

- Uranium recovery to extract (or *mine*) uranium ore, and concentrate (or *mill*) the ore to produce 'yellowcake'
- Conversion of yellowcake into UF_6

- Enrichment to increase the concentration of uranium-235 (U^{235}) in UF_6 (to either civil levels c. 20 per cent max or weapons-grade levels – around 80 per cent, 93 per cent ideally required by weapons manufacturers)
- Deconversion to reduce the hazards associated with the depleted Uranium Hexafluoride (DUF_6), or 'tailings', produced in earlier stages of the fuel cycle
- Fuel fabrication to convert enriched UF_6 into fuel for nuclear reactors
- Use of the fuel in reactors (nuclear power, research or naval propulsion)
- Interim storage of spent nuclear fuel
- Reprocessing (or *recycling*) of high-level waste (currently not done in the USA)
- Final disposition (disposal) of high-level waste

APPENDIX B

IRAN'S NUCLEAR POWER FUEL CYCLE

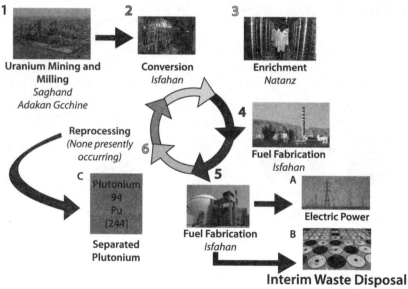

1 Uranium Mining and Milling
Saghand
Adakan Gcchine

2 Conversion
Isfahan

3 Enrichment
Natanz

Reprocessing
(None presently occurring)

6

4 Fuel Fabrication
Isfahan

C Plutonium
94
Pu
[244]

Separated Plutonium

5 Fuel Fabrication
Isfahan

A Electric Power

B Interim Waste Disposal
Anarak

APPENDIX C

THE NUCLEAR WEAPONS CYCLE

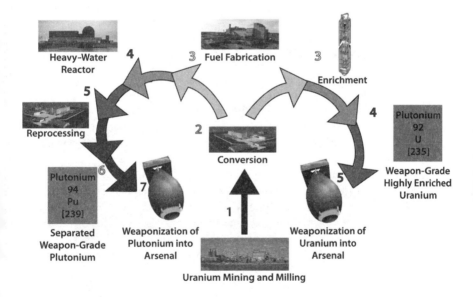

Source: http://www.isisnucleariran.org/sites/weapons-fuel-cycle

NOTES

CHAPTER 1: IN THE BEGINNING WAS THE ATOM BOMB: NUCLEAR POWER AND THE POST-WAR WORLD

1. *The Fulton Sun*, http://century.guardian.co.uk/1940-1949/Story/0,,127720, 00.html [accessed 16 July 2012].
2. UN GA Resolution 1 (1) 'Establishment of a Commission to Deal with the Problem Raised by the Discovery of Atomic Energy', January 1946, in *UN Official Document Search*, http://documents.un.org [accessed 11 January 2007].
3. UN GA Resolution 192 (III) 'Prohibition of the Atomic Weapon and Reduction by One-Third of the Armaments and Armed Forces of the Permanent Members of the Security Council', 19 November 1948, in *UN Official Document Search*, http://documents.un.org [accessed 10 January 2007].
4. See C.F. Barnaby, *Preventing the Spread of Nuclear Weapons* (Pugwash Symposium, 1969).
5. 'Atoms for Peace Speech', in *IAEA*, http://www.iaea.org/About/history_speech.html [accessed 23 June 2006].
6. Confidential Security Information, 'Summary of Reactions to President Eisenhower's Speech Before the General Assembly, December 8, 1953', 16 December 1953, p. 1.
7. 'Confidential Letter Addressed to the President of the United States', 6 December 1953, in *Digital National Security Archive*, http://nsarchive. chadwyck.com/nsa/documents/NP/00137/all.pdf [accessed 6 February 2007. Link no longer working].
8. Although Iran's reaction has remained unlocatable.

9. Confidential Security Information, 'Summary of Reactions to President Eisenhower's Speech Before the General Assembly, December 8, 1953', 16 December 1953, p. 1.
10. Confidential Letter, 'Let's Open the "Simple Case" of the Peaceful Atom', in *Digital National Security Archive*, http://nsarchive.chadwyck.com/nsa/documents/NP/00140/all.pdf [accessed 23 January 2007. Link no longer working].

CHAPTER 2: TWO CENTURIES OF LOSS: IRAN AT THE ADVENT OF NUCLEAR POWER

1. Abbas Milani, *The Shah* (New York: Palgrave Macmillan, 2011), p. 86.
2. Abbas Milani, *The Shah*, p. 82.
3. Ibid., p. 87.
4. For a fuller discussion, see Ruhollah K. Ramazani, *Iran's Foreign Policy 1941–1973: A Study of Foreign Policy in Modernizing Nations* (Charlottesville: University of Virginia, 1975).
5. Abbas Milani, *The Shah*, p. 91.
6. For a fuller discussion, see Homa Katouzian, *Mussaddiq and the Struggle for Power in Iran* (London: I.B.Tauris, 1999).
7. Mohammad Reza Pahlavi, *Mission for My Country* (London: Hutchinson, 1961), pp. 125–6.
8. Ibid., pp. 124–5.
9. Cyril E. Black, 'Challenges to an Evolving Legal Order', in Richard A. Falk and Cyril E. Black (eds), *The Future of the International Legal Order*, Vol. 1, *Trends and Patterns* (Princeton: Princeton University Press, 1969), in Ramazani, *Iran's Foreign Policy*, p. 11.

CHAPTER 3: THE PEACOCK WANTS TO STRUT: NUCLEAR POWER UNDER THE SHAH

1. US Department of State, 'Atoms for Peace Agreement with Iran', *Department of State Bulletin* 36, 5 April 1957, p. 629.
2. Nuclear power reactors are rated by their electrical output (MWe). Research reactors do not produce electricity, so they are rated by their thermal output, which means the full title here should be 5 MWt. The power produced by a 5 MWt plant is 5 MW (of heat): that is every second it produces 5 million joules of heat energy. Only about one-third of that can be converted into electricity. So this plant would produce 5 MWt or 1.7 MWe. For the sake of the reader 'MW' will be used for both in the expectation that the reader remembers the difference.
3. Etemad interview, 2009.

4. Daniel Poneman, 'Nuclear Policies in Developing Countries', *International Affairs (Royal Institute of International Affairs 1944-)* 57/4, Autumn 1981, p. 570. See also Homi. J. Bhabha, 'Science and the Problems of Development', *Science* 151, 4 February 1966, p. 545.
5. Ervand Abrahamian, 'Structural Causes of the Iranian Revolution', in *MERIP Reports* No. 87, *Iran's Revolution: The Rural Dimension*, May 1980, pp. 21–2.
6. Ibid.
7. Louis Kraar, 'The Shah Drives to Build a New Empire', *Fortune*, October 1974.
8. See below for a fuller discussion.
9. Author interview with Akbar Etemad, London, 2007.
10. Ibid.
11. Khazaneh interview via email, September 2011.
12. Ibid.
13. Poneman, 'Nuclear Policies', p. 568.
14. In contrast, by the second half of the 1970s Iran's long-term external debt was some $7.5 billion as against some $15 billion of foreign exchange assets. Jahangir Amuzegar, *Iran's Economy under the Islamic Republic* (London: I.B.Tauris, February 1993), p. 6.
15. UN Department of International Economic and Social Affairs, Statistical Office, *World Energy Supplies 1973–1978* (New York: United Nations, 1979), pp. 246–60.
16. Poneman, 'Nuclear Policies', p. 569.
17. *National Security Archive*, Secret, Memorandum State, 'Memorandum to the President for the Visit of the Shah', *Collection: Iran Revolution*, 8 November 1977, p. 3.
18. Pahlavi, *Mission*, p. 288. While the point is valid it should also be noted that the high rate of oil consumption, domestically at least, largely resulted from huge state subsidies on oil, and internal mass consumption and waste was a consequence of very low consumer prices set by the state.
19. *New York Times*, 17 May 1962.
20. Ibid., pp. 85–6.
21. *New York Times*, 31 December 1977.
22. Pahlavi, *Mission*, p. 288.
23. Ibid.
24. Poneman, 'Nuclear Policies', p. 576.
25. Anne Hessing Cahn, 'Determinants of the Nuclear Option: The Case of Iran', in Onkar S. Marwah and Ann Schulz (eds), *Nuclear Proliferation and the Near-Nuclear Countries* (Cambridge, Mass.: Ballinger, 1975), p. 192.
26. Akbar Etemad, interview by author, London, 22 December 2007.

NOTES

27. Daniel Poneman, *Nuclear Power in the Developing World* (London: George Allen & Unwin, 1982), p. 86.
28. Harold Nicolson, *The Meaning of Prestige* (Cambridge: Cambridge University Press, 1937), p. 9.
29. 'June 1974 – First Nuclear Test – International Reactions', in *Keesings World News Archive*, http://www.keesings.com [accessed 10 March 2007].
30. For a fuller discussion on the treaty, see Edwin Brown Firmage, 'The Treaty on the Non-Proliferation of Nuclear Weapons', *The American Journal of International Law* 63/4, October 1969, pp. 711–46.
31. For a fuller discussion, see Hugh Gusterson, 'Nuclear Weapons and the Other in the Western Imagination', *Cultural Anthropology* 14/1, February 1999.
32. CIA, Directorate of Intelligence, Office of Political Research, Research Study, 'Managing Nuclear Proliferation: The Politics of Limited Choice', Secret, excised copy, December 1975, p. 13.
33. Richard K. Betts, 'Incentives for Nuclear Weapons: India, Pakistan, Iran', *Asian Survey* 19/11, 1979, p. 1054.
34. Pahlavi, *Mission*, p. 132.
35. For a fuller discussion, see Ali M. Ansari, 'The Myth of the White Revolution: Mohammad Reza Shah, "Modernization" and the Consolidation of Power', *Middle Eastern Studies* 37/3, July 2001, pp. 1–24.
36. Ibid.
37. Pahlavi, *Mission*, p. 145.
38. Ibid., p. 136.
39. Scott Sagan, 'Why Do States Build Nuclear Weapons? Three Models in Search of a Bomb', *International Security* 21/3, Winter 1996/97, pp. 73–4.
40. Ibid., p. 307.
41. CIA, 'Iran: An Overview of the Shah's Economy', Confidential, Memorandum, 16 October 1974, p. 4.
42. Cahn, 'Determinants', p. 192.
43. Poneman, *Nuclear Power*, p. 92.
44. Author interview with Reza Khazaneh, London, 2010.
45. Ibid.
46. *AG Friedensforschung*, http://www.ag-friedensforschung.de/regionen/Iran/bushehr.html [From German] [accessed 5 August 2011].
47. Khazaneh interview by email, December 2011.
48. Etemad interview, 2009.
49. Etemad correspondence, December 2011.
50. Ibid.
51. The US Atomic Energy Commission also agreed to supply Iran with fuel for two 1,200 MWe light-water reactors and signed a provisional agreement to supply fuel for as many as six additional reactors with a total power capacity

of 8,000 MWe. In October 1977, the State Department announced that Iran would buy eight nuclear reactors from the USA for generating electricity.

52. See next chapter.

53. 'Uranium Enrichment: How to Make an Atomic Bomb', *Cosmos Magazine*, 22 August 2006, http://www.cosmosmagazine.com/news/579/uranium-enrichment-how-make-atomic-bomb [accessed 2 November 2011].

54. 'How to Build an Atomic Bomb', *The UnMuseum*, http://www.unmuseum.org/buildabomb.htm [accessed 2 November 2011].

55. See Appendix A.

56. Etemad correspondence, December 2011.

57. See next chapter.

58. The arrangement is a complicated one. Eurodif was formed in 1973 by France, Belgium, Spain and Sweden. In 1975 Sweden's 10 per cent share in Eurodif went to Iran as a result of an arrangement between France and Iran. The French government subsidiary company Cogéma and the Iranian Government established the Sofidif (*Société franco–iranienne pour l'enrichissement de l'uranium par diffusion gazeuse*) enterprise with 60 per cent and 40 per cent shares, respectively. In turn, Sofidif acquired a 25 per cent share in Eurodif, which gave Iran its 10 per cent share of Eurodif. The Shah lent $1 billion (and another $180 million in 1977) for the construction of the Eurodif factory, in return for the right to buy 10 per cent of the site's production.

59. As regards the latter stages of the fuel cycle, including fuel fabrication and reprocessing, work had begun at a laboratory scale before the revolution hit.

60. Interview with Reza Khazaneh, London, 2010.

61. Ibid.

CHAPTER 4: ARMS AND THE SHAH: NUCLEAR WEAPONS UNDER THE SHAH

1. Abbas Milani, *The Shah*, p. 71.

2. Ibid., p. 237.

3. 'Follow-Up on the President's Talk with the Shah of Iran', Secret, Memorandum, Documents from the US Espionage Den. v. 8:4, 15 June 1972, p. 1.

4. Ibid., p. 4.

5. Kenneth Rush, 'State Visit of the Shah of Iran', Secret, Memorandum Department of State, 20 July 1973, p. 3.

6. Abbas Milani, *The Shah*, p. 327.

7. Cahn, 'Determinants', pp. 197–8.

8. *New York Times*, 7 October 1976.

9. Pahlavi, *Mission*, pp. 306–7.

10. Ibid., pp. 307–8.

11. Norman Dombey, 'The Nuclear Non-Proliferation Treaty: Aims, Limitations and Achievements', *New Left Review* 52, July–August 2008.

12. Treaty of the Non-Proliferation of Nuclear Weapons. http://www.un.org/en/conf/npt/2005/npttreaty.html [accessed 23 April 2008].

13. Ibid.

14. Author interview by telephone with Adeshir Zahedi, London, 2008.

15. Sagan, 'Why do States Build Nuclear Weapons', p. 77.

16. 'June 1974 – First Nuclear Test – International Reactions', in *Keesings World News Archive*, http:www.keesings.com [accessed 6 April 2007].

17. 'Additional Safeguards Agreement in Iran', in *IAEA*, http://www.iaea.org, p. 1 [accessed 23 April 2007].

18. Etemad correspondence, December 2011.

19. Cahn, 'Determinants', p. 200.

20. *William C. Potter*, 'The NPT Review Conference: 188 States in Search of Consensus', *The International Spectator* 3, 2005, p. 20, http://cns.miis.edu/pubs/other/potter051118.pdf [accessed 23 January 2007. Link no longer working].

21. Etemad interview, 2007.

22. Pahlavi, *Mission*, p. 113.

23. Lefever, *Nuclear Arms in the Third World*, p. 53.

24. See, for example, Department of State, declassified Document, 'Assessment of Indian Nuclear Test', 5 June 1974, p. 1.

25. Lefever, *Nuclear Arms in the Third World*, p. 53.

26. John K. Cooley, 'More Fingers on Nuclear Trigger?', *Christian Science Monitor*, 25 June 1974, in Cahn, 'Determinants', p. 199.

27. *New York Times*, 24 June 1974.

28. Shahram Chubin, *Iran's Security Policy: Intentions, Capabilities and Impact* (Carnegie Endowment for International Peace, 1993), p. 101.

29. Lewis A. Dunn, 'Half Past India's Bang', *Foreign Policy* 36, 1979, p. 85.

30. Sagan, 'Why do States Build Nuclear Weapons', p. 78.

31. For a fuller discussion, see Bahram Navazeni, *Gahshomar-e siyasat-e khariji-ye iran: Az Day Mah 1357 ta mordad mah 1367* (Tehran: Markaz-e Asnad-e Enqelab-e Islami, 1381/2002).

32. A. Kapur, 'Nth Powers of the Future', in *Annals of the American Academy of Political and Social Science* 430, p. 90.

33. *New York Times*, 23 September 1975. As Epstein notes figures of 20 or 30 are likely to be figurative; it is more likely that it would take just 2 or 3.

34. *New York Times*, 2 October 1975.

35. Abbas Milani, *The Shah*, p. 325.

36. Etemad interview, 2007.

37. Ibid.

38. Dale R. Tahtinen, *Arms in the Persian Gulf* (Washington: American Enterprise Institute for Public Policy Research, 1974), p. 2.

39. Leslie M. Pryor, 'Arms and the Shah', *Foreign Policy* 31, Summer 1978, p. 57; Military sales to Iran were valued at $524 million in 1973, $3.91 billion in 1974, $2.6 billion in 1975 and $1.3 billion in 1976 – a cumulative total of $8.3 billion.

40. Ibid.

41. For an idea of just how vast military spending was, see Appendix C.

42. Sagan, 'Why do States Build Nuclear Weapons', p. 55.

43. Joseph Kraft, *Washington Post*, 27 April 1975.

44. US Department of State, Bureau of Intelligence and Research, 'Contribution to N.I.E 4-1-65', 4 October 1965, p. 3.

45. Alvin J. Cottrell and James E. Dougherty, 'Iran's Quest for Security: U.S. Arms Transfers and the Nuclear Option', in *Institute for Foreign Policy Analysis Foreign Policy Report*, May 1977, p. 3.

46. 'Memorandum for C.D. Jackson', Secret Document, 31 December 1953, p. 1.

47. Secretary of Defense Melvin Laird to Secretary of State et al., Top Secret, excised, 'Stopping the Introduction of Nuclear Weapons into the Middle East', 17 March 1969, p. 1.

48. Ibid., p. 2.

49. Ramazani, *Iran's Foreign Policy*, p. 301.

50. Pahlavi, *Mission*, p. 213.

51. IAEA GOV/2007/58. 1975 – for the establishment of a laboratory to study the spectroscopic behaviour of uranium metal (Germany), p. 3.

52. Etemad interview, 2007.

53. CIA, Directorate of Intelligence, 'Managing Nuclear Proliferation: The Politics of Limited Choice', December 1975, p. 12.

54. Secret Memorandum, Henry Kissinger to The President of the United States, 'Strategy for your Discussion with the Shah of Iran', 13 May 1975, p. 1.

55. United States, Energy Research and Development administration, 'Iran: Atomic Energy Programme', mimeo, in *Digital National Security Archive*, October 1976, p. 3, http://nsarchive.chadwyck.com [accessed 2 July 2007].

56. Quester, 'The Shah', p. 21.

57. See Appendix A.

58. BBC News, 'In Depth. The Nuclear Fuel Cycle', http://news.bbc.co.uk/1/shared/spl/hi/sci_nat/05/nuclear_fuel/html/mining.stm [accessed 11 July 2012].

59. Office of Assistant Secretary of Defense for International Security Affairs to Secretary of Defense, 'Nuclear Energy Cooperation with Iran (U) – Action Memorandum', n.d. [Late June 1974], enclosing Atomic Energy

Commission and Department of State memoranda, Confidential, with handwritten note attached, in *The Nuclear Vault: The Iranian Nuclear Program, 1974–1978*, http://www.gwu.edu/~nsarchiv/nukevault/ebb268/index.htm [accessed 12 December 2011].

60. US Embassy Tehran cable 5389 to Department of State, 'Iran's Intentions in Nuclear Matters', 1 July 1974, Confidential.

61. Special National Intelligence Estimate 4-1-74, 'Prospects for Further Proliferation of Nuclear Weapons', 23 August 1974, http://www.gwu.edu/~nsarchiv/nukevault/ebb268/index.htm [accessed 12 December 2011].

62. Poneman, 'Nuclear Policies', p. 573.

63. *Washington Post*, 9 August 1977.

64. Sidney Sober, 'Your Meeting with the Shah at Blair House', Confidential Briefing Memorandum, *National Security Archive*, 9 May 1975, p. 1.

65. Abbas Milani, *The Shah*, p. 331.

66. *Washington Post*, 6 June 1975.

67. Etemad interview, 2007.

68. Abbas Milani, *The Shah*, p. 2.

69. Section 123 of the Atomic Energy Act, http://nnsa.energy.gov/aboutus/ourprograms/nonproliferation/treatiesagreements/123agreementsforpeace fulcooperation [accessed 9 March 2012].

70. Etemad interview, 2010.

71. Waiting for the Iranians to 'Put All their Cards on the Table', US Embassy Tehran cable 5397 to State Department, 'Audience with Shah', 20 June 1977, Confidential.

72. Quester, 'The Shah', p. 23.

CHAPTER 5: SLOW DECLINE, QUICK FALL: THE END OF THE SHAH'S PROGRAMME

1. Quester, 'The Shah', p. 93.

2. Ibid., p. 95.

3. Ibid.

4. 'US-Iranian Peaceful Nuclear Cooperation Agreement', Secret Telegram, 17 October 1978, in *Digital National Security Archive*, http://nsarchive.chadwyck.com [accessed 8 September 2007].

5. Khazaneh interview, 2010.

6. Quester, 'The Shah', p. 95.

7. Abbas Milani, *The Shah*, p. 310.

CHAPTER 6: CHILDREN OF THE REVOLUTION: A YEAR OF CHAOS – 1979

1. Author phone interview with Mohsen Sazegara, December 2008.

2. Author phone interview with Dariush Homayoun, December 2008.

3. The idea had been around since at least the mid-nineteenth century (first espoused by Molla Ahmad Naraqi) but was deemed radical and supported only a handful on the fringes of Shi'i thought. For a fuller discussion of the *velayat-e faqih*, see Ruhollah Khomeini, *Velayat-e Faqih* (Tehran, 1361/1982).
4. 'Message to the Pilgrims' (Message sent to Iranian pilgrims on Hajj in Saudi Arabia from Khomeini in exile in Najaf), 6 February 1971, in *Islam and Revolution: Writings and Declarations of Imam Khomeini* (Mizan Press, 1981), p. 195.
5. *The New York Times*, 22 January 1979.
6. 'Death of Ayatollah Khomeini', in *Keesings World News Archive*, June 1989, http://www.keesings.com [accessed 15 October 2007].
7. Khazaneh correspondence, December 2011.
8. William Branigin, 'Iran Set to Scrap $34 Billion Worth of Civilian Projects', *The Washington Post*, 30 May 1979.
9. *Washington Post*, 30 March 1979.
10. Poneman, *Nuclear Power*, p. 96.
11. 'Scale-down for Iranian Nuclear Programme', BBC Summary of World Broadcasts, 28 May 1979.
12. *New York Times*, 22 January 1979.
13. 'Iran's Reconsideration of its Nuclear Policy', BBC SWB, 19 July 1979.
14. Khazaneh correspondence, December 2011.
15. Poneman, *Nuclear Power*, p. 96.
16. *Wall Street Journal*, 10 April 1979.
17. 'Iran: In Brief; Nuclear Energy Policy', BBC SWB, 11 April 1979.
18. *The New York Times*, 1 August 1979.
19. There are conflicting reports as to the exact percentage of work completed on the plants, but this appears to be the general median.
20. 'Iran, W German Nuclear Power Contract', June 1979, in *Lexis-Nexis*, http://www.lexis-nexis.com [accessed 24 August 2007].
21. 'Nuclear Stake Frozen', *Facts on File News Digest*, 31 December 1979, p. 976 E2, in *Lexis-Nexis*, http://www.lexis-nexis.com [accessed 9 August 2007].
22. *Kayhan*, 20 June 1980 [From Persian].
23. *Newsweek*, 'Iran's Growing turmoil', p. 42.
24. Brumberg, *Reinventing Khomeini: The Struggle for Reform in Iran* (Chicago: University of Chicago Press, 2001), p. 65.
25. Shirin Sedigh Deylami, 'Strangers Among Us: The Critique of Westoxification in Perso-Islamic Political Thought', University of Minnesota, Political Science, p. 67.
26. *Washington Post*, 30 May 1979.

NOTES

CHAPTER 7: RESTART ALL ALONE – 1980-9

1. Author interview with Abulhassan Bani-Sadr, Versailles, January 2010.
2. *Nucleonics Week*, 1 October 1981.
3. *Nucleonics Week* 23/12, 25 March 1982, p. 3.
4. Khazaneh interview, 12 January 2010.
5. Over the coming years Iran repeatedly requested that Kraftwerk restart activities at Bushehr, and each time, Kraftwerk just produced the fax. Khazaneh interview, 2009.
6. Richard Johns, 'Middle East's Uneven Nuclear Progress', *Financial Times* (London), 16 June 1982, p. 28, in *Lexis-Nexis*, http://www.lexis-nexis.com [accessed 27 May 2007].
7. Ann Maclachlan, 'Iran Seeking Way To Finish Bushehr Plant But Bonn Denies Exports', *Nucleonics Week* 27/44, 30 October 1986, pp. 4–5.
8. *New York Times*, 19 February 1980.
9. *Kayhan International*, 24 March 1982.
10. *Resalat*, 11 August 1981 [From Persian].
11. 'Iranian Nuclear Power Project', BBC SWB, 6 July 1982.
12. *Democracy Now*, 3 March 2008, Stephen Kinzer on US–Iranian Relations, the 1953 CIA Coup in Iran and the Roots of Middle East Terror.
13. Majid Khadduri, *The Gulf War* (Oxford: Oxford University Press, 1988), p. 89.
14. Richard Lehman, 'The U.S. Stake in Iran', confidential memo, 23 February 1980, in *Digital National Security Archive*, http://nsarchive.chadwyck.com [accessed 8 October 2007].
15. *The Washington Post*, 9 September 1982.
16. IAEA GOV/2004/83.
17. Anthony Parsons in Majid Khadduri, *The Gulf War* (Oxford: Oxford University Press, 1988), p. 8.
18. *Nuclear News*, October 1985.
19. *Islamic Republic News Agency (IRNA)*, 8 September 1984.
20. *Nuclear News*, October 1985, p. 76.
21. Khazaneh correspondence, December 2003.
22. *Nucleonics Week*, 30 October 1986, pp. 4–5.
23. *IRNA*, 1 December 1986.
24. *Nuclear News*, December 1986, pp. 17–18.
25. In total Iraq was to carry out eight attacks on Bushehr throughout the war: 24 March 1984, 12 February 1985, 4 March 1985, 5 March 1985, 12 July 1986, 17 November 1987, 19 November 1987 and 19 July 1988. Damage to the facilities was estimated at $2.9–4.6 billion.
26. UN Document A/39/865, Letter dated 85/02/14, 'From the Permanent Representative of the Islamic Republic of Iran to the United Nations

Addressed to the Secretary-General', 15 February 1985, in *UN Official Document Search*, http://documents.un.org [accessed 28 August 2007].

27. UN Document S/17133, Letter dated 85/04/27, 'From the Permanent Representative of the Islamic Republic of Iran to the United Nations Addressed to the Secretary-General', 26 April 1985, in *UN Official Document Search*, http://documents.un.org [accessed 26 August 2007].

28. Ibid.

29. Ibid.

30. Ibid.

31. Ibid.

32. Ibid.

33. UN Document A/42/829, Letter dated 87/11/20, 'Effects of Atomic Radiation: Note', 30 November 1987, in *UN Official Document Search*, http://documents.un.org [accessed 26 August 2007].

34. UN Document A/42/789, Letter dated 87/11/20, 'From the Permanent Representative of the Islamic Republic of Iran to the United Nations Addressed to the Secretary-General', 20 November 1987, in *UN Official Document Search*, http://documents.un.org [accessed 26 August 2007].

35. UN Document A/42/829.

36. Douglas Glucroft, 'The Atomic Energy Agency is Considering Completing the Bushehr Power Plant', *Nucleonics Week*, 25 March 1982, in *Lexis-Nexis*, http://www.lexis-nexis.com [accessed 23 March 2007].

37. *Nuclear News*, October 1985, p. 41.

38. *Middle East Defense News*, 29 April 1991.

39. *Kayhan*, 11 November 1986 [From Persian].

40. Hunter, *Iran and the World*, p. 66.

41. *Middle East Defense News*, 5 December 1988.

42. For example, in 1988 US pressure forced Argentina to abandon proposed collaboration in which Buenos Aires agreed to help with converting the TNRC reactor from HEU fuel to 19.75 per cent LEU, and to supply the LEU to Iran (this was delivered in 1993).

43. *The Nation*, 8 November 1984.

CHAPTER 8: IRAN'S ISLAMIC BOMB? NUCLEAR WEAPONS UNDER THE ISLAMIC REPUBLIC

1. Interview with Soltanieh, Vienna, 2009.

2. 'Iran Trains Nuclear Engineers in Pakistan', Middle East *Defense* News, 5 December 1988.

3. UN Document A/C.1/41/PV.24, 'Verbatim Record of the 24th Meeting: 1st Committee, Held on 29 October 1986, New York, General Assembly, 41st Session', 31 October 1986, in *UN Official Document Search*, http://

documents.un.org [accessed 7 August 2007]; all subsequent quotations from this speech can be found here.

4. UN Document A/C.1/41/PV.24.

5. UN Document A/41/468/ADD.1, 'Review of the Implementation of the Declaration on the Strengthening of International Security: Report of the Secretary-General', 10 November 1986, in *UN Official Document Search*, http://documents.un.org [accessed 19 August 2007].

6. For example, UN Document A/44/800, 'International Decade for the Eradication of Colonialism: Report of the Secretary-General', 27 November 1989, in *UN Official Document Search*, http://documents.un.org [accessed 15 August 2007].

7. 'The Convention on the Physical Protection of Nuclear Materials', May 1980, in *IAEA*, http://www.iaea.org/Publications/Documents/Infcircs/Others/inf274r1.shtml [accessed 30 September 2007].

8. Etemad, 'Iran', p. 224.

9. Iran was also suspected of undertaking an air raid on the nuclear centre at Tuwaitha on 30 September 1980.

10. Leonard S. Spector, *Nuclear Ambitions: The Spread of Nuclear Weapons, 1989–1990* (Boulder, CO; Oxford: Westview Press, 1990), p. 207.

11. 'Internal IAEA Information Links the Supreme Leader to 1984 Decision to Seek a Nuclear Arsenal', in *Institute for Science and International Security*, 20 April 2012.

12. David Albright, *Peddling Peril: How the Secret Nuclear Trade Arms America's Enemies* (New York: Simon Spotlight Entertainment, 16 March 2010), p. 71.

13. Yossi Melman, Meir Javedanfar, *The Nuclear Sphinx of Tehran: Mahmoud Ahmadinejad and the State of Iran* (New York: Carroll & Graf, 2007), p. 99.

14. See Appendix A.

15. IAEA GOV/2003/75, p. 5.

16. IAEA GOV/2004/83.

17. I am hugely indebted to David Albright's excellent treatment of this issue in David Albright, *Peddling Peril: How the Secret Nuclear Trade Arms America's Enemies* (New York: Simon Spotlight Entertainment, 16 March 2010).

18. IAEA GOV/2007/58.

19. IAEA GOV/2004/83. Iran would later tell the IAEA this was to create the nuclear fuel necessary to power the Bushehr reactors once they became operational.

20. IAEA GOV/2007/58, p. 3.

21. David Albright, *Peddling Peril*, p. 71.

22. *Peddling Peril*, p. 75.

23. IAEA GOV/2007/58, p. 3. Iran has admitted this series of meetings to the IAEA.

24. Ibid.
25. David Albright, *Peddling Peril*, p. 77.
26. Ibid.
27. Ibid.
28. IAEA GOV/2007/58, p. 3.
29. Ibid.
30. That year, Iran brought a Fuel Fabrication Laboratory (FFL) at Isfahan into operation without informing the IAEA (it subsequently informed the Agency in 1993 and provided it with design information in 1998).
31. IAEA GOV/2007/58, p. 2.
32. Ibid.
33. 'Iran on Verge of A-bomb, Jane's Weekly Indicates', in *Christian Science Monitor*, 26 April 1984.
34. *New York Times*, 26 April 1984.
35. *The Associated Press*, 14 June 1989, Wednesday, PM cycle 'Iran Rejects Nuclear Arms', in *Lexis-Nexis*, http://www.lexis-nexis.com [accessed 24 September 2007].
36. *The Associated Press*, 9 January 1984.
37. Ali Ansari, 'Iran and the US in the shadow of 9/11 Persia and the Persian Question Revisited', in Homa Katouzian and Hossein Shahidi (eds), *Iran in the 21st Century: Politics, Economics and Conflict* (London: Routledge, 2008), p. 108.
38. William O. Beeman, *The Great Satan vs. The Mad Mullahs: How the United States and Iran Demonize Each Other* (Westport, CT: Greenwood, 2005), p. 8.
39. Ibid., p. 9.
40. 'Hashemi-Rafsanjani Speaks on the Future of the Revolutionary Guards Iranian Revolutionary Guards Corps', Tehran Domestic Service, 0935 GMT, 6 October 1988, translated in *FBIS-NES*, 7 October 1988, p. 52.

**CHAPTER 9: RESTART FOR REAL: THE PROGRAMME
GOES LIVE - 1989-2002**

1. *Middle East Defense News*, 29 April 1991. Several non-executive vice-presidents were appointed with the 1989 constitutional reforms.
2. *IRNA* in English, 1 September 1991.
3. *Tehran Times*, 29 February 1992.
4. Anthony H. Cordesman, Khalid R. Al-Rodhan, *Iran's Weapons of Mass Destruction: The Real and Potential Threat* (CSIS, 2006), p. 116.
5. For example, a January 1992 attempt to buy a fuel fabrication facility and a Uranium Dioxide conversion plant from Buenos Aires. Mark D. Skootsky, 'U.S. Nuclear Policy Toward Iran,' 1 June 1995 in www.nti.org [accessed 20 August 2011].

6. *Nucleonics Week*, 25 October 1990.
7. *The Associated Press*, 6 November 1991.
8. IAEA GOV/2004/83.
9. *The Associated Press*, 'China Releases Details of Nuclear Program with Iran', 4 November 1991.
10. *Nucleonics Week*, 29 September 1994.
11. *Dallas Morning News*, 28 September 1995.
12. *Sunday Telegraph*, Con Coughlin, 'Iran: Article Highlights Danger of Iran's Nuclear Weapons Program', 23 February 1997.
13. *El Independente*, 5 February 1990, p. 2; in *Nuclear Developments*, 16 March 1990, p. 2.
14. See, for example, *Keyhan*, 19 July 1990.
15. *Middle East Defense News*, 29 April 1991.
16. *Voice of the Islamic Republic of Iran*, 17 September 1991.
17. Ali M. Ansari, *Confronting Iran*, p. 70.
18. *IRNA*, 23 September 1990.
19. Ibid., p. 104.
20. *Voice of the Islamic Republic of Iran Network 1*, Tehran, 21 April 1994 [From Persian].
21. Mark Hibbs, 'Minatom Says It Can Complete One Siemens PWR in Iran in Five Years', *Nucleonics Week* 35/39, 29 September 1994, p. 3.
22. Ibid.
23. Ibid.
24. Khazaneh correspondence, September 2011.
25. Official Kremlin International News Broadcast, 26 January 1995, in BSWB [accessed 15 August 2011].
26. See Ali M. Ansari, *Confronting Iran*, pp. 155–6 for a fuller discussion.
27. Khazaneh interview, September 2011.
28. Ibid.
29. *Nucleonics Week*, 9 October 1997.
30. *Nucleonics Week*, 21 May 1998.
31. Ibid.
32. *Iran News* (Tehran), 'US Again Uses the Same Failed Policy', 30 July 1998, pp. 2, 15; in 'Tehran Paper on US, Israeli Attempts To Impede Ties', FBIS Document FTS19980806002608.
33. *IRNA* (Tehran), 5 August 1998; in 'Tehran Paper Attacks US Resolution Against IAEA', FBIS Document FTS199805001091, 5 August 1998.
34. *BBC*, 'Russia to Triple Number of Nuclear Experts in Iran', 15 January 1999.
35. *The Current Digest of the Soviet Press*, 11 May 2000, p. 20, in *Lexis-Nexis*, http://www.lexis-nexis.com.

36. Russian Minister Rejects US 'Economic Pressure' Over Iran, ITAR-TASS (Moscow), 1 June 2000, in FBIS Document CEP20000601000135, 1 June 2000.
37. Yekaterina Kats, 'Ekozashchita Group Co-Head Slivyak Interviewed on Nuclear Technology Exports', *Segodnya* (Moscow), 16 March 2001, in FBIS Document CEP20010316000106, 16 March 2001.

CHAPTER 10: PROLOGUE TO THE NUCLEAR CLASH - 1989-97

1. *Voice of the Islamic Republic of Iran*, 6 November 1990 [From Persian].
2. *Xinhua General News Service*, 26 October 1991.
3. *The Times of London*, 29 September 1990.
4. *The Daily Mail*, 25 January 1992.
5. *Washington Times*, 8 May 1995.
6. *Vision of the Islamic Republic of Iran Network 1*, 'Director of Iran's Atomic Energy Organization outlines Tehran's policy Tehran, 2 March 1995 [From Persian].
7. 'Nuclear Chronology: Iran, 1993', Nuclear Threat Initiative, available at http://www.nti.org/e_research/profiles/Iran/1825_1870.html [accessed 30 October 2007. Link no longer working].
8. *The Associated Press*, 6 November 1991.
9. *IPS-Inter Press Service*, 27 September 1994.
10. *Voice of the Islamic Republic of Iran Network 1*, 21 April 1994 [From Persian].
11. *Vision of the Islamic Republic of Iran Network 1*, 28 February 1995.
12. *New York Times*, 3 January 1995.
13. *Vision of the Islamic Republic of Iran Network 1*, 28 February 1995 [From Persian].
14. http://www.un.org/disarmament/WMD/Nuclear/1995-NPT/pdf/NPT_CONF199503.pdf [Link no longer working].
15. *Federal News Service*, Prepared statement by Michael Eisenstadt before the senate foreign relations committee subcommittee on near east and South Asian affairs subject, 'Iran under Khatami: Weapons of Mass Destruction, Terrorism, and the Arab-Israeli Conflict', 14 May 1998.
16. *New York Times*, 'Iran May Be Able to Build an Atomic Bomb in 5 Years, U.S. and Israeli Officials Fear', 5 January 1995.
17. Anthony H. Cordesman, Khalid R. Al-Rodhan, *Iran's Weapons of Mass Destruction: The Real and Potential Threat* (CSIS, 2006), p. 111.
18. China was technically not obligated to report this as it was not yet a member of the NPT in 1991, but Iran was obligated under its IAEA Safeguards Agreement to report the acquisition of the material.
19. IAEA GOV/2004/83, p. 4.
20. Ibid.

21. Ibid., p. 5.
22. IAEA GOV/2007/58, p. 4.
23. Ibid. Between 1994 and 1999, Iran had a total of 13 meetings with members of the network.
24. The IAEA, however, was not convinced that Iran did not pursue further development of the P-2 design and called on Iran in September 2005 to provide more information on the history of its P-2 developments. IAEA GOV/2005/67.
25. *Daily Mail*, John Laffin, 'Iran and a nuclear gift from the gods' 25 January 1992.
26. *Financial Times*, 29 January 1992, p. 4.
27. *Washington Post*, 17 November 1992, p. A30; in Michael Eisenstadt, 'Living With a Nuclear Iran?', *Survival*, 3 August 1999, pp. 124–48.
28. *Vision of the Islamic Republic of Iran Network 1*, Tehran, 18 December 1994 [From Persian].
29. Leonard Spector, 'Does Iran Have the Bomb?', *The American Spectator*, February 1996.

CHAPTER 11: AGHAZADEH'S MISSION: ACCELERATION - 1997-2002

1. Khazaneh interview, 2010.
2. Ibid.
3. IAEA GOV/2007/58, p. 4.
4. IAEA GOV/2004/83, p. 6.
5. IAEA GOV/2007/58, p. 4.
6. *Vision of the Islamic Republic of Iran*, 6 July 2000.
7. 'In the Shadow of the Mullahs,' *The Jerusalem Post*, 11 January 1998.
8. *Israel Wire*, 10 December 1998, http://www.israelwire.com [accessed 15 June 2010. Link no longer working].
9. *CNN*, http://edition.cnn.com/2002/ALLPOLITICS/01/29/bush.speech.txt [accessed 11 July 2012].

CHAPTER 12: CRISIS - 2002-3

1. Author interview with Ali Jafarzadeh, 28 May 2009. It is widely suspected that the MKO received the information from the Israelis, who believed that it was better coming from an Iranian opposition group than Israel.
2. Interview with Olli Heinonen, Vienna, 2009.
3. IAEA GOV/2003/40, p. 2.
4. Interview with Former UK Ambassador to the IAEA Peter Jenkins, UK, 2009.
5. See IAEA GOV/2003/40, pp. 2–3.
6. Ibid., p. 7.

7. Interview with John Bolton, Washington, 2009.
8. Ibid.
9. پرونده هسته ای به خاتمی تقدير تقدی خاتمی ازتلاش تيم مذاكره كننده هسته ای و ارايه گزارش حسن روحانی از
   ['Khatami's appreciation of the efforts of the Nuclear Negotiating Team and Hasan Rowhani's report on the nuclear dossier to Khatami'], 2005 [From Persian].
10. Ibid.
11. Ibid.
12. Bolton interview, 2009.
13. Jenkins interview, 2009.
14. Ibid.
15. This fear had recently created one of most controversial and potentially important events of the nuclear crisis. In the early months of May 2003, Iraq had been so recently and comprehensively destroyed by US military power, Iran (reportedly) offered the USA a significant package of concessions to resolve the nuclear crisis and overall relations between the two countries. Tehran proposed to end support for Lebanese and Palestinian militant groups, to help to stabilize Iraq following the US-led invasion and to make its nuclear programme more transparent. In return, Tehran asked Washington to end its hostility, to end sanctions and to disband the MKO and repatriate its members. The offer was prepared in Tehran, by Iran's Ambassador to France, Sadegh Kharrazi, came in an unsigned letter, passed via the Swiss Ambassador, Tim Guldimann, in Tehran (Washington's conduit to Tehran in the absence of formal relations between the countries). It was passed both to the State Department (where Guldimann also briefed officials on his conversations with the Iranians) and to Republican Congressman Robert Ney of Ohio, who passed it on to President Bush's Deputy Chief of Staff, Karl Rove. Believing the letter to be genuine and to have been approved by the highest authorities, the US State Department was keen on the offer, but was over-ruled by Vice-President Dick Cheney's office (while those such as Bolton thought the offer a 'fantasy') which rejected the plan. 'We don't negotiate with evil' was the response.
16. See IAEA GOV/2003/63.
17. Bolton interview, 2009.
18. Jenkins interview, 2009.
19. 'Rowhani to Khatami', 2005 [From Persian].
20. Speech by Supreme National Security Council Secretary Hasan Rowhani to the Supreme Cultural Revolution Council, 'Beyond the Challenges Facing Iran and the IAEA Concerning the Nuclear Dossier', *Rahbord*, 30 September 2005, p. 32 [From Persian].
21. 'Rowhani to Khatami' [From Persian].

NOTES

22. 'Estefadeh-ye solhamiz az enerzhi-ye hasteh'i' *Rahbord*, Fall 2003 [From Persian].
23. Taha Hashemi, 'Khoruj az en-pi-ti mosave ba ta'sir-e bishtar-e propogand-ha-ye Amrika ast', *Aftab*, 30 September 2003 [From Persian].
24. Besharati, p. 315 [From Persian].
25. 'Friday Prayer Leader Calls for Withdrawal from NPT', *Tehran Times*, 20 September 2003.
26. 'Asgar-Owladi, dabir koll-e Mo'talefeh-ye Islami: Emza'-e protocol-e elhaqi rah-e jadidi bara-ye ferestadan-e jasusan beh keshvar ast', *Resalat*, 9 August 2003 [From Persian].
27. George Perkovic, 'For Tehran Nuclear Programme is a Matter of National Pride', *Yale Global*, 21 March 2005.
28. Ibid.
29. 'Rowhani's Speech to the Council', pp. 31–2 [From Persian].
30. Saideh Lotfian, 'Nuclear Policy and International Relations', p. 162.
31. 'Rowhani to Khatami', 2005 [From Persian].
32. Ibid.
33. 'Rowhani to Khatami', 2005 [From Persian].
34. 'Rowhani's Speech to the Council', p. 22 [From Persian].
35. Ibid., p. 37.
36. Nicoullaud interview, Paris, January 2010.
37. Ibid.
38. 'Rowhani's Speech to the Council', pp. 11–12 [From Persian].
39. Nicoullaud interview, 2010.
40. Ibid.
41. Ibid.
42. In fact, Rowhani made two phone calls. After discussions with Seyed Mousavian, the two men decided that it would be best to speak to the president and the office of the Supreme Leader to get permission for some sort of compromise on suspension. It had dawned on the Iranians that if the negotiations collapsed there would be security as well as political consequences (Iraq was still uppermost in everyone's mind). Rowhani's first call was to Khatami. He outlined the situation – and the very real possibility that the talks would collapse – to which Khatami told him to avoid this outcome at all costs. He then spoke to the Office of the Supreme Leader, which also agreed that the talks should not be allowed to fail. Hassan Rowhani, *Amniyat Melli va Diplomasi-ye Hastehi Iran*. Tehran: Markaz-e Tahqiqat-e Estaratejik-e Majma'-e Tashkhis-e Maslahat-e Nezam, (2012), pp. 176–7. Seyed Hossein Mousavian, *The Iranian Nuclear Crisis: A Memoir*, Carnegie Endowment for International Peace (12 July 2012), p. 140 (Kindle Edition).
43. Nicoullaud interview, 2010.
44. See IAEA GOV/2003/75 a fuller discussion.

45. 'Rowhani to Khatami', 2005 [From Persian].
46. 'Rowhani to Khatami', 2005 [From Persian].
47. Nicoullaud interview, 2010.

CHAPTER 13: FROM TEHRAN TO PARIS AND BEYOND - 2003-5

1. 'Rowhani to Khatami' [From Persian].
2. IAEA GOV/2004/11.
3. Heinonen interview, 2009.
4. IAEA, 'Director General Comments on Iran Report,' *IAEA.org*, 25 February 2004.
5. 'US Again Accuses Iran of Hiding Nuclear Program,' *Middle East Online*, 26 February 2004.
6. Jenkins interview, 2009.
7. The IAEA officially confirmed the discovery in August 2004 and in August 2005 confirmed that the HEU traces had indeed come from Pakistan.
8. 'Edamah-ye mozakerat ba azhans manf'ati bara-ye Iran nadarad', *Jomhuri-ye Islami*, 14 March 2004 [From Persian].
9. 'Ejbar, na Ejma', *Jomhuri-ye Islami*, 14 March 2004 [From Persian].
10. *Associated Press*, 31 October 2004.
11. 'Majlis-e haftom va protocol-e elhaqi', 14 March 2004 [From Persian].
12. *Keyhan*, 14 March 2004 [From Persian].
13. *Middle East Online*, 'Iran Puts Off UN Nuclear Inspection Mission,' 12 March 2004.
14. 'Rowhani's Speech to the Council', p. 17 [From Persian].
15. 'Rowhani to Khatami', 2005 [From Persian].
16. The February discovery of HEU traces on the centrifuges at Natanz was officially confirmed by the IAEA in August shortly before the Board Meeting.
17. Jenkins interview, 2009.
18. The Iranians also considered the Paris Agreement, and its aftermath, a great success. In fact, they wanted to build on the agreement, and their intense diplomacy resulted in the November 2004 IAEA Board Resolution (adopted on 29 November) one of the most positive resolutions (in Iranian eyes) on the programme to date. Iran's corrective measures on several past breaches were confirmed, as was the fact that all declared nuclear materials in Iran had been accounted for, with no diversion to prohibited activities. Critically, the Paris Agreement was confirmed with an emphasis on the voluntary, not legally binding, nature of enrichment suspension as a confidence-building measure. Finally, the resolution stated that the Iranian case was removed from the Board of Governors' provisional agenda. As far as the Iranians were concerned, Rowhani's plan was being implemented in full and the November 2004 resolution was a successful example

of crisis management. Seyed Hossein Mousavian, *The Iranian Nuclear Crisis: A Memoir*, Carnegie Endowment for International Peace (12 July 2012), pp. 211–12 (Kindle edition).
19. 'Rowhani to Khatami', 2005 [From Persian].
20. 'Rowhani's Speech to the Council', p. 26 [From Persian].
21. Ibid., p. 28.
22. Ibid.
23. 'Rowhani's Speech to the Council', 2005 [From Persian], pp. 26–8.
24. Ibid., p. 16.
25. Ibid., p. 38.
26. Interview with Nick Burns, Boston, 2009.
27. Burns interview, 2009.
28. Ibid.
29. Jenkins interview, 2009.
30. Bolton interview, 2009.
31. Ibid.
32. Ibid.

CHAPTER 14: ENTER AHMADINEJAD: REVERSING INTO THE FUTURE - 2002-5

1. Jenkins interview, 2009.
2. Crisis Group, Middle East Report no. 51, 'Is there a Way Out of the Nuclear Impasse?', 23 February 2006, p. 3.
3. Crisis Group report, 2006.
4. *Mehr News Agency*, Iran's Statement at IAEA Emergency Meeting, 10 August 2008, available at http://www.fas.org/nuke/guide/iran/nuke/mehr080905.html [accessed 11 July 2012]; in Anthony H. Cordesman, Adam C. Seitz, *Iranian Weapons of Mass Destruction: Doctrine, Policy and Command* (CSIS), http://csis.org/files/media/csis/pubs/090112_iran_wmd_policy.pdf [Link no longer working].
5. Khamenei himself repeated the *fatwa* in explicit language on several subsequent occasions – for example, on 4 June 2006. '[The West claims] that Iran is after a nuclear bomb. This is untrue and is a pure lie. We do not need nuclear bombs. We do not have any target against which we can use nuclear bombs. We believe that using nuclear weapons is against Islamic rulings (*ahkam*). We have explicitly announced this. We believe that imposing on our people the cost of producing and stockpiling nuclear weapons is absurd. Production of such weapons and their preservation is very costly and we do not see it [as] right to impose these costs onto our people.' Ali Khamenei's speech, 4 June 2006, http://farsi.khamenei.ir/speech-content?id=3341&q= [accessed 11 July 2012].

NUCLEAR IRAN: THE BIRTH OF AN ATOMIC STATE

6. 'Ayatollah Vows Iran's Nuclear Program will Go On', *The Associated Press*, 3 June 2008; 'Iranian Supreme Leader Vows to Pursue Nuclear Program', *Voice of America News*, 3 June 2008.
7. 'Rowhani's Speech to the Council', p. 34 [From Persian].
8. Crisis Group interview, September 2005.
9. 'Iranian President's UN Speech', *BBC News*, 18 September 2005.
10. Jenkins interview, 2009.
11. In the words of a Russian foreign policy adviser, 'Russia has no incentive to formally join this process. It's a dead end.' Crisis Group report, 26 February 2006.
12. Jenkins interview, 2009.
13. Ibid.
14. *The New York Times*, 13 March 2006.
15. IAEA GOV/2004/11.
16. IAEA GOV/2005/87. When put together in the presence of a neutron detonator, two highly enriched uranium hemispheres become a bomb.
17. Jenkins interview, 2009.
18. Bolton interview, 2009.
19. Burns interview, 2007.
20. Ibid.
21. Ibid.
22. 'Iran Cautious over US Talks Offer', *BBC News*, 1 June 2006.
23. Crisis Group interview with Iranian Official, 2 March 2009.
24. Author interview, Ali Ansari, 31 March 2009.
25. Larijani interview with *Jam-e Jam television*, 16 July 2005.
26. Burns interview, 2007.
27. *New York Times*, 12 April 2006.
28. Crisis Group interview, 28 March 2009.
29. 'Iran Turns Away IAEA Inspectors', *Global Security Newswire*, 21 August 2006.
30. Bolton interview, 2009.
31. Full text at http://www.un.org/Docs/sc/Security Council_resolutions06.htm [Link no longer working]. The resolution exempted the Bushehr project in order to secure Russian support.
32. Full text at http://www.un.org/docs/sc/Security Council_resolutions07.htm [Link no longer working].
33. *Los Angeles Times*, 3 September 2007.
34. IAEA GOV/2007/58.
35. See below.
36. Burns interview, 2007.
37. Burns interview, 2007.

38. Full text at http://www.un.org/docs/sc/SecurityCouncil_resolutions08.htm [Link no longer working].
39. Burns interview, 2009.
40. Trade statistics show that in 2006 EU exports to Iran fell by 13 per cent overall, 'Global Security: Iran', House of Commons Foreign Affairs Committee, fifth report of Session 2007–2008.
41. 'Iran Unmoved by Threats over Its Atomic Program', *The New York Times*, 12 June 2008.
42. *International Herald Tribune*, 8 September 2008.
43. Much Iranian trade has also been redirected through the Gulf states, where the presence of a large diaspora community (between 200,000 and 400,000 in Dubai alone) facilitates such activity.
44. Author interview, Ali Ansari, 31 March 2009.
45. Author interview, Iranian Ambassador to the IAEA, Ali Asghar Soltanieh, Vienna, 21 November 2009.
46. Ibid.
47. IAEA GOV/2008/4.
48. 'Bush Raises the Stakes over Iran Bomb with Warning of "Holocaust"', *The Times*, 29 August 2007.
49. 'George Bush's Memoirs Reveal How He Considered Attacks on Iran and Syria', *The Guardian*, 8 November 2010.
50. 'US Generals "Will Quit" If Bush Orders Iran Attack', *The Times* (London), 25 February 2007.
51. See *IRNA*, 26 October 2005, 14 December 2005 and 11 February 2006.
52. Author interview, Prime Minister's Spokesman, Mark Regev, Jerusalem, 12 September 2009.
53. Author interview, Giora Eiland, Tel Aviv, 10 September 2009.
54. Author interview, Israeli Diplomat, Jerusalem, 13 September 2009.
55. Author interview, Israeli Diplomat, 8 April 2009.
56. Ibid.
57. Author interview, Giora Eiland, Tel Aviv, 10 September 2009.
58. Interview with White House Official, 2010.
59. Interview with FCO Official, 26 June 2010.
60. IAEA GOV/2009/8, http://www.iaea.org.
61. *Iran: Nuclear Intentions and Capabilities*, December 2007, p. 7.

CHAPTER 15: ENTER OBAMA: NUCLEAR DÉTENTE? - 2008-10

1. Brian Knowlton, 'In Interview, Obama Talks of "New Approach" to Iran', *The New York Times*, 12 January 2009.
2. Riedel interview, Washington, 2009.
3. Riedel interview, 2009.

4. *The Washington Post*, 27 January 2009.
5. *CBS News*, http://www.cbsnews.com/8301-503543_162-4759248-503543.html [accessed 11 July 2012].
6. 'Obama Extends to Iran an Olive Branch on Videotape, Issuing a Holiday Message of Peace', *The New York Times*, 20 March 2009.
7. http://www.state.gov/r/pa/prs/dpb/2009/04/121499.htm [accessed 11 July 2012].
8. *Global Insight*, 7 April 2009.
9. Ali Akbar Dareini, 'Iran Leader: Don't Vote for Pro-Western Candidates', *Associated Press*, 18 May 2009.
10. Ibid.
11. Interview with FCO Official, 26 June 2010.
12. Interview with White House official, Washington, 9 September 2009.
13. The Iranian insisted that the nuclear issue be dealt only within the framework of the IAEA. Soltanieh interview, 2009.
14. Interview with White House Official, 2009.
15. Ibid.
16. Ibid.
17. Iran claims it did not have any obligation to declare the plant to the IAEA any sooner because it was no longer implementing the modified code 3.1 and was therefore only obliged to inform the IAEA of a plant's existence six months before putting nuclear material into it. Author interview with Soltanieh, 2009.
18. Interview, FCO Official, 2010.
19. Soltanieh interview, 2009.
20. Unclassified administration document entitled, 'Public Points for Qom Disclosure', unspecified date, available at http://www.politico.com/static/PPM41_public_points_for_qom_disclosure.html [accessed 11 July 2012].
21. *CNN*, 25 September 2009. The Agency inspected the plant the following month and declared all findings consistent with Iranian declarations though Western diplomats and intelligence remained sceptical.
22. Crisis Group interview with French Official, Paris, 16 September 2009.
23. Interview with US Official, 6 October 2009.
24. Interview with US Official, 28 September 2009.
25. Ibid.
26. *New York Times*, 24 September 2009.
27. Interview with US Official, 28 September 2009.
28. Interview with US Official, 6 October 2009.
29. Ibid.
30. Ibid.
31. Interview with US Official, 6 October 2009.

32. Interview with FCO Official, 2010.
33. Interview with US Official, 6 October 2009.
34. Interview with FCO Official, 2010.
35. Interview with EU Official, 2009.
36. Interview with FCO Official, 2010.
37. Soltanieh interview, 2010.
38. Crisis Group interview with British Diplomat, UK Permanent Representation to the E.U, Brussels, 5 October 2009.
39. IAEA GOV/2010/10, p. 3, paras 11–13.
40. Interview with FCO Official, 2010.
41. 'Rowhani's Speech to the Council', p. 23 [From Persian].
42. Soltanieh interview, 2010.
43. IAEA GOV/2010/62. Given the February IAEA report of 2,065 kg and an enrichment of rate of enrichment was 117 kg/month since then.

CHAPTER 16: THE END OF DIPLOMACY? THE NON-DIPLOMATIC ALTERNATIVE - 2010-12

1. Khazaneh interview, London, 2009.
2. 'Israeli Test on Worm Called Crucial in Iran Nuclear Delay', *New York Times*, 15 January 2011.
3. *Financial Times*, 10 December 2010.
4. Interview with French Official, 2010.
5. IAEA GOV/210/46.
6. *Reuters*, 14 September 2011, http://af.reuters.com/article/energyOilNews/idAFLDE68D06L20100914?sp=true [accessed 25 September 2011].
7. Soltanieh interview, 2010.
8. Julia Damianova, 'Nuclear Negotiations with Iran End in Failure', *Los Angeles Times*, 21 January 2011.
9. IAEA GOV/2011/7, pp. 3–4.
10. Ibid., p. 4.
11. Crisis Group interview with a Western Military Officer, Beirut, September 2009.
12. Seymour M. Hersch, 'Our Men in Iran', *The New Yorker*, 6 April 2012.
13. IAEA GOV/2011/54.
14. 'How I Would Check Iran's Nuclear Ambition', *Washington Post*, 5 March 2012.
15. Icana.ir, 6 April 2012.
16. *Kayhan*, Iran, 8 April 2012.
17. Ibid.
18. Javad Heydarian, 'Iran, West head for showdown', *The Diplomat*, 20 February 2012.
19. *Wall Street Journal*, 'Tehran Hardens Nuclear Stance', 13 June 2012.

20. *Agence-France Presse*, 'Iran, world powers fail to reach Moscow break-through', 20 June 2012.

CHAPTER 17: CONCLUSION

1. Seyyed Hossein Mousavian, 'Iran and the West: The Path to Nuclear Deadlock', *Global Dialogue* 8/1–2, Winter/Spring 2006.
2. http://2012.republican-candidates.org/Romney/Iran.php [accessed 11 July 2012].
3. Gusteron, 'Nuclear Weapons and the Other', p. 115.

BIBLIOGRAPHY

LITERATURE IN ENGLISH

Abrahamian, Ervand, *Iran Between Two Revolutions* (Princeton: Princeton University Press, 1982).

Afrasiabi, Kaveh, *After Khomeini: New Directions in Iran's Foreign Policy* (Boulder, CO and Oxford: Westview, 1994).

Albright, David, *Peddling Peril: How the Secret Nuclear Trade Arms America's Enemies* (New York: Simon Spotlight Entertainment, 2010).

Alikhani, Hossein, *Sanctioning Iran: Anatomy of a Failed Policy* (London: I.B.Tauris, 2000).

Amuzegar, Jahangir, *Iran's Economy under the Islamic Republic* (London: I.B.Tauris, 1993).

Ansari, Ali M., *Confronting Iran: The Failure of American Foreign Policy and the Roots of Mistrust* (London: Hurst & Co., 2006).

Ansari, Ali M., *Iran, Islam, and Democracy: The Politics of Managing Change* (London: Institute of International Affairs, Chatham House, 2006).

Arjomand, Said Amir, *The Turban for the Crown: The Islamic Revolution in Iran* (New York and Oxford: Oxford University Press, 1989).

Ashcroft, Bill, *Key Concepts in Post-Colonial Studies* (London: Routledge, 1998).

Bakhash, Shaul, *The Reign of the Ayatollahs: Iran and the Islamic Revolution* (London: I.B.Tauris, 1985).

Barnaby, C.F., *Preventing the Spread of Nuclear Weapons* (London: Pugwash Symposium, 1969).

Barnaby, Frank, *How Nuclear Weapons Spread: Nuclear-weapon Proliferation in the 1990s* (London: Routledge, 1993).

Beeman, William O., *Language, Status and Power in Iran (Advances in Semiotics)* (Bloomington, IN: Indiana University Press, 1986).

Beeman, William O., *The Great Satan vs. the Mad Mullahs: How the United States and Iran Demonize Each Other* (Westport, CT: Greenwood, 2005).

Bensahel, Nora, and Byman, Daniel L., *The Future Security Environment in the Middle East* (Santa Monica, CA: RAND, 2003).

Bill, James A., *The Eagle and the Lion: Tragedy of American–Iranian Relations* (New Haven, CT and London: Yale University Press, 1989).

Brown, Carl L. (ed.), *Diplomacy in the Middle East: The International Relations of Regional and Outside Powers* (London: I.B.Tauris, 2004).

Buchta, Wilfried, *Who Rules Iran? The Structure of Power in the Islamic Republic* (Washington, DC: Washington Institute for Near East Policy and Konrad Adenauer Stiftung, 2000).

Byman, Daniel, *Iran's Security Policy in the Post-Revolutionary Era* (Santa Monica, CA: RAND, 2001).

Calabrese, John, *Revolutionary Horizons: Regional Foreign Policy in Post-Khomeini Iran* (Basingstoke and New York: Macmillan/St Martin's, 1994).

Campbell, Kurt M., Einhorn, Robert J., and Reiss, Mitchell B., *The Nuclear Tipping Point: Why States Reconsider their Nuclear Choices* (Washington, DC: The Brookings Institution, 2004).

Carter, John J., *Covert Action as a Tool of Presidential Foreign Policy: From the Bay of Pigs to Iran-Contra* (Lewiston, NY and Lampeter: Edwin Mellen Press Ltd, 2006).

Chelkowski, Peter, and Dabashi, Hamid, *Staging a Revolution: The Art of Persuasion in the Islamic Republic of Iran* (London: Booth-Clibborn, 2000).

Chen, Zak, *Iran's Nuclear Policy and the IAEA: An Evaluation of Program 93+2* (Washington, DC: Washington Institute for Near East Policy, 2002).

Chubin, Shahram, *Iran's Security Policy: Intentions. Capabilities and Impact* (Washington, DC: Carnegie Endowment for International Peace, 1993).

Chubin, Shahram, *Whither Iran? Reform, Domestic Politics and National Security* (Oxford: Oxford University Press, 2002).

Chubin, Shahram, and Tripp, Charles, *Iran and Iraq at War* (London: I.B.Tauris, 1988).

Clawson, Patrick (ed.), *Iran under Khatami: A Political, Economic, and Military Assessment* (Washington, DC: Washington Institute for Near East Policy, 1998).

Clemens, Walter C., jr. (ed.), *World Perspectives on International Politics* (New York: Little Brown & co., 1965).

Cordesman, Anthony, *The Gulf and the West, Strategic Relations and Military Realities* (Boulder, CO and London: Westview, 1988).

Cordesman, Anthony, and Al-Rodhan, Khalid R., *Iran's Weapons of Mass Destruction: The Real and Potential Threat* (Washington, DC: Center for Strategic and International Studies, 2006).

Corsi, Jerome R., *Atomic Iran: How the Terrorist Regime Bought the Bomb and American Politicians* (Nashville, TN: Cumberland House, 2005).

Dekmejian, Hrair R., *Troubled Waters: The Geopolitics of the Caspian Region* (London: I.B.Tauris, 2003).

Delpech, Therese, *Iran and the Bomb* (London: Hurst & Co., 2006).

Derrida, Jacques, *Spectres of Marx* (London: Routledge, 2006).

Ehteshami, Anoushiravan, *After Khomeini: The Iranian Second Republic* (London: Routledge, 1995).

Ehteshami, Anoushiravan, and Hinnebusch, Raymond (eds), *Syria and Iran: Middle Powers in a Penetrated Regional System* (London: Routledge, 1997).

Ehteshami, Anoushiravan, and Varasteh, Mansour (eds), *Iran and the International Community* (London: Routledge, 1991).

Ehteshami, Anoushiravan, and Zweiri, Mahjoob, *Iran and the Rise of its Neoconservatives: The Politics of Tehran's Silent Revolution* (London: I.B.Tauris, 2007).

Esposito, John L.R., and Ramazani, Ruhollah K., *Iran at the Crossroads* (New York: Macmillan, 2001).

Fawcett, Louise (ed.), *International Relations of the Middle East* (Oxford: Oxford University Press, 2005).

Fawcett, Louise, and Hurrell, Andrew (eds), *Regionalism in World Politics: Regional Organization and International Order* (Oxford: Oxford University Press, 1995).

Feldman, Shai, *Nuclear Weapons and Arms Control in the Middle East* (Cambridge, MA: MIT Press, 1997).

Fischer, David, *History of the International Atomic Energy Agency: The First Forty Years* (Vienna: IAEA, 1997).

Fuller, Graham E., *The Center of the Universe: The Geopolitics of Iran* (Boulder, CO and Oxford: Westview, 1991).

Ganji, Babak, *Politics of Confrontation: The Foreign Policy of the USA and Revolutionary Iran* (London: I.B.Tauris, 2006).

Giddens, Anthony, *Modernity and Self-Identity: Self and Society in the Late Modern Age* (Cambridge: Polity, 1991).

Halliday, Fred, *The Middle East in International Relations: Power, Politics and Ideology* (Cambridge: Cambridge University Press, 2005).

Halliday, Fred, *Iran: Dictatorship and Development* (Harmondsworth: Penguin, 1979).

Herzig, Edmund, *Iran and the Former Soviet South* (London: Royal Institute of International Affairs, 1996).

Hettne, Bjørn, Inotai, András, and Sunkel, Osvaldo (eds), *Globalism and the New Regionalism* (Basingstoke: Macmillan, 1999).

Hinnebusch, Raymond, *The International Politics of the Middle East* (Manchester: Manchester University Press, 2003).

Hinnebusch, Raymond, and Ehteshami, Anoushiravan (eds), *The Foreign Policies of Middle East States* (Boulder, CO and London: Lynne Rienner, 2002).

Howard, Roger, *Iran in Crisis? Nuclear Ambitions and the American Response* (London: Zed Books Ltd, 2004).

Hunter, Shireen, *Iran and the World: Continuity in a Revolutionary Decade* (Bloomington, IN: Indiana University Press, 1990).

Hunter, Shireen, *Strategic Developments in Eurasia after 11 September* (London: Frank Cass, 2004).

Hunter, Shireen, *Iran After Khomeini* (New York and London: Praeger, 1992).

Hunter, Shireen, and Malik, Huma, *Modernization, Democracy, and Islam* (Westport, CN: Praeger, 2005).

Hunter, Shireen (ed.), *The Politics of Islamic Revivalism: Diversity and Unity* (Bloomington, IN: Indiana University Press, 1988).

Jafarzadeh, Alireza, *The Iran Threat: President Ahmadinejad and the Coming Nuclear Crisis* (New York: Macmillan, 2007).

Katouzian, Homa, *Mussaddiq and the Struggle for Power in Iran* (London: I.B.Tauris, 1999).

Katouzian, Homa, and Shahidi, Hossein (eds), *Iran in the 21st Century: Politics, Economics and Conflict* (London: Routledge, 2008).

Keddie, Nicki R., *Modern Iran: Roots and Results of Revolution* (New Haven, CT: Yale University Press, 2003).

Khadduri, Majid, *The Gulf War* (Oxford: Oxford University Press, 1988).

Kile, Shannon N., *Europe and Iran: Perspectives on Non-Proliferation* (Oxford: Oxford University Press, 2005).

Kinzer, Stephen, *All the Shah's Men: An American Coup and the Roots of Middle East Terror* (Hoboken, NJ: John Wiley & Sons, 2003).

Kissinger, Henry, *The White House Years* (New York: Little Brown & Co., 1979).

Kapuscinski, Ryszard, *Shah of Shahs* (London: Picador, 1986).

Lefever, Ernest W., *Nuclear Arms in the Third World: U.S. Policy Dilemma* (Washington, DC: The Brookings Institute, 1979).

Marschall, Christin, *Iran's Persian Gulf Policy: From Khomeini to Khatami* (London: Routledge-Curzon, 2003).

Marwah, Onkar, and Shulz, Ann (eds), *Nuclear Proliferation in the Near-Nuclear Countries* (Cambridge: Ballinger Publishing Co., 1975).

Maull, Hanns, and Pick, Otto (eds), *The Gulf War: Regional and International Dimensions* (London: Pinter, 1989).

Melman, Yossi, and Jafandar, Meir, *The Nuclear Sphinx of Tehran: Mahmoud Ahmadinejad and the State of Iran* (New York: Carroll & Graf, 2007).

Milani, Abbas, *The Shah* (New York: Palgrave Macmillan, 2011).

Moin, Baqer, *Khomeini: Life of the Ayatollah* (London: I.B.Tauris, 1999).

Morgenthau, Hans J., *Politics among Nations: The Struggle for Power and Peace* (New York and London: McGraw-Hill Publishing Co., 1992).

Mousavian, Seyed Hossein, *The Iranian Nuclear Crisis: A Memoir* (Carnegie Endowment for International Peace, 12 July 2012).

Muller, Harald (ed.), *A European Non-Proliferation Policy: Prospects and Problems* (Oxford: Clarendon Press, 1987).

Nicolson, Harold, *The Meaning of Prestige* (Cambridge: Cambridge University Press, 1937).

Northedge, F.S., *The International Political System* (London: Faber, 1996).

Northedge, F.S., *The Use of Force in International Relations* (London: Faber, 1974).

Nye, Joseph E. (ed.), *The De-escalation of Nuclear Crises* (Basingstoke: Macmillan, 1992).

Pahlavi, Mohammad Reza, *Mission for My Country* (London: Hutchinson, 1961).

Parker, John W., *Persian Dreams: Moscow and Tehran Since the Fall of the Shah* (Washington, DC: Potomac Books Inc., 2009).

Poneman, Daniel, *Nuclear Power in the Developing World* (London: George Allen & Unwin, 1982).

Pranger, Robert J., and Tahtinen, Dale R., *Nuclear Threat in the Middle East* (Washington, DC: American Enterprise Institute for Public Policy Research, 1975).

Quester, George, *The Politics of Nuclear Proliferation* (Baltimore, MD: John Hopkins University Press, 1973).

Rahnema, Saeed, *Iran After the Revolution: Crisis of an Islamic State* (London: I.B.Tauris, 1996).

Rajaee, Farhang, *Iranian Perspectives on the Iran–Iraq War* (Gainesville, FL: University of Florida, 1997).

Ramazani, Ruhollah K., *Iran's Revolution: The Search for Consensus* (Bloomington, IN: Indiana University Press, 1990).

Ramazani, Ruhollah K., *The Persian Gulf and the Strait of Hormuz* (Alphen aan den Rijn: Sijthoff & Noordhoff, 1979).

Ramazani, Ruhollah K., *Iran's Foreign Policy 1941–1973: A Study of Foreign Policy in Modernizing Nations* (Charlottesville, VA: University of Virginia, 1975).

Ritter, Scott, *Target Iran: The Truth about the White House's Plans for Regime Change* (London: Politico's, 2006).

Samore, Gary (ed.), *Iran's Strategic Weapons Programmes: A Net Assessment* (London: Routledge, 2005).

Schirazi, Asghar, *The Constitution of Iran: Politics and the State in the Islamic Republic* (London: I.B.Tauris, 1997).

Spector, Leonard S., and Smith, Jacqueline R., *Nuclear Ambitions: The Spread of Nuclear Weapons 1989–1990* (Boulder, CO and Oxford: Carnegie, 1990).

Tarock, Adam, *Iran's Foreign Policy since 1990: Pragmatism Supersedes Islamic Ideology* (New York, NY: Nova Science Publishers, 1994).

Timmerman, Kenneth R., *Countdown to Crisis: The Coming Nuclear Showdown with Iran* (New York, NY: Three Rivers, 2006).

Timmerman, Kenneth R., *Weapons of Mass Destruction: The Cases of Iran, Syria and Libya* (Los Angeles, CA: Simon Wiesenthal Center, 1992).

Ungerer, Carl, and Hanson, Marianne, *The Politics of Nuclear Non-Proliferation* (St Leonards, NSW: Allen & Unwin, 2001).

United Nations, *A Zone Free of Weapons of Mass Destruction in the Middle East* (United Nations, 1996).

Venter, Al J., *Iran's Nuclear Option: Tehran's Quest for the Atom Bomb* (Havertown, PA: Casemate, 2005).

Von Grunebaum, G.E., *Modern Islam* (Berkeley and Los Angeles, CA: University of California Press, 1962).

Zangeneh, Hamid, *Islam, Iran and World Stability* (London: Macmillan, 1994).

CHAPTERS IN BOOKS

Ansari, Ali, 'Iran and the US in the shadow of 9/11: Persia and the Persian Question revisited', in Homa Katouzian and Hossein Shahidi (eds), *Iran in the 21st Century: Politics, Economics and Conflict* (London: Routledge, 2008).

Ashcroft, Bill, Griffiths, Gareth, and Tiffin, Helen, 'Discourse', in Ashcroft et al., *Key Concepts in Post-Colonial Studies* (London: Routledge, 1998), pp. 149–57.

Cahn, Anne Hessing, 'Determinants of the Nuclear Option: The Case of Iran', in Onkar Marwah and Ann Shulz (eds), *Nuclear Proliferation in the Near-Nuclear Countries* (Cambridge: Ballinger Publishing Co., 1975), pp. 185–204.

Etemad, Akbar, 'Iran', in Harald Muller (ed.), *A European Non-Proliferation Policy: Prospects and Problems* (Oxford: Clarendon Press, 1987), pp. 203–27.

Lotfian, Saideh, 'Nuclear Policy and International Relations', in Homa Katouzian and Hossein Shahidi (eds), *Iran in the 21st Century: Politics, Economics and Conflict* (London: Routledge, 2008), pp. 158–80.

JOURNALS

Abrahamian, Ervand, 'Structural Causes of the Iranian Revolution', in *MERIP Reports* No. 87, *Iran's Revolution: The Rural Dimension* (May 1980), pp. 21–6.

Ansari, Ali M., 'The Myth of the White Revolution: Mohammad Reza Shah, "Modernization" and the Consolidation of Power', *Middle Eastern Studies* 37/3 (July 2001), pp. 1–24.

Barnaby, Frank, 'The Nuclear Arsenal in the Middle East', *Journal of Palestine Studies* 17/1 (Autumn 1987), pp. 97–106.

Betts, Richard K., 'Incentives for Nuclear Weapons: India, Pakistan, Iran', *Asian Survey* 19/11 (1979), pp. 1053–72.

Betts, Richard K., 'Paranoids, Pygmies, Pariahs and Nonproliferation', *Foreign Policy* 26 (Spring 1977), pp. 157–83.

Bhabha, Homi J., 'Science and the Problems of Development', *Science* 151 (4 February 1966), pp. 540–51.

Deylami, Shirin S., 'In the Face of the Machine: *Westoxification*, Cultural Globalization, and the Making of an Alternative Global Modernity', *Polity* (2011) pp. 43, 242–63, doi:10.1057/pol.2010.27; published online 17 January 2011.

Dombey, Norman, 'The Nuclear Non-Proliferation Treaty: Aims, Limitations and Achievements', *New Left Review* 52 (July–August 2008).

Dunn, Lewis A., 'Half Past India's Bang', *Foreign Policy* 36 (1979), pp. 71–89.

Epstein, William, 'Why States Go – and Don't Go – Nuclear', *Annals of the American Academy of Political and Social Science*, Vol. 430, *Nuclear Proliferation: Prospects, Problems, and Proposals* (March 1977), pp. 16–28.

Gusterson, Hugh, 'Nuclear Weapons and the Other in the Western Imagination', *Cultural Anthropology* 14/1 (February 1999), pp. 111–43.

Johnstone, Diana, 'Little Satan Stuck in the Arms Export Trap', *MERIP Middle East Report*, No. 148, *Re-Flagging the Gulf* (September–October 1987), pp. 1–18.

Kapur, A., 'Nth Powers of the Future', in *Annals of the American Academy of Political and Social Science* 430 (March 1977), pp. 84–94.

Leventhal, Paul, 'Nuclear Terrorism', *Science* (New Series) 233/4770 (19 September 1986).

Majd, Mohammad G., 'Land Reform Policies in Iran', *American Journal of Agricultural Economics* 69/ 4 (November 1987), pp. 843–8.

Pajak, Roger F., 'Nuclear Status and the Policies of the Middle East Countries', *International Affairs* 59/4 (Autumn 1983), pp. 591–606.

Poneman, Daniel, 'Nuclear Policies in Developing Countries', *International Affairs (Royal Institute of International Affairs 1944-)* 57/4 (Autumn 1981), pp. 568–84.

Power, Paul F., 'The Mixed State of Non-Proliferation: The NPT Review Conference and Beyond', *International Affairs (Royal Institute of International Affairs 1944-)* 62/3 (Summer 1986), pp. 477–91.

Pryor, Leslie M., 'Arms and the Shah', *Foreign Policy* 31 (Summer 1978), pp. 56–71.

Quester, George. H., 'The Shah and the Bomb', *Policy Sciences* 8/1 (March 1977), pp. 21–32.

Sagan, Scott, 'Why Do States Build Nuclear Weapons? Three Models in Search of a Bomb', *International Security* 21/3 (Winter 1996/97), pp. 54–86.

Schelling, Thomas C., 'Thinking about Nuclear Terrorism', *International Security* 6/4 (Spring 1982), pp. 61–77.

LITERATURE IN OTHER LANGUAGES

Bani-Sadr, Abulhassan, *Quelle Revolution Pour l'Iran?* (Paris, 1980).

Richard, Y., *Le Shi'sme en Iran* (Paris, 1980).

LITERATURE IN PERSIAN

Bani-Sadr, Abulhassan, *Khiyanat be Omid* (Paris, 1361/1982).

Bani-Sadr, Abulhassan, *Bayaniyeh-ye Jomhuri-ye Eslami* (Tehran, 1358/1979).

Khatami, Mohammad, *Bim-e Mowj* (Tehran, 1372/1993).

Khomeini, Ruhollah, *Velayat-e Faqih* (Tehran, 1361/1982).

Khomeini, Ruhollah, *Hokumat-e Eslami* (Najaf, 1350/1971).

Khomeini, Ruhollah, *Tali'eh-e Enqelab-e Eslami* (collected interviews by Khomeini in Paris, Najaf and Qom, 1362/1983).

Navazeni, Bahram, *Gahshomar-e Siyasat-e Khariji-ye Iran: Az Day Mah 1357 ta Mordad Mah 1367* (Tehran: Markaz-e Asnad-e Enqelab-e Islami, 1381/2002).

Rowhani, Hassan, *Amniyat Melli va Diplomasi-ye Hastehi Iran* (Tehran: Markaz-e Tahqiqat-e Estaratejik-e Majma'-e Tashkhis-e Maslahat-e Nezam, 1391/2012).

Sadr, Mohammad Baqer, *Jomhuri-ye Eslami* (Tehran, 1358/1979).

MEDIA SOURCES

Associated Press (AP) news archive

BBC Summary of World Broadcasts (BBC SWB) archive

BIBLIOGRAPHY

Christian Science Monitor
CNN
Enqelab-e eslami newspaper
Kayhan newspaper
Kayhan International
Keesings World News Archive
Le Monde Diplomatique newspaper
Lexis-Nexis
Middle East International (MEI)
Nuclear Engineering International
Nuclear News
Nuclear Power
Nucleonics Week
Resalat newspaper
Reuters news archive
The Guardian newspaper
The Independent newspaper
The New York Times newspaper
The Times newspaper
Voice of Amercia (VOA)

OFFICIAL ARCHIVES

National Archives of the United Kingdom (Public Record Office)
National Security Archive at the George Washington University
UN Document Records

INDEX

INDEX

Amano, Yukiya, 266, 267, 275
Amir Kabir, Mirza Taghi Khan, 10
Amir Kabir University, 167
Amrollahi, Reza, 97, 109, 112, 113,
    144, 148, 154, 163, 164, 283
    AEOI, appointment as head of,
        103–104
    Aghazadeh, replaced by, 142
    AQ Khan deal, 123–125
    covert facilities, 147
    Khatami, endorsement of, 142–143
    nuclear programme, restart of
        under Rafsanjani, 132–136
    Russians, negotiations with over
        Bushehr, 138–140
    Saghand, discovery of uranium
        deposits at, 151–152
Anglo-Persian Oil Company, 9
Arak heavy-water plant, 164, 167,
    168, 176, 177, 179, 197, 206,
    242, 251, 255, 281
Argentina, 18, 19, 36, 73, 115, 116,
    134, 138
Asfia, Safi, 16
Atomic Energy Organization of Iran
    (AEOI), 27, 55, 117, 121, 148,
    151, 179, 180
    Aghazadeh, change of direction
        under, 141–144, 163–168
    Bushehr project, 137, 139–141
    costs, accusations of spiralling, 85
    founding of, 20–24
    inspectors, banning of, 205
    nuclear fuel cycle and supporting
        infrastructure, work on, 44–47
    nuclear programme, cancellation
        of, 95–97
    nuclear programme,
        'normalization' of, 132–135
    nuclear programme, restart of,
        102–103, 105, 112, 115
    projects, initial, 36–41

scientific personnel, build up of,
    35–36
Stuxnet, 264–265
uranium-enrichment programme,
    206, 261
uranium-enrichment programme,
    covert, 125–126, 158–159
'Atoms for Peace' programme, the,
    4–5, 52, 66, 71
Australia, 66, 185, 205

Bani-Sadr, President Abolhassan, 98,
    103, 105
Barbarossa, operation, 7
Basij, the, 199
Bazargan, Mehdi, 92, 95, 96,
    105, 106
Beijing, *see* China
Bhabha, Homi, 18,
Blair, Tony, 180
Blix, Hans, 110, 148
Bolton, Ambassador John R.
    belief that Iran is seeking a bomb,
        183, 226
    desire for regime change in Iran,
        205–206
    diplomatic differences with
        Europeans 184–185
    discussions with Powell over EU
        ministers' trip to Tehran, 194
    IAEA Board, September 2003,
        186–188
    Iran, negotiating with, 232
    MKO revelations, 2002, 180
    US policy towards Iran, change of,
        214–215
Borujerdi, Ala'eddin, 205
Brazil, 36, 56, 116, 224, 287
    Tehran Declaration, 261–262, 263
Brill, Ken, 186–188, 203
Bullard, Sir Reader, 7, 48
Burkina Faso, 55

INDEX